Presented to :-

Major David Collins
        RMR (Retired)

from the Army Rugby Union

Aldershot.   6th January 1993.

        David Murray.

        Secretary
        Army Rugby Union.

THE HISTORY OF ARMY RUGBY

THE HISTORY
OF
ARMY RUGBY

by
JOHN McLAREN

THE ARMY RFU

First published 1986
Consultant editor: Derek Wyatt

Printed and bound in Great Britain by
Butler & Tanner Ltd, Frome and London

ACKNOWLEDGEMENTS

I feel somewhat diffident in being called the author of this history, as so many people have contributed to its composition and without their invaluable help this book could not have been published.

I owed a great debt to the late Col Peter Upcher who handed over to me an immense amount of material and letters which enabled me to start off on the right track. My wife and I have very happy memories of the weekend we spent with Peter, and his wife, Rona.

The history also owes an enormous debt of gratitude to the inspiration and enthusiasm of the late Brig Tony Ridings who gave me considerable encouragement throughout and recently, to Brig Peter Crooks, who overcame various problems in a calm and confident manner. Similar, I imagine, to his performance as full-back for the Army, the Combined Services and Durham.

I must thank Sylvia Nash for the magnificent way she contributed in producing the history in its finished form. Her devotion to the task and helpful advice was constantly appreciated.

My thanks also to Jo Greenwood who undertook the initial typing and to John Leighton of the Graphics Office School of Infantry who designed the dust cover.

In the last stage of production the meticulous attention to detail and the utter professionalism of Mary Lou Grimberg in checking the manuscript was nothing less than outstanding.

I must not forget Col Mike Hardy who by a mixture of devious charm and spurious flattery persuaded me to compile this history, nor his half-back partner for England, Brig Dennis Shuttleworth, now President of the Rugby Football Union, for his wise and constructive advice.

In carrying out my research, I was indebted to the staff of the Guildhall Library, London, the Colindale Reading Library and the RMC Sandhurst Library. My thanks are also extended to editors and contributors of Corps and Regimental journals.

The Army RFU are extremely grateful to the Sport and General Press Agency for assistance with the photographs.

To the many (some sadly no longer with us) who contributed to the history: Brig A R Aslett, Maj Gen A R Birtwhistle, Lieut Col N S Bruce,

Maj J D Braisby, G J Bryan, Brig B T V Cowey, Col M J Campbell-Lamerton, Lieut Col J R Cole, Lieut Col W Clarke, Lieut Col Jo Crewe-Read, Brig T P Crawley, Maj P L Cutler, R Cherry, Lieut Col P E Y Dawson, H L V Day, Mrs Davies, Lieut Col J Dalrymple, Lieut Col G J Dean, Lieut Col A R Evill, Gen Sir Anthony Farrar-Hockley, F J V Ford, R Folliard, Maj H G Greatwood, Brig W D C Greenacre, H C Harrison, Brig T G H Jackson, Lieut Col B A L Jones, Lieut Col W W Knock, Maj Gen Sir Douglas Kendrew, Lieut Col R Leyland, Diana Morgan, C M Middleton, H MacIlwaine, Lieut Col C L Melville, Lieut Col A L Novis, Y Price, Rt Rev V J Pike, Col M J Paterson, Maj W S Philips, Maj Gen C Purdon, Col M U Ryan, Maj I P Reid, D Rhys, Lieut Col H L T Radice, Brig M S Taversham, S Stephenson, Maj N T Slater, Brig G Taylor, Brig C Tyler, Mrs C M Usher, J R B Worton, A R F Wright, Derek Wyatt, The Secretary, Royal Navy RFU and The Secretary, Royal Air Force RFU.

Finally, my sincere and heartfelt thanks to my wife, Mary, who has given me immense support during the production of the history and has been a tower of strength with her encouragement and understanding.

John McLaren
Heytesbury,
January, 1986

The ARMY Rugby Union wishes to record its thanks and appreciation to the Directors of Stewart Wrightson for their help and support in the production of this history.

CONTENTS

30 YEARS ON

I remember, my son, the matches,
  In the half century year
And the might of the men of those days,
  Make me shed a silent tear.

For they ran with the speed of greyhounds,
  They tackled like grisly bears,
Their limbs were knobbly with muscles,
  And matted with thick black hairs.

They never barged in the line out,
  Or knocked the ball back to their threes,
Or lay on the ground for hours,
  Holding the ball with their knees.

Three-quarters never ran backwards,
  Or crowded out their wing
And they never blamed their forwards
  When they couldn't heel the thing.

Ah things are not what they used to be,
  Don't you agree with me, Sir?
'My boy,' said the ancient patriarch,
  'You'll find that they never were.'

                              Anon.

Foreword

By
The President of the Rugby Football Union
Brigadier D W Shuttleworth OBE ADC
1985–86

I enjoyed every moment of my rugby playing career in one of the Army's rugby regiments, my subsequent service as an Army Rugby Union administrator and my time as an Army representative on The Rugby Football Union Committee. Now as the 78th President of The Rugby Football Union I feel honoured and privileged to be invited to write the foreword to this *History* of rugby in the Army.

The record of the British Army is packed with stories of courage, feats of valour, battle honours, team-work, Regimental and Corps pride. Such tradition stems from the skill, spirit and determination to succeed, and the fitness and ability of units to fulfill their roles. One major factor contributing towards the drawing together of all these fine qualities is the playing of team games; they demand interdependence, unselfishness, physical fitness, high morale, determination, leadership, character, self-discipline and inventive initiative. Although in historical terms the game of rugby football has only developed since the middle of the nineteenth century there is no other sport which more completely combines all these qualities, or contributes more to the moulding of the character of the British soldier who plays.

The History of Army Rugby recounts the highlights of the game and its personalities at different levels in the Army throughout the past 130 years. The book makes fascinating reading and illustrates the quality of person playing the game. For example, in one Regimental XV after the First World War there were holders of two DSOs, five MCs and two MMs. During the 'Golden Era' between the two World Wars there were no fewer than 44 serving soldiers who gained International honours. At all levels, and in a variety of ways soldiers have figured prominently in the game throughout the world.

A great deal of effort by many people has gone into the compilation of this History. I hope they will accept our gratitude for their efforts and forgive me for not mentioning them all individually. However, I wish to pay particular tribute to Mr H L V Day, Mr U A Titley and

Lieut Col P G Upcher DSO who all, before their deaths, contributed so much to researching and preparing the background material. I wish also to pay tribute to the late Brig N T Ridings CBE who organised the production of the first manuscripts of the History and gave us a firm base on which to proceed to publication. Finally, I thank Lieut Col John McLaren OBE for editing and writing the History so expertly and with such dedication.

On a personal level the History has reminded me of the pleasure I have had in the game, of great men I have played with and against in the Army and the other Services and of lasting friendships through rugby football. I am sure it will give equal pleasure to others who have participated in rugby in the Army and, indeed, to all those who love our game.

BEGINNINGS

The Guards and the Cavalry played the earliest recorded game of rugby in the Army, in a setting best remembered for the ill-fated Charge of the Light Brigade and the dedication of Florence Nightingale. The match was at Balaclava on 27 March 1855 – right in the middle of the Crimean War (1854–56).

Both the year and the location are significant.

The year establishes how quickly the Army adopted a new sporting idea. For although it was just over thirty years since William Webb Ellis had picked up the football and run with it at Rugby School in 1823, that was the first time that the possibility even of an alternative method of play had been introduced and the principles had been talked over for so long afterwards that it was 1841 before the different game was brought in at Rugby School itself. It was 1861 before it really attracted wider popularity.

The location of this first recorded Army game might seem strange at first. The date was also significant, being exactly a year after that on which Great Britain and France had entered this war with Russia, and less than six months after the Battle of Balaclava and the noted Charge (25 October 1854) – part of a terrible year in bad conditions. In such circumstances an army would be expected to be more seriously occupied, but it will be seen in this history that soldiers can sometimes relax amid conflict. During the two later world wars, in fact, it was acknowledged that the game of rugby was kept alive mainly by Service teams.

Until the formation of the Rugby Football Union in 1871 there was no universal code of rules for the rugby-style game. Rugby School football was designed to be played only there, and at all other places where Old Rugbeians had spread the gospel the game had to be very much modified, so each club had its own set of rules. Until 1860 very few 'foreign' matches were played, but when strangers met on the football field the first event was a discussion by captains to decide how the game should be ordered.

The Army generally played the Eton game (normally eleven a side) and the match in the Crimea was between a Guards XI and a Cavalry XI. It is not recorded who won. The first Army side using rugby-type rules was that of the Royal Military Academy, Woolwich, where a club was formed in 1860, though football was already a popular pastime there in 1856/57.

The matches played were in the rugby idiom by teams representing the 2nd Battalion and the 3rd Battalion of the Grenadier Regiment of Foot Guards at Lord's Cricket Ground in March 1859. The first game, on 1 March, was played twenty-five a side (this being the proper number for an important match at that time) and ended in a draw. A return was ordered for 9 March, but with fifteen a side. The presence of several senior Army officers at these encounters suggested to some that the War Office was interested in football as an exercise and a diversion for soldiers.

In 1862 the 53rd (Shropshire) Regiment beat the 8th (King's) Regiment in a rugby game at Aldershot Camp by one goal: the teams were twenty a side. During the following February Rossall School played the School of Musketry, Fleetwood, in a thirteen-a-side game. Although Rossall used the Rugby rules intermittently, this particular meeting seems to have taken place under Harrow rules.

It was in 1864/65 that the RMA, Woolwich, met Richmond for the first time, home and away, a fixture which lasted for several seasons. At the first match Woolwich won by one goal to nil. The margin of victory, we are told, would have been greater but for the high wind, which defied attempts at place kicking. At this time, and indeed until the eighties, matches were won on goals only. A try was no more than that – a try at goal. A side might spend the whole afternoon in front of their opponents' goalposts, gaining tries one minute, and yet lose the match by a freak dropped goal. Various schemes for a points system were advanced in the seventies (one of the more popular was five points for a goal however kicked, three points for a try, one point for a touch-in-goal, one point for forcing an opponent to touch down in defence), but for many years the best that could be got from a goalless game, or one where the numbers of goals were equal, was a 'draw in favour'.

The Royal Military College (as it then was) at Sandhurst had come into prominence in 1860/61 with a season of football activity, and by the mid-1860s both they and the RMA, Woolwich, were becoming stronger, with first-rate fixture lists embracing many of the best clubs in London and the suburbs.

Woolwich and Sandhurst met each other for the first time in 1876 and Woolwich won. The development of rugby at these two establishments is examined more fully later, with Corps and Regimental histories, and the results of their encounters may be found at the end of the next chapter. On 16 December 1876, the RMA went to Cooper's

Hill to play the Royal Indian Civil Engineering College. The Engineers had a 'try' disallowed because three Woolwich men were absent from the field at the time!

There was other interest in various places during this period. In 1866/67 the 8th Depot Battalion at Colchester was said to have a good side, playing a combination of Eton and Rugby rules. A club called the Royal Artillery Band was to have a brilliant season in 1874/75, but it did not last long. In Ireland, where the Association game was almost unknown, two Army sides were enjoying the company of such great clubs as Landsdowne, Dublin Wanderers and Dublin University. These were the 94th Regiment and the 93rd (Sutherland Highlanders), the latter one of the most popular teams ever to play in Ireland. In 1878/79 the 21st Lancashire Rifle Volunteers played a match against the well-known Oldham Club. And from overseas came the news that a game had even been played in the Bhulan Pass, Afghanistan by Maj Gen Biddulph's Army.

Several prominent players emerged at this time. C W Sherrard and C A Crompton, both of the Royal Engineers, had the distinction in 1871 of becoming the first soldiers to gain International honours. Both played for England. F B G d'Aguilar, another Sapper, played for England in 1872; F T Maxwell and H W Renny Tailyour, also Sappers, took the field for Scotland, and a Gunner, R P Maitland, was also capped for Scotland. R D Garnons-Williams, Royal Fusiliers, gained one cap for Wales in 1881. International caps were awarded regularly to Army players right up to the end of the century.

Renny Tailyour, who played for Scotland against England in the first International at Kennington Oval on 4 February 1872, was described as a forward of fine stature and one of the keenest players on the field. He also had the skills to play for Scotland against England at Association Football and was in the Royal Engineers' team against the Wanderers in the first English Cup Final, but was on the losing side. However he gained his Cup Final medal in 1875 when the Royal Engineers won the FA Cup by beating the Old Etonians 2–0 at Kennington Oval.

Garnons-Williams also divided his interests and he played Association Football for Wales as well as rugby. He was to be a casualty of the First World War, being killed in action – still commanding his battalion at the age of fifty-nine – at Loos on 27 September 1915.

1878 was a significant year for Service rugby, as on 13 February the Officers of the Army played the Officers of the Royal Navy for the first time, at Kennington Oval. The Navy won the match by a goal and a try to a goal.

The Army selectors made a generous contribution towards the Navy victory by selecting as captain R Bannatyne who was serving overseas at the time and received no notification of his selection! Another player arrived late, but at least took part in the game. An account of the match appeared in a newspaper called *The Broad Arrow*:

A fine exhibition of football delighted the somewhat small number of spectators. Bush scored the first try for the Navy from a scrummage near the line. The goal was kicked by Orford. A band of naval spectators who had taken up their position beneath a white ensign mounted on the roof of a drag greeted this score with great cheering. The greasy state of the ground was not favourable for any great display of running. Encouraged by a cry from their supporters 'Come on Navy, Force the Passage of the Straights' the Navy mounted great pressure and scored a touch down. In the second half the Navy scored a second try. Wrench of the Army took advantage of some bad passing by the Navy and scored the Army try: The goal was kicked but this ended the scoring and the Navy deservedly won the first match between the Services.

The teams were: *Army* – back: C F Crombie (37th North Hampshire Regt); threequarter-backs: C H Coke (86th Royal County Down Regt), J N Cowan (Royal Engineers); half-backs: F C Heath (RE), A J C French (76th Regt of Foot); forwards: A R Barker (Royal Artillery), A J Street (unidentified), J Spens (85th King's Light Infantry), I W Urquhart (108th (Madras Infantry) Regt of Foot), G Campbell (77th (East Middlesex) Regt). I G Adamson (108th Foot), Gould-Adams (1st (Royal Scots) Regt), T H Manser (Army Hospital Corps), S Ogilvie (unidentified), R A Bannatyne (RA) (captain – absent). *Royal Navy* – F Campbell, C Bishop, E Daniells, C Hart, P Bush, J Startin, D Henderson, J Orford, C Trower, R Montgomerie, J Bennett, F Thring, H Goldfinch, C Bayly, C Walters.

Although an increased amount of rugby was being played in the Services, no further matches took place between the Army and the Navy until 1905, after which year was launched the Inter-Service Championship.

The Calcutta Cup

The Army can be proud that it played a part in the conception of this famous trophy.

Its history is well known to the majority of rugby followers, but briefly it came about from the days when the 3rd (East Kent, The Buffs) Regiment were great supporters of the Calcutta Club and, with the 62nd (Wiltshire) Regiment, took a very active part in establishing rugby in India. The early games were played with an Association ball until the Bombay Gymkhana gave the club two rugby balls which lasted until a supply was received from Rugby.

By 1873 the Calcutta Club had a membership of 137 and there was a free bar which was very popular. Members and friends treated themselves to such an extent that the free bar was discontinued – not surprisingly – and this led to an immediate decline in membership.

Rugby was played from October to February but it was found that the excessive hardness of the turf during the winter months did not add to the enjoyment of the game, so the winter season was dropped.

The Buffs arrived in 1873, but when they left in 1876 enthusiasm waned again and the club was temporarily disbanded. It was suggested, however, that the name of the club be perpetuated by presenting the Rugby Football Union with a cup to be competed for annually by England and Scotland. The offer was accepted and the Calcutta Cup was first competed for in 1879.

The cup itself was brought to England in 1879 by Mr G A J Rothney, one of the founder members of the Calcutta Club.

Forming the Army Rugby Union

Three men in a boat have their place in literature. The Army Rugby Union owes its inception to three men in a train.

There were always several Service players in the Blackheath XV and at the end of the 1905/06 season three of these were returning by train after playing for Blackheath against the West of Scotland in Glasgow. They were Lieut J E C 'Birdie' Partridge (Welch Regt), Lieut W S D Craven (Royal Field Artillery), and Lieut C G (Clive) Liddell (Leicestershire Regt).

Partridge originated the idea, which came to him while he was reading a newspaper item regarding the final of the Association Football Cup. Craven and Liddell supported him; a proposed scheme was put down on paper then and there, and it was completed before the end of their long journey.

On 12 November 1906, a meeting was held at which it was decided to form an Army Rugby Union, and the Hon Secretary who had been appointed, Capt R E G Waymouth, wrote to the War Office requesting sanction by the Army Council for its formation.

There is no doubt that the chief credit for the setting up of the ARU must go to Lieut (later Maj) Partridge. Few players could have had wider experience of rugby at that time than 'Birdie' Partridge. He learnt the game at Dulwich College, and from that solid foundation went on to play for Newport, Blackheath, Pretoria, Transvaal, South Africa (one cap, 1903), London Welsh, the Welch Regiment, the Army, and in an England trial.

On 31 December 1906, the Army Council approved the formation of the ARU and agreed the members of the first committee. They were: Lieut H E Lindsay (7th Dragoon Guards), representing the Cavalry; Capt Waymouth (Royal Garrison Artillery), and Capt Craven, representing the RA; Capt R F A Hobbs and Lieut R A S Mansel, representing the RE; Capt C E Wilson (Queen's), Lieut Partridge and Lieut G H Birkett (South Wales Borderers), representing the Infantry; and Lieut T H Robinson, representing the Royal Army Medical Corps. Two additional members were also approved, representing the Infantry and the Army Service Corps. It will be seen that Lieut Liddell's name does not appear on the committee, as by then he had joined the 2nd Battalion the Leicestershire Regiment in India.

On 10 August 1907, Field Marshall the Duke of Connaught consented to be President of the ARU.

For some reason there was no ARU Committee meeting in 1907 and the first one was held on 16 June 1908. The following decisions were made:

1. Army teams should wear red shirts and stockings and white shorts; these are the same colours as are worn today.
2. Railway fares of teams competing in the Army Cup should be paid for by the ARU, and £50 was to be distributed to units for this.
3. Fixtures against Oxford and Cambridge Universities should be arranged before arranging the Army and Navy match.
4. An executive committee should be elected. Those elected at that meeting were: B A Hill (Army Ordnance Corps), W B Purdon (RAMC), G H Birkett, Secretary, W C Wilson (Leicestershire Regt).

On 21 January 1907, the Rugby Union had donated to the Army a most handsome cup for inter-unit competition and entries were immediately called for. Twelve teams responded. In the final at Aldershot the 2nd Battalion the West Riding Regiment (later the 2nd Bn Duke of Wellington's Regt) beat the Training Battalion RE 5-0. The trophy was presented by General Sir John French.

At a meeting on 5 September 1908, Lieut Partridge and Lieut Wilson were elected to serve on a selection committee to choose a combined Army and Navy side to play the Australians on 28 October that year. The Australians won the match 8-6.

Also in 1908, it was agreed to accept an invitation to play the Slade Bordelais Université Club on 7 February 1909. That match was won by the Army, 9-6.

The first Secretary of the Army Rugby Union proper was Lieut Birkett, but he was ordered overseas in 1908 and handed over to Capt J Rainsford-Hannay (Queen's), who held office until 1919/20. He was also the ARU representative on the Rugby Union Committee and nobody could have worked harder or done more to help Army rugger than he.

In 1911 founder members Craven and Liddell returned home from abroad and both joined the ARU Committee. Craven was made captain of the Army side in place of the third founder member, Partridge.

This was the beginning of the Army Rugby Union as we know it today. It is clear from the minutes of the meetings that the activities up to 1914 were dependent on the interest and the time given up by a comparatively few officers such as Birkett, Rainsford-Hannay, Partridge, Hill, Purdon, Wilson, Craven, Liddell and Robertson. Army rugby players owe a deep dept of gratitude to them.

ROYAL MILITARY COLLEGE SANDHURST
AND
ROYAL MILITARY ACADEMY WOOLWICH
(THE 'SHOP')

HISTORICAL ORIGINS AND CHANGES IN TITLE

1741: founding of The Royal Military Academy, Woolwich

1799: founding of The Royal Military College, Marlow

1812: The Royal Military College, Sandhurst

1947: amalgamation under new title – Royal Military Academy, Sandhurst

Intensive research has so far revealed that the first Army team to adopt the laws as played by Rugby School was the Royal Military Academy, Woolwich. Although football was already a popular pastime at the RMA in 1856 no regular club was formed until 1860. It seems likely that their play was according to the code of the nearby Blackheath Preparatory School.

Although the Royal Military College, Sandhurst must have formed – like Woolwich – one of the oldest clubs in existence no regular records were kept in the early days. The actual date of the foundation of the club is obscure. The standard of rugby both at Woolwich and Sandhurst improved steadily in quality and each acquired a fixture list which included most of the best clubs in the Metropolitan area. Probably the outstanding season for the Woolwich Cadets was that of 1875/76 when they won eight and lost three games scoring 14 goals to nil. They were now playing on a new ground in front of the Artillery Barracks and had adopted a jersey of black, blue and yellow as their colours.

In 1876 the RMA, Woolwich, generously offered a £150 Challenge Cup for annual competition by clubs who were members of the Rugby Football Union. Although at the time competitive rugby was regarded with disfavour by the Union, the offer was accepted and a sub-committee drafted a set of rules to control the competition. However, according to one account, owing to the opposition of the Commandant of Woolwich the offer was withdrawn; another source states that the offer was rejected by the sub-committee who found there were technical difficulties too great to overcome!

The first game between Woolwich and Sandhurst took place in 1876 and resulted in a win for Woolwich.

In March 1890 The Royal Military College Rugby Football Club joined the Surrey Rugby Football Union.

From 1930–39 both Sandhurst and Woolwich had strong fixture lists which included Harlequins A, Wasps, and Old Paulines. Members of the Royal Family frequently honoured with their presence the annual match between Woolwich and Sandhurst.

W F ('Horsey') Browne was captain of the Sandhurst team in 1923 and it is of interest to read the following report on this great player.

Seldom if ever, has the RMC side had a better Captain. Full of enthusiasm and energy he knows the game well and was an excellent coach . . .

An article in the RMC magazine commented on the standard of play of boys coming from rugger schools:

Last year it was found necessary to comment on the fact that players, from "Rugger" schools came up to the RMC with little or no knowledge of the art of tackling. The same is true of this year's players. This is regrettable, because it means that these players will never learn to tackle properly. We endeavour to teach them here, but in the majority of cases it is too late.

The 1927/28 season was one of the most successful in Sandhurst history; they played 21 games, winning 20 and losing one, and scored 419 points against 123. During this period a certain J D G Niven from Stowe School was one of the forwards; he was later to become famous in other fields! In the 1928 Woolwich–Sandhurst match brothers played on opposite sides; F R Ievers was centre threequarter for Woolwich and G M Ievers was full-back for Sandhurst.

Matches were played annually against the Royal Naval College Greenwich and Royal Air Force Cranwell. Also in 1927 Sandhurst had as visitors Ecole Speciale Militaire St Cyr, whom they beat 11–3.

During the war Sandhurst (OCTU) had a regular fixture list which helped to keep rugby alive.

The following article written by the late Lieut-Col Roy Leyland (the Army, Lancashire, England) sums up clearly Sandhurst rugby today:

After the war, long established fixtures were revived between Blackheath, Richmond, Harlequins, Rosslyn Park, London Scottish, Oxford Un Greyhounds, Cambridge LX Club and Army Trials XV, Corps and Regimental sides, and Commandants XV were introduced.

Post war teams are difficult to compare with pre war 1939 vintage years because of the difference in ages, physique and quality of opposition and the tendency to see the performances of the past through rose-tinted spectacles.

However, allowing for the inevitable interference of academic and military activities with sport and the great improvement in the quality of Club Rugby, RMA Sandhurst has established and maintained a high reputation for standard of play and sportsmanship. Its contribution to Service, University and County and International Rugby is clearly indicated by the number of ex-Cadets awarded International Caps and the over fifty who have gained Army Caps and the many to be found regularly in County sides.

During the 1950/51 season at Sandhurst the XL Club was formed. The object of the Club was to include all members of the 1st XV, 2nd XV and other promising players, with the aim to foster the spirit and knowledge of Rugby Football.

The old Sovereigns competition was abolished and an Inter-Company League was introduced.

The Academy fixture list was widened further to include the Royal Military College, Kingston, Canada and the The Military Academy, West Point, USA.

ROYAL MILITARY ACADEMY WOOLWICH V ROYAL MILITARY COLLEGE SANDHURST
1876-1939

1876 Woolwich	–	1896 Sandhurst	8-6
1877 drawn	–	1897 Sandhurst	10-3
1878 drawn	–	1898 Sandhurst	10-5
1879 drawn	0-0	1899 Woolwich	8-0
1880 Sandhurst	14-3	1900 Sandhurst	16-0
1881 drawn	0-0	1901 Woolwich	16-3
1882 Sandhurst	13-0	1902 Woolwich	6-5
1883 Woolwich	3-0	1903 Sandhurst	5-3
1884 Sandhurst	18-3	1904 drawn	5-5
1885 Sandhurst	13-6	1905 Woolwich	14-0
1886 Sandhurst	11-0	1906 Sandhurst	16-0
1887 Sandhurst	17-0	1907 Sandhurst	16-5
1888 Sandhurst	17-0	1908 Sandhurst	33-8
1889 Sandhurst	23-3	1909 Woolwich	17-8
1890 Sandhurst	27-0	1910 Woolwich	45-9
1891 drawn	0-0	1911 Woolwich	25-0
1892 Sandhurst	5-3	1912 Sandhurst	23-11
1893 drawn	0-0	1913 Woolwich	21-16
1894 Sandhurst	11-0	1914-15 no matches	
1895 Woolwich	3-0	1916 Woolwich	12-5

1917 Sandhurst	21–4	1932 Sandhurst	8–3
1918 Sandhurst	11–5	1933 Sandhurst	8–0
1919 Sandhurst	17–6	1934 Sandhurst	12–0
1920 Woolwich	13–8	1935 Sandhurst	24–3
1921 Woolwich	8–3	1936 Sandhurst	11–5
1922 Sandhurst	11–5	1937 Sandhurst	16–7
1923 Sandhurst	14–6	1938 Woolwich	21–0
1924 Woolwich	17–3		
1925 Woolwich	12–6	*played 61*	
1926 Sandhurst	11–6	Royal Military College Sandhurst won 35	
1927 Sandhurst	8–3		
1928 Woolwich	18–16	Royal Military Academy Woolwich won 19	
1929 Woolwich	41–10		
1930 Sandhurst	14–3	drawn 7	
1931 Sandhurst	36–0		

THE DUKE OF WELLINGTON'S REGIMENT

HISTORICAL ORIGINS AND CHANGES IN TITLE

1702: The Earl of Huntingdon's
Regiment of Foot

1751: 33rd Regiment of Foot

1782: 33rd (or 1st Yorkshire West
Riding) Regiment of Foot

1787: 76th Regiment of Foot ('The
Hindoostan Regiment')

1853: 33rd (Duke of Wellington's
Regiment)

1881: 1st Bn The Duke of Wellington's
(West Riding Regiment)

1881: 2nd Bn The Duke of Wellington's
(West Riding Regiment)

1920: The Duke of Wellington's Regiment (West Riding)

The great rugby tradition in the Dukes really began with the preliminary moves of that untraditional operation – the Cardwell Reforms. As far as the Regiment was concerned the basic effect of these measures was the combination of the 33rd and 76th Foot to form the 1st and 2nd Battalions of the Duke of Wellington's (West Riding Regiment) in 1881.

The 2nd Battalion of the Regiment – late 76th – was the real initiator of serious rugby in the Dukes. When stationed at Halifax, Nova Scotia, in 1881, the battalion team had success in local matches. In 1893 the battalion moved to South Africa and remained in Natal for three years. There the rugby team was supreme, winning the two open challenge cups – the Murray and the York and Lancaster – three years in succession.

In 1905 the 2nd Battalion returned home from Dinapore and the 1st Battalion moved to India. 1907 was a year of triumph for Regimental rugby. The Army Union Challenge Cup competition was played for the first time and won by the 2nd Battalion against the Training Battalion RE; while in India the 1st Battalion won all three of the presidencies Open Rugby Challenge Cups – those of Calcutta, Madras and Bombay. The captain of the 1st Battalion team was the Adjutant, Capt E M Liddell. The 2nd Battalion, after other successes, again won the Army Cup in 1914. Two of the heroes of the 2nd Battalion team of those days are still well remembered. One was Lieut R O'D Carey, a tall amiable Channel Islander of considerable charm and a marked sense of the ridiculous. The other was Lieut R J A Henniker, later Maj Sir Robert Henniker, Bt.

After the First World War the Regiment took some years to get its rugger organised. The 2nd Battalion was serving in Ireland under the same melancholy circumstances which overshadow the Army now.

In 1923 2nd Lieut C K T ('Bull') Faithfull, an old Wellingtonian, joined the battalion and under his inspiring leadership the battalion rugger team began to take shape. He was a great front row forward and was also very fast. There is little doubt that he would have gained many more than the three International caps that he did, had he not sustained one of those insidious knee injuries early in his playing career. In 1925 the legendary W F Browne, 'Horsey' to his innumerable friends, joined the battalion. A product of Campbell College, he had captained the Sandhurst team.

In October 1927 the 1st Battalion moved to Devonport and began to battle seriously for the Army Cup. Both in that season and in the succeeding one the team encountered the 1st Battalion the King's Own in the semi-final. The latter were the eventual winners of the Cup and both years they just beat the Dukes.

In 1903 H C ('Bonzo') Miles was posted to the 1st Battalion. He also was an inspired leader with the most impressive drive and enthusiasm, and it was under his captaincy that the 1st Battalion team at last won the Army Cup in 1930/31 and in 1932/33.

In 1938 the 1st Battalion returned from Malta and provided three members of the Army team in the 1938 Inter-Services Championship: Lieut J Harrison as centre threequarter; 2nd Lieut F J Reynolds, capped for England in 1937, as fly-half and 2nd Lieut C F Grieve, an Oxford Blue and Scottish International, at full-back.

The semi-final of the 1939 Army Cup was played against the Welch Regiment on the Leicester club ground. It was a fine sunny afternoon favouring open football. The Welch Regiment who had a strong back division which included two Welsh Internationals – Lieut B V T Cowey and 2nd Lieut J Ford – won 25-3.

The Second World War now intervened and while the Regimental magazine records many games of rugby played by all the Dukes battalions all over the world, it is not until the first season after the war that we can take up again a coherent story of Regimental rugby. Indeed, the 1945/46 season saw a great deal of rugby played.

The first Battalion, then in Palestine, recorded a victory against the Haifa District Police and also the winning of the 1st Division Sevens when they beat the 2nd Battalion the Sherwood Foresters by 16 points to three in the final.

Out in India, Lieut-Col Jack Dalrymple had trained a useful 2nd Battalion XV and seven Dukes players helped 16th Infantry Brigade win the Cawnpore Cup.

Serious post-war Regimental rugby did not start until the 1946/47 season when the Depot, now called 33 Primary Training Centre (DWR), won the Northern Command Sevens.

The season 1948/49 found the 1st Battalion, now amalgamated with the 2nd Battalion, stationed at Strensall. The XV was well balanced with youth and the not-so-young blended together. Second Lieuts Hardy and Shuttleworth were just starting their rugby careers; Pte Turnbull – the first of the Dukes' great players from the Rugby League – had joined, and the brothers Birch and Cpl Frost were a strong front row despite their average age of thirty-eight. C F Grieve was captain, Maj Davidson was in the back row and Capt F J Reynolds in the centre – all three having been persuaded out of retirement. Coaching was in the experienced hands of Majs Gordon Upjohn and Bob Moran.

In this season 2nd Lieut Shuttleworth won the first three of his twenty-two Army caps and it is interesting to note that his partner at fly-half for the Army was 2nd Lieut Nim Hall.

In the 1951/52 season Hardy and Shuttleworth played together for England in the Calcutta Cup match. This is an Army first – the half-backs in an International coming from the same regiment.

The late fifties proved three glorious seasons for the Regiments in Northern Ireland: they won the Ulster Junior and Senior Leagues and were runners-up in the Ulster Cup. As a tribute Ulster put out a full province side for the Regiment's farewell match at Raven Hill. The Dukes won a thrilling match. The Regiment had a superb squad of players during this period, Rugby Union and League National Servicemen and the first taste of Fijian players. Some of the squad during this golden age were: Majs Hardy, Shuttleworth and Hoppe, Capts Gilbert-Smith, Cowel and Cambell-Lamerton, Lieuts Arnold, Cambell-Lamerton (younger brother), Davies, Edwards, Greenway, Ried and Shenton, Cpls Davis, Dickens, Keegan, Scroby, Sabine and Renilson, plus a Fijian contingent of Basu, Cagilaba, Parrat, Ponijiasi and Waquabaca.

Between 1964 and 1968 the Dukes won the Army Cup in four successive years. The inspirations during this period were the intelligent and enthusiastic captaincies of Capt Ian Ried and Capt Dick Mundel, plus the experienced coaching of Maj David Gilbert-Smith and the dedicated play of people like Cpls Dickens, Hemmings and Ponijiasi. The threequarter line during this period of Lieuts Edwards, Walker, Newell and Westcob was electric. Maj Mike Hardy played at full-back in the winning 1966 side and so finished his Regimental playing career.

In 1969 the Regiment moved to Hong Kong and enjoyed some excellent rugby under the coaching of Maj Mike Campbell-Lamerton.

They won the FARELF Cup twice, beating the New Zealand Battalion on both occasions, and got eight Regimental players into the Colony side for the Asian Cup Competitions. (Hong Kong got into the finals twice losing to Japan each time.) Maj Reid, Sgts Basu and Cagilaba and Cpls Cuss and Waquabaca played some superb rugby during this period.

Returning to the UK in 1972 the Regiment won the Army Cup and Sgt Dickens achieved a Regimental record by winning his fifth Army Cup winner's medal.

In recent years the Dukes have won the Army Cup in 1975, 1978, 1979 and 1981 and were runners-up in 1976 and 1983. The Regiment's rugby tradition remains with stars like Sgt Williams and familiar Regimental names in the younger editions of Shuttleworth, Grieve and Isles.

THE ROYAL LEICESTERSHIRE REGIMENT

There were two periods covering about ten years in Regimental rugby history when the Tigers were a power in the Army Cup; the first and greatest was just before the First World War, from 1908 to 1912 inclusive, and the second was in the early 1930s, from 1932 to 1936.

Lieut Clive Liddell, later to become Gen Sir Clive and Colonel of the Regiment, became a founder member of the Army Rugby Union in 1906.

Before the First World War the eight winners of the Army Cup were all Infantry battalions of Line Regiments and the 1st Battalion the Leicestershire Regiment (as it then was) was the most successful, winning the Cup in 1908, 1911 and 1912; they were beaten in the final after extra time in 1910, and beaten by the Welch in the 1909 semi-final.

They did not enter a team in 1907, the inaugaural year, as both battalions were in India. That year Liddell joined the 2nd Battalion there, and he trained and led them to two wins in the Madras Cup, in 1908 and 1909.

The 1st Battalion returned to England in the summer of 1907 and were stationed at Shorncliffe where 2nd Lieut Walter Wilson (who had already played for the Army and England that year) joined them. He was a very good centre threequarter who, although he played for the Army against the Navy in 1908, 1909, 1910 and 1911, did not play for England again after 1907.

Also serving with the 1st Battalion was Capt Brock, a very good centre, and Lieut 'Tough' Yalland, who besides being a good forward himself was a good leader and trainer for forwards. These three formed a very good nucleus for a Regimental team and started hard training and match practice forthwith. Although these three practised and played a great deal with the Regimental side, they also managed to find time to play first-class rugger. All three played for Richmond and the Army, though Brock was only capped once and that was against the Navy in 1909 – playing in the centre with Wilson. Yalland also played for the Army but did not get a cap against the Navy; he did however play for Hampshire.

The battalion entered for the Army Cup for the first time in the 1907/08 season, won 33–0 in the first round, 26–0 in the second and 16–0 in the semi-final. In the final, a very hard game at Aldershot, they beat the 1st Battalion the Welch Regiment by one goal to a dropped goal. It is interesting to note that their line was not crossed once in an Army match that year.

The 1908/09 season saw the start of a most successful half-back combination between Ptes Smitten and Fisher, which lasted for at least another three years and helped the battalion to win two more Army Cups.

They won the first round 12–5 and the second 36–5. The semi-final was played at Cardiff. Perhaps this helped the Welch but they deserved to win a hard fought battle 9–0 and they went on to win the Cup. There was no score at half-time but the inability of the Leicesters' forwards to win the ball in the tight scrums gave few chances to their brilliant outsides and resulted in their first defeat in the Army Cup.

In 1910 the Leicesters and the Gloucesters had the great honour of being the first two Army sides to play at Twickenham before the then Prince of Wales, later King George V. Again the Leicesters had reached the final without a point being scored against them. It was a tremendous defensive battle with everybody playing as hard as he possibly could. All their forwards played well and so did the backs, with Wilson and Brock outstanding. After forty minutes each way there was no score and fifteen minutes each way was then ordered. Eventually in the second half of extra time Cpl James of the Gloucesters, the tallest man on the field, hurled himself at the line. He was tackled by a Tiger, landed on his head over the line, but managed to ground the ball, which acrobatic feat won the Cup! This, therefore, must have been the first score by anyone playing in an Army Cup or Army match at Twickenham.

In the 1910/11 season the Leicesters won 74–6 in the first round, 49–0 in the second and 7–0 in the semi-final against the Welch. In the final against the Life Guards their forwards were the same as those who had played in the previous final. Of the backs, Kitchen regained his place as full-back and Lieut Rolph replaced Brock, on whom age was perhaps beginning to tell. The game was played mostly in a blizzard and saw the last appearance of Lieut Wilson, the captain, and also of Lieut Yalland, the leader of the forwards. The Leicesters won 14-0.

At the start of the 1911/12 season the prospects looked black; six replacements, including those for Wilson and Yalland had to be found. However, Liddell had returned home from India to captain and train the side and Nott and Pte Walker, who both also played soccer and hockey for the battalion, now started to play more rugger, and proved such an excellent pair of threequarters that they played for the Army.

Twenty-two played that year and they scored 60 points without a beating. Everybody felt it would be Liddell's year – and they were right. Their line was only crossed once and the two other scores against them were penalties. They beat the 1st Battalion the Gloucestershire Regiment 13-3 in the semi-final and 2nd Battalion Welch 6-3 in the final, after extra time.

In October 1912 the battalion moved from Aldershot to Fermoy in Southern Ireland. In the second round they beat the 2nd Battalion the Duke of Wellington's Regiment 16-0. Their backs Osborne, Rolph, Nott and Walker all played very well; Osborne, running very fast, scored two excellent tries and Walker one. In the third round the Life Guards got their revenge and deservedly won 10-0.

Looking back, the Leicesters were lucky to start with such outstanding players as Wilson, Brock and Yalland, two good halves in Smitten and Fisher and later outstanding replacements in Liddell, Nott and Walker, none of whom ever seemed to be injured for vital games. Furthermore, they were lucky in having ideal stations for winning the Army Cup in Shorncliffe and Aldershot. Also, from the Regimental point of view they were perhaps fortunate that Wilson was never again selected to play for England after 1907.

Between the Great Wars

The Tigers' success in the Army Cup was, in a way, surprising because unlike two of the other most successful sides prior to the Second World War – the Welch and the Dukes – their other ranks preferred to play soccer rather than rugger. In India the Regiment won the Madras Association Football Cup as many as five times.

For over ten years after the First World War the Regiment had little success in the Army Rugby Cup because the Home battalion, the 2nd, was concentrating on soccer very successfully. The Regiment is one of the few to win both the Army Rugby and Association Football Cups.

The 2nd Battalion was runner-up in the 1926 Association Cup Final and won the Cup in 1927.

But the fact that interest in rugby and the ability to play good rugby by a regimental side was not dead, was shown in 1927 when the 1st Battalion won the Egypt Command Cup, beating Royal Engineers Egypt by 10–3 in the final. Unlike most good Army Cup sides, when so many of the team came from the Officers' Mess, six of this team (RQMS Cave, CSM Smitten, CSM Havilland, CQMS Morson, Sgt Hately and Sgt Dand) all came from the Sergeants' Mess.

Soon after the 1927 successes of the 1st Battalion at rugby in Egypt and of the 2nd Battalion at home at soccer, the two greatest rugby players the Regiment ever had, Tony Novis and Joe Kendrew, joined the 2nd battalion in Catterick, Tony in 1929 and Joe in 1931. Some of the Battalion's best sides now included nine or even ten officers, but there was an Army Rugby Union Rule that a maximum of eight officers could play in an Army Cup side. They were therefore occasionally in the peculiar position of not being able to play their best side in the Army Cup.

The 1931/32 season was Kendrew's first with the Regiment and confidence was growing in the ability of the team. They had a bye in the first round, won the second 8–3, the third 19–0 but in the fourth had a very hard fight against the King's Own, beating them 7–6. In the final at Aldershot they played the Welsh Guards, who deservedly won an unspectacular game by 11–3. The Cup was presented to them by the Prince of Wales, later King Edward VIII, their Colonel-in-Chief.

In November 1932 the battalion moved from Catterick to Londonderry, Northern Ireland; because of the travel involved and their past record, for the next four years they were exempted from playing in the first two or three rounds of the Army Cup. They reached the semi-final against the Welsh Guards, the Cup holders, with some confidence and won 9–3.

In the final they played the 1st Battalion the Duke of Wellingtons' Regiment at Aldershot. The Dukes' Commanding Officer was none other than Lieut-Col Walter Wilson who had captained the very successful Tiger side from 1908 to 1911 inclusive! The Dukes won 19–8, although they had been losing at half-time.

Novis was injured early in the 1933/34 season and took no part in games for the Regiment, the Army or for England. Kendrew was injured in the British trials, so neither of them played in the fourth round against the South Wales Borderers. Thanks to an excellent dropped goal by Haynes the team managed to win 4–0. In the semi-final against the Welsh Guards, though Novis was still injured, Kendrew was fit again and they were strengthened in the pack by the play of Lieut Drummond, who had recently returned from the 1st Battalion in India and had already played for the Army, Leicestershire and Leicester. After a close game they lost 11–14.

The battalion entered the Army Cup in the third round of the 1935/36 and 1937 competitions. Both matches were played in 1936 against the Welch, winners of the Cup in 1935, 1937 and 1939. Both matches were lost; in the first at Londonderry by two dropped goals and a penalty goal to nil; and in the second at Belfast by 6–0, a try and a penalty. Both games were hard fought and after the first match the Leicesters were the first team for three years whose line the Welch had failed to cross. In the second match the recently joined Sandhurst Blues, Lieuts Marriott, a threequarter and Army player, Marshall, a forward, and Daniells, a scrum-half, all played well.

This period between the two great wars finally ended successfully when in 1939 the 1st Battalion in India beat 2nd Welch 6–3 in the final of the Calcutta Rugby Cup.

After the Second World War the Leicesters never established themselves again as a top-class rugby regiment. H O Godwin played for England in 1959 and it was the fourth International cap to be awarded to a member of the Regiment whilst serving. Only two other Infantry regiments, the Duke of Wellington's Regiment and the Welch Regiment have had more Internationals.

THE WELCH REGIMENT

(The spelling varied between Welsh and Welch until 1921 when 'Welch' was finally authorised.)

The Welch Regiment played a consistently important part in the development of Rugby Union Football, not only within the British Army but also in many countries throughout the world.

It is fitting that this story should start in the year 1893, for although rugby was played in the Welch Regiment before that date, it was the year that Wales won the coveted Triple Crown for the first time and this created a great deal of enthusiasm for the game in the Regiment.

In the year 1893 the 2nd Battalion the Welch Regiment were stationed in Deccan in India and it was that year that the captain of the battalion 1st XV, Capt L Brandreth, proposed that Rugby Union Football be given up and the whole energy of the battalion be devoted to Association Football! This created a minor sensation. The proposition was defeated.

From that day on rugby was always the first game of the Regiment. The following year in 1894 under the captaincy of the same Capt Brandreth, the 2nd Battalion the Welch Regiment won the Bombay Cup and held the trophy for eight consecutive seasons. In the same year the 1st Battalion were stationed in Pembroke Dock enjoying Welsh rugby. However, when the war in South Africa broke out they set sail for that other hallowed rugby land. It was in 1903 that one of the most famous rugby characters in the history of the Army Rugby Union joined the 1st Battalion, namely Lieut J E C Partridge. 'The Bird' or 'Birdie', as he was affectionately known, had been playing rugby with Newport. He arrived in the 1st Battalion after the rough going of the South African campaign and at that time the battalion had a company of mounted infantry. 'Birdie' himself holds the unique record of being the only Welshman to be capped for South Africa. He gained a full South African cap against a touring British XV. That cap is still to this day in the Regimental museum at Cardiff, along with many other rugby relics belonging to members of the Regiment.

The 2nd Battalion maintained a wonderful record in India by winning the Calcutta, Bombay, Poona and Madras Cups for several years. In 1908 they left India for South Africa and several members of the battalion played for the Orange Free State in the Currie Cup Competition. Whilst they were stationed at Bloemfontein they won the Roden Cup.

In 1910 the 2nd Battalion left South Africa for Wales. They quickly settled down to their task of regaining the Army Rugby Cup and in the 1911/12 season they once again reached the final, only to lose yet again to their old rivals the Leicestershire Regiment. In the same season the battalion won the Pembrokeshire County and West of Llanelli Cups.

In the final the following year, 1913, they defeated the Gloucestershire Regiment nine points to three. Four of the players – Capt Partridge, Lieut Gransmore, Cpl Murphy and Pte Fisher – had played for the 1st Battalion when they won the trophy in 1909.

In 1920 the Army resumed their Inter-Service matches against the Royal Navy, and the honour of representing the Service was extended to all ranks. CSMI C W 'Charlie' Jones, a forward of outstanding ability, was the first other rank to be awarded his Army cap. He went on to represent Wales against England, Scotland and France, and to this day he is well remembered in both Regimental and Army circles.

In 1920 this same battalion was stationed in Dublin and played such teams as Trinity College, Monkstown, Bective, Palmerston and Landsdowne. Whilst the 2nd Battalion were enjoying such tremendous success in the UK, the 1st Battalion won the All India Rugby Cup in 1924 and 1925 and the Cawnpore and Calcutta Cups in 1926. They left India in 1927 and after eight months in Aden they arrived at Southampton in November to end a tour of service abroad which had begun in 1909.

1927 saw the 2nd Battalion in China and in January 1928 a unique event occurred in the history of rugby football with the visit of the British Army rugby team to Japan. The majority of the players were from the 2nd Battalion and the captain of the side was Capt B U S Cripps. The team were the guests of the Kanto Rugby Union and were met with a great welcome and the most lavish hospitality wherever they went. Five matches were played before crowds varying from 8000 to 20,000. The Army won four games and the other game was drawn. Prince Chichibou, the Crown Prince, was present at most of the games and took a great personal interest in the tour. He was most anxious to get the game established in Japan. Lieut-Gen Sir Charles Coleman, a former Colonel of the Welch Regiment, was a member of that touring team. In memory of such a unique and enjoyable tour the British Army (Shanghai) presented a trophy to be competed for annually by the rugby XVs of the Japanese universities.

A letter from the Secretary of the Japanese Rugby Union, written long after the event in around 1960, confirmed that the trophy had been competed for annually by the teams of the Kanto Rugby Union, which is the area governing the capital city of Tokyo. So it was presented really to the best team in Japan. Unfortunately the trophy was destroyed during the heavy bombing of Tokyo during the war – a tragic ending to a gesture of friendship. However, in his letter, the secretary said that some of the honourable Japanese gentlemen who had played in those games were still living and still met to reminisce about the tour.

Between 1920 and 1924 and 2nd Battalion played in five consecutive Army Cup Finals and won the trophy four times. One of the outstanding players of this period was Capt R M Phillips who played for the Army and played in a Welsh trial as an outside half. Remarkably he had not played rugby before he joined the Regiment, having been to a soccer school.

Once again back in India the 2nd Battalion confirmed their reputation by winning the following trophies:

All India Cup	1931, 1933
Calcutta Cup	1931, 1932
Bombay Cup	1932, 1933

Another piece of rugby history was made in 1936 when the Welch Regiment with the aid of the MEs constructed a rugby ground at Landi Kotal and became the first regiment to play rugby in the Khyber Pass.

On that historic note we leave the 2nd Battalion and turn our attention to the form of the 1st Battalion. From 1930 until 1934 the 1st Battalion went through a building-up process and it was not until 1934 that the team really got into its stride. This period also coincided with the return to England of several of the famous 2nd Battalion players who had by now completed their seven-year tour in India. The 1st Battalion had a captain who had the ability to make the mediocre player good and the good brilliant and to accomplish this by sheer inspiration and personal leadership. Brig B T V Cowey took over the captaincy of the 1st Battalion when he was a subaltern and blended them into a team whose achievements became equal to those of the famous 2nd Battalion side of the 1920s. He achieved all the honours available to him; he was the first officer of the Welch Regiment to play for Wales, and he also became a Barbarian. He dedicated himself to the Welch Regiment and Army rugby.

The spectacular exploits of this 1st Battalion team really started in the 1934/35 season when after a tour of South Wales the team returned to Aldershot to contest the Aldershot Command Final against the King's Own. 'Bun' Cowey, who was injured in the Wales v England match, was not available and for the first time in memory the Welch Regiment played that game without an officer in the side. Irrespective of the absence of officers the team managed to capture the Command Trophy!

The final of the Army Rugby Union Cup was played at Aldershot against the South Wales Borderers and after a very exciting all Welsh final the result was victory for the Welch Regiment by 11 points to nil. Later that year the 1st Battalion threequarters, namely Lieuts B T V Cowey, B E W McCall, Ptes Jimmy Delaney and Curly Williams, broke the Army record in Aldershot by winning the 4 × 110 yards relay in a time of 44.15 seconds! This was a fine achievement after such a hard rugby season.

The 1936/37 season again brought the Army Cup back to the Regiment. 'Bun' Cowey, who had once more taken up the reins, led his side to a glorious win over the Welsh Guards in the UK Final in front of a record mid-week crowd of over 5000 spectators at the famous Cardiff Arms Park. It was a most exciting game and the civilian critics were amazed at the speed and handling expertise of the Welch three-quarters. The Army Final was played against the 1st Battalion the Prince of Wales Volunteers whom the Welch beat 13-7.

The 1937/38 season was not a success as far as the Army Cup was concerned, for in the semi-final round the battalion lost to their old foes the Gloucesters.

The 1938/39 season opened with a fine win over the Dublin Wanderers, followed by three good wins in Belfast. The team then crossed the Irish Sea to take on Waterloo, who were captained by H B Toft, the English captain; also included in the Waterloo side were J Heaton and two other Internationals. The game was a thriller, thoroughly enjoyed by a large crowd. The final result was 10 points to three in favour of Waterloo.

The team now returned to Ireland and before the third round of the Army Cup they defeated Bective Rangers in Dublin and played a draw with Queen's University in Belfast. The team then travelled to Leicester to play their old rivals the 1st Battalion the Duke of Wellington's Regiment in the semi-final and defeated them 25 points to three. The scene was now set for the final against the 2nd Battalion the Gloucestershire Regiment who were the holders. This proved a clash of styles, for the Gloucesters had three of the Army pack, including Lieut Tony Arengo-Jones, whilst the Welch had three of the Army backs in Lieut Champion, Sgt Ibbitson and Pte Jimmy Delaney, as well as their two International wings, 'Bun' Cowey and John Ford. The Gloucesters pack was extremely hard and tough but the well drilled Welch side not only held them but defeated them by six points to three.

It shows the strength of the Welch Regiment rugby that a member of the Regiment played in the position of wing threequarter for Wales in each season from 1934 to 1939 inclusive: B T V Cowey 1934–35, B W McCall 1936, W H Clements (4th Bn TA) 1937–38, and E J V Ford 1939.

The outbreak of the Second World War saw the 1st Battalion in Palestine and the 2nd Battalion in India. It was in between training for war in the desert that the 1st Battalion managed to fit in a few games, and naturally first and foremost was rugger. In April 1940 the 1st Battalion XV took to the air for the first time and flew to Cairo to play a New Zealand XV. After a truly magnificent game they lost by 11 points to nine. Very little rugby was recorded in the 1st Battalion from that date until after the war but there is no doubt that during lulls in battle games were arranged and played between 'international' sides.

Immediately after the Second World War many local rugby competitions were introduced and the Welch Regiment played a significant part in the revival. The 1st Battalion, who had ended the war stationed in Italy, entered the CMF Competition and were narrowly defeated in the final by a very strong South African Divisional team. At the same time the 4th Battalion, who had in their midst Maj Bill Clements, a British Lion and Welsh International man, won the BAOR trophy. This battalion was commanded by Lieut-Col Geoff Burnett, who was a very active member of the Swansea Club, and the team was captained by Maj A Davis.

The 1st Battalion returned to the UK in 1947. However, it was not until 30 October 1948 that they embarked once more upon the Army

Cup trail. The team improved steadily and in the quarter-final of the competition they defeated the Welsh Guards at Burtons Court, Chelsea. The scene was now set for the first of many encounters with the Royal Signals and on the 29 January 1949 they lost by 19 points to 14 in the UK Final. The 1st Battalion had a very interesting side that day and apart from Majs John Ford and Monty Champion, who had both played in the 1939 final, they included John Lane of Newport and Roy Bish of Aberavon. In 1951 the battalion left for Korea and during a spell in the line they played a game against the Kiwis.

> The Kiwi guns fired steadily throughout the game – the shells passing low over the ground. The crash of gunfire, the scream of shells and the cries of supporters, combined to produce a memorable symphony. The spirit and high standard of play shown in the game promised well for the future of Bn rugby, though a number of discoveries will no longer be with us.

After Korea the battalion moved to Hong Kong; the first season was rather a drab affair but once more 'Bun' Cowey appeared, this time as Commanding Officer of the 1st Battalion. In that particular season the battalion won the FARELF Cup, the Hong Kong Land Forces Cup, the Blarney Stone Sevens, the Tamar Cup and the Brigade Shield. The final of the FARELF Cup was the real highlight of the season, for their opponents – the Fijian Infantry Regiment – had not lost a game for four years, but they had not reckoned with the Welch who, in a genuinely thrill-packed game, ran out the winners by 11 points to 10. That game is still a talking point in Hong Kong rugby circles.

It was in 1956 that the 1st Battalion captured for the fifth time (tenth time for the Regiment) the Army Cup that had managed to elude them since the end of the Second World War. Inspired by the Commanding Officer and ably led by Capt John Davey it gave the Regiment a great deal of satisfaction to dispose of the Royal Signals in the quarter-final.

It was with great sorrow that the rugby history of this famous Regiment was brought to a close in 1969. The 1st Battalion had seen many fine players and like the 2nd Battalion had earned their share of rugby glory.

In 1969 the Welch Regiment and the South Wales Borderers amalgamated to become the Royal Regiment of Wales. It was a fitting coincidence that, having been won in the 1968/69 season by the South Wales Borderers, the Army Rugby Cup was already based in the Officers' Mess.

THE GLOUCESTERSHIRE REGIMENT

HISTORICAL ORIGINS AND CHANGES IN TITLE

1694: Colonel Gibson's Regiment of
Foot
1742: 28th Regiment of Foot
1782: 28th (or North Gloucestershire)
Regiment of Foot
1881: 1st Bn The Gloucestershire
Regiment

1756: 2nd Bn 3rd (or East Kent) Regiment of
Foot (The Buffs)
1758: 61st Regiment of Foot
1782: 61st (or South Gloucestershire)
Regiment of Foot
1881: 2nd Bn The Gloucestershire
Regiment

In 1910 the 2nd Battalion reached the Army Final and Cpl James hurled himself over the line to score the only try of the match; he was the first soldier to score a try at Twickenham and he won the match for the Glosters. H Berry was another tower of strength in the side and gained four International caps for England but, being an other rank, he was debarred from playing for the Army. He is however, surprisingly enough, the only Gloster ever to gain International Honours while serving in the Army.

The 1st Battalion reached the semi-final in 1912 when the Leicesters got their revenge by winning 13 points to three. In 1913 and 1914 the Glosters again reached the final but again had to be satisfied with being runners-up. Nevertheless they had imprinted their name on Army rugby.

After the 1914–18 war the 2nd Battalion were sent out to India where they remained until 1929. During the tour of duty they won the Calcutta Cup in 1927.

On returning to England they were posted to Gravesend and had little opportunity to play Service sides so they arranged fixtures with London club XVs. They managed to defeat these sides through fitness rather than by ability and these games helped to improve the standard of play.

The battalion was fortunate in that about sixty per cent of the recruits enlisted into the Regiment were Gloucestershire men from Bristol, Gloucester and the Forest of Dean. A large proportion had played rugby at schools and small clubs and some were even schoolboy Internationals.

The standard was such that in the first two years after returning from India only one officer was able to win a place in the Regimental side and for the next three years there were only two officers playing. Most of the men in the Regiment are of medium-sized physique, and

so it was decided to form a team which would play an open game –
throwing the ball about – backed up by fast-moving forwards.

The battalion made good progress playing this type of rugby and in
1932 they won the Eastern Command Rugby Cup and reached the
semi-final of the Army Cup, in which they were beaten in a replay by
the Welsh Guards.

Finally in 1938 they reached the final. Fifteen coaches and numerous
private cars were packed with supporters, and on arrival at the ground
there were many ex-members of the Regiment who had travelled by
bus, train and cars to add their vocal support. Amongst these followers
was Gen A W Pagan who had played in the winning team of 1910.

The Welsh Guards were a strong all-round side and a thrilling game,
described on page 194, was won by a fine penalty kick taken by
Arengo-Jones. The battalion reached the final again in 1939 but could
not beat the Welch Regiment.

During the war the 1st Battalion, after serving in Burma, returned
to Calcutta, where playing conditions are of interest. The season was
short, from July to September during the monsoon. Games were
mainly of twenty-five minutes each way, and the kick-off timed for
between five and six o'clock in the evenings. Conditions were of two
kinds – either very dry and dusty with a fairly hard ground which
favoured open play, or after a monsoon downpour very wet and
muddy. One local hazard was 'Calcutta Pink Eye' which afflicted Service teams especially; when the mud dried a fine dust was formed,
particles of which inevitably got into the players eyes. The composition
of the soil caused an infection which developed into a most painful
and unsightly form of conjunctivitis. Teams were known to be deci-
mated by this. In the 28th this infection was combatted fairly successfully; all members of the team bathed their eyes with a saline solution
immediately on return to barracks after the game. It was a case of first
stop – the MI room and the eye bath under the watchful eye of the
medical sergeant rather than the wet canteen for a beer.

By 1946 the 28th were in Doolali. A few matches were played locally
and a tour of Bombay resulted in two defeats and one victory.

The Regiment did not win the All India Cup but they won the
Calcutta Cup three times and were five times runners-up. They also
have the distinction of being the only Regiment whose 1st and 2nd
Battalions both won the Calcutta Cup.

In recent years the Regiment has not been able to reach the high
standards of previous years but it is encouraging to see that there has
been a marked improvement in the early 1980s.

THE SOUTH WALES BORDERERS
24th REGIMENT

HISTORICAL ORIGINS AND CHANGES IN TITLE

1689: Sir Edward Dering's Regiment of Foot
1751: 24th Regiment of Foot
1782: 24th (or 2nd Warwickshire) Regiment of Foot
1881: The South Wales Borderers

The Regiment was associated with the Army Rugby Union from it's inception in 1906, which was only proper for a regiment drawing its soldiers in the main from the rugby football fanatics of the mining and steel valleys of South Wales and Monmouthshire.

Indeed the first Secretary of the ARU was a South Wales Borderer, Lieut-Col G H Birkett, a fine player who, but for recurrent injury problems, would undoubtedly have played for the Army. He led the 2nd Battalion of the 24th in the Regiment's first Appearance in the final round of the Army Cup in 1908/09 when they lost to the 1st Battalion The Welch Regiment.

Thereafter the World War and overseas service combined to prevent serious participation until the season of 1922/23 when the 1st Battalion built a really good side and commenced a successful five-year spell. The 24th were lucky to have at this time an outstanding captain and coach in Capt C A ('Muddy') Baker. Baker played for the Army whilst still a gentleman cadet at Sandhurst and was a regular member of the North Midlands County XV.

In the final in 1925 the battalion's opponents were the Royal Horse Guards from Windsor. The 24th won by 16 points to three; tries were scored by Drummer Ward, Pte Rees and Capt Baker. Capt Baker converted two and kicked a penalty goal. Apart from his contribution to the scoring, Baker had dominated the game with his defensive and tactical kicking.

In the 1925/26 Army Cup Final the 24th as holders emerged as victors for the second successive year against the Welsh Guards by 10 points to three. The following year the very strong Regimental XV prepared for the Army Cup campaign with some good civilian opposition. They beat Waterloo 1st XV twice by 14–0 and 16–3 and drew 11 all with Liverpool who had two Internationals playing. The 24th's progress in the Army Cup competition was marked by victories over

2nd (Pack) Brigade RA (14-0), 2nd Battalion Welch (18-0), 1st Battalion Duke of Wellington's (6-0), the Welsh Guards (11-0) and the Durham Light Infantry by 21 points to three.

The final was played at Aldershot on 16 March 1927 and the 24th's opponents were the Royal Engineers, Aldershot. The 24th won for the third year by a score of nine points to eight.

News that the 1st Battalion was to move abroad and that it was likely to be the last year for some time that they would enter for the Army Cup competition put a special significance on the 1927/28 season.

The final against the 1st Battalion The King's own Royal Regiment proved to be a desperately close-run thing. The final whistle blew with the score at 15 points to 14 to the 24th.

The 24th's feat in winning the Army Cup for four successive years was to remain unique until 1968 when the Duke of Wellington's Regiment matched it. Despite many more fine XVs it was also the last time the Cup was won by the Regiment until the final year before amalgamation with the Welch Regiment to form the Royal Regiment of Wales. During this period Capt Baker had been the outstanding player and personality of this most successful side. His personal contribution on the field of play had often been decisive.

The 24th had been lucky to be able to build and keep a XV for the six years necessary to perform this feat. They also had some outstandingly good players: L/Sgts W Thomas and D Jones had played for the Army along with Capt Baker, and Lieut A C Martin was to play for the Army in 1931 and gain a Hampshire County cap.

The rugby balls from the four finals, strangely round to modern eyes and blackened by age, are to be found in the regimental museum at Brecon as a monument to this great achievement.

In 1932/33 the 1st Battalion continued to provide twelve members of the Army XV in Hong Kong whilst the 2nd Battalion moved from Portsmouth to Catterick. On arrival they received the news that their opponents in the first round of the Army Cup were to be the Gloucesters, one of the semi-finalists of the previous year. This game was played on 1 November and turned out to be a match between the big and powerful Gloucester forwards and the 24th's fast and clever backs. On that day might triumphed and the Gloucesters won by 11 points to three. Having departed the Army Cup, the battalion toured Wales and ended up with the creditable record for the season of: played 15; won 10; lost five (including the three matches on tour).

In 1934 the 2nd Battalion set out on a most successful season. Apart from the Service matches, they had a Christmas tour of South

Wales, during which matches were played against Bridgend (6–21), Newport Police (3–5) and Glamorgan Police (9–29). This tour, though not successful from the result point of view, was invaluable in getting the team fighting fit for the Army Cup. Their path to the final was littered with famous regiments: Gloucesters 9–3; Leicesters 18–6; Duke of Wellington's 33–10 and Welsh Guards 6–3. The final was played against the Welch Regiment and resulted in a defeat by 0–11.

The 1st Battalion, meanwhile, had decided that as Rawalpindi did not have a rugby ground one had better be built! Rough it was but it did provide somewhere for the inter-company games to be played and trials to be held. Indeed battalion matches were played against the 2nd Battalion the Welch Regiment (won 9–8) and a combined Royal Tanks Corps XV (drawn 0–0). The following year better things were in store, for the 1st Battalion sent a team to Calcutta to play in the tournament there and then to Bombay for the All India tournament. They reached the semi-final of the Calcutta tournament to be beaten 11 points to nil by Calcutta Football Club who went on to win the tournament. In the All India tournament the 24th reached the fourth round and forced the Madras XV to extra time before losing 3–0. The forwards had supplied plenty of the ball but the inexperienced backs had not been able to use it.

After barren rugby seasons in Rawalpindi and Waziristan, the 1st Battalion moved to Landi Kotal to find a grass pitch which had been made by the 2nd Battalion the Welch Regiment. The 24th started their usual preparations, in the form of Company competitions, to find a battalion XV to take part in the District Competition at Peshawar. A promising side emerged with big, fit and fast forwards and quick, clever backs, including Capt D L Rhys who had contributed so much to the 2nd Battalion's efforts in the past and whose experience was invaluable. The first game was played in a sea of mud, against Peshawar and was distinguished – according to a diarist – 'more by the robust nature of the play than by any scientific brilliance'. The 24th won this game by five points to nil thanks to a centre-threequarter try that was converted. The second round was at Risalpur against the RAF who were reputed to be a formidable combination. This time the ground had been baked as hard as concrete but, with a plentiful supply of the ball, the 24th backs were able to shine and scored five tries to the RAF one. Place kicking proved to be difficult and only one of the five was converted to make the final score 17–3. In the final the 24th beat the Royal Corps of Signals to win the Peshawar Cup and thus completed a limited but unbeaten season.

After the start of the Second World War, rugby was played whenever possible and the 2nd Battalion managed a number of games in England and Northern Ireland.

The start of 1945/46 season saw the 1st Battalion stationed in Kent, whilst the 2nd were still in Germany. In October 1945 the 1st Battalion moved to Palestine and then set out to build a rugby XV to live up to the Regiment's pre-war exploits. It was one of the best in the Regiment's history.

In the first season they played 15 matches; won 15 and scored 328 points to 34. The star players also gained higher honours; Lieut Morgan, L/Sgt Owen and Pte Gravelle were picked for the local Army XV. No less than ten members of the side played in an area XV which beat the 6th Airborne Division and seven players represented 'Wales v Ireland' in Jerusalem.

The highlight of this season was a tour to Cairo. Three matches were played, two against RAF sides and one against the Cairo Army. The RAF were disposed of 50-0 and 23-3 but the Army XV provided much stiffer oposition. Kelleher scored an opportunist try for the 24th which was converted and gave the battalion a 5-0 lead at half-time. The Army XV had a big and talented pack and had the better of the 24th in the set pieces but it was different in loose play and soon after half-time some brilliant play saw Sgt Walkamer touch down with three opponents clinging to him. Near the end the 24th scored a third try to clinch the result at 11 points to nil.

The 6th Battalion, in India, had also been keeping the 24th rugby flag flying. In 1943 they won the 36th Division Cup and only just lost to the Welch in the Bombay Gymkhana Tournament. In October 1945 they moved to Sumatra where they were unbeaten, although they were pressed hard by a battalion of the Duke of Wellington's Regiment.

In May 1946 the 1st Battalion moved to Cyprus and began the 1946/47 season by beating three combined XVs by a total of 99 points to nil. In January 1947, in search of sterner opposition, the battalion XV set off on a tour of Palestine and Egypt. The first game of the tour was against the 3rd Battalion Grenadier Guards at Lydda. The game was abandoned after twenty-five minutes, with the score at 14-0 to the 24th, because of an alarm which required the presence of the Grenadiers in Tel Aviv. RAF Aquir and the 1st Division XV, the next two opponents, were disposed of 23-0 and 38-0 respectively; the hooking of Pte Smith was an outstanding feature of the latter game. Cairo provided matches against the RAF Heliopolis (35-6), GHQ 2nd Echelon (23-0) and the Cairo Casuals (25-3). In these matches it was the backs who impressed, as they revelled in the springy green turf of the Bezira Sporting Club. The slick play of the half-backs Lieut Dennis Wilson and Capt Don Mackney was well supported by the elusive Kelleher and the strong-running Lieut Stan Humphries in the centre.

After Cairo it was back to Palestine for the final two matches of the tour, which were thought likely to provide the severest tests. 6th Airborne Division were first, and for the first time for two seasons the 24th found themselves in arrears. A tremendous forward effort, however, provided the 24th with enough of the ball for L/Cpl Williams on the right wing to get over for three tries, and make the battalion's record safe with a score of 21-6. Palestine Police were confident of taking the battalion record as they themselves had been unbeaten in 1946/47. Despite a growing injury list, the 24th contained the larger Police forwards, with Capt Owen, Sgt Evans and Lieuts Priestly and Connell prominent, and once this was settled the backs won the game 14 points to nil. The season ended with three more matches in Cyprus, all of which were won, and an outstanding side remained unbeaten. The team, led by Capt D R Morgan, had played 14 and won 14 (points for: 362; points against: 15). As a final flourish, the 24th won the Jerusalem seven-a-side tournament for the second year.

In March 1949 the 1st Battalion moved to Khartoum and there, yet again, refused to be daunted by heat and hard ground. The grass was kept alive by flooding the pitch to a depth of about four inches with Blue Nile water every week! Only half the battalion was available at any one time as the other companies were in Eritrea, but two representative matches were played against RAF Khartoum and a local Combined Services XV and both were won. 1950 found the whole battalion in Eritrea busy chasing Shifta and with no rugby opposition. Despite an altitude of 6000 feet, company games continued whenever possible. Towards the end of 1952 serious trials began in order to find a battalion XV for their return to the UK in October. For the 1953/54 season saw the majority of the previous year's XV was available.

The situation at the start of the season 1954/55 was uncertain. Several of the star players of the previous year remained but many others had gone. An early start was made and trial matches began in August so that by September a promising team had been produced. Second Lieut Yates led the XV at centre with Sgt Webb and Cpl Morgan remaining in the backs, whilst Cpl Davidge and Pte E Miles were still amongst the forwards. The season started well with high-scoring wins and the 24th progressed again to the fifth round of the Army Cup with victories over the King's Shropshire Light Infantry (32-0), 11th Armed Division Column RASC (12-0), 2nd Regiment RHA (9-0) and 1st Battalion Grenadier Guards (14-0).

Back in Germany the Army Cup semi-final versus 30th Heavy Anti Aircraft Regiment RA was won by six points to nil and so, for the second successive year the 24th were in the BAOR Final. Their opponents were 1st Battalion the Royal Welch Fusiliers, largely an unknown quantity but who had good forwards and in Sergeant Glenville Jones, of 24th 1947/48 XV fame, they had a tactician and a kicker who demanded the utmost respect. The match resulted in a 3-3 draw. The conditions for the replay were perfect, which was in marked contrast to those of the original match, and although the RWF forwards again gave a splendid display an early try by Pte Browning on the 24th right wing was the only score and the BAOR Cup belonged to the 24th again.

The final against the Depot and Training establishment RAMC took place at Aldershot. The RAMC had a good all-round side and brilliant half-backs in Fulton, who was a Scottish International, and Maeckelburghe – a County player. Such was their class and speed that despite the 24th forwards exerting considerable pressure, every time the RAMC got the ball they looked likely to score. They eventually did score two tries and two goals to nil.

An unfortunate aspect, from the 24th's point of view, was that due to a miscalculation three star players, Gareth Curtis, Hendy, and Loveridge, had played for a Depot XV in the UK Army Cup and were therefore barred from playing for the battalion when they joined it after Christmas. Curtis's great speed and the elusiveness of Hendy would have made a great contribution to the 24th back play.

In the autumn of 1955 the 24th sailed for Singapore and Malaya for a three-year tour of duty. They were welcomed with great enthusiasm by the local rugby fraternity, despite efforts to play down their reported reputation. Many of the stars of the previous year had left, including Cpl Glyn Davidge, Cpl Norman and 2nd Lieut Eddie Yates and, although Curtis and Hendy were now available, much team building and acclimatisation had to be done. Reinforcements had come in the return of Capt Napier and the arrival of 2nd Lieut Paul Wilkinson and Pte Jenkins who had captained Tredegar.

The 24th's apprehensive approach to rugby in Malaya was justified when the first three matches were lost, albeit by narrow margins. The campaign for the FARELF Cup saw the 24th safely through to the fourth round but at that stage they drew the 1st Battalion the Fiji Infantry Regiment who had a team of outstanding and extrovert athletes and – what was more – were impervious to a temperature in the nineties. The 24th hung on until half-time, keeping the score to 6-8 in favour of the Fijians but late in the game the size, speed and fitness of the Fijians took their toll and the final score rose to six points to 29.

The 1956/57 season started well for the battalion with victories over Selangor Club, Singapore Cricket Club and 1st Battalion the King's Own Scottish Borderers. Gareth Curtis had now been released from the Army, which was a severe blow, but many of the previous year's XV remained, reinforced by Pte Jeff Crocker of Rhymney and by a new Medical Officer, Capt 'Nim' Campbell, RAMC, who had been capped for Scotland but who was actually born in Wales. The FARELF Cup Competition proved a great disappointment, for after a really good game against the Rhodesian African Rifles in the first round – won by 21 points to three – in the second round the 24th played badly against the 1st Battalion KOSB, whom they had already beaten that season, and they lost by 10 points to five.

The 1958/59 season found the 1st Battalion in Brecon and the rugby team reinforced by the bulk of the previous year's depot team. To ensure that the battalion team was ready for the start of the Army Cup Competition, fixtures were played against Pontypool United, Pontypridd, Newbridge and Newport United.

After an easy first round of the Army Cup against 22nd Light Anti Aircraft Regiment RA, much stiffer opposition was found in the following rounds; but the battalion reached the semi-final, which was played on Rorke's Drift Day at Brecon, and by beating the Welsh Guards they were once again qualified for the final.

The UK Final was played at Aldershot, the 24th's opponents being 1st Training Regiment Royal Signals. The 24th had arrived at this final without their line being crossed and the Signals had had only one try scored against them, so a stern defensive battle was anticipated. The Signals won by a single drop goal and the 24th were the losers, despite not conceding a try in the whole competition.

In October 1963 the 24th moved to Hong Kong. The Rugby XV played three matches in Wales before leaving, of which the best performance was in losing only 6–9 to a full strength Abertillery side. On arrival in Hong Kong the 24th insisted on a month to become acclimatised and then took on a representative side from the Army in the colony. This match was won easily by 32 points to nil and as a result eleven battalion players were selected for the Hong Kong Army XV for the Triangular Tournament. The eleven players were: six backs – Sgt Freeman and his brother Pte Brynley Freeman, L/Cpls Long and Kukuve, another Fijian Cpl Buakula who had developed into a fast strong wing, and Bandsman Jenkins at full-back; in addition Capt Isaac was appointed captain of the Army XV and took with him Lieuts

Ensor and Howes, Pte Jenkins and L/Cpl Ralph. The 24th's team was not beaten for the remainder of the season and developed into one of the best since the end of National Service. They played 12 matches, won 10 and drew two (those against Hong Kong Club and Hong Kong Police), scoring 267 points against 27.

However the climax to the season came when, having won the Hong Kong Cup with some ease against 49th Regiment RA (34-0), they learned that their opponents in the final of the FARELF Cup were to be an HQ FARELF XV who had actually beaten the 1st Battalion the New Zealand Infantry Regiment, the favourites. The final was played at the Hong Kong Football Club stadium under flood lights. The Borderers won the match 15-0.

During the summer of 1968 the battalion went to the maritime provences of Canada for a training exercise. Rugby in Canada is a growing game and this was evident as soon as the battalion arrived; despite the heat of a Canadian summer three games were quickly arranged. All three were won, although the last was a cliff-hanger and depended for victory on a last-second try. These matches were tremendous entertainment for those present and provided torrid but valid preparation for the Regiment's final year of rugby before amalgamation with the Welch Regiment.

By an odd quirk of fate, or maybe the efforts of the manning gremlin, the Autumn of 1968 saw 24th rugby in the hands of Maj David Cox, a distinguished Welch Regiment player and in his day a deadly kicker of goals; whilst two of the very best 24th players, Lieuts Mike Howes and Chris Ensor were with 1st Battalion, the Welch Regiment! The Army Cup campaign started well with wins over Depot Regiment RE (26-6), the Life Guards (19-0), 30 Signal Regiment (30-6) and the Guards Depot (19-0). At this stage of the season the battalion arranged a South Wales tour and played fixtures against Glynneath (14-18), Cross Keys United (19-10), and Rhymney (12-9). Fortified by this successful foray into Wales the battalion XV returned to Lydd to resume its attempt on the Army Cup.

The UK Final was once again reached and featured the 24th versus the Welch Guards. The game was postponed on two occasions but when it was eventually played the 24th won 9-8.

The elusive Army Cup was to be competed for in BAOR against 7 Signal Regiment. An early penalty goal gave the Signals hope but the UK half of the competition had produced much the more competitive rugby and the 24th were not under pressure from then on; tries were scored by Cpl O'Brien and L/Cpl Llewellyn, the latter converted by Lieut Tudor Williams who also scored a penalty.

This was a highly emotional moment for the 24th for not only had they won the Army Cup – after having come so close on numerous occasions – for the first time for forty years but also they had achieved this success in their final year of existence. Great credit was due to Lieut Tudor Williams who had trained and captained the XV, and who, through his personal play, had also contributed so much to the stability of the side.

In the summer of 1969 the South Wales Borderers amalgamated with the Welch Regiment to form the Royal Regiment of Wales 24th/41st Foot. Such a combination of Army rugby history should ensure that the Welsh hold on the Army Cup is, if anything strengthened! Shortly before this amalgamation the SWB presented a Challenge Cup to be awarded to the winners of the UK final of the Major Units Army Cup Competition.

THE ROYAL REGIMENT OF WALES

(1969: The South Wales Borderers (24th Foot) amalgamated with the Welch Regiment (41st and 69th Foot) to form the Royal Regiment of Wales.)

On 11 June 1969 two famous rugby-playing regiments, the South Wales Borderers and the Welch Regiment, amalgamated to become the Royal Regiment of Wales. The new Regiment was to be custodian of an outstanding rugby reputation. Between them its two forbears had won the Army Rugby Cup no less than fifteen times and had been runners-up on eight occasions.

The amalgamation of the two rugby sides ensured a high standard from the outset and the team was managed by Maj John Davey, who had captained the Welch Regiment side which had won the Cup in 1955/56. Some of the better players left as the two regiments combined, but a strong nucleus existed to make the first challenge for the Army Cup.

The final in 1970 was held at Aldershot where the 1st Battalion the Royal Regiment of Wales met the 1st Battalion Welsh Guards. Following a short tour in South Wales disaster struck the side, five players went down with influenza and although representations were made to postpone the game these were rejected 'in the most sympathetic manner'. The final was described thus by *The Times* rugby correspondent: 'the game did not have a great deal of skill but enormous enthusiasm and was greatly enjoyed by both teams and their partisans'. The battalion lost 18 points to six and it was from this game that a young player emerged who was later to make his mark on Army and Welsh club rugby. He was Pte John Davies.

The season 1970/71 started well enough – Capt Ken Roberts had become team manager and under his guidance the ability of the players increased. However the battalion were ordered to Northern Ireland in November and preparations for the Cup games and friendly matches against the Irish were carried out against a backdrop of riots, road blocks and patrolling. Despite these setbacks the battalion again reached the Army Cup Final and again their opponents were the Welsh Guards. Sadly, the Aldershot bogey struck again and the side played without their captain, Capt Andy Keelan, or their outside half, Pte Wyndham Lewis, who up to then had been playing brilliantly. The deficiency was not helped by torrential rain that preceded the match and thwarted the hope that the fast-running backs would outpace the opposition. In the event it was a good final with both teams giving their all, but the result was decided on penalty kicks in the Guards' favour and the final score was six points to three.

The 1970s and early eighties are still fresh in our memories and the Regiment can be well satisfied with their record over this decade, having won the Army Cup three times and been runners-up seven times.

THE KING'S OWN ROYAL REGIMENT

The story of the King's Own and rugby football is incomplete without the inclusion of Alfred Aslett. Aslett, leaving Clifton in 1918 where he had played rugger for the school for three seasons, spent two years at Sandhurst. Here, playing for the college of course, he was also selected to play for the Army in one match and thus became one of the very few cadets to achieve this honour.

During eight years Aslett was to play for the Army twenty times and eventually for England in six International matches. It was said that in his prime defending 'threes' did not tackle Aslett, they bounced off him!

Rugby in the Regiment was started seriously in 1920 by two outstanding personalities. The CO, Col Hugh Headlam, brought in from the York and Lancasters, was almost a fanatic about the game and, it is said, played rugger himself at forty-two whilst CO; the Adjutant, Ray Somerville, was another fanatic. These two had prepared the ground for Aslett, when in 1921 he joined the Regiment.

But the story of King's Own rugger must go back to twenty years before the Dublin days of 1920–23. In 1900 a young officer from the militia commission in the Cameronians was posted as a Regular Officer to the Regiment. He was 2nd Lieut J M Young, who as a boy had captained Sedbergh. As perhaps the first of several rugger enthusiasts in the Regiment he formed a team in the 1st Battalion at Aldershot on its return from Singapore in 1900. All the other rank players had to be taught the game, mostly by Jim Young; yet a year later, with this very inexperienced young team he challenged the remainder of the Aldershot Command.

The match was played at the Officers Club. Hockey goal posts were used, slender uprights being tied on to the hockey posts. On several occasions the referee had to stop play in order to explain the rules more fully to some of the players on both sides.

In 1903 Jim Young was selected for a Scottish trial but, owing to being posted abroad to Malta to the 1st Battalion which had now returned to Foreign Service, he was unable to accept the invitation. Jim Young eventually commanded the 1st Battalion in Aldershot, Palestine and Cairo from 1929 until 1933 when he retired.

The Regiment's first essay in the Army Rugby Cup was not auspicious. The team was beaten 48-0 by the Welch Regiment and again in the following year - also by the Welch - but by a smaller margin. By now the team had emerged from being just a good regimental side into being a well-known one. It was getting accustomed to big crowds, big occasions, and limelight. But Aslett kept his head, insisting on military duty first, and rigorous training and modesty.

In 1926 the 1st Battalion got into the semi-final of the Army Cup, losing 8-13 to the Welsh Guards. It won the semi-final in the 1927/28 season against the Dukes, only to lose the final against the South Wales Borderers.

In 1927 the battalion had moved to Aldershot where fixtures against the many units stationed within a five-mile radius were easily arranged. In the three years at Aldershot the Army Cup was won at last, the Welsh Guards going down 21-9; in the following season the Cup was won for the second successive year when the Royal Engineers were defeated 3-0.

In the Aldershot period Sgt Morton, who had joined as a boy in 1916, was capped for the Army in 1928, 1929 and 1930. He eventually became RSM and later, Quartermaster. He died in 1971 aged seventy-one.

During the years from Aslett's advent up to 1930, Sandhurst continued to supply new officer player material in the persons of John Brennan, Claude Lincoln and Hugh Wright, all of whom played for the Army; while in the following decade Anderson and Burke joined the 2nd Battalion, both Regimental players-to-be.

Few of the other ranks enlistments knew anything about rugby football on joining the Army and had to be taught the game. In the Aldershot period, more than fifty per cent of the team had been playing for only three years.

The 2nd Battalion had spent five years in Burma, its first peacetime station after the 1914-18 War. Two years in Mavmyo, 3500 feet up, permitted a little rugger and the Adjutant, Capt R C Matthews, started to build a side during the rains. The Battalion moved to Rangoon in March 1922. Matthew's work bore fruit and a good side developed. Some outstanding players were Lieut Hargreaves (who also played for the battalion at soccer, both as goal-keeper and centre forward, and hockey) and Lieut Card, who was a great little threequarter, and he too represented the battalion at rugger, soccer and hockey. In the same season Capt de Cordova took over the captaincy when Matthews, having finished his adjutancy, was posted home. De Cordova was a bustling forward and a year previously, when a captain at the Depot, had played for Lancashire.

When the battalion finally returned to Lichfield after a tour of duty in the Sudan Lieut R N Anderson (later to be Lieut-Gen Sir Richard and also Colonel of the Regiment for fifteen years) and Lieut Burke took over the building of a side. Anderson had a few players available from the Rangoon side of the six years previously, and some from Aslett's side left in England. Sgt Cooney was still serving, as were Drummer Turner, who also played in the Regimental soccer side when it won the Army Cup in 1934, and Sgt Evans, Lieut Robins (younger brother of the England cricketer, R W V Robins) and Lieut Lugard, who were all outstanding players. In its first season the team was to astonish the Army – and itself – by reaching the fourth round of the Army Cup. In 1936 the 2nd Battalion reached the final.

By winning the Army Cup in 1936, the King's Own became only the second regiment in the British Army to win both the Army Cups, rugby and soccer. For the same battalion to appear in both rugger and soccer Cup Finals in the space of three years was a significant achievement. From this great team Lieut Robins and five other ranks played for the Army, Robins being captain.

Sir Richard Anderson has recalled that after the 2nd Battalion's rugger team's successful – and surprising – first year at Lichfield following its return from the Sudan, he did not again make fixtures with other regimental teams, but only with civilian clubs. He argued that to play a 'friendly' with some other regiment, and possibly to be beaten, would give his team an inferiority complex if it happened to be drawn against that same regiment in the Army Cup! He topped off his argument by expressing the belief that the civilian clubs, mostly filled with ex-University players (though not necessarily 'blues'), played a more scientific game than the military sides and that his team – even when defeated – would gain much skill and learn more finesse from the civilian masters of the game. In the rough and tumble of military rugger tactics and technique might not be considered so important.

Although since 1945 the Regiment (amalgamated in 1959 with the Border Regiment to become the King's Own Royal Border Regiment) has never been able to match the successes of the late twenties and the thirties, it made a valuable contribution to Army rugby.

THE KING'S OWN SCOTTISH BORDERERS

HISTORICAL ORIGINS AND CHANGES IN TITLE
1689: The Earl of Leven's Regiment of Foot ('The Edinburgh Regiment')
1751: 25th (Edinburgh) Regiment of Foot
1782: 25th (or the Sussex) Regiment of Foot
1805: 25th (or King's Own Borderers) Regiment of Foot
1881: The King's Own Borderers
1887: The King's Own Scottish Borderers

Hawick, Gala, Melrose, Langholm, Selkirk, Kelso, Jedburgh – all names to be respected in the world of rugby. It is not surprising therefore that rugger should be a 'natural' for the King's Own Scottish Borderers who recruit from the six counties of the Scottish Border.

It was with great surprise, therefore, that in 1960 the serving members of the Regiment learned from Col E D Jackson, the officer who had introduced rugby to the Regiment in 1905, that for his efforts he had been taken aside by his superiors and warned 'we are a soccer Regiment and to start rugby is sheer heresy'! Fortunately he perservered and by the outbreak of the First World War rugby was gaining a foothold in the Regiment. In the early 1920s rugby became established as a Regimental sport, drawing its followers in the main from soldiers who had not played before – a feature of Regimental rugby that continued after the Second World War when almost every successful XV contained one player new to the game that season. The rugby Officer's notes in the Regimental magazines show that 'turbulence' is not something new – virtually every season a new team had to be welded together and a pattern evolved where the XVs played with success in non Army Cup matches but were usually beaten in an early round in the Cup itself.

In the period 1924–26, the 2nd Battalion in Egypt eventually beat the Duke of Wellington's Regiment to become Middle East Champions. The team that won the title contained five future Commanding Officers: E G Miles (who later became Colonel of the Regiment); W G Mattingley (who later commanded KOSB); and R A H Kappey, W A H Maxwell and J B A Hankey (who later all commanded TA battalions of the Regiment).

By the late thirties the Regiment had become sufficiently well known as a 'rugby regiment' for the Depot to enter the Selkirk Seven-a-side Tournament and for the 1st Battalion to undertake a Border Tour in

1938. On paper this team looked the strongest ever but the outbreak of the Second World War prevented it from entering the Army Cup.

Far from damaging Regimental rugby the war years gave the game a tremendous fillip. Both the 4th and 6th Territorial Battalions contained established Border players. They played each other several times and fierce argument rages to this day about the outcome! Tragically the 6th Battalion lost two of its Scottish Trialists (Capt Jock Dun and Pte Crozier) in action after D-Day but was sufficiently blessed with talent to retain the Divisional Championship up to the moment of its disbandment in 1946.

With the end of hostilities in Europe in May 1945 the Battalion became part of the British Army of the Rhine. Again a rugby team was built up – two games against their sister 4th Battalion resulted in a win for each side – and the 6th Battalion went on to win the Championship of the 15th (Scottish) Division. This was achieved shortly before disbandment in early 1946.

Three members of that team went back to club rugby and won International honours: Dod Burrell and Stewart Coltman for Scotland and Garry Price for Wales (as a Rugby League Pro). But for the casualties suffered in battles of 1944–45 there would undoubtedly have been more.

Former members of the side continued to serve the game, which was so much a part of unit life, as referees, coaches, administrators. In May 1977 Dod Burrell, captain of the 1943/44 side, lead the cream of British rugby to New Zealand as manager of the 'Lions'. We can be sure that a little of the spirit of the King's Own Scottish Borderers went with them.

In the competitive years of the fifties and the era of National Service, the stations in which the battalion served should have militated against any real success in rugby. The fame of the Border player was such that other Regiments and Corps serving in the UK would seek him out, and in order to induce him to enter their ranks, would even offer to allow him to return home at weekends to play for his club! This could not be done by the battalion which served in Hong Kong, Malaya, Northern Ireland and Berlin.

Tradition, however, dies hard in the Borders and sufficient men turned down such offers to produce a series of XVs that, by and large, swept the board wherever they were stationed. The XV formed in Hong Kong after the battalion returned from Korea defeated every team in sight including the Hong Kong Club XV, most of whose players had almost defeated an Army XV two days before.

The Malayan Tour of 1954–57 showed the real playing strength available to the Regiment during National Service. The XV were runners-up in the Far East Cup in 1956 and winners of it in 1957.

On arrival in Berlin in 1959 – their first opportunity to enter the Army Cup since 1938 – a council of war made its aim the winning of the Cup in the second season (1960/61). This aim was not only achieved in 1961 but also in 1960 and on each occasion their opponents were once again the Dukes. In 1962 the latter obtained their revenge when they defeated the KOSB XV in the UK Final.

A period of service in Aden, where the XV again swept the local board, cost the Regiment dearly as virtually a generation of players received injuries on the field which put them out of the game for good. The Regiment also had the distinction of being invited to go to Kenya to enter the East African Sevens Tournament in 1962, which they won.

Brigadier Frank Coutts not only played three times for Scotland but in 1977 was elected President of the Scottish RFU. The other two International Caps were D D Valentine and R B Shillinglaw.

THE WELSH GUARDS

Raised 26th February 1915
(The following is taken largely from a history of rugby in the Welsh Guards by the late Brig W D C Greenacre, CB, DSO, MVO and Maj W S Phelps, MBE.)

The Welsh Guards hold one of the best records of any regiment in the history of Army rugby. They have won the Army Cup eleven times and in 1964 completed a hat trick of victories in the competition. In addition the 1st Battalion have been runners-up on eight occasions and the 2nd Battalion have been runners-up once.

The Welsh Guards were raised in 1915 and though a lot of rugby football was played in the Reserve Battalion in England, there is no record of much football being played in 'Flanders fields'.

In 1921 Capt Geoffrey Crawshay was posted to the Guards Depot and set about reviving the interest in the game, and his immense enthusiasm, energy and coaching resulted in the Regiment winning its first Army Cup in 1923.

Two other men also played a major part in this success. Mr T Vile, the ex Welsh International and a famous rugby referee, whose coaching and advice was invaluable, and Lieut Gavin Young, a first-class forward and a fine captain.

Rugby football was now well established in the Regiment and Captain Crawshay created a close relationship with the London Welsh Club. Mention should also be made of his own club, Captain Geoffrey Crawshay's Welsh XV, which was founded in 1922. What he wanted to produce was a Welsh XV who would play rugby to the limit of their ability in the spirit of the Barbarians but not attempting to win regardless.

After being runners-up twice since their win in 1923, the 1st Battalion achieved their second Cup victory in 1932 when they beat the 2nd Battalion Leicester Regiment 11–3.

Welsh Guards rugby benefitted greatly from the support of the late Duke of Windsor who, as Prince of Wales and Colonel of the Regiment, frequently attended Cup ties and took a personal interest in the activities of Welsh Guards players.

It is no secret that the strength of any team is the strength of its reserve, and the Guards Depot provided unfailing support and training facilities for the potential players in Regimental XVs of the Household Division.

It is surprising that T E (Tommy) Rees, a fine full-back who was capped four times for Wales, was the only member of the Regiment to gain International honours whilst serving in the Army, though Lieut W D C Greenacre played in a Welsh trial in 1924 as did Sgt F Pates, Gdsman I Wilcox and Gdsmn W Phillips. Sgt T Boast had a trial for England. W C Powell was not capped until after leaving the Regiment.

During the Second World War, the following represented their countries in war Internationals: Capt Peter Hastings – England and L/Cpls G Williams, H Pimblett and C Jefferies all for Wales.

The 2nd Battalion had been ordered into 'suspended animation' by June 1947, but before going into 'limbo' they reached the final of the Army Cup and were beaten 10–3 by a strong RAMC side.

During the period of National Service, though they received some excellent players, whenever possible they relied purely and simply on regular soldiers, and it was because of this policy that they benefited in the seasons to come.

The 1st Battalion in Palestine upheld the fine tradition of the Regiment by winning the Palestine Cup on several occasions. The major influence of these victories was CSM Dando whose general know-how and fine physical attributes made him a natural captain.

In the 1960s the Regiment came into its own. The 1st Battalion suffered a narrow defeat at the hands of the 1st Battalion the King's Own Scottish Borderers in 1960/61, but this was followed by a famous hat trick of victories: 1962 beating 1st Battalion Duke of Wellington's Regiment 9–6; 1963 28th Company Royal Army Ordnance Corps 9–6 and in 1964 1st Battalion Somerset and Cornwall Light Infantry 25–3. This was to be the high point of their play. There had to be a falling off as key players were posted to extra Regimental employment. Career planning for good games players is always a headache for the Commanding Officer – should a key player be kept simply in the hope of winning another pot? That is a question he is always asking himself, particularly in peacetime when prowess on the sports fields has to replace the glory of wartime medal winning. If a team captain could retain a nucleus of about ten of the previous season's team, then he would consider himself fortunate. Season 1964/65 was to see the Battalion side again win the UK section of the Army Cup but the old foe, 1st Battalion Duke of Wellington's Regiment, was to prove too good in the final, winning by 11 points to six.

A period of rebuilding now had to take place; the season 1965/66 was spent in Aden where rugby was of secondary importance to security. On return in November 1966, followed by disembarkation leave, it was too late to enter the Army Cup competition. It was therefore somewhat surprising in 1967/68, with a young inexperienced side, to find the battalion XV winning the UK Final. They then came a cropper, however, in the Army Final against a very fine side from – yes, once again – the 1st Battalion the Duke of Wellington's Regiment, who won by 20 points to 3. However, there was a nucleus of experienced and up-and-coming players who would soon combine.

The season 1968/69 saw defeat at the hands of the South Wales Borderers in the UK Final. Success was not far away though because the following season Angus Wall had returned from Oswestry and Charles Guthrie was on the scene as organiser. CQMS Hearne captained a side which contained many young players, some just arrived from the Junior Leaders Battalion, who proved too good for the Royal Regiment of Wales, winning by 18 points to six, after what most Welsh spectators described as one of the best Army Cup Finals seen at the Aldershot Stadium.

Season 1970/71 found the 1st battalion once again in BAOR. Having scored a comfortable victory in the BAOR Final under Don Hearne's leadership and with Charles Guthrie playing again, they met the 1st Battalion the Royal Regiment of Wales in the Army Final at Aldershot and won in extra time 6-3.

Hopes were high for a third successive Army Cup victory in 1971/72. Although Don Hearne had left the battalion after a wonderful record of success, Dai Bowen proved to be an able captain who welded together a young but very talented side. However the RRW beat them in the BAOR Final. Virtually the same team made amends in 1972/73 by beating 7 Signal Regiment by 22 points to nine in the Army Cup Final at Aldershot. In 1982 they again won the Cup, beating 21st Engineer Regiment 12-6. Being runners-up to 7 Signal Regiment – who thus gained their revenge – in 1984, they completed a brilliant era of Welsh Guards rugby.

The Regiment can indeed be proud not only of their successes in the Army Cup but of their contribution to all aspects of Army rugby.

CORPS OF ROYAL ENGINEERS

HISTORICAL ORIGINS AND CHANGES IN TITLE

(officers)	*(non-commissioned ranks)*
1716: Corps of Engineers	1787: Corps of Royal Military Artificers
1787: Corps of Royal Engineers	1813: Royal Sappers and Miners

1856: amalgamated under one title – Corps of Royal Engineers

In the 1870s the Royal Engineer Football Club was a power in the land. In 1872, '74, '75 and '78 they reached the final of the FA Cup and in 1875 they won it.

In 1878 the REFC played its first recorded rugby match against the RMA (The 'Shop'); the report on the match reads: 'Played at Chatham on Thursday, October 24th and resulted in a draw, the Academy scoring 1 try, four touches against 1 try ...'.

The Royal Engineer team was:
  backs – Lieuts Cairns, Druitt;
  threequarters – Lieut Cowan;
  halves – Lieuts Bond, Massey;
  forwards – Lieuts Hedley, Gordon, Rice, Dumbleton, Leverson, Stanton, Williams, Thomson, Jackson, Long.

This RE v RMA annual fixture was the only football match played under Rugby Union Rules until 1885.

In 1886 the fixture list was extended and in 1889 Rugby Union was really established with six fixtures, of which only one was lost. The rise in rugby skills was unfortunately matched by a fall in Association skills, both codes being played by the REFC. This gave rise to heated correspondence in the RE journal and for some time the introduction of hockey was blamed! An extract from one of the later letters sums up the situation:

It would be a great pity if we gave up Association football because we have done so badly of late.

It appears to me that there is another cause besides hockey which may partly account for our weakness. Of late years several RE matches have, I believe, been played under Rugby Union Rules. I think this can hardly fail to weaken us. In the years in which we were strongest most of our men had been accustomed to Rugby

H.M. The Queen   PATRON

1985–86
Brigadier D W Shuttleworth OBE, ADC
President Rugby Football Union

Brigadier F H Coutts CBE DL
President of the Scottish Rugby Union 1977-78

The Stewart Wrightson Trophy

Winners. Army Challenge Cup 1907   2 Bn West Riding Regiment DWR
Back row: Finnigan, Swift, Robinson, Thompson, Garside, Martin, Flaherty
Middle row: Egerton, Ramsden, Gillgallon, Denton, Curtis, Goddings, G Lister
Front row: J Lister, Brown   *Thompson did not play in final*

Army v Royal Navy, December 1907
Back row: Stevens, Robertson*, Newton*, Furber, Grischotti, Begbie, Huntingford
Front row: Wilson*, Rogers*, Hill*, Partridge*, Smidt
Sitting: Purdon*, Turner, Caddill*
*International

Army Cup Final 1910
2 Bn Gloucestershire Regt 3 v 1 Bn Leicester Regt 0
James, standing on his head, scores the only try of the match in extra time. The first try scored by a soldier at Twickenham

Army Rugby Cup and Aldershot Command Rugby Cup 1913
Winners: 2nd Bn The Welch Regiment
Back row: Bristowe, Fisher, Garrington, Jones, Murphy, Thomas, Bagnall, Howe, Daley
Seated: Jones, Davies, Gransmore, Lacey (Capt), Partridge, Daniel, Baker, Foreman
Front on floor: Edwards, Secombe

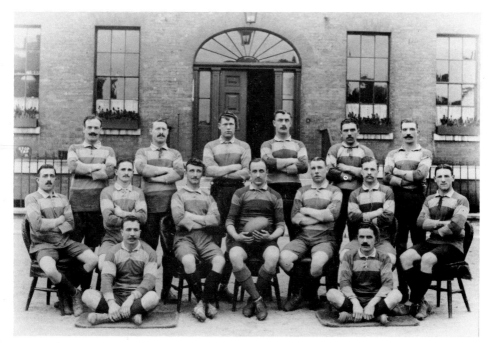

Army Rugby Cup 1912–13
Runners-up: 1 Bn T.he Gloucestershire Regiment
Back row: Spragg, Atkinson, Organ, Nash, Strong, Ible
Seated: Turner, Bayliss, Travill, Duncan, Nicholls, Organ, Green
Front on floor: Murray, Stephenson

Aldershot Cup 1913–14
Winners: 1 Bn The Gloucestershire Regiment
Back row: Giles, Forbes, Nash, Clevelly, Warrick, Wilson, Hill
Seated: Organ, Nicholls, Ible, Duncan, Yalland, Organ, Sherwood
Front on floor: Murray, Stephenson

King George V meets the Army Team in 1921

Army Rugby Cup 1920–21
Winners: 2 Bn The Welch Regiment
Back row: Lane, Beynon, Price, Makin, Gransmore, Lawler, Not Known, Payne
Seated: Phillips, Dunn, Jones, Lindsey Brabazon (Capt), Daniel, Morgan, Payne

Rules; they all however, on joining, gave up Rugby and stuck to the Association Rules. It appears to me that something may be said, in favour of our taking, as a Corps, to Rugby instead of Association Rules; but I cannot help thinking it is a mistake to attempt both.

The results of the 1889/90 season which sparked off the correspondence were:

Association Rules: played 30 won 6 drawn 6 lost 18
Rugby Union Rules: played 6 won 5   lost 1

It will be remembered that the REFC was an Officer's Club, though soldiers were apparently invited to play on occasions.

In the 1892/93 season the Corps played 16 Rugby Union matches and the REFC appointed a Rugby Secretary in addition to the Association Secretary. In 1895/96 season the Rugby fixtures (22) outnumbered the Association fixtures (13) for the first time.

The accounts of matches at this time conjure up pictures which must please the modern young player:

> The services of a referee were procured on the spot. "No appeal" was decided upon but not conformed to; indeed tongues readily lent their natural aid, and if play disappointed the eye, the whistle seldom failed the ear.

> There were no serious accidents although a College player had to retire in tatters, our collaring was too gentle.

> Shortly afterwards an interval of five minutes was found necessary to allow the Wanderers back to effect a change of nicks, his own being somewhat rent. This performance did not take place in public.

> Just before time Kelly had the misfortune to put his knee out and he had to be conveyed home on the trench cart.

Blackheath had been regular opponents of the Corps since 1887 and were always referred to as 'The Heathens'. It is not really clear whether this was an affectionate term or not.

In 1907 the *Supplement* to the RE journals reports:

> An endeavour is being made this year to introduce Rugby Football into the Army by the establishment of an Army Rugby Cup Competition. Members of the Committee include Captain R.F.A. Hobbs, DSO., RE., and Lieut R.A.S. Mansel, RE.

The Training Battalion beat the King's Dragoon Guards by 11 points to three; they 'had the assistance of seven officers, all well versed in the game, and this advantage ensured their victory'. Of these seven officers Hobbs was an England player and both he and Gowlland were Army caps.

The next reported result shows that the Training Battalion RE met the RE Depot and District Battalion in the semi-final and won 3–0.

The game was perhaps more of a vigorous than a scientific exhibition, but on the whole there was little to choose between the teams.

The final was played at Aldershot on 6 April 1907 between the 2nd Battalion West Riding Regiment and the Training Battalion RE.

The RE were beaten by 1 goal to nil in the final. The prediction of the old Blackheath player that we should see "plenty of vigour if not much skill" was completely fulfilled. But it was all quite chivalrous vigour, the officers by precept and example showed that it was not so very difficult to tone down the inclination for excess in finishing a tackle.

By 1914 two more players had gained International honours; Gowlland playing for Scotland in 1908, 1909 and 1910 and Scobie in 1914. The war years virtually brought rugby to a halt, though a few games were played.

Rugby really opened up again in the 1919/20 season and the Corps began most impressively, beating Harlequins 21–5, Blackheath 33–6 and Richmond 19–0.

In 1922 the School of Military Engineering and the RE Depot decided to combine with United Services Chatham and to pool their fixtures.

It will be obvious that this arrangement will be highly beneficial to the RE Officers at Chatham who play rugger, since not only are the facilities for getting a game greatly increased for all but the more experienced players will get first class football, thereby not only making way for others to play in the A and B sides, but at the same time bringing their own play to the notice of Army and County Selection Committees.

Only Corps matches were retained as purely RE fixtures.

Rugby restarted after the Second World War in the 1946/47 season.

This was the era of the National Service player, and the Corps produced two National Service Internationals, Bazley and Michie. Two other National Servicemen, Bartlett and Marques, gained International recognition after they had left the Corps. G W Payne was the last capped Corps player.

Of recent years the outstanding players were Hamish Bryce and Andy Hoon who captained both the Army and Combined Services. Bryce also captained Scotland B and was reserve for Scotland for several seasons.

These random reflections show that the Corps has had some great players and many good players but they had to wait until 1983 to win the Army Cup – seven times runners-up is no substitute for a win. Nonetheless the Royal Engineers can be proud that three members of the Corps were the first Army players to be awarded International honours.

THE ROYAL REGIMENT OF ARTILLERY

The meeting which began it all was held at the Royal Artillery Mess, Woolwich, on 14 July 1924, with Capt A B van Straubenzee in the chair. Its main decisions were:

> 1. That a Club to be called 'The Royal Artillery Rugby Football Club' should be formed.
> 2. That the Club should be for past and present Officers, NCOs and men of the Regiment.
> 3. That Club colours should be white shorts and white jerseys with the Gunner badge on the left breast.

These simple and straightforward decisions record the creation of what was to become at one stage a club of monumental proportions. In its heyday there were over 900 members playing at unit level in various parts of the world and even today twenty-eight teams take part in its annual inter-unit knockout trophy – the MacIlwaine Cup. It is also interesting to note that the meeting ran true to form right from the outset, electing in their absence Maj-Gen Gilman as President and Lieut Baker as Hon Secretary and Treasurer!

It was perhaps inevitable that, drawing their young officers from Woolwich jointly with the Sappers, the first representative fixture to be established by the Gunners was the annual match against the Royal Engineers. At first it was an 'officers only' affair; it was not until that inaugural meeting of the RARFC in 1924 that it was proposed that 'the annual match against the Royal Engineers shall be no longer for officers only and that the Sappers be approached to agree to this'. The first recorded fixture was played at Woolwich on 11 December 1887. The Sappers won 24-0.

From 1921/22 this fixture remained the highlight of the Gunner rugby season, and was played without interruption until the outbreak of the Second World War. By 1938/39 the Sappers had won 10 matches and the Gunners six. Two matches had been drawn, and the Sappers won the last match before the outbreak of hostilities in a 'hard, keen, fast game by a goal, a dropped goal and three tries to a goal, a dropped goal and a penalty goal' (18-12).

'The first post-war Gunner–Sapper match was one worthy of previous encounters.' So reads a press release of the time. It goes on to say

[it] was an excellent hard-fought game, but the Sapper forwards seemed to be more dangerous in line-out and in the loose, and generally had more bustle about them than their Gunner counterparts. However, the result (RA 13 – RE 11) was fair indication of the way play went.

The RA v RE match is now one of the oldest fixtures in the Army rugby calender. It has achieved a standing far beyond that of any other RARFC fixture, and perhaps of any other inter-Corps match.

The MacIlwaine Cup

In 1912 a twenty-three-year-old subaltern named Alfred Herbert MacIlwaine was gazetted into the Royal Field Artillery and posted to Deepcut. On his arrival he found eight officers who could play rugger and so set about creating a team by recruiting selected soccer-playing NCOs and men to make up a XV. This team forced its way into the finals of the Aldershot Command Cup and the semi-finals of the Army Cup.

MacIlwaine was a tremendous personality who had begun his rugby with the 2nd Northumbrian Brigade, RFA (TA), but he was determined to be a regular Army Gunner.

He was to gain four Army caps and five for England and he played in a famous match between the Combined Services and the South Africans, where he was a member of a fine pack led by Norman Wodehouse, RN. The Combined Services only just lost by 18 points to 16.

MacIlwaine was first capped for England in 1912, but in 1913 he was transferred from Aldershot to County Tipperary. He wrote of that time: 'It was while unloading our horses and guns at Waterford that we first heard the song "It's a long way to Tipperary", sung by an old Irish woman'. He hunted with the Tipperary Hounds and then would jump on his Triumph motor-cycle and make for Dublin – 100 miles away! – to play for Monkstown. The team consisted of about fifty per cent soldiers from the Curragh and fifty per cent Sinn Feiners.

After the England–Ireland match in Dublin in 1920 he was told by the selectors not to play for the Army against London Scottish the following Saturday, but as captain of the Army side he ignored the request and sustained a badly crocked right knee which put him out of the Scotland match on the next Saturday and very nearly ended his Army career. The Army did, however, insist that he captain their side again, in March 1921 against the Navy.

In 1925, following his retirement from active rugby, MacIlwaine presented a silver cup to the RARFC for inter-brigade competition, in order to encourage all ranks to learn the game and to play it in the right spirit. The significant feature of the MacIlwaine Cup, as it very soon came to be called, was that right from the outset teams were restricted as to the number of officers they might play. The President of the RARFC, Lieut-Gen Gilman, agreed that the Cup should first be played for after Christmas 1925, under the same rules as were in force for the Army Cup, except that only six officers might represent a brigade instead of the eight allowed for Army Cup fixtures. In 1928 it was agreed that officers who had represented their unit in one round of the Cup should still be eligible to play for that unit for the remainder of the season, but they would not be eligible to play for any other unit.

The competition for the Cup was suspended during the war years and it was not competed for again until the 1946/47 season. But in 1947 – like a phoenix from the ashes – the subject of eligibility rose again, stronger and more pressing than ever before. In this season it was decided that infantry officers serving with or attached to RA units should be eligible to represent those units in the competition, but that TA units would not be able to compete.

The MacIlwaine Cup – more than anything else – has been the inspiration for the wide-spread support and enthusiasm for rugby in the Royal Artillery. Despite continuous amendment to its rules, its original aim remains unchanged and is perhaps more than ever valid today. The term 'the MacIlwaine Cup' will never disappear from the Gunner rugby vocabulary, and the contest for which it is the coveted trophy will remain the foundation of the Gunner rugby year.

The 1923/24 season saw the first true expansion of the fixture list beyond the Gunners v Sappers match. On 28 November 1923 the RA XV lost by 8–18 to the Brigade of Guards, the latter being the first 'all ranks' team the Gunner side had played. This was followed by a match against the Guards Depot on 8 December in which the RA fielded its first 'all ranks' representative side and won by 17–6, Prob/Artificer Cathie scoring two of the tries and G E S Proes dropping a goal.

1925/26 was a golden season. In it, Capt A H MacIlwaine presented his Cup. On Salisbury Plain the newly formed YOs Rugby Football Club, composed of young officers serving at the School of Artillery played two fixtures a week under the captaincy of J K MacFarlan, against local Field and Medium Brigade sides, RAF stations, RE and the Welch Regiment A XV.

A feature of the 1927 season was the firm establishment of a match between the RA YOs and the RE YOs. The match had been instituted the previous year and had been won by the Gunners in the last minute 14–9. This year the score was a good deal more predictable, the Gunners winning 19–6.

In 1931, ten years after the first Gunner–Sapper match to be played after the First World War, the Gunner side was perhaps at its most eminent. In addition to E W F de V Hunt – by now an established International player – at full-back, the side boasted the Army half-back pair, G G J Fenton and F R Ievers as well as J W Wainwright, the Army left wing, A Vaughan-Jones, the Army hooker – soon to be capped for the United Services and to gain three International caps for England – and R G S Hobbs.

'Pooh' Hobbs was capped four times for England in 1932 and played variously for Richmond, the Army, the Barbarians and Kent. In 1955 he was promoted Major-General and while GOC 1st Division was elected a Junior Vice-President of the RFU. In 1960 he became Senior Vice-President, and in 1961, while President of the Regular Commissions Board he succeeded 'Tommy' Voyce as President of the RFU. From 1953 until 1967 he acted as Chairman, and later as President of the RARFC, and it was due to his guidance and enthusiasm for the game that Gunner rugger became endowed with a unique quality in the great years of National Service after the Second World War.

1931 also saw the Military College of Science lose their four-year tenure of the MacIlwaine Cup, the 11th Field Brigade, with Hobbs and Hunt, proving too much for them. However, the following year the 3rd Light Brigade took the trophy in a match described as one which 'will, or should, go down in history as one of the best finals of all time'. In particular the tackling was such that it succeeded in neutralising even Hobbs, and although reduced to fourteen players shortly after half time, they not only held onto a slender 5–3 lead but increased it by a try, thus winning 8–3.

The 1938/39 season, the last before the War, saw the club's fortunes on the ebb. By now the Regiment was very short of experienced players. The club captain was R K Jones in the centre where he was partnered by B M O'Brien, J B Ragg and F B Powell-Brett; although in the match against the Sappers O'Brien and Ragg were replaced by D C

Bevis and J H F Mermagen. K B Eddison was the full-back. The forwards were lead by F J L Cary, the Hampshire wing forward, with Nesbitt, Weldon, Rees, Palmer, Ashmore, Head, Brooke, Barton, Donegan and Simpson all gaining caps during the season. Taylor and Mead were the regular half-backs, although Pearson and Montgomery were also capped during the season. With the 'giants' of the previous generation gone and only Cary regularly playing first-class rugger the club found itself in a position known only too well by competitive sides today: a reputation to live up to with insufficient time and opportunity to bring on new, less experienced players, all of whom seemed to have arrived at once! Even the MacIlwaine Cup brought about a reversal of fortunes, with 18th Field Regiment (the first of the new nomenclature of units) taking the championship away from 9th Field Brigade for the first time for four years. The season finished on 8 March and with it went the fortunes of the clubs promising young players, many of whom were to lose their lives in Hitler's war.

At the first post-war AGM the chair was taken by one to whom, next to MacIlwaine, the RARFC perhaps owes more than to anyone else. Maj-Gen F W H ('Ambrose') Pratt had played for the side in the first Gunners–Sappers match to be fully covered in the club records. Now he was to provide the primary link between the pre- and post-war traditions. For three vital years he served as the club's President, and continued to give his wise counsel at general meetings until as late as 1953. But it is as a supporter of the players themselves, and as a referee, that he will be best remembered. Until 1953 he was the first choice to handle most MacIlwaine Cup Finals and he remained a staunch supporter of the club until his death in 1960.

The first post-war MacIlwaine Cup competition was held in 1946/47. The original plan for the competition was to have had the finalists in the CMF and BAOR zones play each other, the winning side to play the UK zone winners. However, the weather in BAOR put paid to this. In the event the winners of the CMF final, played at Udine in north-east Italy, played the UK finalists, and beat them. Unfortunately it was then impossible for them to play the BAOR winners as they were disbanded shortly after their UK victory! The cup was therefore awarded jointly to 5th Field Regiment, the victims of the 'axe', and 4th Regiment RHA, the BAOR winners.

It was in the 1952 season that 'caps' were finally abandoned in favour of a club tie, the former having become so expensive that none could afford to buy one! Eligibility to wear this tie is to this day confined to those who have played for the Regiment in the RA v RE match, and to certain others on the recommendation of the Selection Committee.

Throughout the 1950s the club had been fortunate in having the services on its committee of a number of distinguished players from the pre-war era. In addition to Maj-Gen Pratt and Maj-Gen Hobbs, Brig Proudlock, Lieut-Col Tremenheere, Lieut-Col Barnaby and Lieut-Col Lawson all served in an executive capacity or as selectors, and it was largely due to their efforts and guidance that the club continued to grow and prosper.

Fifty-three teams entered for the MacIlwaine Cup in 1953. Of these twenty-one took part in the BAOR section, the remainder played in the UK. The final was won by 2nd Regiment RHA who beat the RA wing Mons OCS by 17–8 in extra time, the score being 8–8 at the end of forty minutes each way. In the same year the club side had its best post-war season to date, seven matches were played and only one, that against the RNC, Greenwhich, lost. The side had been steadily improving, thanks to area trials, careful selection and the efforts of Bruce Neale, who was to play for the army a total of seventeen times, captaining the team on three occasions, and who also gained three England caps.

By 1963/64 the club had lost only three games in two seasons and a new source of young players, the Junior Leaders Regiment, was beginning to emerge. This Regiment had won the Junior Cup three times in a row, a run of success largely due to J M Jones, the Army 2nd row forward who, with J S Landau (the club captain), P R Dunchesne and C G A Munty, had provided the impetus for what was to be, perhaps, the finest year to date of the RARFC, the season 1964/65. An opening tour of Dorset brought them victories over Dorchester (29–0) and Blandford (20–9). The side then went into its standard fixture list in which it looked like never losing a match, and at the end of the season had scored a total of 132 points with only 36 against.

In addition to the standard fixture list there was one extra match of great significance. In 1962 the Royal Marine RFC had written to suggest that an RM v RA past and present match should be played in 1964 to honour of the RM Tercentenary, the RA being preferred over other possible opponents for this fixture as being the Corps with the closest association with the RM. This match was played at the Richmond ground on Saturday, 14 November 1964 and was won by the Gunners, 17–6. The Marines had H J Mainwaring and B J Jones at full-back and centre respectively (both Welsh Internationals), G H Waddell the Scottish International fly-half and S J S Clarke the then England scrum-half with thirteen International caps. In addition they had R M Roberts and D J R Brown, the Royal Navy wings, R Challis, the London Scottish hooker, K I Ross, the Scottish International 2nd row forward and

J Barry the Royal Navy No 8 forward. The Gunners had no Internationals, and only two non-serving RA players: D Wardle (Vale of Lune) and R V Francis (Old Paulines) as the half-back pair. Both sides scored four tries, both missed four kickable penalties and a one-point difference in the scores seemed to the Gunners supporters anyway to be a very fair result. The Marines suffered grieviously from the loss of a forward in the first half and Brown on the wing in the second, but a word must be said for the fitness of the Gunner team: there was not a single stoppage for a Gunner injury.

The 1965/66 season saw a milestone established. The RA scored their fourth victory in a row over the Sappers to bring level the score in matches. By now they had lost Landau, Nicholls, Muntz, Wilkes, Davis, Miller and Lalakonacoi, from the side which had been such a consistent success for three consecutive years.

History was made the following year when 7th Regiment RHA became the first Gunner unit to reach the final of the Army Cup; they were beaten in that match at Aldershot by the 1st Battalion Duke of Wellington's Regiment.

The same year saw the last appearance of Gen Hobbs as President of the club. He had been President for fourteen years and had guided the club through the turbulent days of National Service to an all-regular side which, in 1964, had possibly the best season of its long existence. His place as President was taken by Maj-Gen McMeekin with Lieut-Col Heaven, himself a former player/Secretary of the club, as Chairman.

In 1967 the club side had a difficult season with only two of the previous year's team to call upon. However, at unit level the UK Final of the Army Cup was, for the first time, an all Gunner affair, 7th RHA beating the School of Artillery. 7th RHA also won the MacIlwaine Cup again, with 14th Light Regiment the runners-up. Three players were capped for the Army: Dick Williams, Freddie Williams and Gareth Davies.

Northern Ireland now began to take its toll on players' availability and team training and, although the club continued to win more games than it lost, this general turbulence denied the side the opportunity to settle down to exploit its full potential. However, in 1970 a resurgence of form began, with the club beating RMCS Shrivenham, RAOC, R Signals, R Marines, RCT and RE, they lost only to RMA Sandhurst, 12–6. Finally in 1985 the Army Cup was won when 7th Regiment RHA beat the 1st Battalion the Royal Regiment of Wales 7–6 in an exciting final.

The minutes of the general meetings of the RARFC are contained in a brown covered book with blue pages. On the front cover are engraved a crown and the letters GR. Beneath them has been stuck the label, now as brown as the book, bearing the legend 'Royal Artillery RFC, Minutes of Meetings 1924-'.

This legend shows an unconcious faith in the future, but perhaps the owner of the unknown hand which wrote it might have been a little less confident had he known that the Second World War was to interrupt the club's fortunes for seven consecutive years. However it has been said that rugby football is a game which embodies in sport the more admirable graces and virtues of everyday life: strength both mental and physical; toughness and chivalry; self-confidence without selfishness; fierce rivalry governed by good comradeship; a respect for discipline and co-ordinated endeavour, rather than senseless anarchy; and honest laughter rather than vengeful rage. Viewed thus it is less remarkable that the club's strength and fortunes are in no way diminished and that its future remains as bright as its distinguished past.

In 1970/71, the Centenary of the founding of the Rugby Football Union, the Kings of Arms granted the Union a Coat of Arms and a motto. The motto reads *Rugbeia Floreat Ubique* - 'Let Rugby flourish everywhere'. The Royal Artillery, which proudly bears the same word *'Ubique'* as its battle honour can take equal pride in the fact that the RARFC continues to play its part in the fulfilment of this aim.

THE ROYAL CORPS OF SIGNALS

HISTORICAL ORIGINS AND CHANGES IN TITLE
1920 (June): Corps of Signals (from the Royal Engineers Signal Service)
1920 (August): Royal Corps of Signals

The start of the Royal Signals' success in Army Rugby began in 1945/46 when it was decided to form a rugby club at Catterick and to open a clubhouse at the old Sergeant's Mess at Scotton Ground, Catterick, the home of 1st Training Regiment. In the 1946/47 season the Corps were extremely fortunate to have amongst them an outstanding enthusiast of rugby football in Maj Gordon Fraser.

Gordon Fraser got to grips with the many problems facing him with immense enthusiasm and drive. His own love of the game and brilliant organising ability resulted in the production of a strong fixture list and the development of an excellent club spirit.

The Corps, with its Depot and Training Centre had a great advantage in being located in Yorkshire, as there were a large number of rugby clubs of varying standards which made for fixtures to meet all standards. The side was known as Royal Signals (Catterick), and drew on all players from all regiments. It was run on the lines of a civilian club, playing Saturday matches against leading clubs throughout the season. Amongst the sides were: Durham, Fylde, Gosforth, Harrogate, Halifax, Huddersfield, Percy Park, Waterloo and also Oxford University Greyhounds and Cambridge University LX Club. Their best season was probably 1951/52 when 28 matches were played: 23 won, four lost, one drawn for 451 points to 149.

Several records were created in civilian competitions. The Yorkshire Cup was won twice, once in 1951/52 when they beat Halifax 11 points to 10; this was the first time a Service side had won in the seventy-three years of the competition; it was won again in 1953/54 when Roundhay was beaten 17 points to three.

The Kelso (Borders) Seven-a-side Cup was won in 1954/55 when Langholm were beaten 22-0 in the final. This was the first time the Cup had been won by an English side since its inception in 1920. The Signals won it again in 1957/58 in a very close game in which they beat Jedforest 16–13. The Huddersfield Seven-a-side competition was won three times; in 1948/49, 1955/56 and 1957/58 and they were runners-up five times, which itself was a record.

Once the Signals (Catterick) side was established, many famous players came into the Corps. Seven players gained International honours whilst serving in the Corps between 1947 and 1957. However it should not be forgotten that the first Corps player to play for England was E H Sadler in 1933.

The Corps also had its share of Rugby league players, including Phil Jackson, Billy Boston and Brian Gabbitas. A considerable number of players played county rugby. Twenty-seven played for Yorkshire and the total number is considerably more.

The Corps have won the Army Cup nine times; on the first occasion in 1947/48 by a side representing the Signal Training Centre; thereafter on seven occasions by 1st Training Regiment and in 1984 by 7 Signal Regiment. Five of these victories were in six years: 1948/49, 1949/50, 1950/51, 1952/53 and 1953/54. This raised a storm of protest which unfortunately caused an investigation into the Signals' rugby affairs. It was unfortunate because, although there was some controversy at the time, in retrospect it was no more than a storm in a teacup. The side comes from units which trained the highest technical trades in the Corps; it had the quality players, as can be seen from the personalities who served in the Signals. More important Maj Fraser demanded a high standard of training and approach which, as any rugby officer whose team has won the competition will appreciate, is essential.

Returning to the competition in 1955/56 they won the Army Cup in 1957 when they beat the 1st Battalion the Welch Regiment 15–3, and in 1959 when they beat the Royal Scots 12–9.

Spectators and supporters play their part too. The Signals achieved yet another record in Operation '1000 or BUST'. They moved 1098 members of the Regiment in a special train and seventeen coaches to Aldershot for the 1956/57 final.

In recent years the Corps were unable to achieve the successes of the magnificent era of the 1940s and 1950s until 1984, when 7 Signal Regiment won the Army Cup, beating the 1st Battalion Welsh Guards 9–3.

ROYAL ARMY MEDICAL CORPS

HISTORICAL ORIGINS AND CHANGES IN TITLE

Medical Orderlies (other ranks)
1855: Medical Staff Corps   *(officers)*
1857: Army Hospital Corps   1873: Army Medical Staff
          1884: amalgamated under one title – Medical Staff Corps
                    1898: Royal Army Medical Corps

The Royal Army Medical Corps did not really make its mark on Army rugby until shortly after the 1939–45 War. That it did so to marked effect then was due to one man, of whom the Corps journal wrote:

> The personal interest taken by the Commandant of the RAMC Depot in their training and the lectures which he gave on every aspect of the game have been rewarded by vastly improved play and success.

The Commandant was none other than Brig H L Glyn-Hughes – a name known, respected and indeed loved throughout the rugby world. Within a year of his taking command of the RAMC Training Centre they won the Army Cup for the first time. Until then the semi-final was the furthest they had reached; although many outstanding players were serving, they never seemed to be together in one country! Indeed what was possibly the best half-back pair the Corps had seen saw no Army Cup success. They were Ben Duggan (who spent a whole season as Haydn Tanner's reserve for Wales without ever getting a cap) and E Rees. Rees, a seventeen-year-old bugle boy, after a couple of seasons with Aldershot Services (then a powerful club side) was posted overseas on reaching man's service, thus spoiling what many thought would have been an outstanding rugby career.

After Brig Glyn-Hughes' departure, Corps rugby slumped a little and although the RAMC side appeared in two finals, both were lost, the first to 1st Training Regiment Royal Signals, Catterick in 1949/50 and the second to the Welsh Guards in 1951/52. Eventually success came again when in 1955 the Corps won the Cup for the second time with a side containing no less than nine players capped by the Army.

D W C (Doug) Smith managed that memorably successful Lions tour of New Zealand in 1971, whilst Dr Jackie Matthews' performances for Wales are now a legend. More recently M G (Mick) Molloy's partnership with Willie John McBride for Ireland was probably the best 'engine room' of all contemporary International packs. The other Irishman of that time, Moroney, was paid the highest compliment by the last Springboks to tour the UK when they named him as the best prop they encountered.

In recent years RAMC Rugby has no longer been the power that it was, although it has regularly continued to supply players for the Army side. When one looks at the declining standards of the civilian Hospitals Cup competition the answer is clear for all to see. Young doctors today have to spend so much more time studying for examinations for higher and higher qualifications that rugby is suffering! Perhaps the Corps needs another Glyn-Hughes. They have, however, proudly provided thirty-five Internationals, which is more than any other Corps has done.

ASC/RASC/RCT RUGBY
1897–1985

HISTORICAL ORIGINS AND CHANGES IN TITLE

1869: Army Service Corps
1918: Royal Army Service Corps
1965: Royal Corps of Transport

It is very difficult to trace the actual day the Corps first played a representative game of rugby. The first acknowledged Army Service Corps 'quality' player was Lieut O'Brien Butler, who played for Ireland and the Army in 1897/98. However no mention is made of this fact in the Corps journals of the day. Nor is the fact that in 1907/08 Lieut A G C De Smidt represented the Army. The sporting notes in the journal were devoted to the other code.

The first major report on ASC rugby appeared in a full-page article of the *Sporting and Country House Supplement* of *The Tatler* on 28 March 1917. It highlighted the record total of points scored by any team in the United Kingdom in the course of one season. Played 22, won 22, points for 1046, points against 27. The article states:

> The ASC has, at the hour of writing, taken on and beaten every possible opponent except the Welsh XV, (which, even with expense of the journey guaranteed, cannot get to town; while the ASC cannot of course, go to Wales), and the unbeaten Devonport US team with which arrangements for a match are now in progress. So that the ASC could scarcely have done other than it has done in the absence of opponents of real class.

Three players were given special mention:

> Jones is now the best heavy stand-off I think I have ever seen ... Cpl H Wagstaff is the best player. He is in fact, the brains of the whole thing. Without him the 1,046 would be, perhaps, 500. Alone of this team he does not do the obvious. We have had many internationals as good as he during the century – but he will never be in the class of Gwyn Nicolls, and H H Vassal, M G Macleod or the late Basil Maclear, though he is easily the best back seen in wartime football, as Clark is one of the best forwards!

Despite this praise there were many red faces over the article, which also asked, just how could a team be so dominant during the war. Indeed it is rumoured that a question was raised on this matter in the House of Commons.

The first article on rugby to appear in a Corps journal was in March 1922. It was titled 'Rugger' by 'Light Blue and Scarlet'. It gives some indication as to the forming of the Corps XV as it is today.

> Some time ago, a letter was addressed to all stations asking for the names of officers and men who played "rugger", so that the Corps team (apart from the Aldershot team) could be considerably strengthened for Corps matches. I believe several names were forwarded to the Hon Secretary – but, I know of one man, who was this season playing for a county, whose name was NOT received. That should not be. If a Corps "rugger" team is to be put on the field, it should be the best obtainable. To make it so, players from stations, other than Aldershot, must come forward. I maintain, that if the Royal Air Force can raise fifteen such as they now have – the Corps can do the same . . .
>
> This year, the Corps Club gave a grant of £25 towards the expenses of running a Corps team. A similar sum may not be granted in the future if there is nothing to show for it. A start has been made, and a good one too – all it needs now, is the individual support of every one of you.

It was the year 1922 that the Corps produced two outstanding players in Lieuts J A Middleton and H M Hinde. Of Lieut Middleton the following article is reproduced from *The Sporting Life*, it was titled 'Army Rugby Back':

> In J A Middleton, an officer of the RASC the Army has a player who is likely to gain International honours in the near future – if not this season, the next. Middleton (who also has an Irish qualification) took part in the final English rugby trial at Twickenham, but in spite of his distinct promise, Cumberlege and then Pickles were preferred as Internationals. Now both these players have failed, and consequently the form of Middleton (who also plays for Richmond), will be closely watched in the Army and Navy match at Twickenham on Saturday.

On 7 March 1922, his selection was announced to play for England against Scotland on 18 March 1922. Lieut J A Hinde, a forward played regularly for Richmond, Hampshire and the Army was unfortunate not to get an England trial.

Lieuts Middleton and Hinde were posted to Egypt in 1924. Their departure from the rugby scene drew many accolades for their rugby prowess:

> Truly he [Middleton] and Hinde stand out as the two giants and pioneers of Corps rugby.

> Lieut Middleton was also one of those instrumental in the formation of the Aldershot Services side.

The popularity of the game appeared to be increasing. In May 1923 an article in the Corps journal said:

> One of the features of last season was the amount of keeness taken by the rank and file in the game. At several matches played on the Corps ground, the crowd cheering, and cries of "HLI" and "keep it on the island" reminded one of a "soccer" match – with the froth blown off.

After the Second World War the Royal Army Service Corps recommenced playing inter-Corps rugby football on that delightfully situated sports field in front of the old Buller Officers' Mess. It says much for the planners that when Buller Barracks was rebuilt in the sixties they allowed this playing field to remain and even added a sports pavilion.

The RASC side of the 1950s benefited, as did the rest of the Services, from the influx of National Servicemen. One of the most promising recruits in 1951 was a Pte J D Currie who had not then developed in stature or his full rugby potential. He did not play for the Army although he had a trial, but was later to go on and win twenty-five caps for England and form a memorable second row with R W D Marques who played for the Royal Engineers and the Army in 1954. In this decade six Corps players represented the Army. A notable performer who came on-to the Corps scene in the mid fifties was Frank Fenner who before he was transferred to the RASC had played full-back for the Royal Navy in the Inter-Service matches of 1951 and 1952, and was an England trialist. Frank's stocky figure was to become a permanent fixture as full-back for the Corps, continuing right up to his retirement in the early seventies.

It was during the sixties that the Corps produced two outstanding players, John MacDonald, a fine prop and useful goal kicker, who played eight times for Scotland as well as representing the Army and the Barbarians. The second was Graham Lilley, a fast and fearless back row forward who won twelve Army caps in addition to playing for the Combined Services and the Barbarians.

Capt P R B Mitchell also emerged as the outstanding Corps player, representing the Army and Combined Services in 1948 and 1949. He was a pillar of strength in the Corps side from after the war until 1950, when he was posted to Malaya.

1965 saw the formation of a new Corps – The Royal Corps of Transport – and the 1965/66 season was a good one. After losing to REME in the first outing of the season, victories were recorded against the RAMC, RAOC, RAEC and RE. The side was built around 63rd Parachute Squadron and against RAOC there were eleven from that minor unit in the side. There were two old heads to steer this youthful enthusiasm – Terry Barrett, a former Gloucestershire hooker leading the pack, and as always Frank Fenner captaining the side from full-back. That season was a good start for a new Corps.

Throughout the early seventies good rugby was still played and between 1965 and 1981 seven Corps players won Army caps in the Inter-Service matches. Mike Bowles, a stalwart second row forward played for the Army from 1973 to 1982 and had the honour of captaining both the Army and Combined Services, including the match against the Australian Touring side in 1980.

In the overseas theatres the Corps colours have been carried on many a foreign field. There has always been a RASC/RCT BAOR side and there were RASC representative XVs in Singapore and Malaya.

The Army Cup has seen two Corps sides into the final, the first in 1958 when the 1st (BR) Corps Troops Column RASC met the 1st Battalion the Duke of Wellington's Regiment. The Corps side, which was known affectionately as the 'Corps Sports Column', owed much to the drive and enthusiasm of the then Commanding Officer Peter Taylor, who transformed the Regiment into a very good sporting unit insisting upon, nay demanding, peak physical fitness and complete dedication to the game of rugby football. He welded together a team which had no stars but possessed a determination to reach the final. The Dukes just had too much rugby know-how and won 23–5.

The real giant killers in the Army Cup competition were 63rd Parachute Squadron RCT who as very much a minor unit took on the big boys and were eventually beaten in the final of 1966, again by 1st Battalion DWR. 63rd were led by John Macdonald and were super fit, nothing was impossible, they ran everywhere and tackled everything. It says much for the schooling and attitude of mind that they were able to hold the Dukes to 9–0 because with the exception of their captain they had no stars, but they were a mighty fine team.

No report on RASC/RCT rugby football would be complete without mention of the Eassie Sevens, named after Maj-Gen W J F Eassie CB, CBE, DSO, who was Inspector RASC from 1951 to 1954. This event takes place at Buller at the end of every season and a feature of it until 1973 was the appearance of Gen Eassie himself every year right up to his seventy-third birthday. He was a great supporter and loved Corps rugby. He died on 13 May 1974 aged seventy-four.

ROYAL ELECTRICAL AND MECHANICAL ENGINEERS

HISTORICAL ORIGINS AND CHANGES IN TITLE

1942: The Royal Electrical and Mechanical Engineers (formed from personnel transferred from the RE and RASC)
1949: Corps of Royal Electrical and Mechanical Engineers

In the war years of 1942 to 1945 the Corps, like all other military organisations, devoted its energies to winning the war and rugby football personalities, successes and defeats are largely unrecorded. Games would be played all over the world on an *ad hoc* basis, for recreation and as a means of keeping fit but there was no attempt to organise the game on a Corps basis.

At the end of the war there was time for stalwarts, such as Brig Tyler (later Maj-Gen Sir Leslie Tyler) to put the Corps on the sporting map and he laid the foundations of REME rugby which the Corps has enjoyed ever since. He took over as Commandant of the REME Training Centre at Arborfield in July 1945 and, with the blessing of the first Corps Director, Maj-Gen Rowcroft, formed the REME Arborfield RFC. Its first season 1945/46, showed what could be done with the right sort of leadership and an eye for the talent which lay dormant in the Garrison. So much did the game flourish in that first year that the rugby correspondent of the London evening paper, the *Star*, was moved to report on 9 March 1946 that

> An Army side from Arborfield, composed of officers and men, has appeared amongst the big clubs. This season they have met such teams as the Kiwis, Rosslyn Park, Bedford, Devonport Services, London Irish and Rugby Town and won 22 out of their 33 matches.

Team captains, Joe Starling and Philip Joy were supported by such personalities as Joe Dobie (also general secretary), Bill Bailey, David Lister, John Stewart, Murray Grammar, Ian Priest and Peter Wildman. Three XVs were fielded and the record of the first XV for the 1946/47 season is worth recalling. The results, 13 wins out of 23 games played, speak for themselves. Even the results of matches against Corps sides, organised from pre-war foundations, were no disgrace for the Garrison team.

The highlight of the 1946/47 season must surely have been the match against the touring New Zealand Army side. Normally the Kiwi side did not play against individual clubs but Brig Tyler managed, some say by the promise of a 'good' evening after the match, to get them to Aborfield to play the Garrison side. The whole Garrison turned out to see an exciting game which the Kiwis won 43–3 (Davis scored the REME try). It is confirmed that the evening after the match was 'good'.

The pace in the late 1940s was, however, too fast as the players departed for civilian life or were posted out, and by the end of the decade the Arborfield Club was in decline. Fixtures with most of the main clubs were dropped and at the end of the 1950/51 season the club ceased to field a full team and concentrated on the club sevens.

However, the demise of the REME Arborfield RFC was not to be permanent, and in the mid sixties the posting to Arborfield of Philip Winchcombe (who was skippering the Corps XV) and the return of Dennis Bowen saw its re-emergence. Its fixture list was not as strong as in the late forties but the club continues to this day. Thus with the keen support of Brig Geoffrey Walker, at the time Commandant at Arborfield, the club was revived in time for the 1966/67 season. Success exceeded expectations and it was very satisfactory to find that so much goodwill towards REME Arborfield had survived the 'years of depression'! In this first revival season the club held its own with many others over a wide area and founded a reputation for open and sporting play. The response from the local people was so good that a regular 2nd XV was run and often a 3rd XV. Tours were undertaken to Yorkshire and to Bournemouth. The season ended on a note of great satisfaction, for not only were 37 out of 39 1st XV matches won but the club dinner was honoured by the presence of Mr Duggie Harrison, the RFU President. As a result of reforming the REME Arborfield RFC the Corps XV won all its representative matches, scoring 230 points with only 14 against.

The following two seasons (1967/68 and 1968/69) were successfully devoted to strengthening the fixture list and venturing abroad for a match against RC de Vincennes.

The strength of rugby at Arborfield has had its effect on Corps connections with Berkshire; they are stronger than with any other County side. Thirty-two REME players have represented Berkshire since 1946 when the County first competed in its own right in the County Championships. The first Berkshire XV contained seven REME players and in 1969/70 over half the Berkshire Colts XV came from the Army Apprentices College, Arborfield.

The sevens competitions started in the late 1940s and it is a moot point whether they were regarded as Corps fixtures or Arborfield RFC fixtures. In their heyday they played such teams as Rosslyn Park, Wasps and the Metropolitan Police. One of the most notable successes at that time was in the Middlesex Sevens where, in 1947, REME reached the finals but lost to London Welsh in the first of the final round played at Twickenham.

Though Corps sevens deteriorated with the temporary disbandment of the Arborfield RFC, the mid fifties with National Service saw a revival of Corps fortunes; this was also reflected in the strength of the Corps XV, when outstanding players like Swan (Scotland), Hancock (England), and Morgan (Wales) put the Corps in high standing in the Services rugby scene. Maj Priest, who had given so much to the game, had died the previous year when commanding the Command Workshop REME in Austria, and the Cup for this competition was presented in his memory by the British Troops Austria Rugby Club.

Interwoven in the account so far is Corps rugby, which of course is not purely a UK affair. In BAOR the Corps mounted a BAOR XV as far back as 1946, albeit without the quality of the Arborfield RFC XV – who trounced them 47-0. Over the years the REME UK XV has met the REME BAOR XV on their Easter pilgrimages to Germany; it is always a keen contest. The Corps side in BAOR competes for the Ellis Cup in the inter-Corps matches in Germany.

Like other Regiments and Corps, REME has been instrumental in assisting the start of rugby in various parts of the world. Brigs Dobie and Libby, while serving in Australia in the 1950s, assisted in re-introducing rugby into the Australian Services; and the REME Workshop in Jamaica, in conjunction with the Royal Hampshire Regiment, introduced the game into that part of the world in 1960.

But the record is strongest and the records most complete for the UK Corps XV. The Corps side in the UK has invariably had its base at the REME Training Centre, Arborfield, where a large proportion of its members are usually stationed. In the beginning the strength of the team emanated from the existing REME Arborfield RFC side which, as has already been related, gained strength and experience from a fixture list containing some of the senior clubs in the London area.

The first Corps match took place during the 1945/46 season against the Royal Artillery at Larkhill; REME won by 23-8. Matches against other Corps started in the 1946/47 season and have continued to the present day with few changes. The interest in REME rugby in the UK in 1947/48 was shown in the UK Final of that year. The Corps drew with Royal Signals at Leicester 6-6 but unfortunately lost the replay at

Northampton and thirteen bus loads of spectators travelled from Arborfield to see the replay.

Over the years the Corps, besides playing against other Corps and civilian clubs, has regularly undertaken tours at home and abroad. Formerly the tours were against the West Country which included Penzance and Newlyn and Bridgwater. Nowadays there is the annual tour at Easter to BAOR where matches against the REME BAOR XV, other BAOR XVs and the American Army take place.

After the war interest in rugby in the Corps, other than the well established activities of the REME Training Centre at Arborfield, was stimulated by a competition which started in 1947. The then Colonel Commandant, Maj-Gen Sir Basil A Hill, presented the Corps with a cup for annual competition between Commands in the UK – the Hill Cup. In the 1950s with a reorganisation of Commands in the UK the Hill Cup became a competition between REME unit sides.

XVs were raised in the UK mainly by the training battalions, but large workshops also raised sides. In the fifties the more successful sides were those of 3rd, 4th, 5th, 6th and 7th Training Battalions. 3rd and 5th were at Arborfield, 4th and 6th at Bordon and 7th at Barton Stacey. The successful 7th Battalion side had many first-class rugby league players in its XV – the big problem was getting these players to adapt to line-out work!

REME can be justly proud of their four Internationals, J S Swan (Scotland), J H Hancock (England), H J Morgan (Wales), and B McCall (Ireland). Swan's seventeen caps on the wing is a record for any Army back playing for Scotland and no other Army player has played for Wales in as many matches as H J Morgan's twenty-seven.

Finally, Peter Crooks recalls a remarkable match when playing for Durham against Lancashire in 1953. The International referee Mr R Cooper almost certainly achieved a record for post war rugby games by NOT awarding a single penalty kick! Denys Rowbottom the rugby correspondent of the *Manchester Guardian* reported that: 'The referee clearly appreciated the good spirit of the players and had the play under control.' Peter Crooks says it was a privilege to have taken part in such a game even though Durham were defeated 23–0. Brigadier Crooks, Chairman of the ARU, now represents the ARU on the RFU Committee.

THE LAUNCHING

The years up to the First World War brought the regular organisation of a match between the Army and the Royal Navy that had not been followed through from their previous meeting in 1878. Two interesting situations arose in the seasons before 1914. The Army had a wealth of International talent but met with little success. And there had to be a decision on whom the Royal Marines would play for, giving H C 'Dreadnought' Harrison and E J B Tagg a place in history as the only men to turn out in representative matches for both the Army and the Navy.

A game between officers of the Army and the Navy took place at Queen's Club in 1905 in the presence of the Prince of Wales (later King George V) and the Army won 10-0. In 1906 the Navy welcomed the Army for a match at Devonport and won 17-3 to have their revenge. The first official Inter-Service match, however, was at Queen's Club on 27 February 1907, and made a more fitting launching point for the now traditional climax to the Services' rugby season. It turned out to be a thrilling game that the Navy just won 15-14.

The Army were leading 6-5 at half-time, but on change of ends the Navy took command by means of better forward play, and scored twice. The Army half-backs, three of their threequarters and six forwards were all Internationals, but despite this it was only in the last quarter of the game that they made a spirited counter attack. In his one and only game for the Army, Basil Maclear (Royal Dublin Fusiliers), a legendary figure of Irish rugby, received a pass and, although surrounded by opponents, ran through the Navy side throwing off desperate tackles to score near the post. But Hill (AOC), the captain, missed the conversion that would have won the match.

Earlier Hill had converted a try by De Smidt (ASC) and there were two penalty goals but the Navy scored three tries, all converted. Play on both sides, though, prompted *The Times* correspondent to write:

> Certainly a team chosen from the Army and the Navy would in all probability defeat any team England could put in the field at the moment.

The exciting individual try by Maclear was typical of him. One of Ireland's greatest three quarters, he was a strong powerful man, a fast runner with an exceptional and deceptive swerve that enabled him to break through the strongest defence. His tackling was both ferocious and deadly. In an International career of three seasons he scored a number of such dazzling tries, one of the most notable being a swerving powerful run of nearly a hundred yards through the first Springboks' side, in a match Ireland lost by only 15 points to 12. He did play one game for Ireland as a wing forward, amid gaining eleven Ireland caps.

Maclear, who served for a long time in Ireland and played for Monkstown and Cork County, had, before he was posted there, been given several trials by England, who failed to realise his potential. He had an idiosyncrasy of wearing a pair of white kid gloves which, in Internationals, he changed at half-time, and he also frequently wore a khaki puttee round his waist.

The one appearance Basil Maclear made for the Army stands as a particular memorial to him. He was killed in action at Ypres in 1915.

Such was the high standard of rugby played by those serving in the Army prior to 1907 that sixty-one became Internationals, and between 1907 and 1914 twenty-six gained International honours and played for the Army. A further thirteen received International caps but did not play for the Army.

For all that, the next few years were not encouraging. Two matches were played in 1907, the second on 18 December, and the Navy soundly beat an army side full of Internationals 15–0! Once again the Navy forwards dominated the game and throughout they looked the more dangerous side, with tries by Orr, Rankin and Moir, all converted by Lappage. There was no game at all in 1908, but in 1909 a strong Navy side including six Internationals well and truly defeated the Army 25–0. On that occasion D'O Lyon converted three of the tries by Greig, Manners, Cooper, Warrington-Morris and Burgess-Watson, and remaining points came from a dropped goal by Blagrove. The Army half-backs were completely outplayed and their threequarters saw little of the ball. For his one of the Navy's tries Cooper jumped over the Army's full-back Grischotti (King's Shropshire Light Infantry) for a remarkable score!

Things improved slightly for the Army in 1910, in that they did not have a blank sheet, but they lost again, 19–10, at Queen's Club on 5 March. The Prince of Wales, who was to become King in May of that year, watched the game from the clubhouse and saw a vigorous sporting match with a splendid exhibition of forward play. The Army had the best try of the match, scored by Wade-Gert (RA) from an opening by Gardiner (RMA), but in general the open play by the backs was spoiled by wild passing and poor handling. Gowlland (RE) scored another try for the Army and both were converted by 'Dreadnought' Harrison. Navy scorers were Cooper, Royle (2), Greig and Burgess-Watson, with two of their tries converted by Burgess-Watson and Abercrombie.

At last in 1911 the Army managed a victory, whether or not spurred on by a large and enthusiastic crowd that included the England selectors. The game was again at Queen's Club on 4 March and the Army won 22–13.

This was another exciting game, won by the better-equipped all-round side. The Navy had scored first, but the Army forwards were more effective in the scrum and the line-out. In the open they dribbled in the Scottish style. Pym (RGA), who scored one try, was a very elusive half-back, and R F Simson (RFA – there were two Simsons in this match), who got two tries, had a fine all-round game. Wilson (Leicestershire Regt) also scored two tries and converted one, Griffith (RFA) was another try scorer, and Harrison made one conversion. Navy tries were by Wodehouse and Royle, converted by Abercrombie, who completed their points with a penalty goal.

The Army had to make the most of that win as they could not match it until 1914. The Navy won 16–8 in 1912 and 18–8 in 1913.

Games continued to be at Queen's Club and on 2 March 1912, King George V, accompanied by a new Prince of Wales (later King Edward VIII and Duke of Windsor), attended the match which, it was said, they followed with great interest. The King was known to enjoy football of either code and was particularly knowledgable about rugby and here he and his heir were seen to be appreciating all aspects of the game. The Army forwards played what they called 'the Blackheath game', holding and heeling out and breaking up quickly all the time. The Navy forwards, however, were magnificent in the loose and time and again made surging runs down the field, their D'O Lyon tackling so fiercely that the Army backs began passing widely and too quickly.

'Dreadnought' Harrison was in the Navy team that day and converted two of their four tries, by Collier, Peet, Millar and Eddis. Kellie (RA) scored two tries for the Army and one was converted by Pym.

On 1 March 1913, the King again enjoyed a good game and was amused when a large bulldog – obviously a sea dog! – joined the Navy pack during the first half and had to be forcibly removed. The Army put up a better fight than expected, though the Navy were the better side. A try by Huggan (RAMC) in the corner enabled the Army to score first, but soon the Navy half-backs began to take control of the game and this resulted in a superb try after a thrilling threequarter movement, with Royle scoring under the post. The Navy, despite an Army counter attack, kept control, though R F Simson scored a fine individual try to make up the Army points. Mr F C Potter-Irwin, the referee, did not bother too much about the strict letter of the law, knowing everyone was playing in the right spirit. The Navy scored other tries through Peet, Davies and Lapage and three were converted by Lapage.

Around 1913 it was agreed that the Marines should, in future, always play for the Navy, but for 1914 'Dreadnought' Harrison was back for one more game with the Army, converting four out of their six tries as they beat the Navy 26–14. The handsome Army victory came in rain and fog before the King and Prince Albert (later King George VI). The Army had five Internationals in their pack and the game was a duel between the Army forwards and the Navy backs. The half-time score was 18–3 and although the Navy made a spirited effort in the second half the Army held on. Once again Mr Potter-Irwin let the game take its own course, blowing the whistle only when it was absolutely necessary. There was hardly a penalty! The Army tries were two each by Huggan and Usher (Gordon Highlanders) and the others by MacIlwaine (RFA) and Gowlland, to tries for the Navy by Wodehouse, Simson, Peet and Oakley, one converted by Davies.

Harrison gained three Army caps and two for the Navy, plus four caps for England. He was a big, robust, pugnacious forward, uncompromising in his approach, who went flat out for the full eighty minutes. He was wounded in the First World War, but afterwards became a referee and took charge of the France v Scotland game in 1922.

It is recorded of him that while playing for the Navy in 1909 he was captain of their team and was approached by the Army captain at half-time with the remark that the match was not rugby football but a bloody battle. The Army captain, Partridge, finished up by saying: 'We thought we were playing against a side of Gentlemen.' Harrison's reply was short and to the point. 'We,' he said, 'had no such silly illusions!'

In 1910 the decision was made to play the Army Cup Final at Twickenham and in 1913 it was suggested by the Navy that their annual match with the Army should be played there too. The Army agreed to this, provided the teams were chosen from all ranks, only officers having been eligible to play heretofore. The war intervened and nothing was done about this change until afterwards. An Army Rugby Union minute in 1919 then read:

The meeting was unanimous in ruling that in future all ranks must be eligible in all Army matches, and that no Army Cap should be given except for matches in which the team representing the Army is selected from the Army as a whole irrespective of rank.

TEAMS FOR ARMY INTER-SERVICE MATCHES
1907–1914

It is regretted that forwards cannot always be shown in their correct positions in the pack as the press and match programmes are not uniform in listing the teams.

1907 (Feb) *Army:* W Grischotti (King's Shropshire Light Infantry), A W Newton (R Dublin Fus), B MacLear (R Dublin Fus), A G C De Smidt (ASC), W C Wilson (Leicestershire Regt), T T H Robinson (RAMC), E D Caddell (RAMC), B A Hill (AOC) (capt), R F A Hobbs (RE), J E C Partridge (Welch Regt), G E B Dobbs (RE), G C Gowlland (RE), J R Simson (Highland Light Infantry), F T Turner (RAMC), J R B Bond (Suffolk Regt).
Navy: G H D'O Lyon, W H Lapage, S P Start, H J Orr, D F Moir, P L H Noble, E G Ede, C D Cox, A R Palmer, F M Austin, E W Roberts (capt), C H Abercrombie, F O'B Wilson, C D Dix, H Brown.

1907 (Dec) *Army:* W Grischotti, A W Newton, L M Stevens (Worcestershire Regt), A G C De Smidt, W C Wilson, E D Caddell, W B Purdon (RAMC), B A Hill (capt), J E C Partridge, F T Turner, W L Y Rogers (RA), L Robertson (Cameron Highlanders), W L Huntingford (R Marines), L A Furber (KSLI), R P G Begbie (RGA).
Navy: G H D'O Lyon, G Biggs, A Lappage, H J Orr, D F Moir, L L Greig (capt), F S Carlisle, N H Rankin, F B Watson, F O'B Wilson, J S Wilson, R D Cox, T E Hughes, N D Wodehouse, J H Benbow.

1909 *Army:* W Grischotti, W C Wilson, A W S Brock (Leicestershire Regt), G C Campbell (RE), F W Gransmore (Welch Regt), R H Montgomery (Welch Regt), J C Teague (R Marine Light Infantry), B A Hill, J E C Partridge (capt), G C Gowlland, L Robertson, L A Furber, R P G Begbie, H L Bulkeley (RE), C A Bolton (Manchester Regt).
Navy: G H D'O Lyon, H C E Blagrove, G L D Gibbs, S D Tillard, S F Cooper, L L Greig (capt), E Manners, E W Kirkby, A D Warrington-Morris, F Burgess-Watson, F O'B Wilson, H C Harrison (capt), Wodehouse, E J B Tagg, G Le Page.

1910   *Army:* J H Rohde (RE), J T Simson (RAMC), M J Williamson (RAMC), W C Wilson, R H Wade-Geary (RA), H Gardiner (RFA), J A Pym (RGA), F G Marshall (R Army Chaplain's Dept), W S D Craven (RA), C A Bolton, J E C Partridge (capt), E J B Tagg (RMLI), H C Harrison (RM), G C Gowlland, L Robertson.

Navy: M G H Edwards, H C E Blagrove, G L D Gibbs, G C C Royle, S F Cooper, L L Greig (capt), E Manners, N A Wodehouse, C H Abercrombie, A D Warrington-Morris, F Burgess-Watson, C E Turle, G S Brown, G Le Page, E W Kirkby.

1911   *Army:* B C Quill (Queen's Regt), W C Wilson, R F Simson (RFA), J N Thomson (RFA), J T Simson, H Gardiner, J A Pym, J D Bowie (RAMC), L Robertson, C A S Carleton (Welch Regt), W E Mann (RFA), H C Harrison, R P G Begbie, W S D Craven (capt), A L P Griffith (RFA).

Navy: G H D'O Lyon (capt), F C Peet, G C C Royle, G D Millar, G D Campbell, W J A Davies, F E Oakley, N A Wodehouse, F Burgess-Watson, A H Bissett, G S Brown, R H T Raikes, C R Peploe, C H Abercrombie, W F Wake-Walker.

1912   *Army:* B C Quill, R H Wade-Geary, A S Heale (RAMC), R F Simson, A L Bonham-Carter (King's R Rifle Corps), H Gardiner, J A Pym, W S D Craven (capt), C G Liddell (Leicestershire Regt), R P G Begbie, I M Heath (Indian Army), R H A Kellie (RA), L Robertson, A L P Griffith, C M Usher (Gordon Highlanders).

Navy: G H D'O Lyon, F C Peet, J L Boyd, G C C Royle, K B Millar, W J A Davies, F E Oakley, N A Wodehouse (capt), H C Harrison, W B Hynes, C S Church, M Collier, G S Brown, R H T Raikes, C J F Eddis.

1913   *Army:* C A Baker (RMC), J L Huggan (RAMC), R F Gordon (RA), R F Simson, J N Thomson, C R M Hutchinson (RA), E de S Rideout (RE), W S D Craven, L Robertson, C M Usher, G C Gowlland, A H MacIlwaine (RFA), R Hemphill (RAMC), F H Lacy (Welch Regt), R W Ling (RA).

Navy: C A C Russell, F C Peet, W N Lapage, H R Thomson, G C C Royle, W J A Davies, F E Oakley, N A Wodehouse, H C Harrison, W B Hynes, J S Wilson, R H T Raikes, C H Abercrombie, C J F Eddis, J S Budge.

1914   *Army:* A M Jackson (RE), J L Huggan, R M Scobie (RE), C R M Hutchinson, H J Walker (R Warwickshire Regt), G W Oliphant (West Riding Regt), H Gardiner, L Robertson, H C

Harrison, A H MacIlwaine, G C Gowlland, C M Usher, A L W Neave (Indian Army), E F Boyd (Northumberland Fus), R W Ling.

Navy: C A C Russell, G C C Royle, D J R Simson, A E Thomson, F C Peet, W J A Davies, F E Oakley, N A Wodehouse (capt.), W B Hynes, M Collier, R S Benson, A L Harrison, L B R Wansborough, W F Wade-Walker.

1914–1920

Little is recorded about Army rugby during the First World War years and immediately afterwards. There was some play at the RMA, Woolwich, and the RMC, Sandhurst, though results of their annual fixture show that while no matches took place in 1914 or 1915 they resumed in 1916 and continued.

During the battle on the Somme in 1916 two companies of the 16th Battalion Northumberland Fusiliers set off from their trench behind a high drop-kicked rugby ball. Tragically all but eleven men of the eight platoons who followed it were cut down by machine-gun fire.

Just before another battle on the Somme, at St Quentin in 1918, it has been noted that 20th Light Division organised knock-out contests in rugby and other sports on a particular Sunday, 17 March – St Patrick's Day. Sundays were mostly rest days and this was some relief for the soldiers amid the strenuous weeks.

After the war there was mention in 1919 of an Inter-Services and Dominion Forces Championship. The Army Rugby Union was concerned in 1919 and 1920 about player status in respect of professionalism. One letter read:

> It has been brought to the notice of the ARU that cases have occurred during the war where Inter-Unit rugby football competitions have been held under Northern Union rules for Cups or medals presented by clubs or individuals. I am directed by the Committee of the ARU to point out that soldiers taking part in any such competition in future will forfeit their right to come under terms of the amnesty granted to Army players ...

In the same year it was decided that unless absolutely unavoidable no Northern Union player should be included in any trial match played with a view to selecting representative sides. And in 1920 it was reported that an NCO named Cpl Goode, of the 1st Battalion Gloucestershire Regiment, having played for the Northern Union as a professional, wanted to be re-instated as an amateur. An ARU minute gives their answer:

> It was agreed that there could be no question of re-instatement.

The ARU also had a problem in 1919 over cadet players, summed up in another extract from their minutes:

The Honorary Secretary referred to Blackheath's action in playing Cadets against the Army and asking other Army players to play for them next season, on the plea that the Army has no matches before Christmas. It was agreed a letter be written to the Army Sports Control Board pointing out fully the situation showing that in playing games, whichever side you play for is, or ought to be, a matter of free choice, and therefore the ARU consider the permission given to the Cadets at either colleges (RMA, Woolwich, RMC, Sandhurst) to play for outside clubs and not the Army is not a matter of free choice. The Army is barred from playing these Cadets whilst other clubs are allowed to get propaganda into the Colleges and therefore when the Cadets leave they will naturally play for outside clubs instead of the Army.

For some reason the Army were compelled to curtail their fixtures in 1920 and the ARU had some correspondence with Llanelli Rugby Club about not renewing their fixture for the next season. The club wrote regretting this and the Army regretted it too as Llanelli were considered 'one of the most sportsmanlike sides they had played against'.

BETWEEN THE WARS
PICKING UP THE PIECES - 1919–1928

The Services quickly got to grips with putting the game together after the war. The newly-formed RAF were welcomed into the Service competition, but at the beginning of the period this mainly meant for the Army that they had two opponents to beat them instead of one!

Unable to take up where they had left off in 1914, the Army were afflicted as in other, pre-war, years and lost their first four games against the Navy. Playing the RAF they lost three of the first five. This was partly due to four England players, the halves W J A Davies and C A Kershaw with the Navy and W W Wakefield and C N Lowe in the RAF.

W J A Davies, RN (twenty-two International caps), was an intelligent outside half with a perfect pair of hands, a wonderful eye for an opening, and a deceptive swerve. He partnered Kershaw in fourteen Internationals, winning thirteen and drawing one.

C A Kershaw, RN (sixteen International caps), was a scrum-half with a very fast and long pass and he was one of the first scrum-halves, if not *the* first, to break with the ball in his hands. W J A Davies, his partner, in his book *Rugby Football* writes, 'Kershaw rarely kicked to touch, in fact, during four consecutive years of first class football I doubt whether Kershaw kicked the ball more than a dozen times.'

W W Wakefield, RAF, later Lord Wakefield of Kendal was the greatest rugby player of his time. A forward of immense strength and great speed he revolutionised forward play, and the English back row of Wakefield, Voyce and Blakiston were a formidable trio. He obtained thirty-one caps for England, was captain from 1923–27 and President of the Rugby Football Union in 1950–51.

C N Lowe, RAF, was a brilliant wing threequarter who scored eighteen tries in the twenty matches he played for England.

A match against the French Army was a regular fixture too and the most unsuccessful season was in 1923 when the Army lost to the Navy, the RAF and the French. Despite that, the strength of Army rugby was such that in 1923/24 several fixtures went very much their way. They beat Leicester 15-3, Blackheath 25-6, London Scottish 29-3 and

Richmond 27–3. But during the time of Army decline in the early 1920s it had been suggested that Army physical training instructors might be well advised to introduce scrummaging, tackling and passing into their recruit training syllabus. In 1924/25 the Army beat Bristol 14–3, Harlequins 6–0, Blackheath 6–0 and London Scottish 19–3, and went on to their most successful season in 1926 when they defeated the Navy, the RAF and the French Army!

Twenty-one players received International caps in the years just after the war and a number came very close. Many outstanding county and club players failed to get Army caps, one of these being J H (Jack) Dalrymple (Blackheath and Devon), a fast, determined wing three-quarter, who later became Lieut-Col Dalrymple, ARU Secretary.

From now onwards the Army v Navy matches were all to be played at Twickenham, as decided, and with other ranks allowed in the teams. The first game since 1914 was on 28 February 1920, and took place in the presence of the King and the Prince of Wales. The Navy won 23–11.

CSM C W Jones of the Welch Regiment had the honour of being the first non-officer in the Army side. He was all-round forward and no one worked harder throughout a game. In his career he was to gain six Army caps and three for Wales, some considering he was unlucky not to receive more International recognition. Jones, described as a cheerful man, played for the 2nd Battalion the Welch Regiment in the five Army Cup Finals they reached, four of which they won. He also served on the ARU Executive Committee.

His introductory Inter-Service game, unfortunately, was not otherwise memorable for the Army, who gave a disappointing performance. It was played at a great pace and the tackling was hard, but the Army, though fighting valiantly, were up against a far better team. The Navy forwards were outstanding in their rushes, in the line-out, and in the set scrums. Both of their England players were on view, Kershaw having his first game and partnering Davies, who was their captain.

The Army had in E G W W Harrison (RFA) a fast wing, but he had one fatal fault. He did not go down on the ball but instead took flying kicks at it! Their captain, Scobie (RE), seemed oppressed by the cares of his office. Many of his passes were not only impossible to take but a source of danger to his side. Harrison later represented the UK at the famous 1924 Olympics and played for the Mother Country XV.

For the time being, the matches against the RAF were to take place at various locations and their baptism was at Queen's Club on 6 March of the same year (1920), when the Army defeated them 21–9. The

Army proved to be the better team and deserved their win, in front of the King, Prince Albert and Prince Henry (later Duke of Gloucester).

C M Usher (Gordon Highlanders), who had first played for the Army in 1912 and 1913, was having his opening game for them since the war and he made a colossal difference to the pack, leading it well and inspiring his fellows with the excellence of his play. The Army backs outplayed their opponents and their team led 15–0 at half-time. The best forwards on the field were Usher and Wakefield, who led a fine RAF pack, but the Army backs won the match for their side, playing well together and being faster and cleverer than the opposition. The Army scored five tries, two each by Baker-Jones (RFA) and Wilkins (Tank Corps) and the other by Scobie, three of them converted by Penny (RFA). McLennan (two tries) and Symington (one) were the RAF scorers.

Both sides had problems when the Army next came to play the Navy on 26 February 1921. The game clashed with a Scotland–Ireland International which claimed three Navy men, and they were also without Kershaw, who had influenza. Usher was unable to play for the Army, and they discovered a further difficulty when they took the field. They were not only to be playing the Navy but a section of the crowd also – vociferous noisy young ladies from the School for Naval Officers' Daughters!

The match, which the King again attended, was to prove exciting, with a final score of 11–10 to the Navy. It began in a thrilling fashion when an Army player appropriately named King (RFA) eluded his opposite number and swerved round the full-back to score a fine try. Shortly afterwards he was largely responsible for Worton (RMC) getting a try, he followed this up by dropping a goal, and by half-time the Army had a ten-point lead.

This particularly annoyed Davies, the Navy captain, as he had given special instructions before the game that King was to be marked very carefully! With King having already personally accounted for seven of the points, Davies held a council of war in the interval. This put new life into his team. Stephenson scored a try and then Davies himself kicked a penalty goal from wide out. He was going to take a drop kick when he heard a spectator shout 'Take a place Davies'. He did.

A breath-taking last fifteen minutes followed until, with five minutes to go, Duncan (Queen's Own Cameron Highlanders) fumbled a high kick near the Army line and Eyres, the Navy centre, gathered the ball and scored. Attempted conversions by the Army earlier had been interrupted by the schoolgirls shouting 'Navy, Navy' as the Army took their kicks. This one by the Navy was surrounded by a death-like silence! It succeeded, and the Navy won the game, Davies doing the converting.

The RAF began to get into their IS stride on 5 March at Queen's Club when they beat the Army 26–3. They scored five tries to the Army's one and Lowe was their outstanding player scoring four of them. Wakefield led the RAF pack with great *élan* and they outclassed the more sluggish Army forwards. His happy inspiration to play Lowe in the centre paid off and all his tries came after splendid runs. Smith also scored a try and four were converted by Maxwell, who kicked a penalty goal as well. The Army's try was by King, from a movement that appeared to include not less than three forward passes.

John Worton was selected to play for the Army in this match but the Commandant at Sandhurst refused to grant him permission – he considered he should put the RMC side first!

Usher was back as captain for the Army v Navy match on 4 March 1922. Three of the four half-backs were already Internationals and the fourth, Worton, was to play for England four seasons later, the Army lost again, 7–3.

The King honoured the match with another visit on a day that had seen heavy rain two hours before the match, which made the turf slippery under foot and the ball difficult to hold. Middleton (RASC), the Army full-back, kicked a prodigious length with great accuracy, but Kealey, the Navy back, was his equal. Day (RFA) ran with real determination to score the Army try, but the Navy levelled the scores with a penalty kick by Luddington. It was the genius of Navy skipper Davies that won the match. He found himself with no room to man-oeuvre, so calmly ran a yard or two to his left and pulled up. Before anyone could get at him he screw-kicked a drop for goal that sailed between the posts.

It was at Essex County Cricket Ground at Leyton on 11 March that the Army had their second win of that period against the RAF, aveng-ing the previous year's defeat by a score of 23–8.

At the start, the RAF forwards so dominated the Army pack that Wakefield withdrew himself from the forwards and helped the three-quarters, his attacking runs and tackling being very successful and bringing the RAF their first try, converted by Maxwell. But the Army were on terms 5–5 at half-time after a kick ahead was followed up, and from the turn-round the better Army halves and threequarters began to assert themselves. Worton, at his best, served team-mate Tennant (RA) well and gave the threequarters plenty of opportunities. Tries by Day were initiated twice by Usher and once by Tennant.

Kilgour (Northumberland Fus) and G D Young (Welsh Guards) scored the other Army tries. Day made four conversions. Jones got the RAF a second try.

All the Army backs except Tennant gained International caps and this was perhaps a fitting match for Usher to bow out, as he played his usual forceful game in the forwards, well supported by Young, Ross (HLI) and MacNamara (Royal Inniskilling Fus).

C M (Charles) Usher was a most distinguished player, who began both his Army and International career in 1912, going on to gain ten Army caps and sixteen for Scotland. He captained Scotland as well as the Army and was a dashing and tireless forward, covering the ground like lightning. He was severely wounded during the First World War and was a prisoner for four years, but he recovered so well that he played for a Mother Country XV in an Inter-Services' and Dominion Forces' Championship of 1919. Seven of his Army caps came after the war and ten of his games for Scotland.

At the age of forty-two he was attending an Army match against Blackheath as one of the selection committee. One of the Army players failed to turn up and he was prevailed upon to take his place – the Army won 21–11 and, according to *The Times*, Usher had a splendid game!

The following letter, sent out before the 1923 Navy match, shows how team instructions had obviously improved since 1878 when the captain, of all people, had failed to receive notification of his selection:

Room 102, Horse Guards,
Whitehall, S.W.1.
19th February 1923.

[To: H. L. V. Day Esq.,
    Royal Artillery Mess,
    Woolwich.]

Dear

You have been selected to play for the Army against the Navy at Twickenham on Saturday, March 3rd and to captain the side.

A charabanc will leave the Whitehall entrance to Horse Guards at 12 noon on that day to take players to Twickenham. The team will lunch together on the ground at 1 p.m. After the match the charabanc will return to London taking such players as wish to avail themselves of this transport.

DRESS

Please provide your own *white* shorts and ensure that they are clean. Stockings and a numbered jersey will be provided on the ground.

An Army Cap will also be provided *unless* you are already in possession of one in which case will you kindly forward it to me *at once* in order that the extra date may be put on to it.

Please pay particular attention to your boots (studs, laces etc.)

TICKETS

I enclose 2 complimentary stand tickets. A luncheon ticket (for your personal use for lunch with the team) will be forwarded to you shortly as will two tickets for tea which latter are for use as you may desire.

PRACTICE

It is hoped that you will be able to come to the Royal Military Academy, Woolwich, on Wednesday Feb. 28th for practice with the team beginning at 3 p.m. under Captain A. H. MacIlwaine's direction. The best way to get to the R.M.A. is by train to Woolwich Arsenal, thence by tram to the R.M.A. gate.

Will you kindly answer the following questions *by return of post:—*

  (i) Will you be able to play for the Army against the Navy?

 (ii) Will you be travelling from London by charabanc with the team?

(iii) Was the jersey you played in at Richmond last Saturday of the correct size? and would you like any minor alterations such as shortening sleeves, if so by how much?

(iv) Have you an Army Cap, if so, are you sending it to me now?

 (v) Will you be able to come to the practice at the R.M.A. on Wednesday, February 28th?

Yours sincerely,

Major.
Asst. Hon. Secy.
ARMY RUGBY UNION

For all the careful arrangements shown in the letter, however, due to circumstances beyond their control the Army had to endure an unsatisfactory 1923 season of IS games. They were handicapped by many young players being posted abroad; leading player Aslett (King's Own Royal Regt) was injured in early November and was unable to take part in Service matches; and with the retirement of Usher there was a big need for an inspiring leader.

The Navy won their game on 3 March 16-11, but the Army did well in the early stages, and had their finishing been better they might have built up a winning score. In a game played at great pace and in the best of spirit, before a crowd of 20,000, they scored first despite missed chances. Giles (Welsh Guards) got a try from a line-out close to the line and skipper Day kicked a splendid conversion. Although the touch judges disagreed, the referee allowed the goal. But a wild pass from an Army forward on his own '25' allowed the Navy's Eyres to score a try to start them off and the Army were not left for long basking in their 8-3 half-time lead, secured when a fine passing move-ment ended in Millar (RE) brushing past opposing full-back Gilbert for a try. In the action Gilbert sustained a broken thumb and he had to leave the field.

Undeterred by seven forwards, the Navy scored twice fairly soon in the second half, the second try after a break by Kershaw at half way. After a fourth try – the last three were by Haines, Mackenzie and Davies with Burnett converting two of them – the Army also managed another five minutes before 'no side' to close the gap a little, Millar, their wing, scoring the try which was not converted. The Army worked desperately for a further success but to no purpose. Giles, Rennie (Black Watch), Ross (HLI) and Young worked untiringly in the Army pack, but Worton was outplayed by Kershaw at scrum-half and Day was badly shaken up by a hard tackle.

Aldershot was the ground for that year's RAF match on 10 March. The RAF piled on the agony in the 'Home of the British Army' by not only winning 13-5 but in doing so taking the IS Championship for the first time in only their fourth season!

They held their own in the forwards and possessed a distinct super-iority outside, to be always the most formidable combination. A for-ward rush brought a score in the first ten minutes and then their captain, Wakefield again, who set a fine example and was the outstand-ing player on the field, forced his way over for a try by sheer strength, with several opponents clinging to him. Adams and Lowe were other try scorers and Runham made two conversions. Eventually Worton sent Palmer (Queen's Royal Regt) over for an Army try, which Middleton converted with a splendid kick, but the RAF thoroughly deserved their victory.

In 1924 the Army found their first win against the Navy since 1914, and that successful season was marred only by a later defeat by the RAF. The Army did, however, beat the Navy 19-5 on 1 March and only lost 8-3 to the RAF on 8 March at Uxbridge.

Playing the Navy, the Army forwards excelled, with Browne (Duke of Wellington's Regt), Rennie, Faithfull (also DWR) and Ross being outstanding in the loose. Worton, as usual, worked very hard and his partner Tucker, home on leave from India (Gurkha Rifles), was a marked success, showing the value of the straight run and the hand off when adopted by a big man with a raking stride. Millar made full use of his chances by scoring four tries with excellent determined running. Rennie scored one and Aitken (RE) converted twice. Navy points were from a try by Giffard converted by H S Harrison.

After that showing the Army, with an unchanged side, were confidently expected to beat the RAF, but the latter had other ideas. They had another deserved win by setting a tremendous pace from the start and maintaining it throughout, their forwards breaking quickly and being among the Army backs in a flash, well supported by their half-backs Russell and Medhurst. Chick scored a try in the first two minutes, which was converted by another player rejoicing in the name of Usher – he had played in earlier matches in opposition to his Army namesake. The RAF Usher kicked a very fine penalty goal from 40 yards when the Army were penalised just before half-time.

The Army had scored their try in the first half when Aslett threw a long pass out to Bryan (RE), who went over in the corner, but the RAF had the match under strict control and never allowed the Army pack to show the fire and brilliance so evident against the Navy. The loss of Faithfull at half-time due to a hip injury was unfortunate for the Army but did not affect the pattern overall as neither side scored in the second half.

Brighter times arrived for the Army in 1925. The selectors had a plentiful supply of forwards and it was difficult to know whom to leave out for the Navy match on 7 March. At scrum-half both Powell (Welsh Guards) and Worton were available. In the Army's 11-8 win Powell thoroughly justified his selection.

The Navy led deservedly at half-time 8-3, from tries by Stevenson and Davies, one converted by Forrest, but in the second half it was all Army, with Powell repeatedly outwitting the defence with his long reverse pass. The Army constantly got the ball from the tight scrums. Bryan had scored their first try when he cleverly avoided being crowded into touch, then Millar made an opening for Phillips (Welch Regt) to score in the corner, Powell converting.

That made the teams all square, but Bryan made all the running for Green (Northamptonshire Regt) to score the winning try just on time. The Navy's try by Davies, a brilliant individual effort, crowned an immaculate performance by him in what was his final first-class game.

He was recalled to the Navy side to team up again with his old partner and new skipper Kershaw.

The Army could not follow up that game by beating the RAF at Wembley Stadium on 14 March but saved the match by the skin of their teeth for a 6-6 draw. Thanks to their forwards they enjoyed a much bigger share of the game, but the threequarters kept dropping their passes and any movements they managed to make were slow and mechanical.

Lowe gave the RAF two tries in the first twenty minutes, after running cleverly and with his usual great determination. Powell, however, replied for the Army from a fine break down the wing by Bryan. Tremendous Army pressure after that was resisted by the RAF, with Powell and Phillips almost scoring, but in the last minute Bryan was able to get a pass out to Loch (RE), who dived over to equalise.

The vintage year of 1926 at last saw the Army win the IS Championship, but before beating the Navy 24-10 on 6 March they were given a rare fright by them.

The Navy got a try in the first five minutes and continued to press until Rees (Welsh Guards) kicked a penalty goal for the Army. The Navy hooked the ball in the set scrums three times out of four, but the Army managed to score five tries, two by Bryan, and one each by Aslett, Down (Dorsetshire Regt) and Cass (King's Own Yorkshire Light Infantry), three converted by Rees. The Army tries were all by threequarters and new scrum-half A T Young (Royal Tank Corps) had a share in all five.

In this game, where the packs were evenly matched, with Browne and Ross outstanding for the Army, it was Young who was largely responsible for the Army victory. This was his first inter-service match and he kept penetrating the Navy defence, making early display of what was to be later called his 'magnificent genius'.

Branson and Fricker scored Navy tries that day and Garrett a drop goal.

On 27 March at Twickenham, on which both IS games were centred from that day, the Army had the satisfaction of defeating the RAF 11-0, but although they won the RAF had as much, and possibly more, of the play.

Bryan picked up a ball by his own line and ran almost the length of the field for the Army's first try, but the RAF put them under intense pressure. Aslett, at centre, however, tackled like a demon and Rees, at full-back, by perfect positioning and safe catching proved invaluable to a side in such distress. At last the Army got going and eventually improved on their slender position by Browne and Phillips both adding tries in the last four minutes. Rees made one conversion. The RAF had the misfortune to have what appeared to be a good try disallowed, as the referee ruled that he personally had got in the way of an Army player.

For 1927 and 1928 the Army were to finish off the period in good style, but they began on 5 March 1927, by going down 6–3 to the Navy. They were considerably weakened by the loss of three of their Internationals, Aslett, Clinch (Middlesex Regt) and Rees.

Nevertheless, the Army still had four Internationals in their ranks, but these did not stand them in good stead. In the first half the Army hardly ever managed to hook the ball in the tight scrums, and their backs had few chances. When Young did make a break to the Navy line his pass to Sewell (Northamptonshire Regt) was dropped. Meanwhile, the Navy scored what were to be their winning tries in the first half, through George and Harry. Heavy rain did not help in the second half, but Maxwell (RAOC) broke through cleverly before passing to Bryan, who used his speed to achieve a good try. Yet despite working hard the Army failed to score again.

Against the RAF on 25 March, however, the Army won 22–0 and on a bitterly cold day outplayed the RAF in a poor game. Aslett returned to the Army team but did not have one of his best matches. Young showed flashes of brilliance, though, and his partner Tucker improved greatly on his form against the Navy. Rees was unavailable for the Navy match because of a broken leg so was naturally still out for this one.

A young RAF side rather went to pieces and allowed the Army to score six tries, which came from Bryan (3), Palmer, Browne and Maxwell, with Cass converting two. Palmer, it was said, in trying to take his passes at full speed, fluffed most of them. *The Times* correspondent considered this a commendable fault, adding:

> Still, if he could only combine thought with headlong dash Palmer would be one of the most dangerous wings now playing.

Both IS matches in 1928 were won by the Army for them to regain the championship. They defeated the Navy 11–5 on 3 March and the RAF 18–6 on 24 March, only spoiling that year's record at the end of the month when they were handsomely beaten by a French Army side, which included five internationals.

After a year's absence because of his injury, Rees was with the Army team again as full-back in a star-studded line-up that had five Internationals outside the scrum and three in the pack. For all that, the

Army only just held their own in a match of mistakes against the Navy. It was not until the last quarter of an hour, when they scored two fine tries, that they got on top.

Aslett, the captain, was at his brilliant best and Young, as usual, was outstanding, but the Navy put up a splendid fight against a team with such abundance of talent. They were without their International full-back, but his replacement, Gosling, had an excellent game.

After a try by Townend (DWR), converted by Rees, matched by a Navy try for Freeman, converted by Trentham, the game reached its last twelve minutes with the scores still equal. The Navy were unlucky not to go ahead with a drop at goal, which hit one of the posts. But then Young made a dazzling run and Cole (Loyal Regt) took a long pass and scored the Army's second try. It was not converted. That was not important when Young again made the opening for a further try to consolidate. He sent a 20-yard pass to Aslett, who kicked ahead, and Bryan, following up, caught the ball in his stride and ran to the Navy full-back, before returning it to Aslett for the score.

The genius of Young once again had to turn the tide when the Army played the RAF. Despite their seven Internationals that day, they were slow starters once more and were well and truly outplayed for at least half of the game, never getting really going. They did lose Gibbons (Welsh Guards) in about the first tackle of the game, though, and this possibly had some effect.

Young took charge, turned defence into attack, and started a movement that ended in Bryan scoring under the posts. Rees converted that try and two more of the subsequent ones where Bryan went over again after a well-controlled dribble and Aslett and Townend joined in the scoring. Odbert and Pott found a try apiece for the RAF.

Everyone seemed to have forgotten about the hapless Gibbons once he was injured. According to *The Times*, he remained unconscious in the dressing room for several unnecessary hours until eventually an Army ambulance was called into service from many miles distant.

THE GOLDEN ERA 1929–1939

The build-up from 1926, and regaining the IS Championship in 1928, led the Army into their most successful period. In the ten years up to the Second World War they played 11 matches against the Navy, of which they won eight, with one draw; had another eight wins out of their 11 games against the RAF; and won all three of their matches with the French Army in that time.

Weighing points, the Army scored 131 to 65 in their games with the Navy, 159 to 77 versus the RAF, and 47 to 20 over the French. Outstandingly, most of the points came from tries and conversions. In the total 337 there were only three penalty goals, one dropped goal and two goals from a mark.

A constant flow of prominent players represented the Army and twenty-three gained International honours. Many county sides included service players and their influence on rugby was considerable.

It was entirely fitting that Alfred Aslett, one of the Army's greatest players and their most successful captain, should see them into this memorable decade before having his last match in 1929, and also that he, one outstanding threequarter of the era, should overlap with the other, A L (Tony) Novis of the Leicestershire Regiment. What was Aslett's last IS season was the first for Novis, who himself went on to be a successful Army skipper.

Against the Navy on 23 March 1929, Novis scored two tries and Aslett one as the Army won 17–11 to begin a great season. The game was a clean, vigorous encounter with eight tries scored altogether, others for the Army coming from Townend and Wainwright (RA) compared with Navy ones by St Clair Ford, Stephenson and Carhill, but only one for each side was converted, by Novis and Forrest.

Before this match the band had played not only the National Anthem but the Marseillaise, the latter in memory of the French First World War leader Marshal Foch, who had died on 20 March.

Ten minutes into the game the Army had the misfortune to lose their scrum-half, Young, with a broken collar bone, but Browne came out of the pack and played a fine stand-in's part, once Cole, at outside half, was able to judge the length of his passes. The Army backs mounted a series of delightful movements in which skill, pace and sure handling were evident. Novis, Cole and Aslett were all in great form and Novis made his IS debut with the first try after a swift handling movement.

The Army followed this up on 27 March by defeating the RAF 27-0, a record score that made a fine farewell to the captain, Aslett, who signed off with two of the seven tries that day. The packs were equally balanced, but outside the scrum the RAF defence became increasingly ineffectual and hesitant in the face of such fast determined runners as Cole, Novis, Aslett and Wainwright. The Army scored 11 points in the first quarter of an hour and were on top throughout. Novis also scored two tries and made three conversions. Other tries were by McCreight (RA), Wainwright and Hobbs (RA). McCreight proved a capable substitute for the injured Young.

After helping the Army to retain the IS Championship, Aslett could reflect on a career that began when he captained the Sandhurst XV in 1920 and was immediately snapped up for the Army in their two representative games in 1921. He went on to receive twenty Army caps and in those twenty matches was never in the losing team. A strong determined centre, who could brush aside the most severe defence, he was also a perceptive tactician, which he proved when he captained the team with great success on twelve ocasions.

Though having his first England trial in 1921, Aslett was not capped for his country until 1926, when he thought he was past his best. He gained six caps for England eventually and went on to be a selector for many years. For some time he had few opportunities to play rugby in England anyway. He served in Ireland from 1921 to 1924 and while there played for the Landsdowne Club in Dublin. He said he was offered an Irish cap providing he could find an Irish relative!

In 1922, while playing for Lancashire against Cheshire, Aslett sprained an ankle very severely and unfortunately this injury was a constant hindrance to him for the rest of his career, but around the time of his last match for the Army he captained his Regimental side to victory in two Army Cup Finals, in 1929 and 1930, after they were runners-up in 1928.

Alfred Aslett, an England selector from 1948-59, was elected Vice-President of the Rugby Football Union in 1958, but had to resign because of ill health. He was Director of the Army Sport Control Board in 1946.

In addition to the players already mentioned as particular names to remember from these years, J B (John) Worton merits a place as a strong reliable scrum-half, who was capped ten times for the Army and twice for England. He would probably have played further matches for his country but for A T Young. Worton also took the field for Harlequins and was in the winning team in the first seven-a-side tournament in 1926.

On 1 March 1930, the Army began their defence of the IS title by beating the Navy 16–10, winning comfortably against opponents who lacked pace and never got into top gear, but on 22 March, though they retained the championship again with a 14–8 win over the RAF, they had a hard struggle to overcome the determined RAF defence.

Rice-Evans (Royal Welch Fus) gave the Army a lead against the Navy with a good try in the first few minutes, and further tries were by Rew (RTC), Devitt (Seaforths) and Cole, two converted by Nott (Worcestershire Regt). Townend had a splendid game as a front row forward constantly in support of his backs and it was he who led a forward rush that resulted in Rew gathering the ball and scoring. Webb, the English International, bulldozed himself over the line for a Navy try and St Clair Ford also scored, both converted by Luddington.

The RAF were a different matter, but although their pack, led (with boundless energy) by the great George Beamish, subdued the Army in front and provided their backs with chances galore, these were cast away by indiscriminate kicking. The Army backs, on the other hand, despite having far fewer chances, were able to put them to advantage through greater speed and thrust, especially in the centre, where Novis and Rice-Evans proved too fast and clever for their immediate opponents. The outcome of this was tries for Rice-Evans, Cole, Townend and Wainwright, with one converted by Nott, to give the Army victory, while only Gibbs and White found tries for the RAF, one converted by Gibbs.

George Townend, another outstanding player who had helped establish the Army team, was making his departure with his try in this match. He gained ten Army caps and was first class in any position one would care to name, having two International trials as prop forward, being a number eight for Yorkshire, Devon and the Army, and playing at stand-off half for his Regiment in two Army Cup winning teams. He never received an International cap, however. Lieut-Col Jack Dalrymple said of him that Townend was in his opinion the best all round, 'and I stress, all round', rugby player that the Duke of Wellington's Regiment ever produced, but that he never received due tribute was, no doubt, due to the fact that he lived and breathed the same air as that other powerful personality and rugby genius 'Horsey' Browne.

Townend was said to be a joy to play with, as his confidence and coolness, whatever the circumstances, inspired the team. He was blessed with all the qualities of strength, balance and speed, and was in addition a perfect kicker of the ball, whether punting or place kicking. He once scored 19 points for the Army against the French Army.

Another reason for Townend not gaining International recognition was his sense of duty and loyalty to his Regiment. Generally, whenever International trials took place he had been grossly overplayed. He never missed a Regimental match simply because he had been selected for a higher grade game a few days later. It was finally said of him that he was a true Yorkshireman who had a deep affection for his Regiment.

The years of 1931 and 1933 in the Army's golden era were marred by the tragic deaths of two favourite players, the incomparable 'Horsey' Browne and the 'magnificent genius' A T Young.

'Horsey' Browne was to die of Leukaemia on 23 May 1931. He was only twenty-eight. His death was a particularly great blow to his Regiment, the Army (for whom he gained sixteen caps) and his country, Ireland (twelve caps) as he was previously so amazingly fit. Once, on the same day, he had run in a cross-country race, played rugby, and in the evening won a boxing match. His contribution to the Duke of Wellington's Regiment in the rugby field was second to none.

A lovable character and a man of great charm, Browne was only lacking in height and weight (5 ft 8 ins, 11 stone), which nearly denied him the chance to shine as an outstanding forward. The Irish selectors took a lot of persuading to choose him, because they thought he was too small. What he lacked in stature, though, he made up for by being a great student of the game and an inspiring leader. He played usually in the back row of the scrum and was utterly tireless. In the loose he covered ground at an astonishing speed and he was a desperately difficult man to stop. His energy and determination often carried him through the strongest defence, and as a devastating tackler he rarely failed to get his man.

At the express wish of Adrian Stoop, himself a legendary scrum-half who before the war played fifteen times for England and who was Vice-President of the RFU when 'Horsey' died, 'Horsey' Browne was carried from the Military Hospital at Aldershot to Stoop's House, Hartley Grange, for his last few days, thus to die among friends whom he loved.

The other tragic death, that of A T Young, occurred in India where he had been posted – at Bareilly – on 26 February 1933. He was thirty-one.

Young, who gained ten Army caps and eighteen for England, had some magnificent games for both and was a lively and intelligent scrum-half. He learned his rugby at Tonbridge School and later gained his 'blue' as a freshman at Cambridge. He was very adept at turning defence into attack, as has already been noted, and was like lightning in seizing on a loose ball and breaking away in an elusive manner. At his most brilliant he could be a match winner, but on occasions he was desperately erratic, so that, as a feeder to his outside half, his passes were apt to be high, wide and handsome. This unorthodox, unpredictable and brilliant scrum-half, however, was one of the best players to wear an England and Army jersey.

Shortly after his death, a memorial was unveiled to him in St Augustine's Church, Bexhill, Sussex, in 1934.

By a sad coincidence, 1931 (the year of 'Horsey' Browne's death) was the one year in the decade that the Army lost both of their IS matches. On 7 March they went down 6–0 to the Navy and they lost 16–5 to the RAF.

The Navy, who had previously beaten the RAF, won the IS Championship by seizing two outstanding chances against the Army. The smartness of their scrum-half, Webster, the deadly tackling of St Clair Ford, and the exceptional pace of Lane proved the deciding factors. The Navy also held a pronounced advantage in the scrum. A try each by St Clair Ford and Lane settled the issue.

A newcomer to the Army side, G Taylor (West Yorkshire Regt), had a dazzling game as a flank forward and was relentless in his tackling and backing up, but poor handling prevented the Army making much progress. In the second half Novis created two perfect openings for the wings, only in both cases – with the line at their mercy – for the scoring pass from Novis to be muffed.

The Army were without Novis and Cole for the RAF match, but with George Beamish leading the RAF forwards magnificently to give an impressive performance, the RAF deserved their success. A brilliant dummy and swerving run by McCreight enabled the Army to score first when this was followed by a perfectly timed pass to Troop (DWR), who completed the movement, with Hunt (RA) converting. The RAF, however, immediately came back and a break by Bader (later Sir Douglas Bader of Second World War flying fame and who later that same year lost both legs in a flying accident) was supported by Williams for the latter to score. The RAF led 11–5 at half-time on other tries by Hodder and Coote, Simmons having made a conversion.

In the second half the RAF put in attack after attack and but for the determined tackling of Hunt at full-back would have scored more than once, Coote and Bader being prominent in the RAF raids. They were limited to one more try, by Constantine, converted again by Simmons.

The Army were back on a winning track in 1932 and for the rest of the era, even when losing to one IS opponent, managed to stave off double defeats.

They rose to the occasion on 5 March 1932, and beat a confident Navy side 11-0. Hunt played in the centre and was a great success, as were the new full-back Radcliffe (RE) and new wing threequarter Crawford (also RE). Crawford scored an excellent try, beating two would-be tacklers cleverly with change of pace and swerve. Kendrew (Leicestershire Regt) converted with a good kick from an awkward angle. In the second half brilliant tackling by Radcliffe, Hunt and Novis kept the Navy out, with both the play and captaincy of Novis proving an inspiration to his side. Cole had one of his best games. The rest of the Army's points came from tries by Vaughan-Jones (RA) and Sadler (RCS).

A decisive 21-4 win against the RAF on 2 April was achieved despite the Army being without Kendrew and Vaughan-Jones and losing Tyler (RA), the centre, five minutes from the start after he had scored the first try. On the injury to Tyler Novis moved into his place and Jackson (Indian Medical Service) came out of the pack. The RAF paid a heavy price for poor finishing power and one or two weak links in defence, which let the Army score two tries after Coote dropped a clever goal to give the RAF the lead. There was a valiant effort by RAF skipper George Beamish (there were now two Beamishes in his team), but the Army controlled most of the game in the second half.

Novis, appropriately, scored the try of the match and made one conversion, amid a wealth of tries, after Tyler's, by Hobbs, Cole and Crawford, with other conversions by Sayers (RA) and Hunt. This was Hunt's last IS match and nearly the end of his career. In the 1933 season he was badly injured and never played rugby again. He had played eight games for the Army was full-back and three as a centre-threequarter to earn his eleven caps. He was capped five times for Ireland.

A victory at 19-0 (two goals and three tries) on 4 March 1933, was the most decisive ever gained by the Army over the Navy and was nonetheless impressive because the Navy were never completely out-played.

The Army had a most effective side that year. Prior to the Navy game they defeated Blackheath, the outstanding club team of the season. In the *Rugby Football Annual* of 1933/34 one critic stated that

'The Army would have given any of the national sides of last year a hard game and perhaps more'. Five members of the Army pack were current Internationals, and Sayers was to be capped for Ireland in 1935. Two more Internationals, Hunt and Vaughan-Jones, were not available through injury.

Exhilarating, attacking rugby was produced, with Cole, at stand-off half, in his best form, though his partner Simpson (RE) had a disappointing match. The Army pack eventually took control but the Navy made some spirited counter-attacks until the straight running and rapid passing of the Army backs and skilled combined play broke the Navy defence. Crawford scored four tries and Pike (Royal Army Chaplains' Dept, later to become Chaplain General to the Army) one, two of them converted by Novis. Crawford had an outstanding game on the wing, his opportunism and speed being responsible for his fine scoring.

On 25 March the Army beat the RAF 12–3 to keep hold of the championship, but did not have it all their own way in that game either. Once again George Beamish was in great form, and it was no fault of his that his team, outweighed and outpaced in front, just failed to stay a cracking pace. The Army were handicapped by injuries. Troop left the field with a slipped cartilage. Novis sprained an ankle before half-time, and on returning could only hobble about on the wing. Finally Boast (Welsh Guards) broke his nose and the Army pack was reduced to six.

Great credit must go to the gallant six forwards who, led by Kendrew, never flinched against formidable odds. Dean made a try for Crawford and put the seal on a splendid Army victory by himself darting through the covering defence for another try. One was converted by Kendrew and there was a dropped goal by Croston (RE). Coote scored a try for the RAF.

This was the last IS match for Taylor, giving him his fifth Army cap. He was a speedy aggressive wing forward who was thought to be one of the fastest in England. Outside the Army he played for Lancashire, and when his days of Army rugby were over he continued to play at unit level. At the age of forty-two, when he was Commanding Officer of the 2nd Battalion West Yorkshire Regiment, he led his team to victory in the Malayan Command Cup

For the 1934 Navy match on 3 March the Army had seven changes from the previous season's outstanding side, and were without Novis, who was injured. But they found a number of capable newcomers and beat 16–8 a strong Navy team that included such stalwarts as Elliot, in the stand-off half position, and forwards of high calibre like Hammond, Watkins, Webb, Forrest, Tarr and Crick, the captain.

It was a dull game, with none of the excitement of 1933, but was highlighted by the first appearance of Unwin (Middlesex Regt), who scored a try, and by a typical Crawford try when he broke through a fragile defence to score. Dean jinked his way through for another try. McCreight also got a try and Kendrew converted twice. The Navy made a good fight back with a penalty goal by Forrest and a try by Kirkby, converted by Forrest, when the Army were 11 points up. The Navy try came after a great passing movement. The Army forwards, however, were inspired by Kendrew, who was always ready to take on the opposition, and he was able to finish off the scoring appropriately by converting McCreight's try.

By defeating the RAF 14-3 on 24 March the Army won the IS championship for the third year running, though the RAF gave them a much harder game than was anticipated.

With only fifteen minutes to go the scores were level at one try each, the Army's having been scored by Reeves (RTC), who replaced Pike in the pack. Jennens was the RAF scorer. The Army piled up the remaining points when McCreight, the captain, then scythed through the RAF defence for one try. Hobbs scored one under the posts, and Cowey (Welch Regt), another newcomer who played for Wales earlier in the season, not only scored but was a constant danger to the RAF defence. One try was converted by McCreight. The second Beamish, now the only one of that name in the RAF team, had a great game displaying all the qualities of his legendary brother George.

Novis returned as captain for the 1935 Navy match on 2 March but injuries continued to plague the Army and it was only with a truly heroic effort that they won this game 11-8.

Cowey went off in the first ten minutes and the Army were also deprived of Kendrew before half-time, neither of them taking the field again in that match. To balance up slightly, the Navy's Hammond was also off the field injured for some of the first half. Sayers withdrew from an Army pack which had already been hard pressed to get a fair share of the ball, and in the second half the Army endured a severe pounding, only tenacious tackling saving their line from the Navy assaults. A draw was likely on tries for the Army by Novis and Hobbs, one converted by Sayers, and matching Navy points from tries by Lane and Hammond and a conversion by Gosling, but the issue was decided on a penalty goal by Sayers. There was some regret expressed about a penalty decider - a sentiment somewhat out of fashion today.

Like his predecessor Aslett, and others, Novis scored a try in his last match, which was against the RAF on 3 April, but his Army rugby career had a disappointing ending. Since 1929 he had gained fourteen caps and of the 13 previous games 11 were won, but unfortunately in this his 14th and last game for the Army his team were beaten 6–3.

Although Kendrew and Cowey were still unfit, the Army were expected to beat the RAF, who had already gone down 13–8 to the Navy. But the RAF adapted their play to conditions of heavy rain and were not only tactically superior, their finishing was far better. Brother Beamish, now RAF skipper in his turn, led his pack to go all out from the start. Irens kicked a penalty goal in the first five minutes and it was 3–0 until just before half-time, when Novis equalised following a clever kick ahead.

An RAF try by Walker sealed the Army's fate as he kicked through a startled defence to score, and in the final period his tactical skill played a big part in ensuring victory for his side. Once again a penalty kick was the difference between the teams, but the RAF thoroughly deserved their win.

With the departure of Novis the Army said goodbye to a brilliant, imaginative and constructive threequarter, who played both on the wing and in the centre. He always seemed to do especially well in Service games – as well as his fourteen Army caps he also gained seven for England – and though the last game was lost he could look back on the eleven wins and captaincy in ten games where, under his leadership, the Army won the Inter-Services' Championship three times. As captain he was an inspiration to any side and he was instrumental in raising the play of his Regimental team to a very high standard. He captained the Leicesters' side that reached the final of the Army Cup in 1932 and 1933. An immensely strong runner and a difficult man to stop when at full speed, he toured Australia and New Zealand in 1930 and scored a considerable number of tries. He was also a Barbarian.

In 1933 he Captained England against Ireland and Scotland and in the match against Scotland he outpaced Ian Smith 'The Flying Scotsman' in a race to touch down. Next season, just before the trials he had a serious knee injury which put him out for the rest of the season and finished his International career.

The final Army match for Tony Novis was also the last for Victor Pike, the great Army and Irish International of the 1930s. He went on to become Archdeacon Pike, Chaplain General to the Forces, and a delightful story about him was told by Charles Usher.

After his playing days were over, Pike was leaving the stand following an England–Ireland International match at Twickenham. The greatest indignation an Irish XV can suffer is to give away a push-over try to England, and this was what had happened.

An Irish supporter spotted Victor Pike and, recognising him, shouted: 'Victor, Victor, Ireland should have won.'

'No, not at all, not at all,' said Pike. 'They have lost the habit of prayer.'

'What do you mean, Victor, lost the habit of prayer?'

'Glory be to God,' Pike replied, 'surely they know that the way to stop a push-over try is go down on your knees.'

The historic decade was now half over and several well-known players had left the scene, as recorded, with others to follow, but the Army's triumphant progress suffered no halt as others took their places.

On 6 March 1936, the Army met the Navy with a future England trial full-back, three Internationals in the threequarter line, an International scrum-half, and the Internationals Kendrew and Sayers with future International Melville (Black Watch) in the pack. The Army eventually won 12-3 on four tries to the Navy's one, but with five minutes to go the score was only 6-3 and the issue still open.

The Navy scored first when Hamilton-Hill seized the ball and dived over the line, and despite the loss of Darley they tested the steadiness of the Army midfield backs, with their forwards the livelier in the loose. Darley was injured in a terrific collision with a member of his own side, Hurden, in a game that was one of the fiercest and most gruelling struggles ever seen at Twickenham. The Army subsequently drew level and won with tries by Dean, Rawlence (RE), who got two, and Hobbs.

This was the last of the seventeen games that J R Cole played for the Army, which gained him more caps than almost any other player. His career spanned the years from 1928 and he was accorded special praise by both Tony Novis and Alfred Aslett. Cole, fly-half for the Army and Harlequins, was classed as an imaginative and lively stand-off-half, with an excellent pair of hands and a quick eye for a gap in the defence. Novis has commented that there were few halves who served their centres better than he did, but Cole, strangely enough, never gained International honours. He played in three trials in 1929 and 1930 and was reserve on two occasions but that was all. Aslett considered him 'the best outside half never to play for England'.

After the 1936 Navy match the selectors were far from satisfied with the Army team, and the reserve strength was so strong that for the RAF game on 23 March they dropped three current Internationals, Kendrew (England), Sayers (Ireland) and McCall (Wales). Cole might well have gone on to play in this match, but he, Boast and Watson (Queen's Royal Regt) were also left out. The drastic changes, several of which were regarded as 'astonishing', were, however, successful and the Army won 16–5 to be once more the Service champions.

Wallis (East Surrey Regt) proved a splendid pack leader and although the RAF scored a brilliant try in the first half, through Holland, converted by Coslett, the Army forwards took command in the second half. After Wallis and Rawlence had scored a try apiece Marriott (Leicestershire Regt) broke through a disorganised defence to get a third. Owen (Welch Regt) made two conversions and also scored a penalty goal.

This was the year that Kendrew retired from rugby, at a comparatively early age. He was captain for the Navy match, which therefore saw his last appearance as well as Cole's.

D A 'Joe' Kendrew started his rugby at Uppingham, the famous 'nursery' for players, and had already represented England against Wales and Scotland in 1930 when he joined his Regiment in 1931. He only received seven Army caps but had ten for England and was a most successful captain of his Regimental team, being with Novis in the Leicesters' Cup Final sides of 1932 and 1933. He had toured Australia and New Zealand in 1930 and 1935 and captained England in two of their International matches.

He played for the Territorial Army in 1931 in their first game against the Army.

Kendrew was a strong, fast and very hard-working forward, who played equally well in the tight and the loose. There is a story of him that, appearing at a banquet after an International with a black eye, he said: 'I cast my bread upon the waters early in the game, and it came back to me ...'

He later had a most distinguished Army career, serving during the war in North Africa and Italy, being awarded the DSO with two bars and the CBE. Later he commanded the 29th British Infantry Brigade in Korea and was awarded a third bar to his DSO. From 1956–60 he was GOC Cyprus and was awarded the CB, and in 1963 he was appointed KCMG and became Governor General of Australia.

1937 brought the Army two good wins and the IS title for the eighth time in ten seasons. They defeated the Navy 14–3 on 6 March and trounced the RAF 29–9 on 3 April.

The greater teamwork and speed of the Army overcame the superior weight and stamina of the Navy forwards. Reynolds (DWR), to be capped for England two weeks later, was well marked by his opponents, but that did not prevent him from showing a fine burst of speed which left the defence standing and enabled him to put the Army eight points ahead, and Marriott and Unwin combined well for the latter to score. Howard-Jones (RMC) made one conversion.

The second half was fast and exciting and the Navy replied when Casement picked up a loose ball and scored their try, but Dean, the Army skipper, dodged past the Navy defence to give his team a further try, and Sayers collected a dropped ball to send in Reynolds for his second try.

Against the RAF there were Army tries by Leyland (Army Educational Corps), Reynolds, Marriott, Whitty (Queen's Own Royal West Kent Regt) and an unknown, with Owen collecting 14 points alone by kicking four conversions, a penalty goal and a mark. But the game was not as one-sided as the score might suggest. The RAF could only counter with tries by Halford, Fox and Gascoigne, but resisted strongly against a side that fielded six Internationals. Owen, however, effectively demonstrated the value of a reliable kicker and Reynolds and Leyland were prominent in a number of thrusting breaks. The RAF missed the services of Walker, but Rogers and Cross did fine work for them and it was Rogers who fought his way almost to the line to give Gascoigne his try.

On 5 March 1938, the Navy, who had already beaten the RAF, deservedly broke the long spell of Army ascendancy, getting home by one point, 10-9, in one of the most exciting games for some time. Apparently the Navy and the RAF had met at dinner and swore that one or other of them would beat the Army!

Reynolds was unfit, but the Army had eight players who had been capped by their countries, plus Ford (Welch Regt), who was capped in 1939. They were, though, to miss Owen and his kicking prowess of the previous season.

The Navy scored first through Wickham after an effective foot-rush by the forwards, and a fine conversion was kicked by Crawford. Ford went over for the Army, with the Navy full-back out of position, but the conversion failed. It was 5-3 at half-time, and the Navy had gained the lead against the wind.

Immediately after the interval Ford raced away to score his second try, then Allan (Army Dental Corps) added a third, but again the conversion was missed. In the last minute the Navy made their final effort and after a brilliant break by Vavasour a try was scored by Kirkby wide out. Could Crawford convert again? In utter silence he did and this was followed by a great cheer.

The Army did not let the RAF follow suit on 26 March. That game went to the Army 15-7 and all their points had been secured in the first half. Apart from Harrison (DWR), later an England trialist, all the army backs were Internationals and so were four of the pack. Tries came from Dean and Tarrant (Gloucestershire Regt), one conversion and a penalty from Sayers, and a drop goal from Reynolds.

The Army were the better side, but the RAF came back in the second half and bit into the Army lead with a fine individual try by Moseby, after a 35-yard run, a kick ahead and a good pick up. Holland dropped a goal. The Army kept getting offside and the RAF might have come considerably closer if their place kicking had been better. Reynolds, with his long stride, and Leyland, with his zig-zag dashes, were the best Army outsides.

G J Dean made his farewells with that match, as captain. He only gained one England cap but had eleven Army ones and was captain five times, four of those games being won. He was a very lively scrum-half, who played also for Harlequins and Sussex, and he scored a remarkable number of tries. An all-round sportsman, he contributed to winning the Army Lawn Tennis Doubles Championship (as a lieutenant in 1936 with Tank Corps' colleague Lieut R V Jenkins), and he played regularly for his Regiment's hockey team.

At the end of this magnificent decade the Army blotted their mainly immaculate copybook. On 4 March 1939, they just managed to salvage a 6-6 draw with the Navy, thanks to Arengo-Jones (Gloucestershire Regt) kicking two penalty goals, but on 26 March the RAF surprised everyone by beating the Army with comparative ease, 18-3.

The Navy match was dull and unimpressive and the Army adopted an unenterprising approach, using the touch line largely as a means of advancement as well as defence. Leyland and Unwin outside him combined well, but they had few chances and the rest of the backs lacked both initiative and penetration. Luckily for the Army, Crawford, who kicked so well for the Navy the year before, missed a number this time, and but for that the Navy would have won. Their points, as it was, were from tries by Bridges and Stacpoole.

All the Army could do against the RAF was for Arengo-Jones to kick a penalty goal, giving him the distinction of being their only scorer in that year's two IS matches, which had not brought them a single try. This compared with the RAF's tries by Cobden, Walker and Rogers, a conversion by Cobden, a drop goal by Walker and a penalty by Irens. Walker, the RAF captain, was superb and constantly had the Army defence in trouble, having a part in all three tries. Rogers and Garvin gave the Army's Leyland or Harrison little room to move. The RAF were a much better side in the first half and looked winners from the start.

Roy Leyland, a brilliant attacking centre threequarter, was capped eight times for the Army and three times for England. He was unlucky not to play more often for his country. He toured South Africa with the 1938 British Lions, but was probably at his best when partnered with Jack Heaton in the Lancashire side. It was Tony Novis who rightly called the period from 1929 to 1939 'the Golden Era of Service rugby' and the last year's anti-climax need not be too keenly felt as he was not thinking only of results. He has written of that decade:

One retains a vivid impression of the tremendous enjoyment which everyone seemed to get out of taking part in the game. Although it was hard and vigorous, there was a certain feeling of 'joie de vivre' and not a sense of desperate earnestness which seems to possess players these days.

In addition I think the game was less complicated. There were no such terms as "teach-ins", second phase possession, good and bad ball. Put at its simplest the forwards' job was to provide the backs with the ball and their job was to score tries. Possession was all-important, and kicking to touch only used as a last resort.

The Army was fortunate in having two such outstanding personalities as Major-General Brooke Purdon and Colonel Jock Hartley as co-selectors. Jock was a very large man who had gained his Cap as a forward for England. He had a deep knowledge or the game and was seldom wrong in his opinion of a player. Brooke was the perfect fellow selector for Jock; a former Irish international, he had all the charm which one associated with the Irish....

...Going to Twickenham by coach from the old Metropole Hotel in Northumberland Avenue, the team invariably passed a number of funerals. This became such an established fact that it was accepted as a good omen, and the more funerals passed the better the team's prospects became. On one occasion the number amounted to eight, which ensured a most satisfactory win over a strong RAF side.

It was a memorable period which has never been approached since the War. This is mainly due to the Army being so much smaller than it used to be, also leave is not as readily granted, and many players are serving abroad who previously would have been retained in the UK.

However the spirit of Inter-Services' Rugby remains the same and I am sure that those lucky enough to take part in it enjoy it just as much as those who played in more favoured times.

SECOND WORLD WAR YEARS

Rugby was played at home and overseas throughout the war, and enjoyed by both Union and League players from all three Services.

Games took place as far afield as Singapore, Kuala Lumpur in Malaya, Cairo, India and Burma. There is also a record of rugby being played in prisoner-of-war camps.

One of the finest matches was between the British Army and the French Army in Paris on 24 February 1940. Internationals against France had not been played since 1931, so it was a great occasion to be meeting once more. A game full of thrills resulted in a win for the British Army by 36 points to three.

Despite the French having eleven Internationals in their team they could not compete with the speed and inventiveness of the British, who must have had one of the strongest sides ever to represent the Army: O/Cadet V G J Jenkins (Wales), Lieut E J Unwin (England). O/Cadet P Cranmer (England), Lieut W Wooller (Wales), O/Cadet R H Guest (Waterloo), Lieut F J Reynolds (England), Sgt J Ellis (England), O/Cadet R E Prescott (England), Cpl W H Travers (Wales), Gnr W E N Davies (Wales), O/Cadet T F Huskisson (England), Lieut R B Mayne (Ireland), Cpl G B Horsburgh (Scotland), Capt H J M Sayers (Ireland) (capt), Sgt S Walker (Ireland).

Wooller scored three tries, one after a 70-yard run and another which began in his own 25. Other tries came from Sayers (2), Cranmer, Davies and Guest. Jenkins converted six of the eight. The only French score was in a penalty goal kicked by their captain, Thiers.

At home, just before the game in Paris, two strong sides played each other at Richmond under the titles 'The Army' and 'The Empire'. The Army team had thirteen of the players who were to take on the French, plus P L Duff and A W B Buchanan, later replaced by Huskisson and Walker. The Empire side was a mixed bag of eleven Internationals, including A Obolensky (England), G A Walker (England), H Tanner (Wales), J K Watkins (England), the aforementioned Huskisson, and S R Couchman (England). The Army won 27–9 on six tries, three conversions and a penalty goal to two tries and a penalty.

From 1942 there were a number of Service International matches played between England and Scotland and England and Wales. These aroused immense interest among the general public, who welcomed the opportunity for some relaxation amid the weary days of war. Wales emerged most successfully from these encounters, winning seven and only losing one of their eight games. England, who naturally played most, won six times but lost ten, while Scotland won three and lost five. Detailed results were:

1942	Scotland	21	v	England	6	Inverleith
	Scotland	8	v	England	5	Wembley
	Wales	17	v	England	12	Swansea
	Wales	9	v	England	3	Gloucester
1943	England	29	v	Scotland	6	Inverleith
	England	24	v	Scotland	19	Leicester
	Wales	11	v	England	7	Swansea
	Wales	34	v	England	7	Gloucester
1944	England	23	v	Scotland	13	Murrayfield
	England	27	v	Scotland	15	Leicester
	Wales	11	v	England	9	Swansea
	England	20	v	Wales	8	Gloucester
1945	Scotland	18	v	England	11	Leicester
	England	16	v	Scotland	5	Murrayfield
	Wales	28	v	England	11	Swansea
	Wales	24	v	England	9	Gloucester

The following Army players were awarded Service caps:

ENGLAND			
S Brogden	2	L E Oakley	1
R T Campbell	3	G W Parker	2*
F P Dunkley	3	R E Prescott	12*
J Ellis	6*	H Pimlett	1
A L Evans	2	F J Reynolds	1*
R L Francis	7	E H Sadler	3*
F W Gilbert	3	J Stott	5
P R Hastings	7	E J Unwin	1
C B Holmes	1	G P C Vallence	1
E Hodgson	4	M M Walford	2
T F Huskisson	4*	P W Walker	1
A E Johnston	1	E Ward	11
D L K Milman	2*	E J H Williams	4
C L Newton-Thompson	3		

* indicates a Pre-war International

SCOTLAND

W G Biggart	1	M D Kennedy	1
A W Black	2	J B Lees	1
C R Bruce	3	D Maltman	1
A W B Buchanan	2	J Maltman	3
H H Campbell	2	J R McLure	4
F H Coutts	2	E A Melling	1
J B Craig	1	C L Melville	6*
E C K Douglas	4	W H Munro	4
P L Duff	3*	W C W Murdoch	5*
I N Graham	3*	C M'Lay	1
T Gray	5	J B M'Neil	1
R M Grieve		N W Ramsay	3
J D H Hastie	3*	G D Shaw	6*
J R Henderson	2	J A D Thom	1*
J R S Innes	2	H G Uren	2
T G H Jackson	1	J A Waters	3*

WALES

F L Bevan	1	J Regan	1
D A Brown	1	A J F Risman	4
R G Coleman	1	R Rowland	1
A Davies	3	T Sullivan	4
C H Davies	2*	W E Tamplin	5
W E N Davies	3*	H Tanner	8*
E Evans	2*	H Thomas	2*
R J Flower	3	L Thomas	2
T Foster	7	W H Travers	4*
W G Jones	3	F Trott	2
J L Knowles	2	G Williams	3*
V J Law	4*	R Williams	3
D Phillips	2	S Williams	7*

* indicates a Pre-war International

The Army also played Ireland in Belfast, winning 12–11, 15–0 and 9–5.

A unique match took place in 1943 between a Northern Command Rugby League XV and a Northern Command Rugby Union XV. It was played at Headingly under RU rules – to be won by the League XV 18–11. At the luncheon preceding the game a message was read from the Secretary of the Scottish Rugby Union demanding that no player in the RU side should ever have played Rugby League football.

The RU team, including several Scots, consisted entirely of peacetime RU players.

Just after the war two units of the Parachute Regiment played each other in Java, watched by a large number of Japanese prisoners-of-war.

The enthusiasm for and enjoyment of rugby was maintained at all levels throughout the war years, which were vintage ones for coarse rugby players. They frequently found themselves marking a County or International player, and John McLaren recalls once finding himself marking E C (Claude) Davey, the great Welsh centre who was renowned for his crash tackling. He claims it was the most terrifying experience he had in the entire War!

BACK TO THE RUGBY FIELD 1946–1955

Army rugby started after the war when two matches were played in 1945 against the new British Army of the Rhine (BOAR), both of which the Army won. In December that year they had sterner opposition and were beaten 25–5 by the 2nd New Zealand Expeditionary Force (The Kiwis) at Bristol.

Because of the war, the Inter-Service Competition was not held for six years, but on resuming in 1946 the Army began another successful decade. The golden era was past, but the Army were to beat the Navy by six matches to four, scoring 100 points to 65, and against the RAF they won seven and drew twice, with over double the RAF's points, at 99 to 46. The short period of National Service and operational moves to Korea, Malaya and Suez meant that more men played for the Army during this period than in any previous decade, so the Army were still a power in British rugby.

They began by defeating both the Navy and the RAF with identical scores, 11–6.

The first IS match since 1939 was played on 4 March, 1946, in blizzard conditions, with fine snow and a bitterly cold wind that numbed the hands. Both packs played well, but it was the Army's superiority behind the scrum, with a dazzling threequarter line, that justified the result. The Navy made up in courage what they lacked in experience behind the scrum. The teams were level on tries for the Army by Innes (RAMC) and Gregory (also RAMC) to penalty goals by Vaughan and Hughes, but a minute before time the Army's Munro (RCS) scored the winning try and Ward (Lancashire Fus) kicked the conversion.

Although by beating the RAF, on 23 March, the Army won the championship much of the play in that game was not of a high standard. The Army had one team change, T G H Jackson (RCS) coming in for Drummond (KOSB) in the threequarters, and the RAF missed Bleddyn-Williams.

There was no score in the first half, but after an exciting corkscrew run by Munro a movement by skipper C R Bruce (RA) and Innes resulted in Bruce scoring. A further try was secured by Innes, with Ward converting this and also kicking a penalty goal. The RAF replied

Army (3) v Royal Navy (7) 1922
Back row: MacNamara, Young, Hinde, Middleton*, Davies, Worton*, Aslett*
Seated: Jones*, Baker Jones*, Usher*, Day*, Kilgour*
Front on floor: Ross, Palmer*, Arnott
*International

Army (11) v Royal Navy (0) 1932
Back row: Radcliffe*, Novis*, de V Hunt, Tyler, Crawford, Cole, Simpson
Seated: Troop, Sadler*, Vaughan-Jones, Clarke*, Hobbs*, Kendrew, Withers*, Rew,

At the Army Cup Final 1934
Lt-Col W B Purdon (Secretary ARU), Lady Isobel Gathorene-Hardy
HRH The Prince of Wales
(1 Bn Welsh Guards defeated 5 Royal Tank Corps 4–0)

Army Rugby Cup 1938–39
Winners: 1 Bn The Welch Regiment
Back row: Penell, Lett, Peters, Bevan, Cowell, Baldwin, Pass, Roberts, Evans
Seated: Thomas, Ibbitson, Ford, Cowey (Capt), Owen, Delaney, Champion
Inset – Mackie

Army v Royal Navy 1949
Clancy (Army) (left) gathers the ball from the loose

Army v French Army 1950
Reeve scores Britain's first try

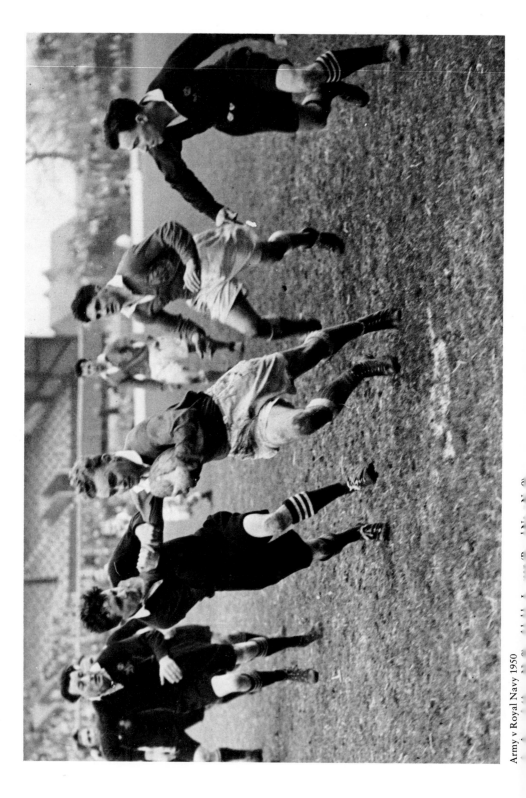

Army v Royal Navy 1950

Army v Royal Air Force 1974
Spawforth under pressure

At The Welch Regiment Museum, Cardiff, 12 October 1985 Welsh Internationals of The Welch Regiment
Left to right: Windsor Major, Bill Clements, Bun Cowey (holding Bird Partridge's South Africa Cap), John Ford, Barney Mccall

Army v Empire 1940
W B Purdon, *'Dreadnought'* Harrison, J Hartley

Army (36) v French Army (3) 1940
Back row: Wakelan, Debon, Edwards, Unwin, Cranmer, Huskisson, Horsburg, Purdon, C Gadney (Referee), Duff
Seated: Davies, Jenkins, Sayers, Wooller, Reynolds, Travers
Seated at front: Guest, Prescott, Walker, Ellis

with a penalty by Lloyd-Davies, followed by the best try of the game, from Parker. The packs were well-matched, with C H Beamish (yes, again the name of Beamish appears) for the RAF and Priest (Army Physical Training Corps) for the Army being prominent in both the tight and the loose.

A bad winter was probably reflected in the 1947 IS matches, where the Army played the RAF first, on 22 March, and did not meet the Navy until 12 April.

In the first of these games recent lack of match practice was evdent and much of the play was untidy, yet there was no lack of excitement before the RAF won 8-0. The Army were short of four Internationals, Glyn Davies (RCS), Jackson, Kirk (RAMC) and Watt (also RAMC) all of whom were unable to play because of injuries. The RAF did not field a full-strength side either. Walter (RA), the Army full-back, played throughout the second half with a broken wrist, and during that half Dangerfield, the RAF wing, was carried off with a broken leg.

The RAF won the game by taking advantage of a wild pass for an opportunist try and following this up with another try from what might be called an 'old-fashioned forward rush'. The scorers were Towell and Horsfall with one conversion by Lloyd-Davies.

For the Navy match only three of the Army backs retained their places. One of the changes brought in Howard-Jones (RTR), who had played rugby up to 1939, and it was recorded as pleasing to see him filling the full-back position again, obviously not least because, in the Army's 19-11 win, he made two conversions and kicked two penalty goals.

The Army pack, with three Internationals in Coutts (KOSB), Valentine (also KOSB) and White (Northamptonshire Regt), won almost all the ball. Joy (REME) had a great day as hooker, and the ubiquitous scrum half and skipper Wilson (Royal Sussex Regt) was in brilliant form. Tries by Matthews (RAMC), Coutts and Danby (RAOC), with the two conversions and one penalty, gave the Army a 16-point lead at half-time, but the Navy fought back in the second half. It was their forwards who scored all their three tries, two by Hosking and one by Carnelly, one converted by Goodman.

An exciting match which was in doubt until the last minute was provided for the King, the Queen and Princess Margaret when they attended the Army v Navy game on 6 March, 1948. The Army, with eight Internationals, were favourites, but one of the Navy's Internationals was D B Vaughan who, as captain and leader of the pack, had very different ideas and played the game of his life. Not only did he score both of his team's tries with power and speed in the break-away but he was unlucky not to get a third. His leadership inspired the Navy side to a 9-8 victory, and it was said that he played one of the most outstanding games in the history of inter-service matches.

A magnificent Navy team effort prevented the Army 'stars' getting into their stride. Fearsome tackling by their backs was sufficient to contain the Army's attacking. Burges kicked a penalty goal for the Navy to open the scoring, but the Army went ahead on a fine try by Jackson, converted by Walter, after Wilson had started the move off with a run of 40 yards and a pass to Jackson in full stride. Soon after half-time, however, Vaughan scored his first try and later made a crushing tackle, grabbed the ball, and raced away on his own to score again. In the last minute Wilson, after a quick heel near the line, was over it in a flash, but Walter missed the conversion that would have edged the Army in front.

Although the final win at 15-8 against the RAF on 3 April does not look as close, the Army had to hang on grimly to their lead in that game. They were 12 points up with twenty minutes left, but at that stage the RAF launched attack after attack. The Army backs were in good form, in particular Matthews and Cameron (RA), who made a number of exciting breaks and both scored after determined runs. Douglas, the RAF wing, also had a superb game, though, and was a constant danger to the Army defence, later getting the two RAF tries, one converted by Smailes. Jackson also scored for the Army and Coutts converted one try as well as kicking a penalty goal.

Princess Margaret and the Duke of Edinburgh were present on 7 March 1949 when the Army beat the Navy by the largest number of points since 1926, at 23-3.

In all departments except at hooker the Army were in control and it was an impressive victory, on tries apiece by Cameron, Cross (RCS), Smith (RAMC) and Jackson, one dropped goal by Cameron and another by N M Hall (RCS), who also kicked a penalty and made one conversion.

At half-time the Army were leading by 20 points to nil. The Navy had a better second half, but could not break the Army defence and had to be content with a penalty goal by their skipper, Hosking. Cross was the best of a sound Army pack.

A penalty goal each was all, however, that either the Army or the RAF could manage on 26 March, to draw 3-3 in a game that turned out to be something of a 'mixed grill'. There were periods full of scrappy play, highlighted by some thrilling moments, but both sides missed scoring opportunities and uppermost in the minds of the majority of spectators was the sustained brilliance of the RAF pack. For the Army, Hall kicked with judgement and accuracy and among the threequarters both Cameron and Reeves (RCS) made some skilful breaks. Coutts kicked the Army penalty – he was now team captain, having taken over for the Navy match – and Smailes scored the penalty for the RAF.

Two players made their appearance on the Army rugby scene midway in the decade and became its prominent personalities. Both were from the Duke of Wellington's Regt. They were Michael Hardy (Ampleforth College) and Dennis Shuttleworth (Roundhay School & Yorkshire Schoolboys) who first met at the Royal Military Academy, Sandhurst and later decided to join the same Regiment. They then played together for England, Combined Services, Barbarians, the Army, Yorkshire Headingly and Blackheath.

They combined to become the best pair of half-backs to play for the Army since the Second World War. Together they played in 11 matches against the Royal Navy, the RAF and the French Army of which seven were won and four lost. Their constructive play and all-round ability played a major part in many an Army victory.

They would have played many more times together but for their being posted overseas. It will be a surprise for some to learn that they only played together in one International when they were in the England side which won the Calcutta Cup in 1951. Previously Mike Hardy had Gordon Rimmer of Lancashire as scrum-half in two matches and later in 1953 Shuttleworth was partnered by another Lancastrian, Martin Regan, in the match against Scotland which England won 26-8.

At outside half Hardy was adept at making a devastating outside break followed by a well-timed pass. He was a splendid handler of the ball and his screw kicking to touch has seldom been equalled.

Shuttleworth was a resilient, unselfish player with immense courage and took a lot of punishment to protect his outside half. A very strong tackler and when at his best would send out a stream of fast long passes. He could judge the pattern of the game with uncanny precision.

Shuttleworth was to gain twenty-two Army caps and two for England, Hardy, eleven for the Army and three for England. They both served on the Yorkshire Rugby Union Committee, The Army Rugby Union Executive Committee and together as the Army representatives on the Rugby Football Committee.

In 1985 Shuttleworth was elected President of the Rugby Football Union and the Army are justly proud of this honour.

The opening of their inter-Service double act was marked by a season where the Army easily retained the championship, continuing to keep the Navy under with a 16–6 win on 4 March 1950, and beating the RAF 11–3 on 25 March without their line being crossed in either game.

A crowd of 15,000 saw the Army demonstrate impressive form against the Navy, where their win was well-earned and they were not at all flattered by the large margin of victory. The Army had three current Internationals in Scott (King's Royal Rifle Corps), Phipps (Royal Hampshire Regt) and Hyde (Northamptonshire Regt) in the threequarter line, but they and the new half-back pair had as their opponents such Navy stars as M C Thomas, Lewis-Jones, Glastonbury and Lawson.

After Hardy had kicked a penalty goal, Scott made a dazzling break and, with a perfect side step, beat more than one would-be tackler to score the first try, which Hardy converted. Ten minutes after half-time the best move of the match was started by Hardy breaking on the blind side, well supported by Neale (RA) and Cross, and resulted in Hardy scoring the second try. Two penalties from the Navy, by Lewis-Jones, brought them uncomfortably close, but the Army showed their superiority with a further try by Cross. Hardy had made a second conversion along the way. He and Shuttleworth combined well in the match and Coutts was an inspiring leader.

The RAF tackled bravely in their match against a powerful and aggressive Army back division and remained on terms when Smailes scored a penalty goal to counter a good try by Hyde. The Army then began to attack with determination and after a dazzling run Phipps scored a try that Coutts converted. Reeves picked up a loose ball and, running 30 yards, added a third try. Hardy directed the game with fine judgement, kicking immaculately and defending soundly. He was the launching pad for many Army attacks.

After their previous successes against the Navy, the Army had an unpleasant shock on 3 March 1951, when the Navy earned a convincing 11–0 win by a splendid combination of enterprising attack and tireless effort. The experience and thrust of Malcolm Thomas and Lewis-Jones in the centre gave the Army a worrying time. The Navy points were from two good tries by Copley and Hall, one converted by Lewis-Jones, with Holgate dropping a magnificent goal from the touch line.

The Army recovered by defeating the RAF 14–0 on 31 March. There was no questioning the Army superiority in that game, most of which was played in a cold wind and rain. The decisive difference between the sides was at half-back. Shuttleworth had one of his best days and his break on the blind side resulted in a try by Hyde, one of two he scored. Hardy played his usual competent game as outside half. Both in attack and defence he was a steadying influence on the Army side. Another try was by Taylor (DWR) and Edwards (RAEC) made one conversion as well as dropping a goal.

After the 1952 season Hardy and Shuttleworth were split up by duty calls and only came together again at inter-Service level in the Navy match of 1955. In the meantime Shuttleworth was around to be in the Yorkshire side that won the County Championship in 1953, and he was a member of IS teams until 1958, though not continuously. He, therefore, played with a number of other outside halves, the most illustrious being Ken Scotland (RCS) at the start of the next decade in 1956.

For their last-but-one season in partnership, Hardy and Shuttleworth enjoyed 1952 wins at 11-3 over the Navy and 9-6 against the RAF so that the Army took the IS title yet again.

On 1 March the Navy missed Thomas and Lewis-Jones, their two Internationals, but it was the superior kicking of Hardy and Edwards that ensured an Army victory. Phipps gave the Army a fine try to open, but Williams, the Navy forward, scored an equally good one. Their try was not converted, however, whereas Edwards made the Army conversion and he and Hardy added penalty goals. Among the Army forwards Gilbert-Smith (DWR) and Dorey (Royal Hampshire Regt) were outstanding in the loose.

The RAF game on 22 March was spoilt by over-eagerness, which resulted in a glut of penalties being awarded. It must be admitted that the Army victory was against the run of play. The RAF with Weighill, their captain, Yarranton and Stirling always in the forefront, contained a hard-working Army pack. The scores were equal on two penalties by Edwards and a try by Greenwood plus a drop goal by Channer, but a minute before the end Phipps suddenly saw an opening and was through like a shot for the winning try.

In the Coronation Year of 1953 the Army retained the championship, but on 7 March they and the Navy could only set a poor game before the Queen and the Duke of Edinburgh. The Army won 3-0 and a bitterly cold day probably explained many handling mistakes. Both sides became frustrated when movements fell apart through bad handling and poor passing. Thomson (RCS) kicked a penalty from 40 yards, but it was the only kick at goal the Army had all afternoon. It was certainly not a match dish 'to set before a Queen'.

The Army only scored a single try in beating the RAF 11-3 on 28 March but this was a distinctly better game than the one against the

Navy. A dull first half was followed by a thrilling second period and there seemed to be no holding the Army. In the circumstances it was surprising that they only scored the one try, by Brewer (RCS). Long passes, short passes and reverse passes were thrown. But the rest of the points were from a conversion and a penalty goal by Thomson and a drop goal by Rees (RCS), the last a magnificent effort from near the halfway line. Neale (RA) captained the side well and fostered a good team spirit, while Shuttleworth was as good as ever at scrum-half and made some telling breaks. Channer gave the RAF a penalty goal.

In 1954 the Army had an experienced side which contained a mixture of Rugby Union and Rugby League players, but had to meet the Navy on 6 March without Boston or P Jackson (both RCS), who were injured, and lost 8-6. When they returned as centres for the RAF match on 27 March and the Army won 16-3 the comment was made: 'If only Boston and Jackson had played against the Navy.'

All the scoring in the Navy game was done in the first half. The best of the Army backs was Michell (Mons OCTU) the scrum-half who had a splendid game, constantly causing alarm in the Navy defence and dropping a beautiful goal from wide out. Edwards, in his fourth season, gave the Army a penalty goal, but England scored one try for the Navy after Copley had crashed through a clutch of Army players and Pearey got another try. One was converted by Glastonbury. Peter Michell later played many times for Cornwall and was captain of the County side and the Territorial Army.

After an ineffective first half, the Army backs sprang to life and made determined efforts to pull the match out of the fire, but the Navy held firm and deserved their victory. Just before the end Michell nearly scored another try that would have been a dazzler, only he was tackled just short of the line. The Army's two wings in this match, Swan (REME) and Bazley (RE), were both Internationals.

With Boston and Jackson returning for the RAF game the Royal Signals were providing four of the Army backs and six players overall. The Army on this occasion played brilliant rugby. At forward they completely outplayed a strong RAF pack both in the loose and the line-out. They launched attacks from their own line and the speed and strategy of their outsides frequently bewildered the RAF team.

Bazley began by scoring a brilliant try, swerving and weaving his way clean through the defence to score under the posts, and later ran 70 yards to get another great try. In between, Swan ran half the length of the field for the second try. A fourth came from Boston, who scored in the corner after he and Jackson combined. Edwards converted twice. For the RAF Smailes scored a penalty goal.

The Army were happy to have Hardy and Shuttleworth reunited in the half-back position for the Navy game on 5 March 1955, but could not manage a win for their last IS game together, and Hardy's final one for the Army. The Navy won 8–3.

The Queen, the Duke of Edinburgh and Prince Charles saw Navy teamwork and good defensive play bring them the match, while the Army, for some reason, had a bad day. They did not play well as a team, their forwards appearing heavy and ponderous compared with the Navy, and their heeling was so sluggish that Shuttleworth was constantly being harassed by the Navy forwards.

A great try put the Army ahead when Bazley came into the centre, slipped past three men with excellent side steps, and dived over the line. It was typical of tries he scored for England and Lancashire, but it had to stand alone in this game. Although in the second half Hardy and Shuttleworth worked the touchline with skill, the Navy defence refused to weaken and eventually they scored their only try, through Prosser. It, however, was converted by Mainwaring, who also kicked a penalty.

The RAF held the Army to a 6–6 draw on 26 March and by doing so they won the championship for the first time since 1947. At half-time the Army were leading 6–0, from a try and a penalty goal both by Lowden (RA), but in the last quarter of an hour the RAF forwards took complete control and matched them exactly, with a try by Blair and a penalty by Channer.

The focus on prominent players of this decade has been on Hardy and Shuttleworth, but others among those named already who could be also called to mind were the captains J M H Roberts, F H Coutts and B A Neale, also A B Edwards and the Irish centre threequarters G C Phipps.

In the linking process over the years several of the players, like Shuttleworth, go on into the next decade, and so does a newcomer, Norman Bruce (RAOC), who had his first inter-Service game against the Navy in 1955. Much more will be heard of him the years which followed.

HOOKERS GALORE! 1956–1965

The second decade after the war, though not as successful as the first, was still good enough in Inter-Service terms.

The Army won seven of their ten games against the Navy and four against the RAF, with two draws. Only playing the French Army were they remarkably unsuccessful, losing each year they met, 1956, 1957, 1958 and 1959, and by a points ratio of 12 to 52.

With National Servicemen only in uniform for two years, choosing the best side was always a problem for the selectors. Each year they had trial games, as many practice matches as possible before the IS Championship, and thereafter usually tried to choose more or less the same side against both the Navy and the RAF. But every year there were naturally a lot of changes in the team from the year before.

During the National Service period, however, there was always a good hard core of Regulars to give the leadership, example and continuity and in any one year a single player captained the side for these games, some doing so more than once to give a total of seven captains in the decade.

The first captain in 1956 was Shuttleworth and he had mixed fortunes. On 3 March he led the Army to a 6–3 victory over the Navy, but on 24 March they were beaten 26–9 by the RAF.

Played in drizzling rain, the Navy match lacked sparkle, though there were several good features and the Army deserved their win. Shuttleworth was now partnered by Ken Scotland at half-back and they combined well. It was a tough battle up front and Robin Roe (Royal Army Chaplain's Dept), Norman Bruce, Inglis (RA) and Gilbert-Smith (DWR) were prominent in many good forward rushes. Edwards, at full-back, had a splendid game, kicking well and tackling like a demon.

The Navy could only find a penalty goal by Mainwaring, but Southward (RA) gave the Army two tries, scoring his first by robbing Mainwaring of a kick ahead and getting the second as a result of strong running.

Shuttleworth played a good captain's game against the RAF, rallying his side well and encouraging them with his own good play, and the Army fought back in the second half with two good tries by J Regan

(RAMC) and Southward. Scotland had kicked a penalty. The RAF, however, were much too good for the Army, combining well and playing fast open rugby, piling up tries by Howard (2), Davies, Willcox and MacGregor, four converted by Beatson, who also kicked a penalty. Of the Army team, Hartley (RE) had to leave the field injured before half-time. The match was notable for the fact that the brothers Shuttleworth opposed each other at scrum-half.

Inglis took over the captaincy for 1957 and was much luckier, apart from the defeat by the French Army. It was only in the last minute that the Army won their Jubilee match with the Navy on 2 March, 6-3, but they won the IS Championship on 23 March with a fine 14-9 victory against the RAF.

The new captain deserved a great deal of the credit for the Army's win over the Navy, as he fostered a tremendous team spirit. Shuttleworth was missed at scrum-half, but the Navy were without Pearey and missed him in both attack and defence. It was not until Waddell moved from centre to outside half that their back play began to click. They did score the only try of the game, through Rodd, and as the Army had a penalty by Scotland it seemed almost certain that the match would be drawn, but in that last minute Scotland dropped a wonderful goal.

As a result of a kicking duel between Scotland and his opposite number Richards, it was not the Army but the RAF who led at half-time in their game, Richards having scored two penalties to Scotland's drop goal. But in the second half the Army found their form and took the IS title on three tries while the RAF only added a drop goal, again by Richards. The excellent wing Southward scored two of the tries and Bruce finished off a good match by taking full advantage of a defensive mistake to score the third. Gerry Murphy (RAChD) the full-back converted one try. Godson (RCS), at centre, played brilliantly and was a constant threat to the RAF defence.

A 3-3 draw with the RAF was the best result the Army had from 1958 for that year's captain Hugh Greatwood (East Surrey Regt). This also had to suffice as a farewell for Shuttleworth, but he marked his last season by scoring the try that made the Army's points.

The Army had gone down 14-0 to the Navy on 1 March. Neither of their hookers, Bruce and Roe, were available and the Army never looked like winning. The Navy pack dominated the game and the Army forwards could not match the fire of their opponents. Mainwaring was sure in a fine defence the Army rarely looked like penetrating, and he frequently came up to make the extra man in attack. A try by Bebb was converted by Mainwaring, who also kicked three penalty goals.

Shuttleworth and Saville (DWR) gave more thrust to the Army side against the RAF on 22 March, though it was a game of missed opportunities. The Army forwards did much better than against the Navy, forcing their opponents to heel slowly and seriously handicapping the RAF's Brace and his partner Richards. By making ingenious use of a short penalty, Shuttleworth surprised the RAF with his try, but Richards dropped a beautiful goal and in the closing stages the RAF missed a great chance when the ball was knocked on with the line at their mercy.

1958 might have seen the departure as a player of Dennis Shuttleworth, but like other personalities in this history he carried on serving the Army Rugby Union, as a member of the Executive Committee, and as the Army's representative in the RFU Committee, of which he is now President. He was also able, some twenty-three years after ceasing to play himself, to take pride in having a son follow in his footsteps by being capped for the Army.

Norman Bruce was appointed captain in 1959 and no one can hold it against him that on results he made an inauspicious start in that respect. For few, if any, Regular Army officers can have had such a distinguished career in International rugby as he, and no one has done more to stimulate enthusiasm for the game or raise the standard of play at all levels in the Service.

He was introduced to the game at the ripe old age of seven in his native Galashiels and at seventeen was a regular member of the Gala pack. During his National Service he was posted as a Drill and PT Instructor to the Junior Leaders' Battalion, RAOC, in 1953. He played for Aldershot Services and Hampshire, and in the 1954 season gained his first Army cap – there were to be twenty-seven altogether.

Bruce joined Blackheath, and while with them gained his first Scottish cap, against France in 1958. Later he transferred to London Scottish. From then on he was an automatic selection as hooker for Scotland and played thirty-one times for them in full International matches, missing only one through injury. He would have had even more caps but for a posting to the Far East in 1964. He played many times for Hampshire – he was their captain in 1959 too – and was elected Vice-President of the Hampshire RFU in 1961. He also played for the Barbarians.

As Army skipper for the first time, on 7 March 1959, Bruce led the side with spirit, particularly during the latter part of the second half of their game with the Navy, when it was only by hard tackling that the Navy kept the Army out and survived to win 6-0.

It was a fast and furious game played in a wonderful sprit, but the Navy set it alight from the start and their Dixon soon scored a try after full-back Mainwaring had made a break, gathering a ball not meant for him. He played his usual prominent role in attack and defence. This was Mainwaring's last match against the Army and this versatile opponent was recognised as a player of distinction. Sharp made many telling breaks and dropped a fine goal from 35 yards.

Again on 4 April Bruce led the Army splendidly and their forwards put up a brave show in a desperate struggle, but the RAF won 11-3. Under skilful guidance they wore down and foiled their opponents by tactical kicking and seizing chances as they came along. Having beaten the Navy they were able to retain the championship their draw had helped them to in 1958. The Army, here with a front row including two International hookers and one who was 'all-but International', were left with one try by D A Williams (RCS), compared with the RAF's tries by Burgess and McGovan, with one conversion and a penalty by Mettler. One commentator thought the Army could have scored on six occasions in the first half!

In 1960 the Army captain was Raffle (RE), which was to be highly appropriate when they won the prize. They defeated the Navy 12-3 and the RAF 6-3, and this successful season meant a good IS debut for another player who was to have an especially distinguished career, Mike Campbell-Lamerton (DWR).

Against the Navy on 5 March the Army once again had an overflow of hookers with Bruce, Godwin (Royal Leicestershire Regt) and Raffle. Effective scrummaging and shrewd kicking by Sharp (RCS) had the Army using the touch line for most of the game. Purdy (RAEC) and Handfield-Jones (RE) scored tries and Sharp two clever drop goals. Fullerton replied with a penalty kick.

The Army won the championship on 26 March in a dull game with the RAF which depended on penalties. Both sides defended well, but attacking movements were spoilt by poor finishing or relentless tackling. Mettler gave the RAF a penalty but Crooks (REME) won the game for the Army with two good penalties. Peter Crooks, at full-back, who had also played against the Navy, was in his first IS season then. He went on to become Brig Crooks, ARU chairman.

Bruce was back as skipper in 1961, but regrettably the Army could not keep hold of the IS title. On 4 March they lost 6-3 to the Navy and on 24 March they came a real cropper as the RAF beat them 19-11.

Although the Navy won on two penalty goals by Thomas, while the Army's Heath (RE) scored a try, the Navy deserved to win a game of missed chances. The Army made a habit of getting off-side and this resulted in the Navy's penalties. Braybrooke (RE), who replaced at half-back an injured Shillinglaw (KOSB), made the break that led to Heath's try.

Despite losing one of their half-backs, Booth, before half-time, the RAF were always the more dangerous team in their match and thoroughly deserved their victory as well. They had three good tries by Jenkins, Glastonbury and Greenhough, two converted by Brown, who also kicked two penalties. Parker (RAEC) and Braybrooke scored Army tries and MacDonald (KOSB) converted one and scored a penalty. Sharp played well as stand-off-half for the Army, but did not always link up with his threequarters.

In 1962, when Greatwood had another season as captain, the Army managed to beat the Navy 9–6 on 17 February by holding on in a close game where a Navy try and a drop goal whittled down the Army's 9–0 lead in the last twenty minutes. That made an exciting finish to a game that had not had many thrills, though both teams had plenty of chances. In the second half Campbell-Lamerton made slashing breaks towards the Navy line and after continuous pressure the Army scored a push over try to add to previous points, try scorers being Vaux (RE) and Heath, with Rosser (RAEC) dropping a goal. Hamilton (try) and Harries (drop goal) scored for the Navy.

But the Army could not regain the championship that year as the RAF played with splendid dash, confidence and skill on 24 March and won their match 19–14. Far livelier than the Army, they amassed 19 points to the Army's three before a counter attack that was left too late. The Army made a desperate effort in the second half, but although scoring two tries, thanks to Moyle (REME) and Braybrooke, one converted by Crooks, they could not break the RAF defence. Crooks and Greatwood kicked a penalty apiece. The RAF points came from tries by Glastonbury, Glashier and Jenkins, Brown converted two and scored a penalty, and Booth dropped a goal.

Spiritual guidance added weight to the 1963 season when the Army chaplain Roe was given the captaincy. The team gave him suitable responses by winning back the championship that the Army was then to keep until the end of that decade.

The presence of Roe and Bruce meant there were again two hookers in the Army team when they beat the Navy 11–3 on 2 March. Both sides set out at a rattling pace, but destructive tackling by Handfield-Jones and Waquabaca (DWR) in the centre and the coolness of Crooks at full-back halted the Navy onslaught.

After a penalty on each side, from Crooks and the Navy's Cormack,

Bruce pounced on a loose ball and timed his pass perfectly for a try by Stone (REME). In the second half the Army scored a wonderful try, a rapid passing movement with Reid (DWR) coming into the line twice resulting in Blinkhorn (RAOC) making an extra man and Moyle going over the line. Crooks kicked a good conversion.

CP Simpson, the first RMA cadet to play for the Army since SL Howard-Jones, made his presence felt against the RAF on 13 April with a late try he converted himself to make the difference between winning 8-6 and drawing. He was a wing of strong physique, six feet six and a half inches in height and over fourteen stone in weight, with a fine turn of speed, and he made best use of this in scoring the only try of the game with a great run in the last three minutes. Before then the Army had just a penalty goal by Stevens (Royal Hampshire Regt), now at full-back, in the balance against the RAF's drop goal by Palin and penalty by Brown.

Campbell-Lamerton became team captain for 1964 and retained the post for 1965, the only player to be skipper for two years running in that period. He kept an unbeaten record thanks to the Army scraping a draw and having some luck on their side in the last match.

His captaincy began in style on 7 March 1964, when the Army easily beat the RAF 19-6 and on 4 April they won 8-0 over the Navy, to retain the championship without, once again, having their line crossed.

Their forwards were far better in the loose than the RAF and Braybrooke, at scrum-half, can seldom have had a better game. The Army were eight points up inside eleven minutes. Splendid handling by the Army backs resulted in some fine tries. Waquabaca at centre was a constant danger and once Braybrooke slipped through the defence to send Mike Stancombe (RE) in for a try, one of two he scored. Others were by Campbell-Lamerton and Reid. MacDonald (RASC) converted two of the tries and also scored a penalty goal. The RAF only managed two penalties, by Jenkins.

The ball used in the Navy game was experimental, being made of chamois leather which repelled the wet. It happened to be a cold and wet day. The Army scored both of their tries, by Guthrie (Welsh Guards) and Moroney (RAMC), after charging down defensive kicks. Though Braybrooke was later badly concussed he had had another good game, handling well in difficult conditions and being very elusive. One try was converted but it is not known by whom.

At the end of this season Bruce said a temporary goodbye as he was posted to Borneo. He had an outstanding record up to that time, having played every year and gaining twenty of his twenty-seven Army caps in that period alone. He would have had more if he had not been injured in 1958.

Despite his playing for the Army and Combined Services many times, captaining both teams on occasions, and breaking the record for the number of International caps won by a Service player with his thirty-one for Scotland, none of these activities prevented him from giving exceptional encouragement and inspiration to the game at Corps and unit level.

His greatest achievement was in 1963 when he produced a team from his small unit (28th Coy RAOC) to take the Army Cup competition by storm. With a total strength of only a hundred or so he obtained twenty-two playing members and his team won the UK Final, collecting the scalp of the Duke of Wellington's Regiment on the way. They only lost the Army Final to the Welsh Guards by a narrow margin. More details on this can be found in the Army Cup section.

Campbell-Lamerton, another great player of that period, whose distinguished rugby career had started in 1950 with Surrey School Boys and Guildford RFC, captained both the Army and Scotland in 1965. He had joined the 1st Battalion the Duke of Wellington's Regiment early in 1953 in Korea. After a continuous stretch abroad his first appearance on the serious rugby scene was for Blackheath in 1955.

In 1956 he was abroad again, in Cyprus, where he sutained a serious injury doing a helicopter rope descent. He was in hospital and the Rehabilitation Centre, Headly Court for nearly a year and it was feared that he would not be able to remain in the Infantry, let alone play rugby. With great resolution and pluck he made sufficient recovery to start playing sport again. Whilst in Ulster he took up athletics to strengthen his legs and came runner-up in the shot and discus in the 1958 All Irish Athletics Championships; by 1959 he had got back into the Dukes 1st XV. In 1960 his big chance came when he played for the Combined Services against the Springboks. In 1961 he won his first cap for Scotland and by 1966 had collected twenty-three International caps and captained Scotland.

He played for Blackheath, Halifax and London Scottish and captained both Yorkshire and Surrey through to the County Championship finals. He also captained the first Combined Services side to beat the French Armed Forces in post-war years.

In 1962 he toured South Africa with the British Lions. On this tour he played a record number of games, 20 out of 25 matches, including all four test matches. In 1966 he captained the British Lions to Australia, New Zealand and Canada; after an unbeaten record in Australia they unfortunately lost all four test matches in New Zealand. He played in five of the six test matches on tour.

He retired from first-class rugby in 1966 as he was posted abroad again. His last big match was captaining the Barbarians at Leicester. He continued playing for the Dukes up to 1971 and in 1968 led the German Club Hanover 78 through to the finals of the European Club championships. He gained thirteen Army caps.

A man six feet four inches and weighing eighteen stone, he had immense power and strength, and no player worked harder during every second of the game; a very unselfish player. Although he obtained every rugby honour possible, he remained a quiet unassuming personality, both on and off the field. He played No 8 on occasions but was at his best in the second row.

He must be justly proud that his eldest son Jeremy won two Army caps against the RN and RAF in 1981 and for the Anglo-Scots v New Zealand. Recently he has become Chairman of the Army selectors.

It was his leadership in the 1964/65 season which contributed greatly to the Army retaining the IS championship.

Again they played the RAF first, on 13 February and that game ended 11-11, the Army saving their skins when Simpson (now Royal Anglian Regt) kicked a penalty goal five minutes from time. Campbell-Lamerton and Eastwood (Royal Army Pay Corps) won a lot of ball in the line-out, while Fisher (RADC), Stancombe and Friend (Devon and Dorset) did valiant work in the loose, but the RAF backs were faster and smarter in attack and at times outplayed their opponents, with the exception of C G Edwards (DWR). He not only scored two tries but defended with great courage. One try was converted by Williams (RA), another new full-back. RAF scorers were Samuel (try) and Brown (conversion and two penalties). A draw was a fair result to a hard, vigorous forward game.

The Army celebrated their Diamond Jubilee by winning the championship with a 5-3 defeat of the Navy on 27 March, but the general opinion was that they were fortunate to win this match. It was an exciting game but both sides missed their chances.

Although the names of Bruce and Campbell have stood out in this decade, and will also appear in the next, others are not forgotten. Of those who have already bowed out, R Roe was another great, being capped twenty-one times for Ireland, and having toured with the Lions in 1955 (South Africa). He was also capped a Barbarian. H G Greatwood and R J Moyle are also especially noted, and J D MacDonald, who continued to make appearances until 1970, earns an extra mention through playing eight times for Scotland, and also for his dedication and enthusiasm in leading his unit to the Army Cup Final of 1966. His Corps had by then changed its name from RASC to RCT.

As previously observed, National Servicemen had helped the Army considerably after the Second World War, but during the first three years without them, 1963, 1964 and 1965, the Army did not lose an Inter-Service match. They therefore looked to the future with confidence.

SCOTS SUPREME 1966-1975

Although the new decade did not start too brightly, the Army had no immediate reason to think their confidence was misplaced. They still had several Internationals, and if their number was being reduced by retirements from the game might there not be more where they came from?

The Army only just lost to the Navy on 19 February 1966, even if they did have to catch up before ending 10-9. It was a fast and enjoyable game, where the Navy scored two tries in the first half, by Godfrey and Hambrook, both converted by Golding, and the Army were left to penalties by MacDonald (2) and J D Drummond (Royal Highland Fus), but when they had kicked their third one the excitement was intense. The Navy, however, rallied well and held on.

With Bruce still away, the Army had a near-namesake and fellow Scotsman in Hamish Bryce (RE), though he had no chance to shine in this match as he was to do later. The Army were handicapped here by his having to leave the field injured, and when he returned he wandered disconsolately among the backs. Moroney had taken on the hooking. Mike Campbell-Lamerton, once again the captain, was in the front row, where, it was said, it was strange to see him. Both sides showed a willingness to move the ball, but most movements were conventional and lacking in guile. Fisher and newcomer Andy Hoon (RE) put up a splendid display of determined covering.

A 12-3 defeat by the RAF on 5 March unfortunately coincided with Campbell-Lamerton's last IS game, but he gave the Army a display to be remembered, underlining how much his all-round forward play would be missed. He was subsequently chosen to captain the British Lions' 1966 tour, the first Services' player to be so honoured. His retirement from first-class rugby was also marked by his being captain of Scotland in that year too.

Despite having a pack with four Internationals, the Army did not do as well as their supporters expected against the RAF, who put up a most convincing performance. They kept moving the ball about continually and were rewarded by scoring three tries. These came from A Jones, Palin and Cunningham, with Jones also dropping a goal. Saunders (RE) scored a try for the Army.

The strength of the Army side in this period was in its pack and almost all the best players came from Scotland. The team was always captained by a forward and from 1966 to 1971 by outstandingly good Scots. Pringle Fisher, a brilliant flank forward who, like Tony Neary, was an outstanding basket ball player, took over from Campbell-Lamerton. He also captained Scotland and retained both posts into 1968. The Army captain therefore captained Scotland for three years running and was capped twenty-five times. The Army celebrated this by going into a hat-trick of IS Championship wins from 1967.

On 4 March of that year they made the Navy their first victims, 6-3. The Navy were unlucky to lose Goodwin in the first quarter of an hour and the strain inevitably took its toll before the end.

The Army got plenty of ball from the scrum and Eastwood (RAPC) and Martin (RE) were most successful in the line-out. Fisher, an outstanding captain, roved with Bale (RAMC) and Hoon to the discomfort of the Navy. MacDonald kicked a penalty goal and Braybrooke gave a reverse pass to Martin for him to score a good try. A penalty by Cunningham put the Navy uncomfortably close and there were frantic efforts on both sides, but the Army were victorious. Bruce returned to the team in sterling form as hooker.

Three changes were made for the RAF match on 1 April and there was no mistake when the Army won 17-6. The Army forwards were in command and the back row, with the captain Fisher outstanding, threatened danger time and again. Braybrooke made the most of getting good ball and had a sparkling game. MacDonald was another member of the forwards who shone in the loose as well as the attack and he was responsible for half of the Army's points, scoring a try himself, converting another, and kicking a penalty goal.

Two other tries were by Jeffray (RMA) and one by Doug Hathorn (Cameronians), who was involved in one of the changes, coming in on the wing. He was later to be Major Hathorn, chairman of the Army Under 21 Committee. His Army playing career went from 1962 to 1968, though he only had one other IS game, in 1966, the same year that he had a Scottish trial and was capped for Barbarians. After being Chairman of the under 21 Committee he was later Lieut-Col in the Army Catering Corps.

RAF points were from two tries by Ross-Jones and Glover. Ross-Jones, the RAF centre, went off with concussion midway through the first half and although he returned to play on the wing his injury obviously affected his team.

In 1968 the championship began for the Army on 17 February with a 3-3 draw against the RAF, in the presence of the Duke of Edinburgh.

The match was lacking in skill but not in vigour and some of the tackling was ferocious.

The Army only had five members of the previous year's side, but Simpson returned at full-back. He was calm under pressure and linked up with his threequarters in the attack whenever possible. Bruce gave the Army a hooking advantage and Eastwood was not outshone in the line-out by the RAF International, Larter, who scored a penalty for his team. Simpson kicked a penalty for the Army.

Another newcomer appeared in this match, Spawforth (REME), but it was to be the last IS game for Fisher. He was unable to play against the Navy because of injury and after this season he was posted abroad.

The Navy match on 23 March enabled Norman Bruce, another great Scottish forward, to step into his shoes and achieve the result that had eluded him in earlier captaincies, just in time for his departure. Winning 9-6, the Army retained the IS title for a second year.

Bruce captained the side well, but it was a game lacking polish. Army finishing was disappointing and many a good movement came to nothing. Graham Lilley (RCT), who had made his IS debut in the RAF match, scored the Army's try here and Simpson kicked two penalty goals, playing soundly at full back. A try for the Navy came from G L Jones and a penalty from Lavelle.

For many seasons Bruce had been one of the Army's outstanding forwards and they were sorry to think this was to be his last game. He held the view, however, that 'a player should put back into the game as much as, or more than, he has been fortunate enough to get out of it', and he has faithfully given practical effect to this principle. His was another name to appear subsequently on the Army Rugby Union Executive Committee, as Lieut-Col Bruce, Chairman of the Selectors.

There may have been a new captain for 1969 but the Scots supremacy remained, as the job went to Hamish Bryce and he held it for all six IS games through 1970 and 1971 as well. He, also a Barbarian and a travelling reserve for Scotland, proved an excellent captain, setting a fine example both on and off the field.

On 8 February 1969, the Army and the Navy drew 3-3 in a somewhat disappointing match. The ground was hard and covered in snow and the game was likewise tremendously hard. The icy conditions were partly to blame for many promising movements petering out, but the Army did score the only try. Campbell went over after running diagonally from a scrum through a defence who evidently expected him to pass! Among Army forwards who all played well, Bryce, Moroney and Lilley were particularly effective. Tuffley gave the Navy a penalty goal.

A total of 47 points were scored from 11 tries, seven converted, without a single penalty when the Army beat the RAF 26–21 on 1 March. Many said it was the most thrilling Inter-Service match they had seen since the War.

In the first ten minutes a hesitant RAF defence gave away two tries from kicks ahead and the Army were 10 points up, then enjoying a fairly definite supremacy until ten minutes into the second half, by which time they led 26–5. At that stage the RAF launched their spirited counter attack and had their supporters wild with delight. Four tries were scored by a revived and invigorated team, and if they had not missed a number of penalty kicks they might well have seized a surprising victory. Army tries were by Campbell (RE), Lilley, Mick Molloy (RAMC), Barstow (Queen's Regt), who got two, and Neck (Welsh Guards), four converted by I S G Smith (RADC). Bevan (2), Howe, Ray and Glover scored for the RAF, with Peter Larter making three conversions.

By winning the championship for the third successive year, the Army came up to the halfway point in this decade with plenty of hope for the good times continuing.

In those few years they had in their pack six players who were Internationals: Campbell-Lamerton, Bruce, Fisher and MacDonald among them won eighty-five caps for Scotland; Moroney and Molloy were together to win thirty caps for Ireland. In addition, Simpson had one cap as a threequarter for England, and at full back now there was Smith, who won eight caps for Scotland.

But there were no Internationals who played in the threequarters or half-backs in this decade. That is perhaps where the weakness was, despite some good individuals like Spawforth, who had twelve games at scrum-half and frequently played very well, Boyle (Parachute Regt), doing well in the centre in thirteen matches from 1967, and Philip Davies (13th/18th Royal Hussars), who had the ability to be the best back and the most dangerous threequarter when he showed up in 1972, although he was only to play seven times.

In 1970 the writing began to appear on the wall.

Since the First World War the Army had in each decade, as has been seen, always won more Inter-Service matches than they had lost, until ten years under review, when they won eight and drew three, which meant losing nine. With four of their wins and two draws already behind them after eight games, they were to find the going tougher now, rarely having a look-in at the IS title and more often finding their cup of misery stirred by a wooden spoon. One of the few consolations was to be that overall in the decade they managed to score more points, 213, than the 205 against them. They were to reach a peak in that respect in 1975 when they beat the RAF by a record 41 to 13.

The Army were optimistic at the start of the 1970 season, but it was soon apparent that they could not produce the form of 1969. They lost 15-9 to the Navy on 7 March, the pack lacking power in the scrummage and their line-out work being cumbersome.

In the second half the Navy soon went ahead and they scored three tries. Lavelle got the first and knocked himself out in the effort! Ryan intercepted an Army pass to score the next one, and finally G L Jones side-stepped through to score under the posts. Tuffley converted all three. MacDonald kicked three Army penalties. Spawforth went off with a broken jaw about ten minutes from the end.

On 4 April the RAF beat the Army 15-12, their forwards gradually asserting themselves, shoving the Army pack in the tight, rucking better and hounding the Army halves into errors.

The Army scored first with a try by Neck, but the RAF countered with four by Farr, Fowlie, Steele and Casey, three of them in the last half-hour. Casey also kicked a penalty. Five minutes before no-side, Tim Lerwill (RMA), who had already given the Army two penalties, dummied and jinked through to score a try, but unfortunately he missed the conversion and just before the whistle he missed a penalty that would have tied the match.

For 1971, despite having some excellent results against the clubs, including a victory over Newport, the Army's form against the RAF and the Navy was disappointing.

Playing the RAF on 13 February there was a 6-6 draw, but neither side made the best of their chances in a game that never rose to any heights. Wilson (RE) was th best of a moderate threequarter line that appeared thoroughly out of form. H Williams (RHA) scored two penalties for the Army, while Steele gave the RAF a try and Dave Hannah got a penalty.

March 6 brought arctic weather and although the Army scored first they were beaten 11-9 by a Navy team who, considering the conditions, played some remarkably good rugby. It might have been significant that this was not only Bryce's last match as Captain but his final IS game, considering the total number of his caps - thirteen!

Fabian of the Navy played one of his many good games and converted one of their tries, which were by Gretton and Ackerman. Newsom dropped a goal. Gatehouse and Ackerman gained valuable possession in the scrum. Neck got a try for the Army and Smith scored two penalty goals, but they could not avoid retaining the wooden spoon.

There was, however, to be a dramatic improvement in 1972. The Army were back as championship winners that year. They beat the RAF 14–6 on 19 February and the Navy 13–3 on 14 March. This coincided with the first season that a try counted for another point, four instead of three.

The Army had a completely new front row in two RAEC props, Johnson and Noel Slater, an Oxford Blue, with Luckey (RA) hooking. Jeffray (now also RA) returned on the wing after an absence of four seasons. They took on an RAF team who were the favourites, having four Internationals, but up to half-time there was little between them.

Spawforth was without any doubt the star of the match. His darting runs, neat kicking and immaculate passes made all the difference to the Army side both in attack and defence. A splendid try scored by the wing, Neck, was due to the enterprising Spawforth, who made a quick break on the open side and, kicking high, regained possession and finally threw a long accurate pass out to Neck.

But the Army forwards held their own against a heavier pack and were surprisingly dominant in the line-out, and the in-coming Philip Davies brought creative running in the centre, while the fine running of all the backs was like a breath of fresh air compared with the form of the previous season.

Apart from Neck's try there were two more, for Lilley and Williams. John Davies (RRW) made one conversion. All the RAF had was two penalties from Larter.

For the Navy match there were some enforced changes in the forwards, but Carroll (RAMC) and the newcomers, Bird (DWR) and Gilbert (also DWR), all gave a good account of themselves. Spawforth, getting plenty of ball from the rucks and set scrums, had another sparkling game and his lively play was an inspiration to his side. In the pack Slater was the best forward on the field, and Hoon, who had that year become team captain, was not only a successful skipper but a constant threat in the loose. The Navy got plenty of ball but never really linked up well with their backs. However, Phillips, the Navy wing, saw little of the ball.

Boyle and Philip Davies found gaps in the Navy defence and the latter scored a fine opportunist try, which was followed by John Davies coming into the line to score another, converted by himself. He then kicked a penalty goal. Fabian gave the Navy a penalty.

A sad footnote was later written to the 1971 and 1972 seasons. One of the Army's players against the RAF in those years, Ron Wilkinson (RAOC), died tragically in September, 1973. A bomb disposal officer, he suffered fatal injuries while dealing with an IRA device in Birmingham and died a few days later.

The Army could not match their 1972 season for the rest of the decade.

In 1973 there was a splendid game with the Navy, watched by 7000 spectators, and the result was in doubt up to the last minute, but the Navy won 10-7.

The Navy forwards were in top form and Easson got a lot of ball from the end of the line-out. Fabian, not for the first time, made a large contribution to the Navy's victory. It was he who came into the line and sent Phillips away to score one of his two tries. Fabian made one conversion. When the Navy were leading 10-3 Hoon, who had a cut over his eye that had to be stitched, returned to the field and headed a tremendous revival, but it was not until injury time that Spawforth scored a try in the corner to add to a penalty goal by Turk (RTR).

This was a season of disappointment for the RAF, which overflowed when the Army beat them 19-9. The Army were the more convincing and better-balanced side on the day.

Phil Davies at centre had another fine game, putting to good use his qualities as an attacking player with an eye for an opening and a good pair of hands to continually find gaps in the RAF defence. He scored a try of his own by charging down a kick and paved the way for other tries by Rea (RAMC), Morgan (REME) and Neck. Turk scored a penalty. Larter kept the RAF in the game with three penalties.

For 1974 the disappointment was again the Army's. They lost 9-4 to the RAF on 23 February and slumped 25-3 against the Navy on 2 March.

Slater was the Army team captain in 1974. For the RAF match the RCT provided three members of the threequarter line, but unfortunately Phil Davies, the outstanding centre, was absent with a knee injury and he was greatly missed.

It was a close game but all credit must be given to the RAF for winning, because their centre, Dunsmuir, was a passenger for most of the match after receiving a hip injury. In the end it was the superior place kicking of the RAF that won the day – the Army missed about five attempts at kicks for goal. Each side had one try scored, by Chris Wright (RCS) for the Army and Wakeham for the RAF, but Larter converted for the RAF and also kicked a penalty goal.

Spawforth, the automatic choice at scrum-half, was replaced for the Navy match by Bell (RMA), a cadet who was a former schoolboy

International. Phil Davies returned to the centre threequarter position. He was to be the best threequarter on the field, but unfortunately his kicking had an off day, though he was the only Army scorer, with a penalty.

At half-time the Navy were 9–3 up, but it was not until the last twenty minutes that they really took control of the game and added their further points. The Army backs and forwards worked hard and tackled well, yet the Navy looked a more talented side. To make matters worse for the Army their hooker, Miller (RAEC), was sent off in the closing minutes. The Navy ran out winners on three tries, by Dunn, Birkett and Merrick, two converted by G Jones, who also contributed three penalties.

Another gloomy season looked like ringing down the curtain on this decade when the Army crashed 19–0 at the hands of the Navy on 1 March 1975. The Navy were the all-round better side and the Army never appeared to settle down. To an extent the score, from a good try apiece by Davies and Armstrong with one conversion and three penalties by Piercey, perhaps flattered the Navy, but they took their opportunities.

The record score of 41–13 against the RAF on 22 March, however, cheered the Army enormously, especially as the RAF had previously beaten the Navy 20–7, albeit that the Navy were then handicapped by having three players injured.

A remarkable victory and the highest-ever Inter-Service score was achieved with almost the same side that had lost to the Navy. But after the earlier game's blank sheet there was a real tonic for that season's RAMC skipper Rea as the Army notched up try after try. G G Davies (RCT) had the rare satisfaction of scoring three, Phil Davies, on the wing, had a splendid game where he scored two himself and made the openings for two more. The rest came from Mike Cuss (DWR), Carroll (RAMC) and Collier (REME). Three of the eight tries were converted by D R Williams (RWF) and Morgan dropped a goal. Howe and Gordon scored tries for the RAF, one converted by Larter, who also kicked a penalty goal.

The list of Army players who may be called to mind over the years is seemingly endless, but note was especially taken in this decade of P A Eastwood and D S Boyle.

Interesting newcomers in the later years were two who were to be future skippers, J M (Mike) Bowles (RCT) and S G (Steve) Jackson (RAMC). And the Army came close to having an International again when Norman Gray (RE) had an England Under 23 trial in 1975.

BACK ON COURSE? 1976–1985

The past ten years have safely kept the Army from sinking back into the 'slough of despond' and encouraged the hope that, even if another golden era is not exactly around the corner, their collection of wooden spoons may be complete.

In 20 Inter-Service matches in this period the Army have won 12 and there has been one draw, leaving them on six games to three with the Navy and better than the RAF by six games to four. The Championship was left as a triple tie in 1975, only the sixth in IS history and the first since 1956. There were to be others in 1978 and 1984, but the Army won the title outright in 1976, 1980 and 1983. And over-all they came out ahead on points once again.

On 21 February 1976, the Army defeated the RAF 6–3 as the first step to winning that year's championship. It was not one of the best service games. The Army side was lacking in initiative and generally sluggish. Bell (now 13th/18th Royal Hussars) and Morgan gave their threequarters plenty of ball, but good RAF covering and tackling snuffed out any Army attack. Morgan dropped a goal and P J Wright (King's Own Royal Border), the full-back, kicked a penalty, against the RAF's penalty by C G Williams.

The Army's G O W Williams (DWR), flank forward, had a lively game and showed considerable promise. He was to impress Army supporters as one of the best flank forwards of recent years and he also impressed the All Blacks when during a recent tour he played against them for Combined Services.

A 15–6 win over the Navy on 13 March cut the previous year's tie to give the Army the title, but it could not be considered an entirely satisfactory result.

Their points were from three penalties by Morgan, one by new full-back Denham (RAOC), and a drop goal by returning Spawforth, to the Navy's two penalties by Piercey, but that meant the Army had won the championship without scoring a try. The *Sunday Telegraph* commented: 'The standard of Services' rugby may be low these days, understandably, but surely not that low'!

In the Navy match both sides were constantly penalised, and had the kicking at goal by both teams been better the score would have been considerably higher. The Navy were leading by two penalties to one at half-time, but Morgan kicked all of his in the second half and finally Spawforth's smart drop goal set the seal.

However the Army won the title and by their doing so that particular year it made a fitting farewell for Spawforth, who was having his last IS match.

He was one of the real characters of Army rugby, an imaginative, enthusiastic player whose natural exuberance for the game was a constant inspiration to his team-mates.

Spawforth had been with the REME since he enlisted and joined their Army Apprentice School (now the Princess Marina College) at Arborfield when he was sixteen. He was a born leader on the rugby field, brimming with self-confidence and drive, and it was appropriate he should captain his county, Berkshire.

He was an ebullient, lively and unorthodox scrum-half, who on his day was a match winner. Quicksilver aggressive breaks from the scrum were a speciality and he kicked astutely in both attack and defence. He was continually attempting different options, and if sometimes they ended in disaster they frequently turned defeat into victory.

This player gained twelve Army caps and probably his best game was the one against the RAF in 1972. That 14–6 win was largely due to his control of the game from the base of the scrum, dangerous breaks and accurate kicking, plus an immaculate service to his outside half. Another game to remember was when he played for Combined Services against the South Africans in 1969. His inspiration was very much in evidence as time and again he outwitted the opposition by varying his play. A few minutes before the end the Services led 6–3, but a famous victory was foiled by the Springboks scoring three times in the closing moments, including injury time.

The Navy had a deserving victory on 5 March 1977, but the Army put up a better fight than their 16–0 defeat indicated.

Yet another Davies appeared. Gareth Davies (QDG/APTC), who played with typical Welsh verve, and he and his half-back partner Norman Drummond (RAChD) frequently tested the Navy's defence. Navy full-back Fabian, however, had a fine all-round game, tackling well and producing kicking that was accurate and well judged. He made the opening for the first try and kicked eight of the Navy points with a conversion and two penalties. Try scorers were Ackerman and Connolly. Paul Dunn, the Navy skipper, was as vigorous and fast as ever and disrupted many Army attacks.

When the RAF match came along on 19 March Jackson was

appointed captain, the first non-commissioned rank and the first three-quarter to be captain since Tony Novis in 1935. Jackson had previously played for England Under 19 and captained them against Wales in 1972/73.

The occasion was celebrated for him by the Army winning 19–13 and, as they had not scored a try in their past three games, by two very good ones from Reynolds (REME), which was in itself refreshing. Both sides missed opportunities to score, though, and it was anyone's game until Atkinson (DWR) kicked his third penalty. He had also converted one of the tries. Hickey got a try for the RAF and Orwin matched Atkinson with three penalties.

Hoon returned from overseas to resume his captaincy in 1978 and 1979, the first year of which marked the Centenary game with the Navy, on 4 March in front of Prince Philip. A suitably exciting game took place, played in a fine spirit with no quarter given. Eventually the Navy, led again by Dunn, had a narrow victory at 17–16 and they deserved it.

Both sides ran the ball throughout and the lead kept changing hands as the teams aimed to outdo each other in scoring and repeat or reverse, as the case may be, the original Navy win of 1878. The Army had tries by Gareth Davies and Kevin A'Hearne (RRW), one converted by Atkinson, and he and McCracken (Corps of Royal Military Police) kicked a penalty apiece. For the Navy, English, Hamlett and Richards got tries and Leigh made one conversion. But at the last the Navy nipped in front when Leigh kicked a final penalty.

There is a special atmosphere to the Navy match which the author described in an article for the Centenary programme. It was headed 'Green with Envy?' and told spectators that if this was their first visit to the Navy v Army match it would soon become crystal clear that it was one day of the year when the term 'Silent Service' did not refer to the Royal Navy!

He can do no better than to reprint it here:

As long ago as 1924, the brilliant Navy and England International, W J A Davies, wrote in his book Rugby Football, 'Our grief was shared by the School of Naval Officers' daughters from Twickenham who were sitting in the corner of the stand where the tries were scored, shouting "NAVY, NAVY" as the Army were taking the place kicks which, luckily for us, were unsuccessful!' I'm not surprised! As an Army man it appears to me their children and grandchildren are in the same excellent voice and the cheers of the Naval supporters and the sounding of Klaxon horns drown the more reserved and refined encouragement of the Army followers!

The west car park resembles the Fleet in review order and a meeting of lost souls. There are tables groaning with sumptuous food and Fortnum and Mason hampers. There is sufficient whisky and gin to sink the largest, if obsolete, battleship.

My wife, an ex-Wren, takes all this in her stride, and between drinking monumental pink gins, is being constantly kissed and embraced by enormous men with red faces wearing dufflecoats, who remind her of parties together in such dubious haunts as Chatham, Plymouth, Dovercourt and Fraserburgh. As a mere 'Pongo' I slink away into the bowels of Twickenham and join my contemporaries! in one of the restaurants where we have a modest lunch washed down with a pint of beer. The raucous laughter and screams of delight from the car park come echoing through the windows.

It is said that Cardiff Arms Park is worth 10 points to Wales. I believe the revelry in the west car park is worth at least 12 points to the Navy. My wife says I am just green with envy. Perhaps she's right!

That the championship should turn out to be a triple tie that year was perhaps appropriate. The RAF were very hopeful of beating the Army, but in their game, eventually played on 22 April after being postponed because of frost, the Army were more reliable on the day and won 16-6, on tries by A'Hearne and Bowles, with a conversion and two penalties by yet another new full-back, B J Abbott (REME), to two penalties for the RAF by Green.

It did not escape Army notice, however, that, tie or no tie, they 'won' a moral championship victory. The RAF had beaten the Navy 15-8 which left the Army on top 'on points' – this would have been the deciding factor in the world of soccer!

Even though they were not to take the IS title in 1979, the Army did have the distinction of being the first winners of the handsome Stewart Wrightson Trophy, donated by the firm of insurance brokers who had become sponsors for the Navy match.

An Army win at 10-3 on 10 March was witnessed by a much larger crowd than usual, for whom the teams provided a game full of vigour and excitement. Hoon led the Army with his infectious enthusiasm and energetic zeal. The only try was scored by Kevin Bassom (RE) after a splendid move along the threequarter line and Bowles kicked two penalties, while the Navy could only find one penalty, from Thomas.

Hoon had his last Army match on 24 March when they played the RAF, but in terms of success the previous game was to be his swan-song. The Army could not keep up the momentum from the trophy win and the RAF beat them 10-3 by seizing their chances.

For one penalty by Bowles the RAF had tries by Orwin and Jenkins, one converted by Green. Orwin scored his try from a line-out and Jenkins got his just before half-time by coming away from the scrum and surprising the Army defence.

Andy Hoon was a player of immense experience and one of the best Army Captains since the Second World War. He was an inspiring leader and a very accomplished forward. With fierce determination he was always in the thick of things and was a player very much respected by opponents.

He started his rugby at Clifton College and finished there as captain of the school XV. He immediately got into the RMA side and played in various positions, either in the second row, as a flanker, or a number eight. From his first Army cap in 1966 he would have gained more than the ultimate twenty-two but for overseas service.

Apart from the Army he played for Combined Services, for Black-heath, Headingly and Bristol, and County rugby for Yorkshire, Dorset and Wiltshire and Berkshire. This modest and unselfish player, who had a magnificent record of sixteen years in first-class rugby, was summed up as a hard working, resolute forward with splendid positional sense and a captain of good tactical sense who led by example.

Tim Sinclair (DWR) stepped into the captain's role for 1980 and on 23 February the Army fairly let themselves go against the RAF, winning 26-7, which was perhaps as well as their game with the Navy on 8 March ended in a 0-0 draw. But they had done enough to win the championship again.

In the RAF match they played good open rugby, scored six tries, and if their kicking had been better the score could have gone considerably higher.

If the Scots were the dominant force in the previous decade, this one might well have been headed 'Welsh Supreme', for in this match seven of the Army players came from the Royal Regiment of Wales alone. Only one of them, A'Hearne, put his name on the scorers' list with a try, but the other points revealed more than a little Welsh influence, if only in the name of Morgan, who made one conversion. Two tries from Gleane (RCS) and one each from Lytollis (also RCS), Reynolds and G O W Williams. Seward scored a try for the RAF and Pritchard dropped a goal.

Despite there being no score in the Navy match it had its exciting moments. A further thrill came in waiting for the last match of the season to see if the title would go outright or be a double tie. The RAF settled the matter, to most people's surprise, when they beat the Navy.

Bowles began his first season as captain in 1981 by seeing the Wrightson Trophy go to the Navy, for their 7–3 win on 7 March. There was consolation, though, when the Army beat the RAF 6–4 on 28 March.

The Army missed one or two chances to score against the Navy before Lovegrove (QDG) kicked their only penalty. The wind occasioned some passes not going to hand and the Army did not make the most of their advantage in the first half. Tomlin levelled the scores with a penalty for the Navy and after twenty minutes their right wing, Harker, gave them the try that won the match. Despite the conditions, it was an entertaining game. The Navy thoroughly deserved to take the prize.

Two sons of famous fathers were in the Army team against the RAF, Guy Shuttleworth (DWR) and Jeremy Campbell-Lamerton (Scots Guards). The latter made his first appearance in the Navy game. Charles Richardson of the Royal Scots and son of an equally famous father, Gen Sir Robert Richardson – an extremely good rugby player himself in his youth, having played regularly for BAOR – also gained an Army cap.

Shuttleworth, like his father in a half-back position, put himself to the fore straight away with the Army's two penalties, the first one giving them the lead after fifteen minutes. A'Hearne scored a good try for the RAF shortly after half-time and if they could have kicked their penalties they would have gone well ahead. As it was, the second penalty by Shuttleworth left the Army with a fortuitous victory after a scrappy game.

Andy Chapple (REME) had a splendid game at full-back, tackling well and looking dangerous when coming into the line. His positioning was very sound. Gleane, on the left wing, put in some devastating tackles and saved an almost certain try. For the RAF their veteran, Peter Larter, was prominent in the line-out.

For 1982 the Army beat the Navy 11–7 but then lost 10–6 to the RAF.

Against the Navy on 13 March the Army owed it to Kevin Bassom that they won the Wrightson Trophy for the first time since 1979, as he scored both of their tries, one the decider. The Army went into the match very much the underdogs, their results in the run-up period being less good than the Navy's. But on the day they played magnificently in a most exciting game.

A long penalty by Barry Abbott (REME), who was said to have the longest kick seen in the Army for several years, gave them the lead after only six minutes and although they could not add to it by half-time despite some attacks they stood firm against Navy pressure. The Army also survived early team disruption when Mason (RRW) sustained a shoulder injury and had to leave the field, to be replaced by Byrne (REME). For all their pressure the Navy only had two near-misses.

In a thrill-packed second half opening spell, the Army went further ahead with Bassom's first try, after he was sent away by Abbott on the left, but before long the Navy's Alcock had reduced the lead to three points again with a try for them. They began to look dangerous and make headway, then drew level with a drop goal by Price. Both teams fought hard to score winning points and supporters were on tenterhooks. The Army were under considerable pressure in the later stages until a Navy pass went astray and Bassom, the left wing three-quarter, intercepted to scoop up the ball and run 80 yards in a first-class solo effort, leaving defenders quite unable to catch him.

The RAF game on 3 April was for a new cup donated under their sponsorship by Windsor Life Assurance Company Limited and the Army had high hopes of taking this trophy too so were surprised to be beaten.

They had a good deal of the play, but after Williams (DWR) scored a try in the first fifteen minutes and Abbott converted they could not find any more points, particularly regretting that in the last twenty minutes they did not take their chances. Basson who scored two tries against the Navy, hardly touched the ball all day. The exitement and the crowd were less than for the Navy match.

Having already defeated the Navy 16-14, the RAF by this further win became Inter-Service Champions for only the ninth time outright since they joined in the competition in 1920. They last had the title in 1979.

In 1983 it was touch and go against the Navy, but the Army scraped home 10-9 to retain the Wrightson Trophy, and they clinched the IS title by beating the RAF 16-7.

The Navy match on 12 March was fraught with excitement as the Army fought back on a half-time deficit of 9-0. The senior service had pressed from the start and looked far the more businesslike team, keeping the ball in the Army half for almost the whole of the first fifteen minutes and only narrowly missing a penalty and a touchdown. One good Army spell brought them a near penalty chance, but the ball hit an upright and the Navy soon took charge again. It was their just reward when flanker Stephen Hughes (Royal Marines) seized on a loose ball to power his way through for a try, beautifully converted by Gerry Price, and half-back Price then kicked a penalty shortly before half-time.

With the Navy continuing to dominate at the start of the second half, and seeming likely to add further points to a lead that already appeared unbeatable, the game could have been virtually over. But the Army steadily began to gain ground, though for another twenty minutes or so they had nothing to show for it. Then, however, Geoff Neild (RE) secured a fairly long penalty kick and they were on their way.

Hopes rose with every fresh attack, only to fall again when another penalty was missed and the Navy retaliated, but fifteen minutes later the gap was closed to just two points by Army right wing threequarter David Johnson (RWF) latching on to the ball when a defender fumbled it and sprinting off for a try, fulfilling a promise of speed he had occasionally shown in the first half. A conversion would have eased some of the tension for Army supporters in the, as always, large and enthusiastic crowd, but the teams never did draw level as in 1982 and it had to be all or nothing. With the minutes ticking away even of time added for stoppages, the Army at last edged in front when Neild kicked a final penalty that settled the match.

The Army played with more assurance against the RAF on 26 March, though that game began scrappily with RAF pressure keeping most of the play their way. Peter Warfield (RAEC) kicked soundly at stand-off-half to preserve the Army line, however, and two well-kicked penalties by Neild helped the Army considerably. So despite the RAF hitting back with a try by Underwood in the left-hand corner, from a smart threequarter move after a scrum, and Orwin succeeding with the second of two penalties just before the interval, the situation was far different from the Navy match.

Prior to the RAF scoring, the Army were showing more teamwork and they built on this in the second half, denying the RAF any more points while taking the game over for themselves once more. The backs gained good possession as 'Willie' Williams (DWR) kept things tidy in the loose and Warfield did not have to rely so much on tactical kicking.

Sustained pressure on the RAF brought the Army their remaining points in two tries. They went ahead again after the captain Gareth Davies (QDG/APTC) made a classic break to pave the way for a fine score by Williams, with Neild, full-back that day, converting. Davies broke again, aided by Brian McCall (REME), for Andrew Kay (DWR) to add the second try.

Thus the Army collected in one year the IS Championship, the Wrightson Trophy and the Windsor Life Cup. Things were looking very good again.

To open the IS contest in 1984 the Army beat the Navy 13-6 on 3 March to take the Wrightson Trophy for a third year, a brilliant start to another season which left hopes high, especially for ARU secretary Lieut-Col Pat Dawson, who would be retiring before the 1985 season.

It was by no means certain that the Army would win this match, for they suffered a blow after only three minutes when Warfield, that year's captain, sustained a cut head and concussion. He went off, returned eight minutes later, but had to leave the field completely in the twenty-seventh minute. During that time Neild had dropped a goal in the sixth minute and kicked a penalty in the tenth, to give the Army a 6-0 lead, despite their playing against the wind in the first half, but after twenty-two minutes the Navy equalised. Their full-back, Henderson, reduced the arrears in the eleventh minute with one penalty and stand-off Barnett followed suit. With the Army disorganised by Warfield's injury the Navy looked set to take over.

Peter Lockett (REME) replaced Warfield, however, and with scrum-half Davies, outstanding in defence and attack, as their inspiration, the team settled down again and prevented the Navy from making any further progress by very fine covering. The Navy, encouraged by drawing level, had been doing all the pressing, but by half-time the scoreboard read: Royal Navy, 6, Army 10. The Army pack had made a determined onslaught against the run of play to push the Navy back and Davies nipped along for the only try of the game!

Still the Navy attempted to pull up again and, with the wind opposing them now, opted to run penalties when kicking against the wind might have missed, which delighted their supporters. But although they made several very good moves across the field and had a lot of good ball they could not budge the Army defence and so had nothing to show for it, whereas around midway Neild fixed the closing score for the Army with a second penalty.

The game was summed up as being a good one in keeping with the traditions of this fixture, the exciting and adventurous Navy side defeated by an Army team performance that was excellent in tactics, organisation and discipline.

All was to rest on the final match when the Navy beat the RAF 10-9 on 24 March and this turned out to be one of those years for a three-way tie as the RAF then overcame the Army 19-15 on 7 April. Once again the Army could claim a moral victory 'on points'.

The high scoring in the Army v RAF game reflects very good play which was never bogged down and for a while the Army looked like retaining the championship outright. Neild had kicked the first penalty within the first minute and a half, but the RAF began to show flair that was to pay dividends later on. Their man Bate nearly broke through with benefit of a high punt, but Neild kicked another penalty.

As the RAF pressed to recover, intent on ensuring the game did not get away from them, they produced a lovely move out of a scrum, the ball going quickly from player to player before Allison, without challenge, could touch down in the opposite corner. Evans converted to make it 6-6 and some of their fans thought it appropriate to mark this with snatches of 'The Dam Busters' March! They were found to be premature when the Army replied three minutes later with a try by Lockett, which Neild converted – Neild had thrust through the defence and passed the ball to Lockett, who darted round and placed it behind a post. At 12–6 no more points were to come in that half, but as both teams produced flowing rugby until the interval it was the Army whose supporters could be the more encouraged, for they had another chance when Kevin Bassom dashed away, only to be halted five yards from the line.

Unfortunately for the Army they faded in the second half, while the RAF continued to think quickly and stay sharp. They soon went on the offensive and before long went ahead for the first time. Evans cut the deficit to three points with a penalty and their England International Rory Underwood made a brilliant run up one flank to touch down by the corner flag, fending off two defenders as he did so. Their only disappointment then was that Evans could not make the conversion, making a good attempt at it from a difficult position and nearly managing it but hitting an upright.

Neild had to go off injured just after that and the Army defence began to look shaky. The Army kept trying to run but two dropped goals by Evans sealed their fate. They could have drawn level or edged in front again if both a try and a penalty had succeeded, but when Lockett crossed the line it was disallowed, leaving replacement Mick Blomquist (RE) only able to narrow the gap a little with the penalty. Overall the result was considered a fair one on the day's play.

It would have been nice to end this Inter-Service section with the Army as IS champions once again, or even another sharing situation, but alas it was not to be, and they really only have themselves to blame. Again in 1985 they began splendidly, keeping hold of the Wrightson Trophy for a fourth year with an 11-6 win over the Navy on 2 March but in a far from brilliant game with the RAF on 23

March they lost 15–12 when they had everything going for them. The RAF became champions in a very high-scoring game with the Navy on 6 April (Easter Saturday), taking the title for the first time since 1982 with their 29–23 win.

The Navy cannot be happy at years of Army dominance, but looked like ending it in their match when it was the Army who started all at sea, with Allen (Royal Marines) giving the Navy an early 3–0 lead with a penalty. This, of course, pleased Navy supporters very much, but Gareth Davies, Army skipper once again, was soon rallying his team to counter the Navy's confidence. Hardly to be faulted himself, he was in everything leading by example and results followed before too long. Lockett was stopped just short of the line as pressure began to pay off, but the Army went in front 7–3 as Davies reacted smartly from a scrum when it seemed a push-over try would be scored, grabbing the ball and steering well to the left, to dive over past staggered Navy defenders, than Angus Mackay (RCT) kicked a penalty.

Efforts for flowing rugby were not helped by a wet day and a greasy ball and there were times when neither team looked confident, but Army spirits soared still higher at the start of the second half as left winger 'Chalky' Atkins (Royal Signals) crossed in the left-hand corner for a superb try out of one of the best moves of the game. The Army team had made up magnificently for their slow start and it was now Navy skipper and full-back Alcock who was warned, for his side could only sort themselves out for an inspired last ten minutes, by which time it was too late for more than another penalty by Allen, despite their showing invention and crispness. By then the Army defence was well organised, to give little away. Apart from Davies, Mackay stood out in the Army team for his first-class tactical kicking at full-back and some sharp tackling and handling.

This result was the best possible welcome for the new ARU secretary, who was none other than former skipper Major Hugh Greatwood, and as it coincided with the Army's acquisition of another International after a gap of fifteen years he would have been justified in harbouring hopes of a splendid season. The RAF game dispelled them!

It was enough to make even strong men weep when the Army virtually threw that match away. The 15–12 score looks close. It wasn't. The Army had a 9–0 lead by half-time and were 12–0 up into the second half, thanks to some fine kicking by John Steele (RA), who notched up all four penalties. How the fly-half must have gnashed his teeth later that all were to go to waste.

The RAF, who by this time had two Internationals in Underwood and John Orwin (also England), were made the favourites in some quarters, but did not seem to be doing themselves any favours and it was the Army who had most of the play. Underwood was closely marked by Atkins, but his team appeared to deny him chances to run the ball. All might have been well for the Army if they had kept working at it and never let the RAF realise any of their potential, but they coasted in the rest of the second half and that was disastrous. The RAF started to press, pinned them back in their own half, and frustration led to penalties, three of which succeeded to bring the score to 12–9. Still all was not lost for the Army, but with two minutes to go captain Davies made a wild pass that missed its object and the RAF won a ruck, Lazenby went over for a try and Worrall converted it. In the time left the Army could not tilt the balance again.

This was a match where the Army could look back on few good handling movements and if the RAF were denying Underwood his Army counterparts were not given much chance either. Some of them hardly ever got going and it was scarcely a memorable day for a young man to make his senior team debut, as Steve Wilkins (RCT) did, up from the Army Under 21 side for his first cap.

After this the Army could only wait in trepidation for the result of the RAF v Navy game and hope that the Senior Service could pull something out of the bag for a tie as in 1984. The scoring on 6 April shows they tried hard to that end, but it was not to be.

Whatever the Army do in the years to come the hope must be that enough can be achieved to hold on to the supremacy of Inter-Service results generally, established by the golden era and other vintage seasons.

This 1985 season marked the tenth win of the championship by the newest service since the annual tournament became three-way in 1920, but in that period the Army have won the title outright 25 times and the Navy 15. On individual wins the Army lead the RAF by 35 to 18 (seven matches were drawn), which leaves a fairly secure margin, but the longer tussle with the Navy has little room for complacency. There, since 1907, the Army have 36 wins and the Navy 29, with three games drawn. That situation alone will add spice to the next few years!

INTER-SERVICE RUGBY – FALKLAND ISLANDS

The Inter-Service Rugby Championship is fast becoming a major annual event in the Falklands Calendar and its the second year the Army played the Royal Navy in what proved to be a hard fought open running game with a more skilful army side winning more good possession and scoring more tries but admitting defeat to a superior boot of the Royal Navy full-back. Final score 9–8 to the Navy.

The game against the RAF was not as close but just as hard fought with a final result of 16–4 to the Army. The Navy then went on to beat the RAF.

TEAMS FOR ARMY INTER-SERVICE MATCHES
1920–1985

1920 *Army v Navy:* W M Shewen (KOSB), H L V Day (RFA), R B Y Simpson (Durham Light Infantry) R MacK Scobie (RE) (capt), E G W W Harrison (RFA), P E R Baker-Jones (RFA), E C Penny (RFA), P H Lawless (Middlesex Regt), W B W Roderick (Coldstream Guards), G Hedderwick (RTC), D Cross, (10th Hussars), C Hyland (Life Guards), C W Jones (Welch Regt), G D Young (Welsh Guards), J S W Stone, (RE).

Navy: C M Evans-Thomas, C M Merewether, A E Thomson, S J G MacKenzie, P W R Weir, W J A Davies (capt), C A Kershaw, K A S Clarke, C F G Hallaran, E R Gardner, W G Agnew R C O'Conor, J S Golding, D R Orr-Ewing, T Woods.

Army v RAF: W M Shewen, R B Y Simpson, R MacK Scobie (capt), W C Wilkins (Tank Corps), I G Fitzmaurice (Tank Corps), P E R Baker-Jones, E C Penny, P H Lawless, W B W Roderick, G Hedderwick, D Cross, C Hyland, G D Young, C M Usher (Gordon Highlanders), W R C Penny (RE).

RAF: K F Damant, J L McLennan, O C Bryson, G M Thomas, P C Scott, A W Mylne, H M Massey, T Smith, I C Little, R H C Usher, C Breese, W C Hicks, A W Symington, G H H Maxwell, W W Wakefield (capt).

1921 *Army v Navy* C S Duncan (Queen's Own Cameron Highlanders), A R Aslett (King's Own Royal Regt), G L Bloxham (RFA), P E R Baker-Jones, Q E M A King (RFA), T B L Tennant (RMA), J R B Worton (RMC), C L G Hyland, A H MacIlwaine (RFA) (capt), R L Brown (RE), N J O Carbutt (RFA), F A Pates (Welsh Guards), K L Herbert (Border Regt), T C Rennie (Black Watch), H M Hinde (RASC).

Navy: C M Evans-Thomas, H W V Stephenson, P R Dearden, W C T Eyres, J S Head, W J A Davies (capt), F E Chevallier, W G Agnew, E R Gardner, W Orr-Ewing, G N Loriston-Clarke, W E G Luddington, A H M Hyslop, H V A Phelps, P Williams-Powlett.

Army v RAF: J A Middleton (RASC), A R Aslett, I J Kilgour (Northumberland Fus), K N Crawford (RE), Q E M A King,

P E R Baker-Jones, W R C Penny, G Hedderick, C L G Hyland, A H MacIlwaine (Capt), R L Brown, T G Rennie, H M Hinde, C M Usher, G M Churcher (RA).

RAF: G M Robb, W Tyrell, C N Lowe, G M Thomas, W Jones, J C Russell, J L T Jones, G H Maxwell, S P Simpson, E H Turner, I C Little, R H C Usher, W C Hicks, W W Wakefield (Capt), T Smith.

1922 *Army v Navy:* J A Middleton, H L V Day, A R Aslett, G V Palmer, (Queen's Royal Regt), I J Kilgour, P E R Baker-Jones, J B Worton (now Middlesex Regt), C W Jones, G D Young, H M Hinde, C M Usher (capt), S Arnott (RAMC), J A Ross (HLI), R J Davies (R Berks Regt), G B MacNamara (R Inniskilling Fus).

Navy: S Kealey, W H V Stephenson, M S Bradey, J M Fitzroy, R M Rowlands, W J A Davies (capt), C A Kershaw, E R Gardner, W Luddington, C F Hallaran, W C T Eyres, A H Maxwell-Hyslop, W G Agnew, H Coyte, P B Williams-Powlett.

Army v RAF: J A Middleton, H L V Day, A R Aslett, G V Palmer, I J Kilgour, T B L Tennant, J B Worton, C W Jones, G D Young, H M Hinde, C M Usher (capt), S Arnott, J A Ross, F Dearden (RFA), G B MacNamara.

RAF: T L Lowe, W Jones, O C Bryson, C N Lowe, H H Storrs, J L T Jones, J C Russell, T Smith, W C Hicks, L Whitworth, E F Turner, R H C Usher, S P Simpson, G H H Maxwell, W W Wakefield (capt).

1923 *Army v Navy:* J A Middleton, R K Millar (RE), R Mack Scobie, H L V Day (capt), Q E M A King, P E R Baker-Jones, J B Worton, H M Hinde, H C Giles (Welsh Guards), P E C Honeyman (R Scots), J A Ross, T G Rennie, G D Young, F Dearden, K L Herbert (Border Regt).

Navy: F Gilbert, W G B MacKenzie, D P Evans, J Burnett, M Richmond, W J A Davies (capt), C A Kershaw, F A Haines, E R Gardner, W E Luddington, R S Benson, E H Harding, W C T Eyres, R C O'Conor, D Orr-Ewing.

Army v RAF: J A Middleton, R K Millar, P E R Baker-Jones, R Jones, (Welch Regt), G V Palmer, P L Wilkinson (RE), J B Worton, R J Davies, G D Young, F Dearden, P E L Honeyman, K L Herbert, T G Rennie, C W Jones, F A Pates.

RAF: C Runham, C N Lowe, O D Bryson, N Carter, C B Riddle, A G White, J C Russell, S P Simpson, R H C Usher, W W Wakefield (capt), C D Adams, T Rose, J G Stephens, E B Coventry, C Collins.

1924   *Army v Navy:* C A Baker (SWB), R K Millar, A R Aslett, L G
Thomas (RE), G J Bryan (RE), B H G Tucker (Gurkha Rifles),
J B Worton, W H Aitken (RE), W F Browne (DWR), G A P
Sanders (RA), C K T Faithfull (DWR), F A Pates, T G Rennie,
J A Ross, G D Young (capt).
Navy: H S Harrison, H W Stephenson. A George, T S Lee, R G
Giffard, F E Chevallier, A E Buchanan, W C Eyres (capt), W E
Luddington, E E Gardner, C F Hallaran, D R Orr-Ewing, R
O'Conor, W S Broom, P B R Williams-Powlett.
Army v RAF: P E R Baker, R K Millar, A R Aslett, L G
Thomas, G J Bryan, B H G Tucker, J B Worton, W H H Ait-
ken, W F Browne, G A P Sanders, C K T Faithfull, F A Pates,
T G Rennie, J A Ross, G D Young (capt).
RAF: J G Stephens, J M Wale, P J Chambers, C C Bryson, C B
Riddle, J C Russell (capt), C Medhurst, R H Usher, C D
Adams, J S Chick, T Rose, F Isaac, F W Sinclair, E C Wackett,
S G Collins.

1925   *Army v Navy:* E E Cass (KOYLI), G T Bryson, M A Green
(Northamptonshire Regt), A R Aslett (capt), R K Millar, R M
Phillips (Welch Regt), W C Powell (Welch Guards), W H Stev-
enson (3/16 Punjab Regt), B M Dunn (Welch Regt), R P G An-
derson (RE), P E C Honeyman, K L Herbert, J A Ross, W F
Browne, T G Rennie.
Navy: E S Satterthwaite, H W V Stevenson, T S Lee, R W Ar-
mytage, W H Wood, W J A Davies, C A Kershaw (capt), G E
Luddington, G C F Branson, J W Forrest, A C Chapman, W G
Agnew, G W Yale, C M Morrell, A A Havers.
Army v RAF: E E Cass, R K Millar, M A Green, I G Loch (RE),
G J Bryan, R M Phillips, W C Powell, W H Stevenson, B M
Dunn (capt), R P G Anderson, P E C Honeyman, K L Herbert,
J A Ross, D Turquand-Young (RTC), T G Rennie.
RAF: W Casy, J M Wale, J Marcy, C N Lwe, P G Scott, J C
Russell (capt), P J Chambers, J S Chick, E F Turner, F W Sin-
clair, T Rose, C M Adams, F V Beamish, W Johnson, E C
Wackett.

1926   *Army v Navy:* T E Rees (Welsh Guards), G J Bryan, A R As-
lett, E E Cass, E E Down (Dorsetshire Regt), R M Phillips, A T
Young (RTC), D S Jones (SWB), B M Dunn, R P G Anderson,
H R Saunders (RA), D Turquand-Young, J A Ross, W F
Browne, J D Clinch (Middlesex Regt).
Navy: S Hoskin, H C Cumberbatch, C R Knapman, R W Ar-
mytage, M Richmond, C R Garrett, G P S Davies, W G Lud-

dington (capt), W Paddon, R D Fricker, G C F Branson, W S Broom, D Orr-Ewing, A A Havers, H T Armstrong.

Army v RAF: T E Rees, G T Bryan, A R Aslett (capt), E E Cass, E E Down, R M Phillips, A T Young, B M Dunn, P E C Honeyman, D S Jones, H McVicker (RAMC), J D Clinch, W F Browne, C K T Faithfull, D Turquand-Young.

RAF: W I N Strong, Lord Bandon, C N Lowe, O C Bryson, P G Scott, P J Chambers, J C Russell, J S Chick, P G Chichester, T Rose, G H H Maxwell, M G Christie, J F Wintour, J F Hampton, C J S O'Malley.

1927   *Army v Navy:* E E Cass, G V Palmer, G J Bryan, J L Proudlock (RA), R B Maxwell (RAOC), B H G Tucker, A T Young, J A Ross, D S Jones, E P Sewell (Northamptonshire Regt), W Thomas (SWB), W F Browne, H McVicker, C K T Faithfull, G B MacNamara.

Navy: K A Sellar, N Kennedy, T S Lee, A George, W H Wood, G M Sladen, G P S Davies, W Paddon, W G Luddington, T G P Crick, E H Harding, J W Linton, R C Harry, W C T Eyres, L B Osborne.

Army v RAF: E E Cass, G V Palmer, A R Aslett, R B Maxwell, G T Bryan, B H S Tucker, A T Young, D S Jones, W S Thomas, E G Chamberlain (Hampshire Regt), F Dowas (DWR), H McVicker, J A Ross, C K T Faithful, W F Browne.

RAF: E S Burns, G D Harvey, O C Bryson, F S Hodder, C P Vines, R V M Odbert, J C Sussell, J S Chick, G H H Maxwell, C J S O'Malley, M G Christie, P G Chichester, J G Franks, C Rollings, F V Beamish.

1928   *Army v Navy:* T E Rees, G T Bryan, A R Aslett (capt), G V Palmer, Sir T G Devitt (Seaforth Highlanders), J R Cole (Loyal Regt), A T Young, G Townend (DWR), W A Morton (KORR), P E Gibbons (Welsh Guards), G E R Bastin (RA), D S Jones, McVicker, C K T Faithfull, W F Browne.

Navy: C G Gosling, H W V Stephenson, A R Freeman, W H Wood, J Plunkett-Cole, G R Cook, S H Carlill, D P Trentham, P B Williams-Powlett (capt), T G P Crick, J W Linton, L B Osborne, J B Morrisey, J Webb, A A Havers.

Army v RAF: T E Rees, G J Bryan, A R Aslett (capt), G V Palmer, Sir T G Devitt, J R Cole, A T Young, G Townend, W A Morton, P E Gibbons, G E R Bastin, H H C Withers, C K T Faithfull, D S Jones, W F Browne.

RAF: T A Hale-Munro, P B Coote, J R H Pott, F S Hodder, C H G Bembridge, R V B Odbert (capt), J C Russell, C J S

O'Malley, G F Cockell, F V Beamish, H A Constantine, C M Adams, J S Chick, G R Beamish, M G Christie.

1929   *Army v Navy:* E W F de V Hunt (RA), J A M Rice-Evans (R Welch Fus), A L Novis (Leicestershire Regt), A R Aslett (capt), J W Wainwright (RA), J R Cole, A T Young, H H C Withers (RE), W A Morton, G Townend, H Rew (RTC), R G S Hobbs (RA), D H Nott (Worcestershire Regt), K M Wright (RA), W F Browne.

Navy: C G Gosling, H W V Stephenson, D St Clair Ford, G M Sladen, W H Wood, C R Garrett, S H Carhill, T G P Crick, (capt), M J Brosnan, W C Thomas, J W Forrest, H T Armstrong, C P Evans, A A Havers, H C Browne.

Army v RAF: E W F de V Hunt, J A M Rice-Evans, A R Aslett (capt), A L Novis, J W Wainwright, J R Cole, C C McCreight (RA), H H C Withers, W A Morton, G Townend, H Rew, R G S Hobbs, G E R Bastin (RA), D H Nott, K M Wright.

RAF: J G Llewellyn, N H White, J R H Pott, R D Cotton, G D Harvey, R V M Odber, J C Russell, A C Hall, V E Maxwell, C D Adams, W H Kirby, H A Constantine, J Clarke, G R Beamish (capt), R W Letchworth.

1930   *Army v Navy:* E W F de V Hunt, Sir J C Devitt, J M Rice-Evans, A L Novis (capt), G Peddie (RA), J R Cole, C C McCreight, G Townend, H H C Withers, H Rew, C H B Rodham (Indian Army) R G S Hobbs, D H Nott, K J McIntyre (RTC), K M Wright.

Navy: C G Gosling, D St Clair Ford, T S Lee, G M Sladen, W H Wood, A E Hargrave, G Webster, T G P Crick, W G Luddington, J W Linton, J W Forrest, C Webb, D Orr-Ewing, E H Harding, R K Hodgkin.

Army v RAF: E W F de V Hunt, G Peddie, J M Rice-Evans, A L Novis (capt), J W Wainwright, J R Cole, C G McCreight, G Townend, H H C Withers, H Rew, C H B Rodham, R G S Hobbs, K J MacIntyre, D H Nott, K M Wright.

RAF: G M Ievers, G R Wright, J R H Pott, R D Cotton, N H White, R V M Odbert, G R A Elsmie, W V M McKechnie, G R Beamish (capt), J W H Kirk, G E S Williams, J Beaumont, D R Gibbs, R L Wallace, A C Hall.

1931   *Army v Navy:* E W F de V Hunt, L J Harris (RE), A L Novis (capt), J M Rice-Evans, A G Martin (SWB), J R Cole, F W Simpson (RE), H Rew, H H C Withers, C L Troop (DWR), R G S Hobbs, E P Sewell (Northamptonshire Regt), E H Sadler (RCS), B W Reynolds (DWR), G Taylor (West Yorkshire Regt).

Navy: C G Gosling (capt), R J F Lane, D St Clair Ford, A E Hargrave, W H Wood, C B Hinde, C Webster, N L Evans, W Paddon, J W Forrest, C Webb, C M Morrell, E H Harding, R S Hawkins, C Light.

Army v RAF: E W de V Hunt, E Bentley (DWR), C C Beaty-Pownall (Leicestershire Regt), J M Rice-Evans, A G Martin, G G J Fenton (RA), C C McCreight, H Rew, H H C Withers, C L Troop, R G S Hobbs, G W Annesley (DWR), E H Sadler, B W Reynolds, G Taylor.

RAF: G M Ievers, N Baunt, F S Hodder, P B Coote, C P Robinson, D R S Bader, G R A Elsmie, A C Wallace, W Reynolds, A E Simmons, H A Constantine, G E S Williams, T N Coslett, Beamish, Christie.

1932   *Army v Navy:* S T A Radcliffe (RE), A L Novis (capt), E W de V Hunt, A W Tyler (RA), J E Crawford (RE), J R Cole, F W Simpson, C L Troop, E H Sadler, A Vaughan-Jones (RA), T H Clarke (Gloucestershire Regt), R G S Hobbs, D A Kendrew (Leicestershire Regt), H H C Withers, H Rew.

Navy: R E Toop, H J F Lane, D St Clair Ford, J S Walsham, T S Lee, W Elliott, C Webster, G C M Falla, J J Casement, C M Morrell, C Webb, J D V Forrest (capt), N L Evans, W Paddon, E Light.

Army v RAF: S T A Radcliffe, A L Novis (capt), E W de V Hunt, A W Tyler, J A Crawford, J R Cole, F W Simpson, H Rew, H H C Withers, C L Troop, R G J Hobbs, T H Clarke, F C Jackson (Indian Medical Service), E H Sadler, H J Sayers (RA).

RAF: R N McKearn, T A B Perselles, P B Coote, S D Slocum, F S Hodder, S Williams, R C M Collard, C St J Beamish, G E Valentine, A E Simmonds, J Lewis, H A Constantine, E A Collyns, G E S Williams, G R Beamish (capt).

1933   *Army v Navy:* S T A Radcliffe, A L Novis (capt), A J Croston (RE), A W Tyler, J A Crawford, J R Cole, F W Simpson, D A Kendrew, V J Pike (R Army Chaplains' Dept), C L Troop, H Rew, A Boast (Welsh Guards), E H Sadler, H J Sayers, P G Hobbs.

Navy: C G Gosling, P D Lewis, J S Walsham, J C Benson, J P Kirkby, W Elliot, C Webster, N L Evans, W Paddon, C Webb, R C Harry (capt), R S Hawkins, T G P Crick, J K Watkins, E G Nixon.

Army v RAF: S T A Radcliffe, A L Novis (capt), A W Tyler, A J Croston, J A Crawford, J R Cole, G J Dean (RTC), D A

Kendrew, V J Pike, H Rew, A Boast, P G Hobbs, C L Troop, G Taylor, E H Sadler.

RAF: R N McKern, H W Mermagen, H J F Le Good, R H A Leigh, P B Coote, S Williams, G R A Elsmie, C Beamish, G E Valentine, J S W Bignal, A L Franks, C G R Lewis, C R Davies, G Beamish (capt), G E Ford.

1934   *Army v Navy:* S T A Radcliffe, E R M Bowerman (East Yorkshire Regt), D H D Courtenay (RTC), E J Unwin (Middlesex Regt), J A Crawford, C C McCreight (capt), G J Dean, H J Sayers, A Boast, P G Hobbs, A J A Watson (Queen's Royal Regt), D A Kendrew, L R Morgan (RAMC), V J Pike, H Rew.

Navy: C G Gosling, P Lewis, J H Bailey, J S W Walsham, J P Kirkby, W Elliot, G H B N Hunter, R J L Hammond, R J H Stephens, J K Watkins, C Webb, J W Forrest, H S Doggett, D J Tarr, T G P Crick (capt).

Army v RAF: S T A Radcliffe, B T V Cowey (Welch Regt), D H D Courtenay, E J Unwin, J A Crawford, C C McCreight (capt), G J Dean, H J Sayers, A Boast, P G Hobbs, A J A Watson, D A Kendrew, R L Morgan, G C Reeves (RTC), H Rew.

RAF: R N McKearn, D Finlay, N G Mulholland, J S McLean, B V Robinson, W A K Igoe, J L Barker, R H S McConnell, C Lewis, J O Holland, L W V Jennens, C E St J Beamish, R H Waterhouse, W V Reynolds, J S Bignal.

1935   *Army v Navy:* S T A Radcliffe, B T V Cowey, E J Unwin, F W Simpson, A L Novis (capt), J R Cole, G J Dean, H H J Sayers, K J McIntyre, P G Hobbs, F W Watson, D A Kendrew, F W Whitcombe (RE), A Boast, I Wilcox (Welsh Guards).

Navy: C G Gosling, H J F Lane, J H Bailey, G M Sladen, G M Wheadon, J S W Walshem, S T S V Welch, R J L Hammond, G P Darling, J K Watkins, C Webb, J W Forrest (capt), E G Nixon, D J Tarr, J W Linton.

Army v RAF: S T A Radcliffe, A L Novis (capt), F W Simpson, E J Unwin, J A Crawford, J R Cole, G T Dean, V J Pike, K J McIntyre, H M J Sayers, P G Hobbs, A J A Watson, F W Whitcombe, A Boast, I Wilcox.

RAF: P W Ashton, J M Thompson, S G Walker, W G A Church, W R Morgan, G A Walker, J L Barker, J O Holland, J S Wilson, W Gascoigne, H J Irens, C Beamish (capt), J S Bignall, W V Reynolds, R H Waterhouse.

1936   *Army v Navy:* S I Howard-Jones (RMC), J R Rawlence (RE), E J Unwin, R Leyland (Army Ed Corps), B E W McCall (Welch Regt), J R Cole, G J Dean, P G Hobbs, C L Melville (Black

Watch), H H J Sayers, A J A Watson, D A Kendrew (capt), A Boast, I Wilcox, C R Owen (Welch Regt).

Navy: C R Knapman, R Hurden, B Marsh, A T Darley, M J P Walters, J S W Walsham (capt), S T S V Welch, E A Hamilton-Hill, R J L Hammond, J K Watkins, N L Evans, C Webb, R S Hawkins, D N D Callaghan, I G Aylen.

Army v RAF: S I Howard-Jones, J R Rawlence, J H Marriott (Leicestershire Regt), R Leyland, E J Unwin, H P L Glass (Sherwood Foresters), G J Dean (capt), G H Whitty (R West Kent Regt), C L Melville, I S Graham (Seaforth Highlanders), W M Inglis (RE), C O'N Wallis (East Surrey Regt), G R Owen, I Wilcox, W Phillips (Welsh Guards).

RAF: P W Ashton, K B B Cross, D M Strong, J M Thompson, D M H Craven, G A Walker, J L Barker, J O Holland, T N Coslett, W Gascoigne, C E St J Beamish (capt), C W Sheppard, M R H White, W V Reynolds, G Geaves.

1937 *Army v Navy:* S I Howard-Jones, E J Unwin, R Leyland, J H Marriott, E R M Bowerman, F J Reynolds (DWR), Dean (capt), H H J Sayers, C L Melville, J H H Whitty C O'N Wallis, A J A Watson, A Boast, C E Owen, W M Inglis.

Navy: J E Stevens, R Hurden, K D'O Nott, B M Goldsworthy, R S Casement, W Elliot (capt), E B Talbot, H C Lyddon, G P Darling, R J L Hammond, C Webb, N L Evans, I G Aylen, D N Callaghan, R G Stovell.

Army v RAF: S I Howard-Jones, E R M Bowerman, H P L Glass, R Leyland, J H Marriott, F J Reynolds, G J Dean (capt), J H Bowman (Coldstream Guards), G Taylor, J H H Whitty, C L Melville, H H J Sayers, A Boast, C R Owen, W M Inglis.

RAF: E I Parsons, P L Halford, A V Rogers, K B B Cross, J M Thompson, W G Moseby, R H Spencer, J O Holland, P S Hutchinson, W F Gascoigne, J A Roncoroni, C W Sheppard, Waterhouse, L Fox, H D Jones.

1938 *Army v Navy:* C F Grieve (DWR), E J Unwin, R Leyland, V H Brookes (Indian Army), F J V Ford (Welch Regt), J Harrison (DWR), G J Dean (capt), A E Allan (Army Dental Corps), C L Melville, H J M Sayers, V F D Tarrant (Gloucestershire Regt), C O'N Wallis, F J L Carey (RA), J Evans (KORR), W M Inglis.

Navy: T G C Jameson, J B Kirkby, A L S Hogg, B M Goldsworthy, W B Whitworth, G W Vavasour, D T Wickham, J K Watkins, R J L Hammond, W H Crawford, H Attwood, H C Lyddon, R G Stovell, D N Callaghan, N L Evans (capt).

Army v RAF: C F Grieve, E J Unwin, R Leyland, J Harrison,

F J V Ford, F J Reynolds, G J Dean (capt), A E Allan, C L Melville, H J M Sayers, V F D Tarrant, C O'N Wallis, F J L Carey, J Evans, W M Inglis.

RAF: E I Parsons, W G Moseby, S J D Robinson, J M Thompson, D M H Craven, G A Walker (capt), J O Sowerbutts, J O Holland, C H Beamish, J S Wilson, J A Roncoroni, R R McPherson, C E St J Beamish, L Fox, A E Simmons.

1939 *Army v Navy:* R N B Holmes (RE), E J Unwin, R Leyland, J Delaney (Welch Regt), D C Bovis (RA), H Ibbitson (Welch Regt), A M Champion (Welch Regt), E W Farmer (Gloucestershire Regt), Owen, N W Ramsay (RE), V F D Tarrant, C L Melville, A J A Arengo-Jones (Gloucestershire Regt), A E Allan, H J M Sayers (capt).

Navy: W J Parker, J S Bridger, G Clayton-Greene, M G MacLeod, J P Kirkby, G W Vavasour (capt), D R de Vere Stacpoole, R G Stovell, E R Bridges, D O B Taylor, H C Lyddon, J S Daglish, J K Watkins, R J L Hammond, W H Crawford.

Army v RAF: R N B Holmes, F J V Ford, R Leyland, J Harrison, D C Bevis, H Ibbitson, J L Chambers (RASC), E W Farmer, C R Owen, J L Melville (Queen's Own Cameron Highlanders), F J Carey, C L Melville, A J A Arengo-Jones, R L France (RE), H J M Sayers (capt).

RAF: E I Parsons, T B Mahoney, G D Garvin, A V Rogers, D C Cobden, G A Walker (capt), T Malmforth, T F T Chapman, L Fox, K P English, H J Irens, J A Roncoroni, W G Gascoigne, C H Beamish, J O Holland.

1946 *Army v Navy:* E Ward (Lancashire Fus), J A Gregory (RAMC), C W Drummond (KOSB), W H Munro (RCS), J R S Innes (RAMC), C R Bruce (RA) (capt), K H S Wilson (R Sussex), E Evans (RA), F C Hill (CMP), A G Horsell (RA), J Kirk (RAMC), D V Phillips (RAC), W R Priest (APTC), R M Fleming (RA), D F White (Northamptonshire Regt).

Navy: G Williams, A E Murray, I Williams, S Peel, W D McLennan, E L Hughes, W K T Moore, R Aitken, H O Evington, M R Neely, J B Doherty, J R C Matthews, D B Vaughan, R J Hammond (capt), N A Waller.

Army v RAF: E Ward, J A Gregory, W H Munro, J R S Innes, T G H Jackson (RCS), C R Bruce (capt), K H S Wilson, E Evans, F C Hill, A G Horsell, J Kirk, D V Phillips, W R Priest, R M Fleming, D F White.

RAF: R H Lloyd-Davies, P H Davies, I Davies, D Parker, S F Dangerfield, M R Channer, P W Sykes, D Bolesworth, C G Gilthorpe (capt), P Plumpton, H P Hughes, E A Styles, L Manfield, C H Beamish, E L Horsfall.

1947   *Army v RAF:* S T J Walter (RA), H J Houghton (RAMC), J Matthews (RAMC), H Thomas (APTC), G Stobart (Indian Army), W O Jones (REME), K H S Wilson (capt), J K Williams (RCS), A E P Joy (REME), F H Coutts (KOSB), A C Burcher (Corps of Royal Military Police), T L Richardson (RCS), D D Valentine (KOSB), P J Martin (SWB), D F White.

RAF: R H Lloyd-Davies, E C K Douglas, A C Towell, C D McIver, Dangerfield, M E Channer, P W Sykes, I P D Skepton, C H Beamish (capt), E L Horsfall, A H Burcombe, K J D Dunlop, T J Pitcairn-Hill, F W Higginson, R G Tilbury.

Army v Navy: S I Howard-Jones (RTR), T Danby (RAOC), J Matthews, W O Jones, G Stobart, H Thomas, K H S Wilson (capt), J K Williams, A E P Joy, G C Mackie (RAMC), J T Bartlett (RE), F H Coutts, D D Valentine, P J Martin, D F White.

Navy: S Peel, W D McLennan, F G Brown, J L Miller, T T Lewis, T C Barras, R F G Meadows, J K Morrison, C R Ransome, R Aitken, P Goodman, D B Vaughan, G R D'A Hosking, A H Dell, D. Carnelly.

1948   *Army v Navy:* S T J Walter, T G H Jackson, J Matthews, A Cameron (RA), I S Gloag (RCS), G R Davies (RCS), K H S Wilson (capt), G C Mackie, J R Phillips (RE), D Bevan (Gloucestershire Regt), F H Coutts, D S Rowlands (RAMC), A G M Watt (RAMC), J K Williams, D F White.

Navy: J A G Mares, T T Lewin, S D Walsh, N O Bennett, E J Horlick, T C Barras, J Burges, W G Harrison, C R Ransome, R R Whalley, G R D'A Hosking, A M Power, D B Vaughan (capt), A Meredith, E P B Sindery.

Army v RAF: J M H Roberts (Welsh Guards), T G H Jackson, J Matthews, A Cameron, J V Smith (Gloucestershire Regt), G Davies, K H S Wilson (capt), J K Williams, G C Mackie, J R Phillips, F H Coutts, D Bevan, A G M Watt, B A Neale (RA), D F White.

RAF: A A Smailes, R G Crerar, G D McIver, L B Cannell, E C K Douglas, I J M Lumsden, W T H Hay, A C Blythe, F W Higginson, W E Thompson, R Stirling, A H Burcombe, E L Horsfall, R G H Weighill (capt), B B Exley.

1949   *Army v Navy:* J M H Roberts, T G H Jackson, A Cameron, P B Reeves (RCS), D W C Smith (RAMC), N M Hall (RCS), D W Shuttleworth (DWR), R Cross (RCS), T R Marshall

(RCS), P M Young (RAMC), B A Neale, F H Coutts (capt), J D Clancy (RAEC), J W Hall (RCS), P R B Mitchell (RASC).

Navy: A C Simmons, T B Norman, T K M Kirby, M C Thomas, R M Holgate, T C Barras, R Thomas, D P W Kelly, M Shirley, P B Sindery, A Meredith, G R D'A Hosking (capt), B P Elvey, C R Ransome, F H Bristowe.

Army v RAF: J M H Roberts, A Roche (RAEC), A Cameron, P B Reeves, W D C Smith, N M Hall, D W Shuttleworth, R Cross, T R Marshall, P M Young, B A Neale, F H Coutts (capt), J D Clancy, J Hall, P R B Mitchell.

RAF: A A Smailes, R G Crerar, I J M Lumsden, R J H Uprichard, R H Ross, G R Tucker, W T H Hay, H K Rees, R G H Weighill, E L Horsfall, E E Rossiter, G G Farley, R Stirling, R Clark, C M Browse.

1950   *Army v Navy:* J M H Roberts, D M Scott (King's Royal Rifle Corps), G C Phipps (R Hampshire Regt), P B Reeves, J P Hyde (Northamptonshire Regt), E M P Hardy (DWR), D W Shuttleworth, R Cross, G G Roche (RE), R F Dorey (R Hampshire Regt), B A Neale, F H Coutts (capt), J L Baume (R Northumberland Fus), J E Keeling (RADC), A G C Jones (RE).

Navy: V A Smith, W J Glastonbury, M C Thomas, B Lewis-Jones, J L Miller, G G Bellamy, J A F Lawson, J P England, H E Jones, D P W Kelly, B P Elvey, D Wilkins, F H Bristowe, A A Craigen, R Aitken.

Army v RAF: J M H Roberts, D M Scott, G C Phipps, P B Reeves, J P Hyde, E M P Hardy, D W Shuttleworth, R Cross, D E Iles (DWR), Dorey, Neale, F H Coutts (capt), J L Baume, J H Keeling, A G C Jones.

RAF: A A Smailes, B P Young, R D Austen-Smith, R G H Uprichard, D H Philips, T L Roberts, W T H Hay, S D Little, R G H Weighill, H K Rees, E E Rossiter, S T H Wright, R V Stirling, A R Rennie, T V Buckthought.

1951   *Army v Navy:* J M H Roberts (capt), T G H Jackson, A E Asquith (RA), W C Major (Welch Regt), J P Hyde, E M P Hardy, D W Shuttleworth, B J B Hazel (RAEC), P J Taylor (DWR), P Batten (14/20 King's Hussars), I Zaidman (RAOC), B A Neale, J L Baume, F R Beringer (RE), A G C Jones.

Navy: F N Fenner, B M Gray, B Lewis-Jones, M L Thomas (capt), R M Holgate, T K M Kirby, J A F Lawson, A Meredith, J McQuade, R Aitken, D T Wilkins, G Stride, J H F Hall, P B Sindery, W L Copley.

Army v RAF: J M H Roberts (capt), W C Major, A B Edwards

(RAEC), D M Scott, J P Hyde, E M P Hardy, D W Shuttleworth, P Batten, P J Taylor, D S Gilbert-Smith (DWR), I Zaidman, B A Neale, B J B Hazel, F R Beringer, A G C Jones.

RAF: A A Smailes, D M Baker, K J Dalgleish, G John, D M Rose, R J H Uprichard, W T H Hay, R E Syrett, R G H Weighill (capt), S D Little, R H Williams, E E Rossiter, S T H Wright, F W Higginson, R V Stirling.

1952 *Army v Navy:* J M H Roberts (capt), G C Phipps, J Broome (RAOC), A B Edwards, A G I Wood (RCS), E M P Hardy, D W Shuttleworth, D S Gilbert-Smith, D F Bland (REME), Dorey, W P Black (RAMC), B A Neale, S G Owen (REME), W K Phillips (REME), B J B Hazel.

Navy: F N Fenner, B M Gray, F J Ryder, R M Holgate, R J Horlick, R A Slater, H P Jones, P B Sindery, D B Vaughan, D P W Kelly, D T Wilkins (capt), J Jenkins, W O Williams, J McQuade, D J Mather.

Army v RAF: J M H Roberts (capt), G C Phipps, J Broome, A B Edwards, A G I Wood, E M P Hardy, D W Shuttleworth, D S Gilbert-Smith, D F Bland, R F Dorey, W P Black, B A Neale, S G Owen, W K Phillips, B J B Hazel.

RAF: A A Smailes, T H Lodwig, J Syme, K R MacDonald, G M Griffiths, M R Channer, D C Wilcox, J Greenwood, R H G Weighill (capt), P S Collingridge, P G Yarrenton, R H Williams, R V Stirling, A H Rennie, P O'K Plumpton.

1953 *Army v Navy:* I H M Thomson (RCS), T J Brewer (RCS), D R Rees (RCS), A B Edwards, R MacDonald (RAMC), J Broome, D W Shuttleworth, D F Bland, W P Black, A M Tippett (Rifle Brigade), R J Robins (RCS), B A Neale (capt), J L Baume, F R Beringer, S G Owen.

Navy: A P Harries, R M Holgate, J Thomas, R A Slater, W J Glastonbury, T E Davies, J B Wallace, G E R Ridd, D B Vaughan (capt), P R Sindery, D T Wilkins, A R Valentine, D R Main, K James, W O Williams.

Army v RAF: I H M Thomson, T J Brewer, J Broome, A B Edwards, R MacDonald, D F Rees, D W Shuttleworth, D F Bland, W P Black, A M Tippett, H G Greatwood (East Surrey Regt), B A Neale (capt), J L Baume, F R Beringer, T Taylor (RAMC).

RAF: A J Priddy, G Rowlands, T R Beatson, I D Farmer-Wright, V R Tindall, M R Channer, Lloyd-Williams, A J Herbert, P S Collingridge, J Greenwood, L Williams, P G Yarrenton (capt), C David, B J Lane, R V Stirling.

1954 *Army v Navy:* A B Edwards, J S Swan (REME), S A Lowden (RA), J M D Chapman (RA), R C Bazley (RE), B Gabbitas (RCS), P J Michell (Mons OCTU), R Higgins (RCS), D M Turner (Queen's Own R West Kent Regt), A M Tippett, R W D Marques (RE), J H Hancock (REME), H F McLeod (R Scots Greys), F R Beringer (capt), D Watchorne (RAMC).
Navy: W J Glastonbury, R F P Carne, R A Slater, M A Pearey, R M Holgate, C G Bellamy, J B Wallace, D G E Saunders, J P England (capt), A R Valentine, I J Jenkins, W L Copley, D R Main, R J Carter, P Badcock.
Army v RAF: A B Edwards, J S Swan, P Jackson (RCS), W J Boston (RCS), R C Bazley, B Gabbitas, R Evans (RCS), R Higgins, D M Turner, A R McCrae (RCS), R W D Marques, J H Hancock, H F McLeod, F R Beringer (capt), D Watchorne.
RAF: A A Smailes, D J McPherson, B Jones, D T Williams, J Bootham, T R Beatson, A W Black, R V Stirling, M U Hughes, C David, P G Yarrenton, J Sewell, J C Collard, G L A Head, D G Naylor.

1955 *Army v Navy:* A B Edwards (capt), D F Rees, P Jackson, B Gabbitas, R C Bazley, E M P Hardy, D W Shuttleworth, J Leleu (Parachute Regt), H G Greatwood, P Lysaght (RA), J R Owen (RAMC), J H Hancock, H F McLeod, N S Bruce (RAOC), P D Cleaver (REME).
Navy: H J Mainwaring, A S Bater, Pearey, S R Bemrose, R F P Carne, R McMenemy, H Redrobe, N R M Moir (capt), A R Valentine, I J Jenkins, W L Copley, J J Rainforth, G P Thomas, R G Waldron, F A Prosser.
Army v RAF: A B Edwards (capt), J Regan (RAMC), P Jackson, S A Lowden, R C Bazley, B Gabbitas, R Evans, J Leleu, H G Greatwood, P Lysaght, J R Owen, J H Hancock, H F McLeod, N S Bruce, D Watchorne.
RAF: W J C Paterson, B M Griffiths, B Howard, M Sullivan. R Blair, M R Channer, R I Shuttleworth, J Collard, T Bleasedale (capt), P S Collingridge, J Sewell, P G Yarrenton, D B Vaughan, M N Munnoch, A D Bain.

1956 *Army v Navy:* A B Edwards, I Southward (RA), T Thomas (RA), M Hartley (RE), J Regan (RAMC), K J F Scotland (RCS), D W Shuttleworth (capt), T G A H Peart (RA), K R F Bearne (RE), D S Gilbert-Smith, H M Inglis (RA), E J S Michie (RE), N S Bruce, R Roe (RAChD), W E Townsend (RAEC).
Navy: H J Mainwaring, R F P Carne, S R G Bemrose, M A Pearey, B J Jones, J N G Davidson, J A T Rodd, F A Prosser,

A R Valentine (capt), J W Clements, I J Jenkins, W L Copley, J Jacobsen, G P Thomas, R G Waldron.

Army v RAF: A B Edwards, I Southward, M Hartley, C S Outram (RA) J Regan, K J F Scotland, D W Shuttleworth (capt), T G A H Peart, K R F Bearne, D S Gilbert-Smith, H M Inglis, E J S Michie, N S Bruce, R Roe, M L Bellow (RASC).

RAF: R A Collinge, G M Sullivan, B Howard, A Davies, S Willcox, T R Beatson, R I Shuttleworth, J Collard, I A A MacGregor, P S Collingridge, T Bleasdale, P G Yarrenton, A D Bain, N M Munnoch, G P Vaughan.

1957 *Army v Navy:* J G M W Murphy (RAChD), I Southward, R Chisnall (RA), A Godson (RCS), R Moyle (REME), K J F Scotland, J Hughes (REME), H Roddan (RE), H G Greatwood, H Morgan (REME), E J S Michie, H M Inglis (capt), N S Bruce, R Roe, N C G Raffle (RFE).

Navy: H J Mainwaring, S R Bemrose, G H Waddell, B Jones, J B Glasson, J N G Davidson, Rodd, Clements, T C Jones, Prosser, Jenkins, D T Wilkins (capt), R Titchen, Thomas, R E Morgan.

Army v RAF: J G M W Murphy, I Southward, R Chisnall, A Godson, R Moyle, K J F Scotland, J Hughes, H Roddan, T G A H Peart, H Morgan, H G Greatwood, H M Inglis (capt), N S Bruce, R Roe, N C G Raffle.

RAF: D Rutherford, J Challinor, J N Blake, D G Simmonds, E R Sanstrom, K H L Richards, L G Kapseras, M M Smith, J B Friebe, R J Dufty, P G Yarrenton, D W Neate, A M Bain, H J Pugh, G P Vaughan (capt).

1958 *Army v Navy:* J G Willcox (East Lancs Regt), R Chisnall, P R G Williams (Welsh Guards), A Godson, R J Moyle, K McLean (RAMC), J Scourfield (RAMC), H L J Morgan, G L B Edgecombe (R East Kent Regt), D S Gilbert-Smith, H G Greatwood, M J Hutt (REME), A F Ricketts (REME), N C G Raffle, R Lightfoot (RAMC).

Navy: H J Mainwaring, J B Glasson, D Dixon, P Gaunt, D I E Bebb, T Hodgson, S J S Clarke, R Titchen, T Jones, F A Prosser, R Hollick, D T Wilkins (capt), J Highton, G T Scott, C Mason.

Army v RAF: J G Willcox, R Chisnall, B Saville (DWR), A Godson, R J Moyle, K McLean, D W Shuttleworth, H J Morgan, G L B Edgecombe, D S Gilbert-Smith, H G Greatwood (capt), R E Young (REME), A F Ricketts, N C G Raffle, R Lightfoot.

RAF: D Rutherford, E R Sanstrom, M R Wade, M J Price, F Carlton, H L Richards, D O Brace, D L Davies, P Rowlands, L H Walker, R G Long, Neate, D H Murphy, E J Jones, G J Dod.

1959 *Army v Navy:* R Davies (RA), M R Handfield-Jones (RE), J J McPartlin (RA), A Thomas (RASC), R J Moyle, G Blackett (RCS), P J Davies (DWR), H McI Paterson (RCS), J Scroby (DWR), S J Purdy (RAEC), H G Greatwood, S R Arnold (DWR), N C G Raffle, N S Bruce (capt), R Lightfoot.

Navy: H J Mainwaring, D B Dixon, M A Pearey, J T Hodgson, D P Gaunt, R A W Sharp, N Bickford, Prosser, J R Marchant, A R Godfrey, D G Wixon, T Jones, Titchen, G P Thomas, G T Scott.

Army v RAF: R Davies, A Thomas, McPartlin, A Whitehorn (RE), D A Williams (RCS), G Blackett, P Davies, S J Purdy, J Scroby, E Thomas (RASC), H G Greatwood, S R Arnold, N S Bruce (capt), N C G Raffle, H O Godwin (R Leicestershire Regt).

RAF: B B Wright, W Burgess, A J Rhodes, D W Phelps, R O Rawson, P E Mettler, D G Brace (capt), P E McGovan, A P Close, L R Evans, G J A Head, R G Long, P W Watson, E Jones, J M Rose.

1960 *Army v Navy:* P V Crooks (REME), R J N Leonard (RE), M R Handfield-Jones, D W A Rosser (RAEC), D A Williams, G Sharp (RCS), P Davies, G D Parker (RAEC), G J B Edgecombe, S J Purdy, M J Campbell-Lamerton (DWR), G W Payne (RE), N S Bruce, H O Godwin, N C G Raffle (capt).

Navy: J R Fullerton, J D Casey, M A Pearey, P T Tyrell, P L Gaunt, G C Derry, J A T Rodd, K I Ross, T Jones, C S Stafford, A R Godfrey, D G Wixon, T L Scott, G P Thomas (capt), J E Highton.

Army v RAF: P V Crooks, R J M Leonard, M R Handfield-Jones, D W A Rosser, D A Williams, G Sharp, R B Shillinglaw (KOSB), S D Parker, G J B Edgecombe, S J Purdy, M J Campbell-Lamerton, M A O'Flaherty (RTR), H O Godwin, N C G Raffle, N S Bruce.

RAF: R J Randall, W Burgess, J S Roblin, P E Mettler, P W Duignan, G W Hackett, D O'Neill, I R Evans, L H Jenkins, P E McGovan, S K Mulligan, A P Close, D H Murphy, R Horwood, P W Watson.

1961 *Army v Navy:* P V Crooks, M H S Heath (RE), D W A Rosser, M R Handfield-Jones, R J Moyle, G Sharp, R Braybrooke (RE), V R Marriott (RAEC), C Renilson (DWR), G D Parker, G W

Payne, M J Campbell-Lamerton, E W Davies (RASC), Bruce (capt), J G Vaux (RE).

Navy: H S Cormack, J D Casey, M A Pearey, P T Tyrell, R D Sinclair, P Francis, J A T Rodd, S G Palmer, B W Goodwin, A P Godfrey, C S Stafford, T Jones, F S Owen, G P Thomas, J E Highton.

Army v RAF: P V Crooks, M H S Heath, D W A Rosser, M R Handfield-Jones, R J Moyle, G Sharp, R Braybrooke, G J B Edgecombe, C Renilson, G D Parker, G W Payne, P H Oulton (Cheshire Regt), J D MacDonald (KOSB), N S Bruce (capt), J G Vaux.

RAF: H J C Brown, C Lewis, J A Roblin, M C Greenhough, R Glastonbury, A Murphy, M Booth, B E Morgan, L H Jenkins, K E Lappin, R King, K J Wilson, A Foster, P Thomas, D Murphy (capt).

1962 *Army v Navy:* P V Crooks, M H S Heath, D W A Rosser, M R Handfield-Jones, R J Moyle, I P Reid (DWR), F Braybrooke, V R Marriott, H G Greatwood (capt), T J Evans (REME), P H Oulton, M J Campbell-Lamerton, J G Vaux, N S Bruce, E A Richards (RAOC).

Navy: H S Cormack, J D Casey, G C Derry, C Gibson, R Sinclair, J Harries, B Hay, W E Rothwell, S G Palmer, R W Hamilton, C S Stafford, T Jones (capt, J Jacobsen, G P Thomas, H Sever.

Army v RAF: P V Crooks, M H S Heath, D W A Rosser, M R Handfield-Jones, R J Moyle, R M Taylor (RAOC), F Braybrooke, V R Marriott, H G Greatwood, D Hearn (Welsh Guards), J B B Cockcroft (Welsh Guards), M J Campbell-Lamerton, J G Vaux, N S Bruce, E A Richards.

RAF: A John, R Glastonbury, H J C Brown, J Keepe, D Harries, C Williams, M Booth, A Wright, L H Jenkins (capt), J V McCarthy, S K Mulligan, R S Glazsher, D Murphy, P Thomas, K J Wilson.

1963 *Army v Navy:* P V Crooks, H Blinkhorn (RAOC), M R Handfield-Jones, T Waquabaca (DWR), R J Moyle, I P Reid, F Braybrooke, C A Lees (Landcashire Regt), G A Stone (REME), R M Stancombe (RE), J M Jones (RA), M J Campbell-Lamerton, J G Vaux, N S Bruce, R Roe (capt).

Navy: H S Cormack, D J R Brown, C G Gibson, P T Tyrell, I F Duckworth, P Francis, M A Pearey, A R Godfrey, W E Rothwell, F A C Prosser, P Cantelo, G D Thorpe, K M Heaton, T J Scott, T E Highton.

Army v RAF: W H F Stevens (R Rampshire Regt), C P Simpson (RMA), M R Handfield-Jones, R J Moyle, H Blinkhorn, I P Reid F Braybrooke, C A Lees, G A Stone, R Eastwood (RAPC), J Jones, M J Campbell-Lamerton, E A Richards, N S Bruce, R Roe.

RAF: G A John, Harries, J D M Greenhow, J J C Brown, S F Leete, R H Palin, M J Dymond, K J H Mallett, L H Jenkins (capt), Morgan, Mulligan, R S Glazsher, K G Wilson, D Dibiase, M J D Steer.

1964 *Army v RAF:* R T Brown (RMA), H Blinkhorn, M R Handfield-Jones, T Waquabaca, C G Edwards (DWR), I P Reid, R Braybrooke, M S Friend (Devonshire and Dorset Regt), R M Stancombe, C Guthrie (Welsh Guards), P Eastwood, M J Campbell-Lamerton (capt), J D MacDonald (RASC), N S Bruce, R D H Bryce (RE).

RAF: F W Burns, P A Kelly, H J C Brown, J Keepe, D G Harries, R H Palin, M J Dymond, B E Morgan, L H Jenkins (capt), K J Mallett, R S Glazsher, S K Mulligan, R Elwig, M L Berry, M J D Steer.

Army v Navy: R T Brown, C G A Edwards, M R Handfield-Jones, T Waquabaca, I L Chapman (RMA), I P Reid, R Braybrooke, M S Friend, R M Stancombe, C Guthrie, P Eastwood, M J Campbell-Lamerton (capt), T A Moroney (RAMC), N S Bruce, R D H Bryce.

Navy: P L Golding, J R Hunter, S Newsom, P Thomas, I F Duckworth, J C Gibson, R Bradley, A R Godfrey (capt), S Palmer, W E Rothwell, T Jones, C Stafford, B W Goodwin, T Scott, C S Sever.

1965 *Army v RAF:* F A Williams (RA), T K Colgate (RAEC), I P Reid, C G Edwards (DWR), C P Simpson (now R Anglian Regt), G Campbell (RE), I A Gordon (Cameronians), R D H Bryce, E Barker (RA), N Kirk (RA), P A Eastwood, M J Campbell-Lamerton (capt), J P Fisher (RADC), R M Stancombe, M S Friend,

RAF: R H Palin, W E Dundon, W J Bevan, H J C Brown (capt), P B Glover, E J Loud, R Hill, J R Mace, M L Berry, M J D Steer, M J C Marson, G J Carter, R J J Coral, A C Thomas, L Samuel.

Army v Navy: M J Rose (RTR), T K Colgate, G Lougher (RAEC), C G J Edwards, C P Simpson, I P Reid, R Braybrooke, R D H Bryce, E Barker, MacDonald, Campbell-Lamerton (capt), Eastwood, J P Fisher, R M Stancombe, M S Friend.

Navy: B D Warn, G C Eustace, S J B Newsom, G Jones, R M Roberts, J D St John Ainslie, B Hay, B W Goodwin, J Hinton, H Sever, A M Davis, T Jones, G R Montgomery, D R A Lloyd Edwards, K A Lavelle.

1966 *Army v Navy:* J D Drummond (RHF), D W Saunders (RE), D Lapidus (RCT), C G J Edwards, D F McF Hathorn (Cameronians), I P Reid, D W Thomas (Welch Regt), T A Moroney, R D H Bryce, J D MacDonald, M J Campbell-Lamerton (capt), P A Eastwood, J P Fisher, A D Hoon (RE), P A D Griffiths (RTR).

Navy: P L Golding, J J Pearson, J C Gibson, D Brown, D E Hambrook, J St John Ainslie, B Hay, B W Goodwin, T L Scott, H Sever, D M Davis (capt), P Masterton-Smith, A R Godfrey, K A Lavelle, R A Hallett.

Army v RAF: J D Drummond, D M F Hathorn, C G J Edwards, D Lapidus, D W Saunders, D Elsbury (Welch Regt), D W Thomas, T A Moroney, P W D de Sausmarez (Coldstream Guards), J D MacDonald, M J Campbell-Lamerton (capt), P A Eastwood, J P Fisher, A D Hoon, P Gilbert (RMA).

RAF: R H Palin, I J A Parsons, A Jones, R Stevenson, P B Glover, M D G Wilkinson, R Hill, E J M Thomas E B Matthews, B Latton, M J C Marson, P J Larter, M J Cunningham, A C Thomas, J V McCarthy.

1967 *Army v Navy:* I J A Lowis (KOSB), J S A Jeffray (RMA), G B L Campbell (RE), C G J Edwards, M J C L Smith (Parachute Regt), I P Reid, R Braybrooke, J D MacDonald, N S Bruce, R D H Bryce, P A Eastwood, L Martin (RE), C G Bale (RAMC), A D Hoon, J P Fisher (capt).

Navy: P McN Cunningham, J J Pearson, S J B Newsom, J C Gibson, J D Casey, C R Tuffley, B Hay, A Holt, T A Gatehouse, B W Goodwin, A M Davis (capt), I R Wilson, R T Lane, A P Hallett, A R Godfrey.

Army v RAF: M J Rose (RTR), J S A Jeffray, D S Boyle (Parachute Regt), C G J Edwards, D M Hathorn, G B L Campbell, R Braybrooke, J D MacDonald, N S Bruce, R D H Bryce, P A Eastwood, L Martin, C G Bale, A D Hoon, J P Fisher (capt).

RAF: Allcorn, P B Glover, A Jones, W J Ross-Jones, W C G Steele, W J Beven, R Hill, E R Norris, A B Stephens, E Thomas (capt), D A Hanna, L V Palmer, R Straughton, L Samuels, R Farr.

1968 *Army v RAF:* C P Simpson, H B W Barstow (Queen's Regt), N B Thomas (RAEC), D S Boyle, J C A Jeffray, D J Treadwell

(RTR), D Spawforth (REME), T A Moroney, N S Bruce, D T Bowen (Welsh Guards), P A Eastwood, L M Martin, J P Fisher (capt), A D Hoon, G D Lilley (RCT).

RAF: E J Black, W C C Steele, A Doherty, G P Frankcom, W J Bevan, C Hilliker, M Dymond, C R Ingram, D J Davies, P Ray, P J Larter, D A Hanna, C Farr, L V Palmer, D J Payne.

Army v Navy: C P Simpson, T Waquabaca, C G J Edwards, D S Boyle, N B Thomas, D J Treadwell, R V Kelly (RMA), R D H Bryce, N S Bruce (capt), D T Bowen, P A Eastwood, M G Molloy (RAMC), C J W Gilbert (DWR), A D Hoon, G D Lilley.

Navy: C R Tuffley, J G Scott, D E Hambrook, G L Jones, J C Gibson, S J B Newsom (capt), J E Davies, A Holt, T A Gatehouse, M T Anthony, A J W Higginson, L C P Merrick, D R A Lloyd-Edwards, A Hallett, K A Lavelle.

1969 *Army v Navy:* T L Williams (SWB), H V W Barstow, N Thomas, D S Boyle, B Neck (Welsh Guards), B G L Campbell, D Spawforth, R D H Bryce (capt), R T Preston (RAEC), T A Moroney, P Eastwood, H G R Taggart (RE), C G Bale, A D Hoon, G D Lilley.

Navy: C R Tuffley, D J R Brown, G L Jones, J C Gibson, D E Hambrook, G Jones, J Davies, B W Goodwin, T A Gatehouse, M T Anthony, A J W Higginson, L C P Merrick, A R Godfrey, A Hallett (capt), J L Milnes.

Army v RAF: I S G Smith (RADC), H V W Barstow, M H Philp (Light Infantry), D S Boyle, B Neck, B G L Campbell, D Spawforth, R D H Bryce (capt), R T Preston, T A Moroney, P A Eastwood, M G Molloy, D T Hearn (Welsh Guards), G D Lilley, A D Hoon.

RAF: M K Howe, P B Glover, R B Smith, A E H Doherty, W C C Steele, W T Bevan (capt), D H Humphreys-Evans, P Ray, D Davies, J B Parker. D Waite, P R Larter, C A Farr, A Turner, V A McCarthy.

1970 *Army v Navy:* I S G Smith, N B Thomas, D S Boyle, D Wilson (RE), B Neck, G B L Campbell, D Spawforth, R D H Bryce (capt), G Miller (RAEC), J D MacDonald, M G Molloy, I Cairns (RCS), R Lennox (RAOC), A D Hoon, G D Lilley.

Navy: C R Tuffley, G P Phillips, G L Jones, A L Toms, D J R Brown, G Jones, J E Davies, A G Ryan, T Scott (capt), M T Anthony, R Wilson, R S Langton, K A Lavelle, A P Hallett, L C P Merrick.

Army v RAF: I S G Smith, N B Thomas, D S Boyle, D Wilson,

B Neck, R Jones (Welsh Guards), A T Lerwill (RMA), R D H Bryce (capt), G Miller, R J Drew (RA), M G Molloy, K Collins (REME), A D Hoon, J S Ashcroft (RE), G H Lilley.

RAF: W Casey, W C C Steele, G P Francom, D G Fowlie, M K Howe, A Gay, P D Hockaday, P R Ray, R Herdman, P Hamlyn, P J Larter, D Hannah, C A Farr, G W Fraser, D H Turner.

1971   *Army v RAF:* J Davies (RRW), D S Boyle, D Wilson, F H Williams (RHA), B Turner (RAOC), G C Relph (RA), D Spawforth, R D H Bryce (capt), G Miller, T A Moroney, A D Hoon, J Carroll (RAMC), J S Ashcroft, R Wilkinson (RAOC), G D Lilley.

RAF: M K Howe, W C C Steele, G P Francom, D Dunsmuir, P Smout, H Price, J Hough, J B Parker, R Herdman, P Ray, D Hannah, M Sedman, G W Fraser, V Harris, A D H Turner.

Army v Navy: I S G Smith, B Turner, D Wilson, D S Boyle, B Neck, J Davies, D Spawforth, R D H Bryce (capt), A R Redwood-Davies (DWR), T A Moroney, J S Ashcroft, I Cairns, C G Bale, A D Hoon, G D Lilley.

Navy: T H Fabian, G P Phillips, G L Jones, D E Hambrook, A L Toms, S J B Newsom, M P Gretton, N A Ryan, T A Gatehouse, J C Ackerman, A P Masterton-Smith, G Clarke, R Easson, L C P Merrick (capt), P Kelly.

1972   *Army v RAF:* J Davies, J S A Jeffray (now RA), D S Boyle, P M Davies, (13/18 Royal Hussars), B Neck, F W Williams (RA), D Spawforth, P M Johnson (RAEC), C Luckey (RA), N T Slater (RAEC), M S Molloy, I Cairns, G D Lilley, A D Hoon (capt), R Wilkinson.

RAF: M K Howe, W C C Steele, G P Frankcom (capt), P Carter, D G Fowler, H Price, R Hill, P Parker, J Young, P Ray, P J Larter, D Hannah, A Dalton, C Farr, A Turner.

Army v Navy: J Davies, B Neck, P Davies, D S Boyle, J S A Jeffray, F Williams, D Spawforth, R J Drew, C Luckey, N T Slater, J Carroll, I Cairns, G Gilbert (DWR), A D Hoon (capt), P J Bird (DWR).

Navy: G Fabian, G Phillips, H Archer, A I Toms, D E Hambrook, H Patterson, J F Davies, C Webb, T A Gatehouse (capt), J C Ackerman, J Q Davis, J Rooke, L C P Merrick, A J W Higginson, R Easson.

1973   *Army v Navy:* M Cuss (DWR), B Neck, P Davies, D S Boyle, J Morgan (REME), A S Turk (RTR), D Spawforth, D Bowen (Welsh Guards), C Luckey, J Thorn (DWR), R Rea (RAMC), J M Bowles (RCT), G D Lilley, I Cairns, A D Hoon (capt).

Navy: G H Fabian, D J R Brown, P Birkett, H C K Archer, G P Phillips, G Jones, J Davies, J C Ackerman, T A Gatehouse (capt), D Pulford, R Easson, R Langton, C A Miller, A J Higginson, L C P Merrick.

Army v RAF: M Cuss, B Neck, P Davies, D S Boyle, J Morgan, A S Turk, D Spawforth, J Thorn, H Elkan (RCS), P M Johnson, G D Lilley, J M Bowles, M G Molloy, R Rea, A D Hoon (capt).

RAF: H Patterson, W C C Steele (capt), D G Fowlie, R Asquith, R F M Souter, C G Williams, W Evans, J G Parker, J Macarthy, R H Elwig, A Dalton, P J Larter, W Fraser, A Turner, P J Warder.

1974 *Army v RAF:* A S Turk, D J Kerr (RAOC), J E Knowles (RCT), R P P Ince (RCT), G G Davies (RCT), J H Morgan, D Spawforth, N J Gray (RE), G A Miller, N T Slater (capt), C L G Wright, (RCS), P A Eastwood, M G Molloy, R E Rea, A D Hoon.

RAF: M K Howe, J Wakeham, P Williams, D B Dunsmuir, I Robinson, C G Williams, H Munslow, G J R Thomas, J Young (capt), J B Parker, R F M Souter, R M Holland, P J Larter, A Dalton, G Bond.

Army v Navy: A S Turk, N J Newell (DWR), P W Davies, R P P Ince, G Davies, J H Morgan, R G Bell (RMA), N J Gray, G A Miller, N T Slater (capt), C L G Wright, P A Eastwood, M G Molloy, R E Rea, A D Hoon.

Navy: D E Hambrook, C R English, P Birkett, H C K Archer, G P Phillips, G Jones, J C Davies, J C Ackerman, T A Gatehouse, W Davies, M H Connolly, C A Miller, A J W Higginson (capt), P Dunn, L C P Merrick.

1975 *Army v Navy:* M Cuss, G G Davies, S G Jackson (RAMC), P Robinson (DWR), P Davies, J H Morgan, D R Williams (RWF), R G C Campbell (RCT), T C Sinclair (DWR), N J Gray, R E Rea (capt), R S Collier (REME), S Peacock (RCS), P Griffiths (Welsh Guards), J Carroll.

Navy: P A M Piercey, N L Armstrong, D E Hambrook, A G Jones, H C K Archer, S E Turner, J C Davies, J C Ackerman, R P Smith, D W R Pulford, T Kelly, J Q Davis, P Dunn (capt), J C K Rook, J E Loveday.

Army v RAF: M Cuss, G Davies, D B Reynolds (REME), P Robinson, P Davies, J H Morgan, D Williams R Campbell, T C Sinclair, N J Gray, R E Rea (capt), R S Collier, S Peacock, R A Spurrell (REME), J Carroll.

RAF: M K Howe, D B Dunsmuir, G Moseley, P Williams, B Knowles, A Green, B Gordon, J Parker, D W Gatherer, S Pickering, A Dalton, G A Fraser (capt), P J Larter, R F M Souter, R M Holland.

1976   *Army v RAF:* P J Wright (King's Own R Border Regt), J Davies (Welsh Guards), S G Jackson, P Robinson, D Kerr, J H Morgan, R G Bell (now 13/18 R Hussars), R G C Campbell, J B Mills (REME), N J Gray, G O W Williams (DWR), W E Bott (RE), S Peacock, R A Spurrell, C J W Gilbert (capt).

RAF: M K Howe, M Smith, P Williams, K Richardson, R Wyatt, C G Williams, B Gordon, S Turner, D Gatherer, S Pickering, G Bond, D Mason, J Orwin, S Cuthill (capt), M Sedman.

Army v Navy: D Denham (RAOC), G W C Newmarsh (Light Infantry), S G Jackson, D Kerr, P Elwell (DWR), J H Morgan, D Spawforth, N J Gray, P M Johnson (RA), R G C Campbell, J M Bowles, W E Bott, G O W Williams, R A Spurrell, C J W Gilbert (capt).

Navy: P A M Piercey, D E Hambrook, A G Jones, H C K Archer, N J Penny, P Birkett, C Vouldon, J C Ackerman, R P Smith, D R W Pulford, C A Webb, B Davies, M J Lane, P Dunn (capt), W A Witham.

1977   *Army v Navy:* G J Denholm (RAOC), P Wright, W A N Atkinson (DWR), S G Jackson, D B Reynolds, N W Drummond (RAChD), G Davies (QDG), P M S Mills (Parachute Regt), C Sexton (RE), N J Gray, G D Lilley, J M Bowles, D M McCracken (CRMP), C J W Gilbert (capt), P D Smith (RAOC).

Navy: G H Fabian, B J Wills, A G Jones, N B Stefanie, T B Newsom, S E Turner, C Vouldon, J C Ackerman, P Norrington-Davies, A Dryburgh, P Dunn (capt), C A Richards, M J Lane, M H Connolly, M K Taylor.

Army v RAF: C F Grieve (DWR), B P Clesham (Light Infantry), S G Jackson (capt), W A H Atkinson, D B Reynolds, N W Drummond, G Davies, P Mills, J Mills, N J Gray, R Spring (Coldstream Guards), J M Bowles, P Smith, C Wright, C J W Gilbert.

RAF: M K Howe, W C C Steele, R Seward, H Batty, J Rogers, A Green, S Grey, S Pickering, J McCarthy, J Parker, W W Jenkins, D Mason, J Orwin, J Hickey, G Fraser (capt).

1978   *Army v Navy:* P Wright, K A'Hearne (RRW), S G Jackson, D E Stevens (RE), D B Reynolds, W A N Atkinson, G Davies, M Jenkins (RRW), R J Matthews (RE), N J Gray, J Baxter

(RA), J M Bowles, D P McCracken, G O W Williams, A D Hoon (capt).

Navy: P R Lea, C R English, J Hopkins, A G Jones, A Hamlett, J Leigh, K H Martin, J C Ackerman, P H Plumb, T H W Davies, R Tinson, C Richards, M Lane, P Dunn (capt), L C P Merrick.

Army v RAF: B J Abbott (REME), K A'Hearne, D Prowse (REME), S G Jackson, D G Reynolds, W A N Atkinson, G Davies, M Jenkins, R J Matthews, N J Gray, J Baxter, J M Bowles, P Smith, G O W Williams, A D Hoon (capt).

RAF: P Bate, M Smith, S Grey, R Seward, S Rogers, A Green, K Pugh (capt), M Jones, A McCrindle, B Dix, W Jenkins, C Rayner, J Orwin, G Still, N Gillingham.

1979   *Army v Navy:* S Armstrong (REMF), K A'Hearne, D C Stevens, S G Jackson, K Bassom (RE), D B Reynolds, G Davies, B Tyler (REME), R G Matthews, N J Gray, R Spring, J M Bowles, P Smith, D R Baxter (RA), A D Hoon (capt).

Navy: P R Lea, C R English (capt), D E Hambrook, G H Fabian, T B Newsom, D Thomas, P Hart, J C Ackerman, C A Hughes, B Goodman, R Tinson, C A Richards, M J Lane, L C P Merrick, M K Taylor.

Army v RAF: S Armstrong, K A'Hearne, D C Stevens, S G Jackson, K Bassom, D B Reynolds, G Davies, B Tyler, R G Matthews, N J Gray, R Spring, J M Bowles, P Smith, G O W Williams, A D Hoon (capt).

RAF: G Williams, S N'Jie, W C C Steele, R Seward, S Rogers, A Green, K Pugh, F Fitzgerald-Lombard, A Rust, M Jones, W Jenkins, J Orwin, N Gillingham (capt), J Ponting, G Still.

1980   *Army v RAF:* S Armstrong, H Gleane (RCS), P Lytollis (RCS), P Rees (RRW), K A'Hearne, J Morgan, M Kaged (RRW), P Williams (RRW), T Sinclair (capt), M Jenkins, A Rapley (REME), H Rundle (RRW), J M Bowles, G O W Williams, M Prosser (RRW), replacement – P A'Hearne for Williams.

RAF: G Williams, P Bate, N Coyne, R Seward, A Fenlan, V Pritchard, R Owen, M Fitzgerald-Lombard, T Allison, W Brown, W Jenkins, J Orwin, N Spencer, N Gillingham (capt), G Still; replacements – M Jones for Fitzgerald-Lombard.

Army v Navy: S Armstrong, H Gleane, P Lytollis, P Rees, K A'Hearne, J Morgan, M Kaged, P Williams, T Sinclair (capt), M Jenkins, A Rapley, H Rundle, J M Bowles, G O W Williams, M Prosser; replacement – Reynolds for Lytollis.

Navy: G Fabian, S J Creighton, A G Jones, C J Bryning, T B

Newsom, J Leigh, A R Davies, J C Ackerman, C A Hughes, J R Nash, P Dunn (capt), C J Folland, M Lane, R J Thompson, C A Hughes; replacement – B Wills for Creighton.

1981 *Army v Navy:* P Warfield (RAEC), K A'Hearne, P Lytollis, S Jackson, H Gleane, G Lovegrove (QDG), G Davies (APTC), T Tarr (RAOC), H Elkan (RCS), S Titterington (REME), J M Bowles (capt), J Campbell-Lamerton (Scots Guards), G O W Williams (DWR), C Christopher (RAOC), C Richardson (Royal Scots).

Navy: G Fabian, J H Harker, J Blackett, P D Tomlin, R M Penfold, G A Price, C Youldon, L J Watson, R H Joy, T H W Davies, A Beatson, M Lane, A J Payne, S J Hughes (capt), T Kelly; replacement – R K Aindow for Kelly.

Army v RAF: A Chapple (REME), K A'Hearne, P Lytollis, S G Jackson, H Gleane, G Shuttleworth (DWR), G Davies R P Tarr (RAOC), H Elkan, S Titterington, J M Bowles, J Campbell-Lamerton, C Christopher, P Griffiths (Welsh Guards), C Richardson.

RAF: P Bate, R Allison, P A'Hearne, G Williams, N Coyne, A Paddon (capt), R Owen, M Whitcombe, Rust, M Jones, M Coptcote, P J Larter, N Spencer, G Thomas, J Orwin; replacement – P Bruckner for Williams.

1982 *Army v Navy:* C Spowart (RE), K A'Hearne, L Horton (RE), M Noel-Smith (Gloucestershire Regt), K Bassom, B Abbott, G Davies, S Titterington, A Mason (RRW), R Audrain (RAOC), J M Bowles (capt), R Travers (RAOC), G O W Williams, C Christopher, D Goddard (RRW); replacement – J Byrne (REME) for Mason.

Navy: G Fabian, T Newson, C Alcock, J Blackett, S Creighton, G Price, C Youldon, W Davies, R Joy, J Hirst, C Folland, M Lane, R Thompson, M Sheldon, M Connolly (capt).

Army v RAF: C Spowart, K A'Hearne, M Noel-Smith, P Lytollis, K Bassom, B Abbott, G Davies, S Titterington, J Byrne, R Audrain, J M Bowles (capt), R Travers, G O W Williams, B McFarlane (RCT), C Christopher.

RAF: P Bate, N Coyne, D Warby, S Lazenby, R Allison, M Milburn, S Worrall, M Whitcombe, A Rust, C Stephenson, N Gillingham (capt), J Orwin, G Thomas, M Coptcoat, G Still.

1983 *Army v Navy:* I Hitchcock (RE), D Johnson (RWF), P Lockett (REME), M Noel-Smith, A Kay (DWR), G Neild (RE), G Davies, (capt), C Harvey (DWR), J Byrne, S Titterington, D

McCracken (APTC), B McCall (REME), G Williams, P Silcox (Grenadier Guards), C Christopher.

Navy: D Powell, S Creighton, P Tomlin, B Wills, T Newson, G Price, C Vouldon, J Hirst, R Joy, L Watson, A Turner (RM), I Russell, G Wood, S Hughes (RM), M Connolly (capt).

Army v RAF: G Neild, D Johnson, M Greenhalgh (RA), M Noel-Smith, A Kay, P J Warfield (RAEC), G Davies (capt), C Harvey, R Bedford (RE), M Knight (16/5 Queen's R Lancers), D McCracken, B McCall, G Williams, C Christopher, S Peacock (APTC).

RAF: P Bate, R Underwood, P Aherne, S Lazenby, R Allison, M Evans, S Worrall, M Whitcombe, P Wheeler, C Stephenson, N Gillingham (capt), J Orwin, G Thomas, M Coptcoat, G Still.

1984 *Army v Navy:* M Blomquist (RE), D Johnson, I Shaw (RAOC), P Warfield (capt), K Bassom, G Neild, G Davies, C Harvey, J Byrne, J Brown (RAOC), S Peacock, R Travers, C Christopher, B McFarlane (RCT), B McCall.

Navy: R Henderson, P Barcilon, C Alcock, G Price, T Newson, S Barnett, C Vouldon, J Hirst, I Thompson, S Lord, D Hadlow, A Turner, R Tinson (capt), M Sheldon, G Wood.

Army v RAF: A MacKay (RCT), D Johnson, P Lockett, P J Warfield (capt), K Bassom, G Neild, G Davies, C Harvey, J Byrne, J K Brown, S Peacock, J M Bowles, C Christopher, B McFarlane, B McCall; replacement – M Blomquist for Nield.

RAF: P Bate, R Allison, I Gosling, P Aherene, R Underwood, M Evans, R Owen; M Whitcombe, M Wheeler, C Stevenson J Orwin (capt), N Gillingham, R Lamb, M Coptcoat, D Parsonage.

1985 *Army v Navy:* A MacKay, D Johnson, N Beazley (RA), P Lockitt, E Atkins (RCS), J Steele (RA), G Davies (capt), N Kessell (RCS), J Byrne, C Harvey, R Travers, S Peacock, C Richardson, M Lewis (RA), N Castleton (RMA).

Navy: C Alcock (capt), R Penfold, R Allen (RM), P Tomlin, S Hampton, M Whittington, R Stevens, T Davies, R Joy, S Lord, D Hadlow, P Elliott, M Sheldon, G Wood, S Hughes.

Army v RAF: A MacKay, E Atkins, M Greenhalgh (RA), P Lockett, S Wilkins (RCT), J Steele, G Davies (capt), N Kessell, J Byrne, C Harvey, G Williams, B McCall, S Peacock, M Lewis, R Travers; replacement – Christopher for Williams.

RAF: S Lazenby, M Aspinall, M Thomas, J Goulin (capt), R Underwood, S Cairns, S Worral, M Whitcombe, K Davies, A Billet, B Richardson, J Orwin, D Gigg, M Coptcoat, G Still; replacement – R Huxtable for Thomas.

THE 'TIGERS' SHOW THEIR TEETH
1907–1914

Although, up until after the First World War, playing in Inter-Service matches was confined to officers, there was no such restriction for Army Cup games at any time. In fact a limit was placed on officer players. Rule 20 for the competition directed that 'the total number of officers playing in any team will not exceed eight'.

The other ranks provided an early lesson right in the first final that it did not matter what rank a player was as long as he was fit. When the 2nd Battalion the West Riding Regiment beat the RE Training Battalion 5–0 at Aldershot the Sappers had their maximum allowance of eight officers, of whom R F A Hobbs had represented the Army and England, G C Gowlland the Army and later Scotland, and G C Campbell the Army. The West Riding Regiment team had only one officer, G C Egerton, and nobody in their side was an International or had played for the Army. They were, however, the fitter of the two sides and played more as a team.

Their pack was good in the tight scrums, executed many good rushes and were always on the ball. Their diminutive half-backs, Pte Brown and Pte Lister, were quick and cunning and constantly outwitted the Engineers' half-backs. Towards the end of the game their Pte Martin scored a try from a forward rush and Pte Swift placed the goal.

These private soldiers of the 2nd Battalion the West Riding Regiment (later to become the Duke of Wellington's Regiment), excelled themselves, and the Infantrymen deserved the Cup, which was presented by Gen Sir John French.

While it was inevitable in the changing times that all ranks would become eligible for all matches, the performance of these men and others probably helped towards that decision being made earlier rather than later.

As stated in the introductory chapter of this history, no time was lost in calling for entries for the first Army Cup contest in 1907 after the presentation of the handsome trophy on 21 January of that year. Twelve units responded, but two of the entries must have been received late as there is no record of them in the draw, which was: Royal Scots Greys v 23rd Field Artillery Brigade; RE Depot v 7th Dragoon Guards;

3rd Dragoon Guards v 2nd Battalion West Riding Regiment; 1st Battalion Welch Regiment v Army Service Corps; King's Dragoon Guards v RE Training Battalion.

It was revealed in the March 1914 edition of *The Men of Harlech*, the Regimental Journal for the men of the Welch Regiment, that the trophy had a hitherto unsuspected background. 'It is not generally known that the present Army Cup presented by the Rugby Football Union originated from the 1st Battalion of the Welch Regiment', said the paper.

One imagines that the well-known 'Birdie' Partridge was responsible for suggesting this gift and it was in some ways more of a loan. There is no record of how the Welch Regiment fared at their first venture in 1907, but they were to win the Cup twice before the First World War, seven times between the wars, and once after the Second World War!

Up to 1914 the winners (five in all) of the eight Cup finals were all Infantry battalions of Line Regiments. Only units stationed at home could compete.

The Leicestershire Regiment, who could not enter a team in 1907 as both of their battalions were abroad, made up for that by winning the Cup in 1908 without having their line crossed and going on to win twice more in this period and be runners-up once, each time with their 1st Battalion.

The Leicesters were well led and trained by Lieut W C Wilson, the Army and England threequarter, supported by Lieut A W S Brock, an Army threequarter, and the forwards were led and trained by Lieut R R Yalland, who played for Hampshire. In the final at Aldershot, a very hard game, the 1st Battalion Leicesters beat the 1st Battalion Welch Regiment by one goal to a dropped goal. Under Yalland's good guidance the Tigers' forwards played well, but it was the greater ability, experience and speed of the centres, Wilson and Brock, that won the game. Cpl Lewis scored the try and Lieut Clarke placed the goal.

In 1909 the 1st Battalion Welch Regiment had their revenge on the Leicesters, deservedly winning a hard-fought semi-final game 9-0. Some said that playing at Cardiff inspired the Welch, but it was their superiority in the tight scrums and their ability to control the game so as to deny the Tigers' backs the chances they had the year before that really won the match for them.

Partridge, who combined playing skills with being a very good administrator, started the Welch Regiment off on their Army Cup successes and captained the 1909 side, well supported by Army players F W Gransmore and R H Montgomery. An all-Welsh final went to the 1st Battalion Welch 6-3 over the South Wales Borderers.

The Welch had no team entered in 1910 because both battalions were abroad. In that year the Leicesters again reached the final without a point being scored against them. The 2nd Battalion Gloucestershire Regiment were the other finalists and this was the year the match moved to Twickenham, where, after extra time the Glosters won 3–0.

In the semi-finals of 1911 the Leicesters beat their old and much-respected rivals the Welch 7–0, to meet the Life Guards in the final, which was played in a blizzard.

The Life Guards looked enormous both in height and weight and excelled in the line-out. The Tigers' forwards, however, did magnificently in the tight scrums, getting the ball on the average about seven times out of ten and passing and backing up extremely well. This allowed their backs the scope they needed. Wilson and the two halves, Pte Fisher and Pte Smitten, who had played together for the past three years, were all outstanding. The Leicesters won 15–0 on one goal (converted by Dalby), one dropped goal and two tries.

Another well-known name, that of Capt Clive Liddell, re-appears now as he returned home in 1911 and started to rebuild and train the 1st Battalion Leicesters' team. He did this so well that in 1912 the holders retained the trophy. After beating the 1st Battalion Glosters 13–3 in the semi-finals they defeated 2nd Battalion Welch 6–3 at Twickenham, albeit with extra time.

The final started badly for the holders because, in the first ten minutes, they were penalised for off-side and the Welch scored. After that the game developed into 'a fast and very strenuous rough and tumble. Twice the Tigers' hopes were raised, first when Fisher dived over the line but the try was disallowed and then Smitten apparently dropped an excellent goal but the ball had touched one of the Welch team. However, within ten minutes of time Pte Walker scored a good try in the corner which was unconverted and so made the scores level.

One of the Welch side had been sent off just before half-time for rough play and being reduced to 14 men was beginning to tell on them. The first half of extra time proved fruitless, but at last, in the second period, after a brilliant forward rush Cpl Illston scored the winning unconverted try for the Tigers and Liddell received the Cup.

There was a reason why the Welch had not been too successful in the recent seasons. They had been moving around too much. In 1909 the 1st Battalion left for Alexandria and in 1910 the 2nd Battalion were returning to Wales from South Africa. But after being runners-up in 1912 the 2nd Battalion the Welch Regiment made no mistake in the 1913 final, beating the 1st Battalion Glosters 9–3.

The Welch brought their mascot, 'Taffy' (a white goat) to the final and it proved a most popular attraction as well as bringing them luck. The Glosters scored first with a try by Pte Bayliss in the first quarter of and hour, but their forwards then appeared to have shot their bolt. Play veered in favour of the Welch and by half-time they were in the lead from tries by Gransmore and Lacey. Gransmore scored again in the second half.

The game suffered from both lots of halves trying to do too much, but Gransmore played well as a threequarter. Lieut Lacey captained the Welch very well and it was he who received the Cup. The evergreen Capt 'Birdie' Partridge led the forwards with great skill and vigour and was admirable in the loose. At least four players, Capt Partridge, Lieut Gransmore, Cpl Murphy and Pte Fisher played in both the 1909 and 1913 winning teams.

After winning the Cup in its inaugural year, the 2nd Battalion West Riding (DWR) Regiment did not appear in the final again until 1914, but they rounded off the pre-war era by having their second win and leaving the Glosters as runners-up for a second year.

The 1907 and 1914 finals were linked by Lieut Egerton playing in both and by the 2nd Battalion West Riding team winning in more or less the same way as they had before, with very fit forwards who played a dashing game in the loose and much superior halves. Scrum-half Sgt Greenhough had an excellent game and combined well with Lieut G W Oliphant, who played fly-half in this match but was a forward for the Army.

Greenhough scored from a scrummage near the Glosters' line ten minutes from the start. Although the Glosters had the better of most of the play they failed to score, through wasting their chances and not giving their Pte Hill, probably the fastest and most dangerous wing threequarter on the field, enough of the ball. In the second half Lieut JHL Thompson scored an unconverted try to give the West Riding team further points, and it was only just before time that the Glosters found the line and scored through Lieut Yalland, the best centre on the field.

Lieut-Gen Sir Douglas Haig presented the Cup and medals.

THE 'DRAGON' SUPREME
1920–1928

After the First World War the Welsh, with an 's', including the Welch, with a 'c', had a monopoly of the Army Cup for nine seasons. Not only were other teams held off from the trophy, but few could get to the final because Welsh units often went in by both routes to vie with each other.

In the 1910/1920 competition there was even the possibility of two sides from the same regiment meeting in the final, for, out of sixteen entries that season, the Welch Regiment was represented by its 2nd Battalion and its 51st Battalion. Both got as far as the semi-finals, but then an extraordinary event occurred. The 51st Battalion was disbanded before further play! This must have acted powerfully on the 2nd Battalion. They went on to win the Cup that year and for the next two years as well.

The 2nd Battalion Welch Regiment defeated Experimental Bridging Coy, RE, 11–0 in their semi-final and went into the 1919–1920 final without any team having scored against them. If the other finalists, 2nd Life Guards, thought they had struck lucky when the disbandment of the 51st Battalion gave them an unexpected walkover they were soon disillusioned. It was the Welch who had everything else going for them and, in a match where their superiority outside the scrum was the decisive factor, they deservedly won the final 9–0.

Although their captain, Daniel, made a capital run he mistook the line and ran out of play before touching down, so the Welch had not scored by half-time. In the second half, however, Daniel made up for it with the break that resulted in Phillips scoring. A further try and a penalty goal (scorers unknown) completed their points.

It is recorded that the victors, with the Band of 2nd Battalion Welch Regiment playing popular airs, received a magnificent welcome on their return to Pembroke Dock, from a large crowd of military and civilian enthusiasts. A minute from an Army Rugby Union meeting of 1919 reveals that there might not have been a cup to present, or that someone might have had to find a new one.

The ARU naturally made approaches to the last pre-war winners, the 2nd Battalion the West Riding Regt, about delivering up the trophy.

They discovered that the unit had changed its name to 2nd Battalion Duke of Wellington's Regiment and was under new command. The Commanding Officer wrote to the ARU saying he had only just assumed command of the battalion and 'would endeavour to trace the Army Rugby Cup'! Evidently, he was successful.

From this time the ARU should have had two trophies for this contest, a new one being introduced immediately after the war for the runners-up in the final. This had been suggested in another letter to the ARU, from Major van der Meyer, Scots Guards. He said he had in his possession a cup donated by a Dutch firm of jewellers for competition between rugby teams drawn from the interned prisoners in Holland. The Armistice was signed before the contest could get under way so he offered the cup to the ARU. It was gratefully accepted, but mysteriously there is no record of it having been presented.

Interest in rugby increased rapidly in the 1920s and during this period sections of the Army established themselves as 'rugby playing regiments'. Some were carrying on the tradition from 1907–1914. Others came to the fore in the 1920s.

The ones that come most readily to mind are the Welsh Guards, the King's Own Royal Regiment, the South Wales Borderers, the Gloucestershire Regiment, the Duke of Wellington's Regiment (West Riding), the Welch Regiment, the Leicestershire Regiment, Training Battalion Royal Engineers, and 5th Battalion Royal Tank Corps, of whom a select few are still a dominant force today. Hardly any other teams succeeded in reaching the Cup Final in the years up to 1939.

With a large number of units stationed in Ireland the 1921 competition was split between those there and those in Great Britain, the winners of each group to meet in the final. This did not worry the 2nd Battalion Welch Regt, who carried on as before and had little difficulty in qualifying from the Ireland units. The holders beat 1st Battalion Leicesters 22–0, 1st Battalion Somerset Light Infantry 20–0 and 2nd Battalion Camerons 17–3.

In the final they defeated Training Battalion RE, Chatham, 31–3. When Lieut-Gen the Earl of Cavan presented the Cup he said it had been 'a splendid match, played in the best spirit'.

The Sappers were unfortunate to have a number of injuries before the game, including injuries to their Army half-backs. In the circumstances they did well with an improvised back division. But honours must go to the victors, particularly their backs, who showed greater skill, speed and initiative than seen from Wales in any of her Internationals. This was a time, when Wales despaired of a revival in their back play.

Beating the 1st Battalion Gloucestershire Regiment 27–8 in the 1922 final brought the hat-trick for the 2nd Battalion Welch Regt, but they had a less easy time arriving at the final than in the previous years. The 1st Battalion Somerset Light Infantry gave them a surprisingly close game in the third round before going out 5–3, and they only won their semi-final 11–8.

The semi-final was a repeat of the 1921 final and the Sappers were obviously looking for revenge. The game was at Birkenhead Park in front of a crowd of 4000 and Training Battalion RE led 5–3 at half-time. It was not was not until the last stages that Benyon scored the winning try for the Welch, which was converted by Dunn.

In the final, which took place in a gale, a first-rate pack of forwards laid the foundation of the Welch success. Behind the scrum the fielding and kicking of Payne was up to International standard, and the two halves, Phillips and Morgan, had one of their best days, as did all the threequarters. The Gloucesters' pack fought all the way, but they got little help from their backs.

It was appropriate that Welsh International Charlie Jones should score the last Welch try and add the conversion himself. Beynon and R L Jones also scored tries, two each. Dunn kicked two penalty goals and made two conversions. Nash scored all the opposition points, with one try, converted, and a penalty.

For 1923 the 2nd Battalion Welch Regiment were in Aldershot to contest the final yet again, but could not make it four wins in a row. They had to hand over the title to the Welsh Guards, who defeated them 6–0.

Progress to the final by the holders was as spectacular as ever. They scored 209 points for only 12 against, by removing 1st Battalion Lancashire Fusiliers (63–0), 2nd Battalion Royal Berkshire Regiment (56–0), 1st Battalion Beds and Herts Regiment (41–0), their old rivals Training Battalion RE, Chatham (14–6), and in the semi-final 1st Battalion SWB (35–6).

The Welsh Guards had only taken up rugby seriously in the 1921–1922 season and after beating 1st Battalion Somerset LI in their semi-final they went into the final very much the underdogs.

But Capt Geoffrey Crawshay, on posting to the Guards Depot, had set about reviving interest and his work paid off handsomely. The final was a great forward match, right from the kick-off. Weight told, however. The Guardsmen must have been a stone a man heavier, yet as well as that they were very fit and fast, breaking like lightning and following up punts ahead in fine style. The Welch halves were marked very closely and the threequarters seldom looked dangerous.

Shortly after half-time Pates forced himself over for the first try and later scrum-half Davies slipped round the blind side for the Guards' second. Payne, the Welch full-back, was outstanding for his fielding, kicking and fearless tackling, but it was not their day, especially for their centre, Beynon, who was injured and left the field, not to return. Despite the intensity of effort, though, the game was played in a sporting spirit.

Roles were reversed when another all-Welsh final occurred in 1924 and the same units were there once more – 2nd Battalion Welch beat the Welsh Guards 7–3 that year!

By coincidence, 2nd Battalion Welch were able to sharpen up on mostly Guards' opposition in the earlier rounds, which might have helped. They began with two easy wins, 47–0 over 1st Battalion Scots Guards and 72–0 against 3rd Battalion Coldstream Guards, but the way became tougher after that. Their next two games were really hard and they only defeated the Royal Horse Guards 6–3 and the Guards Depot 5–0. Their semi-final was also hard-fought – not surprisingly as their opponents were Training Battalion RE, Chatham – the Welch, however, won 16–0.

An exhilarating final was, as before, almost entirely a forward battle, with the Guards making the most of their extra weight. The three-quarters on either side had little room to manoeuvre and spent most of their time getting in a quick kick to touch before being tackled. But in what was to be their last final for eleven years the Welch, personified by Phillips, now had the Guards' measure. Indeed Phillips was match winner for the Welch, scoring all of their points from a try and a drop goal. The Guards only had a penalty from Fisher.

The name on the Cup changed again in 1925 but not the accent surrounding it as the 1st Battalion South Wales Borderers won the final for the first time with little trouble. To set themselves up they beat the defending Welch 12–0 in the fourth round.

In the third round the holders had played a long-awaited match against 1st Battalion DWR, after previously taking a strong side, including some Welsh and Army trialists, to Downside School and being beaten 17–0. Their game with 1st Battalion DWR was something of an anti-climax when the Welch won 31–3, but DWR were without their outstanding forward 'Horsey' Browne and the Welch XV were superior in every department. If their kicking had been better the score could have been a lot bigger.

The Royal Horse Guards reached the final for the first time and their side of twelve troopers and three corporals fought hard to keep the score within bounds, never giving up. But the 1st Battalion SWB won 16-3, largely due to their full-back and skipper, Baker, moving to fly-half and from that position opening up the play splendidly for his team.

Baker had a major share in most of the SWB tries, scoring one himself, making two conversions and kicking a penalty goal. Rees and Ward scored a try each. Teed got a penalty for the RHG.

Yet another all-Welsh final took place in 1926, this time between the 1st Battalion SWB and the Welsh Guards, with the SWB winning 10-3. The Guards had beaten the King's Own 13-8 in one semi-final and 1st Battalion SWB put out 1st Battalion DWR 6-8. The DWR had previously had an exciting second round game with 2nd Battalion Welch, who might have repeated their 1925 win. They were leading 5-3 at half-time and soon after the interval went further ahead with another try, but Haylock, the DWR right wing threequarter, scored a try that eventually gave DWR victory 9-8. They went on to defeat the 1st Battalion Somerset LI 9-0 before falling foul of 1st Battalion SWB.

Baker played the whole of this final at full-back and kicked a magnificent SWB penalty. The game was almost a forward battle throughout and the only really good passing movement led to a try by the SWB threequarter Windsor. Davies got a drop goal to complete their points. Young, Gibbons and Murphy were very prominent in the loose for the Guards. Fisher kicked their penalty, which meant that for the second year the SWB line was not crossed. Much of the credit for that went to 'Muddy' Baker, not only for his play but for his captaincy.

Fired by their double success, the 1st Battalion SWB had their third win of the Cup in 1927 and went one better than 2nd Battalion Welch by retaining it in 1928 as well.

The 1926/1927 season got off to a bad start because so many teams had to cancel their fixtures and help in duties necessary owing to the General Strike. The holders managed to survive and had two rousing games, beating DWR 6-0 and 2nd Welch 18-6 in a local Welsh 'derby', before a narrow semi-final win 9-8.

The other finalists were RE (Aldershot), who had previously won 33-7 over the East Yorkshire Regiment. The 1st Battalion SWB, however, had also tested themselves against civilian clubs, beating Waterloo 1st XV 14-0 and 16-3 and drawing 11-11 with Liverpool, and in the final they had the edge to win 9-8.

It was a hard-fought final and the Sappers gained an early lead. Two good threequarter movements resulted in Pickford scoring two tries, one converted by Hilton, and although Baker kicked another magnificent penalty goal for the SWB just before half-time and scored another shortly after the interval the Sappers held on grimly and it looked as if they would have a memorable victory. But with only four minutes to go Douglas scored to give the SWB their hat-trick. The Sappers were left to reflect that despite scoring two tries to one they were the losers.

Nine years of Welsh superiority were rounded off by the 1st Battalion SWB defeating the 1st Battalion King's Own Royal Regiment by a narrow 15-14 in the 1928 final, but that margin epitomised the struggle they had that season to stay on top.

The Welsh Guards showed extreme reluctance to let them off the hook in their semi-final so that they could even reach the final. The teams had to play two matches, the first at Coventry ending in a draw after extra time. In the replay the 1st Battalion SWB just managed to win 3-0. Meanwhile the King's Own won the other semi-final 16-5 over the 1st Battalion DWR, their strong and fast back division finally overcoming the Dukes' defence, who were unlucky to lose their full-back, who had to go off injured.

That year's final was a great game, certainly one of the best and most exciting since the war, with nearly 3000 people present.

An odd sight met their eyes before play started. Each team had a mascot hanging over the goal post. The Borderers' lucky token was not particularly bizarre, being a much-beribboned black cat. The King's Own were more original – they displayed a huge banana, tied with Regimental ribbons!

In the early part of the game the King's Own played more convincingly and went ahead with a penalty kick by Whelpton, then Abbott made a fine break and sent Hall over for a try. The SWB fought back and scored two tries, by Samuels and Rees. In the second half Baker and Martin scored two more tries for the holders, but the King's Own came back with a try by Abbott, converted by Whelpton.

Now only a point separated the teams, but a forward breakaway enabled Baker to get another try for the Borderers. Excitement was by then intense and in the last minute the ball flashed along the three-quarter line for Abbott to score by the corner flag. Could Whelpton convert? The final whistle was blown as the touch judges were signalling failure, bringing to an end a magnificent game by two very good teams.

As this period continued the Army Rugby Union could see how interest was growing. In 1924 only nine units were members of the ARU and the Rugby Football Union. By 1927 the number had increased to seventy-one.

THE DUKES EMERGE
1929–1939

What appears to have been the first visit to the Army Cup Final by a Prince of Wales since his father attended in 1910 coincided, ironically, with the first win by an English regiment since the First World War. The Prince was at the 1929 final as Colonel-in-Chief of the Welsh Guards. He saw the 1st Battalion King's Own Royal Regiment beat the 1st Battalion Welsh Guards 21–9.

The Guards were clearly as determined to achieve a tenth win for Wales as the King's Own were to avoid being runners-up again. The Guards scored first within minutes of the start with a try by Humphries, but Abbott responded in kind after a good threequarter movement and Whelpton converted for the King's Own to lead by two points. Young kicked a penalty goal to put the Guards ahead again, but just before half-time the King's Own took back the lead when Schofield broke through and Abbott got his second try. It remained 8–6 at the turn-round.

At the beginning of the second half play was entirely in the King's Own '25', but eventually the pressures was relieved and, after an opening made by Aslett and Turner, a try was scored by Slocombe. They nearly threw away the advantage with a dangerous piece of passing in front of their goal, which allowed Greenacre to intercept and dive over to score, but finally Aslett himself deservedly added a try for his side and Hopwood gave the King's Own yet another, from a threequarter movement in which the ball travelled twice along the line. Whelpton converted both of those tries. The Guards had, in the meantime, lost Greenacre with a broken collar bone a few minutes after he scored, and this obviously affected them, but in general it was accepted that the better team won.

The King's Own had defeated DWR 8–3 on their way to that final.

In 1930 there were two powerful incentives to spur the King's Own into keeping the Cup: it was their last season before they were due to go abroad; and their captain, Alfred Aslett, announced his intention of giving up first-class rugby. No more was needed. They became even more determined than the year before. Aslett's decision alone would have been enough and his Regiment very much appreciated his forethought in letting them know, for it probably made the difference between the King's Own winning and losing.

They reached the final with a convincing victory over the 4th Battalion Royal Tanks, 32–3, and but for an equally determined team of Sappers their opponents might next have been the Duke of Wellington's Regiment to re-fight one of the 1929 battles. The Dukes scored 138 points to three in their four Cup games up to the semi-finals of 1930 and were thus firm favourites to beat the Training Battalion RE (Chatham). The Sappers took no account of this and set about showing they had different ideas – to win 16–0!

This promised a good final and an exciting game was watched by a very large crowd. The two packs were evenly matched and the marking and tackling on both sides were so keen that ground was gained chiefly by kicking. Both teams, however, missed opportunities by poor finishing. At the end, with twelve minutes left, the King's Own scrum-half, Wright, began a movement from which Schofield made the vital break and Lowe scored in the corner. The Sappers fought back, but the King's Own held on at 3–0 and deservedly won their second consecutive final.

The 1st Battalion Duke of Wellington's Regiment had no problems in either getting to or winning the 1931 final, a fitting tribute to their great player 'Horsey' Browne, who died later that year.

For some seasons the Dukes had been brimful of good players and they thought it was about time their name was on the Cup, to emulate their predecessors of the West Riding Regiment. So they too set off determined to reach the final, and if possible win it.

Their Commanding Officer was Walter Wilson, he who had played for the Army and England before the war and trained and captained the team of his previous Regiment, the Leicesters, with such success in those days. Skipper of the Dukes' team was 'Bonzo' Miles, a fine leader and trainer of rugger players, Browne, sadly, was now seriously ill, but he was an inspiration to any team, whether it was his Regiment, the Army or Ireland, and his influence continued to be felt.

From this second platform, the Dukes reached the final in five matches in which they scored 181 points to nil. They kept their record clean by beating Training Battalion RE (Chatham) 21–0 in the final.

The Sappers were expected to give a good account of themselves and not only on the strength of their appearance in the 1930 contest. They, with the Irish International H H C Withers in their pack, had earlier in the season beaten the Army trial XV.

But the Dukes outpaced them and were superior in every way, though the Sappers deserved full credit for putting up a gallant performance. Cpl Townend, the Dukes' stand-off-half, played a large part in their victory by pinning down the Sappers in their own half with some accurate kicking to touch.

It was twenty minutes before Bentley scored the first try, which Townend converted, but the Dukes led 11-0 at half-time after further tries by Downs and Troop. In the second half Townend dropped a goal and in the last few minutes came two more tries, by Summers, under the posts, and Dalrymple.

Troop was outstanding in the Dukes' pack, while Townend, who had previously played for Devon as a back row forward, was, with Dalrymple, the best of a lively back division. Withers did his best in a beaten Sapper pack and Lambert, at full-back, played a heroic game but could not stem the tide. The game was witnessed by a crowd of 7000.

The link between the Dukes and the Leicesters was interesting, but they were not destined to meet in a final until 1933. the Leicesters made it into the 1932 final, to meet the 1st Battalion Welsh Guards, who ended the holders' run that year at around the quarter-final stage. The Dukes had little difficulty in reaching the third round, beating the Welch Regiment 12-3 in a hard-fought match, where their forwards dominated and allowed the lively Welch backs to see little of the ball. They then won 16-8 in a fast, exciting game against Royal Engineers (Aldershot). But in the next round they faced the Welsh Guards who, in front of their Colonel-in-Chief, won a scrappy game by being bigger, faster and more bustling. That match was full of infringements and penalties, but the Guards won 9-6 by three tries to two penalties.

The Guards subsequently drew with 2nd Battalion the Gloucestershire Regiment in their semi-final, then won the replay 10-0.

By their arrival, A L Novis and D A Kendrew put new life into the 2nd Battalion Leicestershie Regiment, who won their second and third round games easily but only just beat 2nd Battalion King's Own Regiment 7-6 in the fourth round. In the other semi-final they won 3-0 over the SWB in a snowstorm.

Led by L/Sgt Dunn with great skill and enthusiasm, the Guards played well as a team in the final and deserved their 11-3 win. They had no officers playing and their backs, three lance-corporals and four guardsmen, were not over-awed by their famous opponents.

The Welsh pack kept the ball very close and gave Novis and Beaty-Pownall little chance to show their brilliance. Furthermore, the Guards' halves outplayed the Leicesters' pair, Guardsman Quick at scrum-half living up to his name and frequently smothering his opposition before he could pass. After ten minutes Ward scored the first try

and Elias converted, followed by a try from Brown that sent the
Guards in at half-time 8-0 up. Kendrew kicked a penalty for the
Leicesters, but the Guards went further ahead at the end after a for-
ward rush.

Satisfaction came for the Leicesters in 1933 when they beat the
Welsh Guards in the semi-finals. Meanwhile the 1st Battalion Duke of
Wellington's Regiment were having a smooth journey to that year's
final along the other road.

Scrum-half for the Tigers that season was Lieut Derek Watson, who
was big, strong and remarkably fast for his size. One International,
Novis, was his partner at stand-off-half and the other, Kendrew, led
the pack. The Dukes, however, had a current International, Troop, to
lead their pack and a forward battle was just one feature of a final
that produced a most enjoyable mixture of the best elements of rugby
football. There were also outside movements, developed at high speed
by the backs, with Novis and Robinson as guiding brains for their
respective teams. And the tackling was of the highest order too, in
which Upjohn, Dalrymple and Laing for the Dukes and Allen, Beaty-
Pownall and Barlow for the Leicesters were prominent.

The Leicesters opened in great style, the influence of Novis in the
backs and Kendrew leading the forwards being soon apparent. Novis
had a brilliant first half, scoring a try between the posts and converting
it himself. Dunham gave them a further try from a forward rush ten
minutes before the interval. The Dukes missed an easy penalty in front
of the posts.

From 8-0 down, however, the Dukes rallied splendidly and produced a magnificently powered fight-back. They had begun to take
scrums instead of line-outs and gave the hint that they might gain
forward superiority. Within seven minutes of the re-start Robinson
stole away from a scrum and Bentley touched off a fine passing movement with a first-class try. Robinson followed this up with a reverse
pass to Townend, who sent Laing over. The irrepressible Robinson
then went round the blind side and sent Bentley in for a try, converted
by Laing. The game had been taken away from the Leicesters and
ultimately went 19-8 to the Dukes on two more tries, one for Miles
and a third for Bentley, converted by Holt.

A strong Welsh influence was to prevail again in the remaining six
years up to the Second World War, returning with the 1st Battalion
Welsh Guards when they won 4-0 against the 5th Battalion Royal
Tank Corps after extra time in the 1934 final, watched by the Prince
of Wales.

The 5th Battalion Royal Tanks beat the holders, 1st Battalion DWR

16–11 in one semi-final. In the other the Welsh Guards beat the Leicesters 14–11 after extra time. The Leicesters were without Novis and Kendrew left the field injured during extra time.

Although the Welsh Guards only won the final 4–0, again after extra time, they did so by a stupendous drop goal taken by Boast from near the halfway line. The match-winning kick and his all-round performance earned Boast great credit. He was the Guards captain and also trained the side.

The Royal Tank Corps team had some very bad luck as the final approached. They had played well in the early rounds but their International, H Rew was transferred from the battalion before the final 'due to the exigencies of the Service'!

Even without him the 5th Battalion Royal Tanks scrummaged more efficently than the Guards and got more of the ball, thanks to the excellence of Offord's hooking, and more than once they went very close to scoring. But the Welsh Guards, whose backs were all guardsmen – not an officer nor an NCO among them – that year managed to pull off the final win in the presence of their Colonel-in-Chief to compensate for letting him down in 1929, albeit that they had won since then when he was not there. The Prince of Wales, incidentally, was accompanied at this final, held at what was then the Command Central Ground, Aldershot, by the GOC, Gen The Hon Sir J Francis Gathorne-Hardy, whose name is perpetuated in one of the area's present-day SE District rugby trophies.

For 1935 it is not recorded what happened to either of the previous year's finalists, but a win for Wales was inevitable again as the 1st Battalion the Welch Regiment met the 2nd Battalion South Wales Borderers. The only earlier results for either side known are that 2nd Battalion SWB beat 2nd Battalion Leicesters 16–8 and 1st Battalion Welch Regiment defeated 2nd Battalion King's Own 14–0.

The 1st Battalion Welch Regiment won the final 11–0, their excellent teamwork being undoubtedly the deciding factor in the match. Their hooker completely outplayed his opposite number and in the loose they were very lively. The Borderers were mainly on the defensive and had a difficult task in containing the Welch backs. Jones scored the first try after some straight running and clean handling along the threequarter line. Owen put the Welch further ahead with a penalty goal.

Ibbitson started another movement by breaking through the middle to pass to Delaney, who completed the move with a reverse pass enabling Williams to score. Owen converted the try to give the Welch all their points by half-time. Although they did not score again, however, the Welch did not relax in the second half. The SWB saw a little more of the ball but could not pierce the Welch defence.

It is safe to say there was a good deal of talk about the development of rugby in the Welch Regiment during and after this final, for twenty-six years were bridged by the attendance of two of the spectators. There to congratulate the 1935 winners were 'Birdie' Partridge and F W Gransmore from the winning 1909 side.

The 5th Battalion Royal Tank Corps were back in the final of 1936 and made no mistake this time when they beat 2nd Battalion the King's Own Royal Regiment 11-0. They had already had their revenge on the 1st Battalion Welsh Guards for the 1934 final and the King's Own knocked out the holders, 1st Battalion Welch, to settle their old scores for 1935.

The King's Own beat 1st Battalion Welch 10-6 in the 1936 semifinals, taking advantage of the holders' back division being disorganised by injuries to Cowey, Delaney and Roberts. The Welch hooked the ball in four out of five scrums but could not penetrate the excellent King's Own defence.

In the other semi-final the 5th Battalion Royal Tanks beat the Welsh Guards 7-0, a tactical triumph worked out by their skipper and hooker, Lieut Offord. He knew he had no pace behind the scrum but, on the other hand, none opposed to him, and that was only one consideration. While he knew himself capable in the art of hooking, his pack would be heavily outweighed in the scrummage, and in the line-out the opposition would be a head and shoulders above those of his own eight.

His plan, therefore, was to take scrums instead of line-outs, heel on every possible occasion, and kick to gain ground. It worked like a charm, with the stand-off-half, Peebles, kicking a penalty goal and following up with a drop goal.

Offord had another strategy for the final, but so did the King's Own of course, and from the kick-off it was evident that each side was playing to a plan differing as widely as possible from the other's. The King's Own relied on a powerful back division and opened up the game at every opportunity. The Tanks pinned their faith on a pack of fast and dashing forwards. They were content for their fly-half to kick for touch and place them in a position for dropped goals or a score from a forward rush.

In the game of forwards versus backs, the King's Own developed attack after attack and it seemed only a question of time before they scored, but the excellent tackling of the Tanks, in addition to fine defensive kicking, kept them out. The Tanks, then gradually asserted themselves and Robinson, the scrum-half, dropped a very good goal. This was quickly followed by a try by Offord, from a good forward rush. The King's Own fought back well but the Tanks came on again and Robinson dropped his second goal.

The victory was a tremendous triumph for Offord's single-minded determination to play to a plan, but at least one King's Own player helped to set the seal on a classic game. Their centre, Lieut W V H Robins, also a distinguished Corinthian footballer, not only attracted attention with some determined runs but reminded many of a great player of former days, Basil Maclear (Irish International of the Army v Navy Inter-Service match of 1907) by wearing white kid gloves.

The ground had to be cleared of snow for the final in 1937 and it became very muddy, but despite this both sides kept the game open and handled the heavy and slippery ball well. The 1st Battalion the Prince of Wales Volunteers were an extremely fit and keen side and were well led by Butler. The Welch though were a very experienced side, under the inspirational international captain Cowey.

The Welch gained possession from the scrums with almost monotonous regularity. Their outsides, too, proved the speedier and better-combined force in attack, with Cowey a thrustful centre and Thomas a wing of exceptional pace. Cowey scored a try for the Welch but this was followed by a drop goal from Magee, the opposition centre. Delaney put the Welch ahead again, however, with a try that Owen converted and they sewed the game up when Buss scored from a cross kick, Owen converting again, leaving their opponents to settle the closing points of 13-7 with a late push-over try credited to Greene.

A revival in Gloucestershire Regiment rugby came about in the 1937/1938 season, obviously much welcomed as they had last won the Cup in 1910.

After the holders the 1st Battalion Welch Regiment had beaten 2nd Battalion SWB 22-0 in the fourth round, the 2nd Battalion Gloucesters removed them 9-8 in a semi-final. That was a tremendous game where the Gloucesters, whose points were from three successful penalty goals by Arengo-Jones, clearly had to hang on to win after changing ends 9-3 up.

The other finalists were to be the 1st Battalion Welsh Guards, who had beaten the 1937 runners-up 6-0 in the other semi-final, and a close final resulted where 2nd Battalion Gloucesters only won 3-0, but they thoroughly deserved their hard-earned victory, among other things for the way they marshalled their fans. The Gloucesters were given immense support for the final – in fifteen coachloads and numerous private cars!

Arengo-Jones kicked a penalty goal from wide out to make the only score after ten minutes. Both sides' tackling was of a high standard and although both went close to scoring after that the defences held out. In the second half the Welsh Guards worked the touch line extremely well and kept the Gloucesters pinned down for long periods, but the slender lead was not lost. Both teams were playing like Trojans when the closing whistle went.

After so much success in the period between the wars, it is perhaps not surprising that Wales should triumph again in 1939 to end an era. The honours went to the 1st Battalion Welch Regiment once more and the 1938 champions, 2nd Battalion Gloucesters, finished as runners-up that year, 6-3.

The 1st Battalion the Duke of Wellington's Regiment returned from Malta too late to play in the 1937/38 season, so hoped to make their mark again in 1938/39, and they did reach the semi-finals. But their old friends and rivals the 1st Battalion Welch were there to halt the Dukes' progress, as disorganised by an injury to their player Grieve, they were eventually beaten 25-3. The Gloucesters won the other semi-final 24-3 over the 1st Battalion South Lancashires (previously the Prince of Wales Volunteers) to reach their second successive final.

It was the Welsh who were hot favourites for the final and on paper they should have won easily, as so often happens in Army Cup rugby, this did not work out. Both sides were studded with Army and International players. The Gloucesters, with eleven of the previous season's victorious team still on view, had in their pack three who had played in the Army pack against the Navy the week before – Arengo-Jones, Tarrant and Farmer, while the Welch had the two Army halves – Ibbitson and Champion, the Army threequarters Delaney and Ford, who had also played for Wales, and the Army hooker, Owen. They had in addition their captain, Cowey, who although he had not appeared for the Army or Wales since 1935 was still playing almost as well as ever.

The Gloucesters' halves, Hardy and Dainty, proved just as good as Ibbitson and Champion, and their pack in the tight scrums proved better than the Welch. Unfortunately for the Gloucesters, despite their keeping the Welch restricted to their own part of the field in the second half, Arengo-Jones was not in kicking form and could only score one penalty from five attempts. By half-time the Welch already had their six points from a penalty by Owen and a try by Ford, after Cowey made a good opening. Though the Welch nearly scored again, the game finally finished 6-3 in their favour.

An interesting and amusing tailpiece was added to this final nearly twenty years later.

Owing to an overseas posting, and the matter being overlooked by the Army Rugby Union, the names of the winners for 1939 were not engraved on the Cup at that time. When the 1st Battalion Welch Regiment next won in 1956 their captain, John Davey, noticed the omission and had the trophy engraved 1939 under 1956!

At the onset of the First World War, after only a few years of the Army Cup competition, the trophy could have been anyone's for the taking, but a definite pattern was set between the wars that those 'rugby playing regiments', especially those of Welsh origins, were going to be hard to beat. Would this trend continue after the Second World War?

A rugby tradition in itself was not enough, however. It is a matter of some surprise that the Royal Artillery, who supplied a stream of outstanding players for the Army, including a number of Internationals, never managed to get a team into the Army Final. One reason might be that their players were widely distributed and little or no attempt was made to concentrate them in a particular regiment. The Royal Engineers too, despite reaching the final five times, with four of those bids by their Training Battalion, had also failed to win.

THE CHALLENGE OF THE CORPS
1947–1954

After the Second World War, the Army Cup competition resumed in the 1946/1947 season and now took in the British Army of the Rhine, the Army Final to be between the UK winning team and the champions of BAOR. Different groups certainly began to emerge, not the RA and the Sappers in particular but the RAMC and the Royal Signals.

Although over the years the RAMC had more International players than any other corps or regiment, until 1947 no RAMC side was even mentioned in connection with an Army Cup Final. In that season, however, their Depot and Training Establishment burst forth. This, as seen in their Corps' report, was largely due to the enthusiasm and encouragement of their Commandant, Brig H L Glyn-Hughes, whose name was well known and respected throughout the rugby world and who was a most popular President of the Barbarians.

The RAMC had two great International threequarters, J A Gregory, who played for England, and J Matthews, of Wales. In the forwards they had A G M Watt who gained six caps for Scotland. The Depot only just beat 1st Training Regiment Royal Signals, for the UK title, but win they did, 5–0.

To keep the Welsh flag flying, the BAOR Final was won by the 2nd Battalion Welsh Guards, but that was to be a rarity in the immediate post-war years and the lone appearance by the 2nd Battalion, who reached the final in the only season that the Cup was played for in their short lifetime. Their team was captained by their battalion second-in-command A A Duncan, who had played for the Welsh Guards before the war but was better known as an outstanding amateur international golfer.

After a slow and somewhat ragged start the RAMC forwards, although frequently beaten for possession in the tight scrums, began to get a grip on the final, but the only score in the first half followed a neat interception by Gregory, who side-stepped the full-back to score between the posts. Dewsnip converted the try. The RAMC pressed constantly and had the wind in their favour, yet there was no further scoring before half-time.

Eventually, however, the Internationals Matthews and Gregory showed their class and produced what was virtually an action replay.

Matthews opened a passing movement with a delightful swerving run before passing to Gregory, who again side-stepped the full-back and scored under the posts, with Dewsnip making the conversion as before. The Guards replied with a penalty by Havard, but that was their all and they lost 10–3, though they could be proud of holding such strong opponents to a seven-point margin. The RAMC thoroughly deserved their win and had not had their lines crossed in their Cup matches.

The Royal Signals compensated for their UK Final defeat of 1947 by coming right to the fore in 1948 and staying there for nearly the whole period until the end of the 1950s. It was not their UK runners-up unit 1st Training Regiment that started this off but the Signals Training Centre (Catterick), but 1st Training Regiment soon took over.

Signals Training Centre had little difficulty in getting to the top, apart from a game with the REME Training Centre that had to be played twice. The first encounter was a 3–3 draw, but in the replay the Signals won 11–6 after a hard game. The final was with Royal Engineers (Hameln) but if the Sappers looked to this match to change their Corps' earlier run of ill luck in the contest they were disappointed. Signals Training Centre won 6–0 and it might have been more.

A rather scrappy final had the Signals' backs showing their greater thrust and launching some exciting attacks, while the Sapper forwards held their own in the scrums but lacked speed in the loose. Signals' points came from two tries and both were scored in the second half, by Gaunt and Gloag the two wing threequarters. Both conversions were missed, though, and so were six kickable penalties.

Any team reaching the UK Final in the 1948/1949 season would have faced formidable odds, for the Welch Regiment, the Duke of Wellington's Regiment, and the Welsh Guards were all back in England. This was a period of amalgamations and the 1st and 2nd Battalions of both the Welch and the Dukes were joined into one. For the Dukes two special players, Shuttleworth and Hardy, were just starting their rugby careers, C F Grieve, the old Scottish International, was the captain of their team, and F J Reynolds, the England stand-off-half of 1937–38, was also still a force, playing in the centre.

None of this impressed the 1st Training Regiment, Royal Signals, a great deal, though they were given a hard time. They met the Dukes in the UK semi-finals and from 3–3 the game went into extra time, but then the Signallers won 13–8 and they followed that up by beating 1st Battalion Welch Regiment 19–14 in a tremendous UK Final: a match in which the late Chairman of the History Committee, Brig Riding, played when he was serving is this Welch Regiment.

Yet again a team of Sappers represented BAOR, that year 9th Independent Squadron RE, but only to be overwhelmed by the Signallers 31-3. The final was rather an anticlimax, but it was a refreshing game in that no points were scored from penalties at all. Seven tries for the Signallers came from the following T G H Jackson, their Scottish wing, who also dropped a goal, N I M Hall, the England fly-half (two), Bidgood, Bell (two) and Murphy, one converted by Cross. Five tries were scored in the first half and two in the second, where Tranter added a drop goal. Richardson scored a try for the Sappers.

The 1st Training Regiment, Royal Signals, retained the Army Cup in 1950 with an even more convincing win, 36-0, upsetting the comeback of the RAMC Depot and Training Establishment In a surprisingly one-sided final, in front of their Colonel-in-Chief, the Princess Royal, who presented the Cup, the Signallers scored nine tries, three being converted, and kicked a penalty goal. The RAMC, more accustomed to doctoring others, were too afflicted by their own injuries on this occasion. They were very unlucky to have their captain, the Army, Scotland and British Lions' player D W C Smith, crocked before the game, then their fly-half, Gledhill, and right centre Stevens were off the field for more than half of the final.

Among the RAMC victims on their way to the final were the Welsh Guards. The Signallers beat the 1st Battalion Welch Regiment in the UK Final, meaning that once again an Infantry regiment had been thwarted of the ultimate chance. The 1st Battalion DWR had been defeated by RE (Ripon) in the first round that year, 6-3.

The 1st Battalion Welch left to serve in Korea in early 1951 and were not to play in the Army Cup competition again until 1955, but their Training Centre had a good enough side to beat DWR 6-0 after extra time and to do well in the 1950/51 season, until they came up against the holders, who eventually beat them 12-3.

The Signallers, now captained by 2nd Lieut A C Birtwistle (later Maj-Gen. Birtwistle, Deputy President of the Army Rugby Union), put out the BAOR winners, a strong Welsh Guards' side, 9-3 in that year's semi-finals, to reach their third final in a row. In the other semi-final the previous year's runners-up, Depot and Training Establishment, RAMC, lost out 12-3 to 1st Guards Independent Para Coy (the Parachute Regt), who had as their captain Capt J M H Roberts, a Welsh trialist who was also captain of the Army team.

Although they won the final to achieve the hat-trick, the Signallers had a much more difficult time and only did so 9-6. A steady downpour had made the Aldershot ground a quagmire and safe handling impossible. The Guards adapted themselves much more quickly to these conditions and, despite the Signallers scoring first when Luscombe got a try from a line-out, they soon levelled the scores with a penalty by Cahill, who then kicked another penalty to put the Guards ahead, very much against the run of play.

With time running out Miller dropped a splendid goal for the Signallers, however, and, from a comparatively dry piece of mud far out, Hazell kicked a great penalty goal to give them a deserved win as the quicker and more clever team, but every credit went to Roberts and his men for nearly pulling off a surprise.

Depot and Training Establishment, RAMC, had their revenge on 1st Training Regiment, Royal Signals, in the 1952 UK Final, where they defeated the holders 6–5. But their triumph did not last long as they went into the Army Final against the 1st Battalion Welsh Guards and lost 14–0. The Guards had previously come through a very hard BAOR semi-final with DWR before winning 6–3, and they had reached the final after a total of eight matches that brought them 225 points for only 21 conceded.

The leadership of CSM Dando played a large part in the Guards' victory which, it may be noted, notched up the first win for a regimental side since the war.

Handling on both sides was poor and a number of scoring chances were missed, so the RAMC held their own until half-time, when the only points were from a penalty goal kicked by Williams. But eventually Thomas dropped a goal, Dando followed up with a try, converted by Williams, and Evans got another from a loose scrum. Cahill who played for the Welsh Guards here had been with the Guards Independent Company in the previous final.

An especially interesting final took place in 1953 when 1st Training Regiment, Royal Signals, stormed back to beat the 1st Battalion Welsh Guards 35–0.

The Signallers reached the final in six games by scoring 281 points to 12, but not one member from their 1951 winning team could be seen in the final. The Welsh Guards had come through the BAOR contest by latterly defeating 30th Heavy Anti Aircraft Regiment, RA, 14–6, while in the UK Final the Signallers won 28–6 against 1st Training Battalion, RASC. The Welch Regiment and the Duke of Wellington's Regiment were both unable to play in that season's contest. The RAMC runners-up from the year before were polished off in the second round by 3rd Training Regiment, Royal Engineers.

For those Guards experiencing their second final, this one was very different from the first. After the Signallers opened with the wind behind them and Boston scored two tries, one converted by Dunn, the Welsh could only hope to rally in the rest of the game, but from the interval the Signallers just took complete control to run out easy winners. Boston had a magnificent game and scored six tries altogether, once intercepting a bad pass on his own '25' to run through the opposition and get a try between the posts. Dunn's kicking was outstanding, with a penalty and four conversions. It was difficult to understand that only SQMS Rees of the Signals' team gained an Army cap in 1953. The Guards re-arranged their side in an attempt to stem the tide, Dando going to scrum-half, Roberts to fly-half and Jones to full-back, but to no avail.

Nothing could prevent 1st Training Regiment, Royal Signals, from winning their fifth Army Cup in six years as they had an easy road to the 1954 final and there beat the 1st Battalion South Wales Borderers 11-6.

Three times the Signallers exceeded 50 points, when they overcame 6th Training Regiment, RAC, 84-0, 6th (Boys) Training Regiment, Royal Signals, 56-0, and 11th SME Regiment 53-0, towards a total of 302 points for just three against in reaching the final.

The 1st Battalion the South Wales Borderers were left to represent the regiments because the 1st Battalion Welsh Guards, the Welch Regiment and the Duke of Wellington's Regiment were all elsewhere abroad, but they did it uncommonly well. Before winning 5-0 in a very hard BAOR Final with the 6th Royal Tank Regiment they had defeated 2nd Regiment, RHA, 16-11, 30th HAA Regiment, RA, 3-0, and 21st Field Regiment, RE, 6-0. The RHA match was sticky as the SWB were losing 11-3 with ten minutes to go, but they drew level to earn extra time and there scored a converted try that set them up for that third round win.

The final was played at Hanover in perfect conditions. Both sides had their share of star players. The Signals' centres Jackson and Boston, their fly-half Gabbitas, and the full-back, Dunn, were all outstanding Rugby League players, while up front was Reg Higgins, who was a brilliant forward for Lancashire and later for England and the British Lions. In the SWB team was Glyn Davidge, a future Welsh cap and British Lions' player, Rex Richards, another Welsh cap, and Norman Walker, the full-back who was to gain three caps for Wales.

A beautiful try by Boston opened the scoring and the heavier Signals' pack controlled the tight, but the Borderers were very lively in the loose, with Davidge outstanding. Yates crossed the line for them but was recalled for a previous infringement. Within minutes, however, Morgan had kicked a penalty goal to put them on terms. The half-time score of 8-3 to the Signals was a fair reflection of the play so far, though. They had gone ahead again by launching a brilliant attack that resulted in Manley scoring under the posts, making the kick a formality for Dunn.

In the second half another penalty goal by Morgan brought the SWB within striking distance, but the Signallers scored a further good try to make themselves worthy winners.

The Signallers' wonderful record of wins would not go unnoticed anywhere, and it unfortunately attracted more attention than they could have wished. Protests came from certain quarters that training regiment's had an unfair advantage over other units.

At the Annual General Meeting of the Army Rugby Union on 24 June 1954, the following proposal was received from Mons Officer Cadet School:

That the rules of the ARU Challenge Cup Competition be altered in order to permit the holding of two competitions of equal status. One for the regiments – battalions etc. which include the designation 'Training' in their official title. The other for all other Units.

Or an alternative to the above:

That the rules of the ARU Challenge Cup Competition be altered in order to permit the holding of two competitions of equal status. One for all those stationed in the UK and Northern Ireland. The other for those overseas. This decision to remain so long as the great majority of the Active Army remains outside the UK.

The Hon Secretary reminded the meeting of a similar proposal made in 1950 which had been rejected. He said that the Executive Committee considering the present proposal felt that it had been inspired largely because of the continuing success of Training Regiment, Royal Signals, which had won the Competition five times in the last six years.

The Chairman then read a letter from Maj-Gen Scott who explained that he and Maj-Gen Penney had been invited by the Royal Signals Corps Committee to examine the problem and to put their views to the Army Rugby Union.

The letter stated that they were satisfied that the present predominance of the Regiment arose from no improper means but from a powerful combination of favourable factors, namely:

a. The location in a Rugby playing County and the strong connection which had been built up with local Clubs and Schools.
b. The nature of the training in the Regiment which was for high category trades demanding the type of young man produced by these Clubs and Schools.

c. The abnormally long training period for these trades (6 months).

d. The football reputation which had been built up attracted further keen footballers.

e. A very capable organiser.

Some of these factors might well change and they felt that there was no justification for altering the rules of the Competition to exclude the Unit. They had considered the possibility of a reorganisation at Catterick to avoid concentrating the young footballers in the one Regiment, but had discarded this as militarily unsound. In the circumstances, they were of the opinion that for the present it would be in the best interests of the Army and Corps for 1 Training Regiment not to enter for the Competition. They saw plainly the objections to this course but thought it less damaging than any other which might be considered. The Chairman said that he had gone into the matter at Catterick and was himself entirely convinced that the reasons for 1 Training Regiment's high performance were as set out in the letter.

Lieut-Col Spicer, Mons Officer Cadet School, withdrew his motion.

The Chairman said that any changes of the traditional nature of the competition should only be made after very careful consideration. Conditions were still changing and the time might well come when the balance between active and training Units was restored. He appreciated the action of 1 Training Regiment, Royal Signals, in temporarily withdrawing from the competition. He also thanked them for the excellent football which they had provided in recent years and hoped that it would not be too long before they felt it right to return to the competition.

Finally, the Chairman instructed the Hon Secretary to record fully the reasons for the Royal Signals' decision so that Rugby representatives in all Units would be aware of both them and the circumstances in which the decision was made.

The good sense of the ARU prevailed and the Royal Signals deserve considerable credit for the dignified way they dealt with the situation. All the Rugby followers knew the success of the Regiment was well deserved and their contribution to Army Rugby was considerable.

THE LINE REGIMENTS FIGHT BACK
1955-1964

After their two full attempts to recapture their 1947 glory, Depot and Training Establishment, RAMC, won the Army Cup in 1955, and largely at the expense of Welsh opposition. But for the RAMC there would have been another all-Welsh final.

The Welch Regiment returned from the Far East with a notable rugby achievement behind them. They had beaten 11-0 the Fijian Infantry Regiment who had not lost a game for four years! It must have been something of a shock to them, therefore, when, safely reaching the UK Final, they were defeated 19-0 by the RAMC.

Meanwhile in BAOR the South Wales Borderers were having a very hard fight with the Royal Welch Fusiliers to see who would go into the Army Final on their side. In their first match the score was 3-3 after extra time, but in the replay the SWB won 3-0 thanks to a good try by Browning, their right wing.

The SWB, having been runners-up the year before, must have thought they stood a good chance with the Royal Signals out of the way and the RAMC not having much luck in 1950 and 1952, but like the Welch Regiment they were in for a disappointment as the RAMC won 16-0

The RAMC had no star players such as they had in 1947, but nine of their team had played for the Army, and they soon showed their opponents who was in charge of this operation. The SWB, outweighted and out-hooked in the tight, countered with some magnificent line-out play, fiery foot rushes and adroit kicking, hoping by intense spoiling to unsettle the Depot and force them into mistakes on which they could pounce. Close marking and devastating tackling by the Depot, however, and their coolness under pressure, prevented the Borderers from making very much headway.

Gradually the Depot's well-drilled and intelligently-led pack got on top, and the backs were far more incisive than their opponents. Maeckelburghe made a swift break and accelerating through the narrowest of gaps sent Regan over for a try. Just before half-time Watchorne pounced on the ball close to the line and scored wide out. Rumney converted.

In the second half Fulton, the Depot scrum-half, broke away on his own and weaved and dummied his way through the defence to score a try that Rumney again converted. The SWB came back well and it required all the Depot's skill and energy to hold them, but they could not score and two minutes before time the RAMC got the best try of the match, Byrne crossing the line after the most brilliant passing movement. A game played in a splendid spirit and with fine sportsmanship was won by the Depot because of their excellent teamwork, defence, and the brilliance of their half-backs.

Several interesting features characterised the 1955/56 competition, not least that the 1st Training Regiment, Royal Signals, entered again. They managed to reach the sixth round, but there lost 5-3 to the 1st Battalion the Welch Regiment, whose own progress was not to be halted by anyone that season. The RAMC holders were beaten 8-6 in the fifth round by the 32nd Assault Engineer Regiment, RE.

The Welch Regiment were inspired by their Commanding Officer, 'Bun' Cowey, who had done so much for their rugby, firstly as a player, captain and trainer before the Second World War and then by his enthusiasm and dedication behind the scenes in later years. Although he handed over his command a few weeks before the final his inspiration remained to give the Welch the edge to win 9-8 in the final with the 1st Battalion Royal Welch Fusiliers.

This was the first all-Welsh final since 1935 and the first time since the war that no Corps' team had survived. The match took place at Dortmund and, as the scores suggest, was most exciting. The Fusiliers, who won the toss, took advantage of a cold howling wind that was blowing straight down the pitch and after twenty minutes a break by L/Cpl Thomas resulted in their hooker going over for a fine try. But only three minutes later Hamer of the Welch Regiment collected the ball on the right wing and made a brilliant run to score just inside the left corner flag. So it was 3-3 at half-time.

The Welch Regiment surged ahead in the second half when Parry kicked a penalty goal and Kilminster got a good try, but the foward battle was fiery and robust and the excitement became intense when Thomas (any one of three in their team!) scored a beautiful try for the Fusiliers and Jones (one of two!) made the conversion. At that stage there were only three minutes left, just enough for the Fusiliers to snatch victory with a last moment chance for a drop goal – but Johns mis-kicked.

As these things worked out, 1st Training Regiment, Royal Signals, had their place at the top restored and the opportunity for revenge against the 1st Battalion Welch Regiment when the two met in the 1957 final. The Signallers won 15-3.

On paper they were well matched before they faced each other, with the odds rather in favour of the holders. When they won the UK Final 16-0 over 11th/12th SME Regiment, RE, Chatham, the Signallers rounded off total points of 117 for only three conceded. The Welch Regiment, who won the BAOR Cup 12-0 against 1st (BR) Corps Troops Column, RASC, had thereby amassed 132 points without conceding anything.

From the final at Aldershot the Signallers emerged as worthy winners, but at half-time it was the Welch who had shown as the more attractive and enterprising side. For a while, in fact, they dominated in all departments.

In the second half, however, the Signals' team came to life and grew better and better as the game went on, owing a great deal to Ken Scotland, their captain, who made two of their tries and converted three. Despite intense marking by opposition skipper Davey, he controlled the game in a very competent manner. Scotland made a fine cross kick for Williams to score the first Signals' try and converted this and one by Benson two minutes later. He then made a dazzling break with a fine change of pace to send Williams in for his second try. The Welch could only score just before time when J Davies (one of two in the Welch team sharing both surname and initials) broke on the right and passed to Mathias, who passed inside for Lewis to score in the corner.

Apart from Scotland, Evans the full-back and D A Williams in the threequarters had splendid games for the Signallers, while Davies the Welch centre (the other was the full-back) and Williams at scrum-half played well for their side, with Owen and Thomas always prominent for the Signallers and Davey having an outstanding game as the Welch captain.

The Duke of Wellington's Regiment had not won the Army Cup since 1933 and had not reached the final since the war, so when they made up for that in both respects in 1958 it was a matter for celebration, but especially as it was 1958. For that was the last season that leading players Mike Hardy and Dennis Shuttleworth, the DWR halves, were to play together for the unit. Could the occasion be marked with their first Cup winners' medal?

The most important match that probably decided the Cup was not so much the final as a sixth round tie between the Dukes and the holders, 1st Training Regiment, Royal Signals. The Dukes were stationed at Hollywood, Northern Ireland, that season and to reach the UK Final beat the Signallers 8-0, but by no means easily. They had all their points by half-time, Saville dropping a good goal and

Gilbert-Smith scoring a try with a brilliant piece of anticipation, beating two opponents for a touch down between the posts. Hardy converted. But the Signallers completely dominated the tight and the Dukes hardly ever hooked in the scrum. For all their constant pressure, though, the Signallers could not score.

In the final, in Germany, the Dukes met 1st (BR) Corps Troops Column, RASC, who had won the BAOR Cup 24-6 against the 3rd Royal Tanks, and if their pre-match problems were anything to go by the UK champions could have run out of luck. The Dukes' team had their money stolen, and one player, 2nd Lieut Birch forgot his boots, so he was forced to be a spectator while 2nd Lieut Duckney took his place.

Things like that can often unsettle a team, but when the final started it was obvious that the Service Corps were up against an experienced and well-drilled side who had not let themselves be flustered. Their line-up was formidable enough to worry any opposition. At half-back there were the Internationals Hardy and Shuttleworth; in the pack was the Scottish International Gilbert-Smith; and the threequarters consisted of three Rugby League players and one Union player from Halifax.

The Dukes were to win 23-5 and had their first 15 points before the interval. Saville scored the first try, neatly kicking the ball over the full-back's head to touch down close to the posts, and Hardy converted. Haywood got the next try and Saville converted. Just before half-time Dasent shook off two tackles to score in the corner. Saville made an excellent conversion.

The RASC never gave up and by good tackling restricted the Dukes to a goal and penalty in the second half, all of those points down to Saville, who scored the try and converted it himself as well as kicking the penalty to give him a personal tally of 15 points in the match. Just before the final whistle the RASC scored a good try through Oxley, which was converted by Wakefield.

Shuttleworth was outstanding as the Dukes' captain and he and Hardy controlled the game, giving their dangerous backs plenty of ball. Among the forwards Cowell hooked well, Arnold towered at the line-out, and the back row of Gilbert-Smith, Addison and Shenton dominated the opposing half-backs.

Everyone was delighted that Shuttleworth and Hardy ended their partnership on a Cup-winning note, as they had done so much for the Dukes and the Army. They had now achieved what 'Horsey' Browne, 'Bull' Faithfull and man other outstandingly good Dukes' players had failed to do, although they all tried equally hard.

It was all clearly meant to be, for the 1958/59 season was very different for DWR. The 1st Training Regiment, Royal Signals, got their own back with a 5-0 sixth-round win then that put the holders out and set the Signallers up for another final. They went on to beat 3rd Training Regiment, RE, 48-6 and won the UK Cup with a narrow 3-0 victory over the 1st Battalion South Wales Borderers. The other Army finalists were the 1st Battalion Royal Scots, who had never previously attained those heights.

The Signallers thoroughly deserved their 12-9 win, but the Royal Scots made them fight every inch of the way and at one time looked as if they might pull off a surprise. It was a great game played with immense gusto.

Starting with the wind behind them, the Signallers pressed continuously but could not cross the line. Langton, however, put them ahead with two well kicked penalties, and just before half-time Dalby made a half break. There was a short kick over defenders' heads and Carter raced over the line to score.

Chisholm managed to kick a penalty for the Scots moments before the half-time whistle went, and in the second half, with the wind behind them, the Scots pinned the Signallers down and finally Cook kicked a penalty to make the score 9-6. The last five minutes were full of action as a scrum on the Scots' line enabled the Signallers to 'push over' for another try, but Cook proved with another penalty that the Scots were not yet finished. It was an exciting game indeed.

However many Scotsmen there might have been in Army Cup teams heretofore, the 1959 appearance of the Royal Scots was the first real evidence that their Country's units were not just leaving the competition to the Welsh and the English. Then in 1960 the King's Own Scottish Borderers, newly stationed in Berlin, improved on this by winning the Cup – and then they won it again in 1961. As they had had no opportunity to enter the contest since 1938 this was indeed an achievement.

Triumph for the KOSB was to begin three frustrating years for 1st Battalion DWR of reaching the final without a win of the Cup at all. They made a very promising start in 1959/60 when they were in Northern Ireland by building a sound team with a pack that became a dominant factor and was on occasions unstoppable. During their last few weeks in the province they beat a strong Ulster XV that included such players as J Boyle, S D Irwin, W J McBride and A C Pedlow, the Dukes winning 19-5. On returning to England they then defeated Blackheath 24-0 and Richmond 19-6.

It was therefore expected that the Dukes would have a successful run in the Army competition and they did, reaching the 1960 final after scoring 134 points to nil. They won the UK Cup 32-0 against Mons Officer Cadet School.

That year's final was the first with the Dukes for Mike Campbell-Lamerton (who appeared in the team alongside his brother) and it can only be regarded as ironic, in view of his International career for Scotland, that he should make his Cup debut opposite a Scottish unit, whose own player Shillinglaw, the scrum-half, gained his first International cap for Scotland at Dublin that season.

In the first half, with the wind behind them, the KOSB pinned the Dukes down in their own '25' by long kicks to touch, though the Dukes managed to gain ground by forward rushes and good handling movements. Yet despite keeping up their pressure throughout the KOSB line could not be crossed.

The DWR line was not to be crossed either, but the KOSB were busy notching up points from penalties, the first coming after thirteen minutes from Berry, who had moved to scrum-half while Shillinglaw played instead at fly-half. Once or twice the Dukes went close to scoring, but that was all, and the Borderers went further ahead when MacDonald kicked a penalty from near the touch line.

In the second half the Dukes, now with the wind in their favour, could not cope with the splendidly aggressive tackling and covering of their opponents, and finally gave away a penalty in front of their own posts, enabling Berry to add further points. It was just not the Dukes' day and they were beaten 9-0.

The pundits certainly expected DWR to gain their revenge when it turned out that the same two units would be meeting in the 1961 final. But the KOSB had other ideas and held them off 6-3, displaying real attacking flair and power in a well-disciplined and well-drilled performance.

Playing at Aldershot on a lovely spring day with hardly a breath of wind, the final had the KOSB following a match plan as they had in 1960, denying their opponents the ball, capitalising on their mistakes, giving nothing away, and putting constant pressure on the more talented side.

On this occasion the battle up front developed into a tough struggle with each pack trying to neutralise the other. The Dukes started strongly and pressed the KOSB very hard in their own '25', but the opposition pack proved to be heat-resistant and robust in the line-out and held the more lively Dukes, who were perhaps a little unlucky not to score early on. The KOSB led 3-0 a half-time from a penalty goal.

Curry dropped a smart goal to level the scores, which looked more encouraging for the Dukes than the year before, but after some intense pressure by them the KOSB came more into the game and good tactical kicking kept them down in the Dukes' half. Eventually MacDonald flighted an excellent penalty from the halfway line to win the match.

Without wishing to detract in any way from the excellent performance of the KOSB in winning the Cup in two successive seasons, it is astonishing that they achieved this without scoring a try in either final. But it must, of course, be remembered that they also did not have their line crossed.

The same units seem to meet almost unbelievably often in the Army Cup rounds, if not in the final, and at last in 1961–62 the Dukes blew the whistle on the KOSB by knocking them out in the sixth round. This set the Dukes up for the UK Final, where they beat the 1st Battalion RWF 9–0 in a match spoilt by constant infringements, giving them a record from four games of 101 points to nil.

But in the Army Final they came up against the 1st Battalion Welsh Guards, who completed the frustration the Scots had started. The Guards, coming in via a BAOR Final where they won 14–9 against the 1st Battalion Welch Regiment, had a good close game with the Dukes that stood 6–6 until the last few minutes, but their teamwork and splendid forwards tipped the scales to give them a well-deserved victory in the end at 9–6.

The Guards' forwards kept the ball tight and made some telling rushes. In the set scrums, where Baxter hooked admirably, the Dukes got a lot of the ball, but the tackling of the Guards' backs kept them at bay until a break by Sabine resulted in Marsay scoring a try. Curry kicked a penalty to increase the Dukes' lead, but the Guards drew level with two penalties. At the end the Dukes heeled from a scrum on their own '25' and Hearne, the Guards' great forward, snapped up the ball and passed to Woodward, who scored.

A point of extra interest about the 1962 final is that Dennis Shuttleworth and Mike Campbell-Lamerton were both in the DWR team, almost exactly twenty years before their sons were to play together for the Army at Inter-Service level, as noted in the previous Section.

The 1962/63 season made things worse for the DWR, while the Welsh Guards sailed on towards a second win and then a hat-trick, but they were both linked again by the sudden appearance of a new rugby force in a 'David and Goliath' situation. The emerging team came from 28th Company, RAOC, a unit of only around 120 men, but led by the great Army and Scottish forward Norman Bruce.

A weakened Dukes' side succumbed 12–6 to the RAOC newcomers

Army v French Army 1940
Above: Team and officials saluting National Anthem
Below: Team and officials approach the Unknown Soldier's Grave, Arc de Triomphe

Army Cup 1947
Winners: Training Establishment RAMC
Back row: Verney, Marsh, Watt, Rees, Rowlands, Richmond, Kirk, Houghton, Smart, Forshaw, Godsell
Seated: Kindon, Goulden, Gregory, FM The Viscount Montgomery, Matthews, Glyn-Hughes, Mackie, Robbins, Co
Seated at front: Scott, Davies, Pearce, Dewsnip

Army Challenge Cup 1949–50
Winners: 1 Training Regiment, Signals
Back row: Smith, Holliday, Thomas, Saunt, Fathers, Stewart, Turnpenny, Birtwistle
Front row: Hoskins, Mason, Fraser, Hepper, Reeve, Morphy, Luscombe, Cross, Bidgood

Army (3) v Royal Navy (0) 1953
Back row: Mills (Referee), Thomson, Broome, Robins, Black, Bland, Owen, Tippett, Macdonald, O'N Wallis
Seated: Beringer, Shuttleworth, Neale (Capt), Baume, Edwards
Seated at front: Rees, Brewer

Captain D W C Smith: Scotland, Combined Services, The Army talks to Ted Savage, an outstanding administrator for the Army

Army Cup 1960
Winners: 1 Bn King's Own Scottish Borderers
Back row: Nichol, Anderson, Paterson, Lyall, Shaw, Turner, Tait, Grant, Wilson, Redpath
Front row: Newlands, MacDonald*, Shillinglaw*, Johnston, Robertson MacLeod, Reynolds, Berry, Wilson, Mattingl
* International

Army v Royal Air Force 1961
Back row: (Touch Judge) Braybrooke, Handfield-Jones, Heath, Moyle, Crooks, Vaux, Rosser, Edgecombe, Referee
Seated: Renilson, Sharp, Bruce (Capt), Payne, Parker
Seated at front: Oulton, MacDonald

Army v Royal Navy 1964
Back row: Guthrie, Stancombe, Eastwood, Edwards, Friend, Chapman, Brown, Waqabaca, Hardy (Touch Judge)
Front row: Bryce, Braybrooke, Bruce, Campbell-Lamerton (Capt), Reid, Moroney, Handfield-Jones

The Centenary Match 1978
HRH The Duke of Edinburgh with Andy Hoon, the Army Captain

Army Cup 1967
Winners: 1 Bn Duke of Wellington's Regiment

Army v Royal Navy 1984
Back row: High (Referee), Tucker, Shaw, Byrne, Peacock, Brown, Travers, McFarlane, Lockitt, Ball, Bedford, McKay, Bassom, Blomquist, Silcox, Davies (Coach)
Front row: Neild, D Johnson, Davies, Warfield (Capt), McCall, Harvey, Christopher

Army Cup 1984-85

Winners: 7th Regiment Royal Horse Artillery

Back row: Day, Bradshaw, Vicary, Commander, King, Jubb, Holford, Sharples, Hill, Bennion, Charlton, Bogie

Front row: Syems, Reese, Beazley, Byford, Richards, Lewis, Farley, Gascoyne, Goglan

in the fifth round and Bruce's team went on to reach the UK Final and win it, while in BAOR the 1st Battalion Welsh Guards were defending the Cup strongly. They beat the 1st Battalion Lancashire Fusiliers in the BAOR Final.

It was the first time that an RAOC side had reached the final and Bruce had accomplished this despite the limited strength of his unit and the fact that some of his men were comparatively inexperienced rugby players. But as their captain he was a great inspiration. His spirit was infectious and the team he had picked and moulded did him proud. They were affectionately known as 'Bruce's Private Army'! In the final he himself played in the middle of the back row, from where he cajoled, chivvied and encouraged his team by his own fiery example. And they very nearly pulled off what would have been one of the most staggering results in Army Cup history.

The Bible tells us that Goliath stood 'six cubits and a span' (a cubit being 18 to 22 inches and a span some nine inches) and considering the opposition in this final this is an apt analogy. The Welsh Guards were a more experienced and, of course, heavier and taller side. They were well led by Guthrie. 'Bruce's Private Army' were not in the least deterred, however, by opponents who might easily have crushed them into the ground.

Peel put the Guards ahead with a penalty, but by half-time the RAOC had equalised with one by Richards. In the second half Peel put the Guards in front again with another penalty, a fine kick, and then Ackerman, rapidly following up a missed drop at goal, scored an opportunist try. The Ordnance team developed some fast open attacks and eventually Walker dropped a snap goal, but at 9-6 the Guards held on for a thoroughly-deserved win. The holders remained in possession, yet they and everyone else had been shown what might have been possible in that or any other year.

Completing their hat trick in 1964 gave the Welsh Guards no difficulty after that. This is not to belittle the 1st Battalion Somerset and Cornwall Light Infantry, who put up a courageous performance against them in the next Army Final, played in Berlin, but the Guards won that 25-3, being a very much stronger side.

The Welsh Guards were poised for their third win in a row when they began by beating 12th Regiment RSME 40-0 and took the UK Cup 12-6 over 7th Regiment RHA. The SCLI, to-date the only Light Infantry Regiment to reach the final, did not have an easy path there, but were greatly encouraged by defeating 1st Battalion RWF 13-12 in the fifth round and winning the BAOR Cup 13-6 against 19th Regiment RA.

With a strong wind behind them the SCLI started the final promisingly by soon going three points up when Walker kicked a penalty goal, and things were not too bad for them up to half-time, despite the Guards doing all the pressing, for there only came a try against them five minutes before the interval when Geen crossed in the corner.

But with the wind now helping their side, the Guards took control in the second half and piled up try after try, one a brilliant solo effort by Griffiths, a second from Geen, and others by Davies, Powell, Bowen and Skinner. Davies converted two of them. As if that was not enough affliction, the Light Infantry were without their player Carter for most of the second half. Arundel led the SCLI with immense drive and determination and made certain their stronger and faster opponents never took complete control.

Unknown to them at that time the Welsh Guards' successes were keeping them in trim for a show-down with a rejuvenated DWR that was to colour the next four years.

INFANTRY ALL THE WAY
1965-1973

The 1st Battalion Duke of Wellington's Regiment and the 1st Battalion Welsh Guards met again in the 1965 Army Final, but by then the Dukes had moved to BAOR and this must have changed their luck, while that of the Guards was running out. The Dukes gained revenge for 1962 by winning 11-6.

They began their Cup run in a convincing manner by beating the previous year's BAOR champions, 1st Battalion SCLI, 33-3. Their captain, Dick Mundell, patiently and diligently trained the side to play good rugby and team spirit was the highest priority.

For the UK Cup the Welsh Guards had a very hard and exciting game against 63rd (Para Bde) Company, RASC before eventually just winning 14-11.

The final was played at Aldershot on a very cold day, which resulted in a number of dropped passes due to chilled hands. It was largely a forward battle. The Guards, looking for their fourth win an a row, went ahead in the first half when Guthrie kicked a penalty goal, but determined running by Edwards on the wing enabled him to put the Dukes level when he swerved outside his opposing wing and then inside the full-back.

After half-time the Dukes took the lead, thanks to Edwards, who again slashed his way through to score his third try, having previously quickly followed up a kick to score. Pettigrew converted the last try from near the touch line. The Guards siezed on a defensive mistake by the Dukes and a magnificent passing movement resulted in Phillips scoring a try. It was not converted but was a tonic for the Welshmen, whose half-backs then ran and kicked intelligently to force the Dukes to defend desperately. The Dukes, however, held out for a deserved win. Edwards was their outstanding back and Mundell, Redwood-Davies and Hemmings a formidable front row, with Mundell's leadership an important factor in their victory.

It is perhaps of interest to note here that the limit on officer players for the competition no longer applied and had not done so for several years. This was of particular benefit to the Dukes who, as can be seen in the team lists, often went 'one over the eight', sometimes two, and in the 1965 final had as many as twelve officers playing.

After being left as UK runners-up the year before, the re-named 63rd Para Squadron, RCT, under the leadership of their Army and Scotland player J D McDonald, won their way right into the Army Final of 1966, but they were unable to halt the season-to-season progress of the 1st Battalion The Duke of Wellington's Regiment, who beat them 9–0 to retain the Cup for a second year.

For 63rd Para Squadron, RCT, to be there at all was another piece of giant-killing, as they were very much a minor unit who had taken on favourites. That they kept the Dukes to the eventual score said a lot for the excellence of their team, which was well schooled, had the right attitude of mind, was extremely fit and apparently thought nothing was impossible. Only McDonald was a 'star', but his players backed him up superbly, running all over the place and tackling everything.

In 1967 the Dukes completed a well-deserved hat-trick by beating 7th Regiment, RHA, 14–3 in a final where they were clearly the better team.

They had won the BAOR final over 7 Signal Regiment, after a splendid battle in the previous round with the 2nd Royal Tank Regiment whom they only just defeated. Two Gunner teams contested the UK Final, with 7th Regiment RHA, beating the School of Artillery 12–0.

The Army Final at Aldershot was scrappy in the early play with a succession of missed penalty kicks by both sides in the first half. Eventually Pettigrew gave the Dukes a penalty just before half-time.

The Gunner pack had more than held their own in the first half, but the Dukes now began to win the ball in the tight and the loose. Their captain Reid, at fly-half, took firm control of the match and put the Gunners under considerable pressure. From a five-yard scrum he nipped round the blind side and set up Robinson, the wing, to score far out. Edwards made one of his powerful runs through the middle and scored the second try, but neither was converted. Once again, though, Edwards broke away and evaded a number of defenders before passing to Westcob, who sprinted off to score under the posts, that try being converted. Just before the closing whistle the 7th Regiment RHA full-back kicked a good penalty as some consolation for them, They had covered and tackled with spirit and determination but they lacked the constructive ability and thrust of the winners.

It was now the Dukes' turn to aim for four successive wins and by coincidence they were to meet in the 1968 final 1st Battalion Welsh Guards. The Dukes began impressively by beating 1st Battalion KOSB 27–0, 34 Light Aid Detachment RCT 66–5 and, in the BAOR Final, 7 Signal Regiment 12–3 after a hard match.

Meanwhile the Welsh Guards were rebuilding a young and inexperienced side with great success to win the UK Cup, but although they went on to play really hard under the excellent captaincy of Sgt Hearne in the best final for some years they could not upset the Dukes, who won 20-3.

A strong wind made things difficult for both sides, but with its advantage in the first half the Dukes were leading 9-0 at the interval, from two penalty goals by skipper Reid and a blind-side try by Waquabaca.

When Hill kicked a penalty for the Guards shortly after half-time it looked as if the Guards might make a fight of it, but although they pressed strongly three attempted penalties were missed and the Dukes came back and added more points. Robinson cut through a fragile defence to score a try which Reid converted, the skipper kicked another penalty, and a third try was scored, Pettigrew going over after a good handling movement.

The Dukes had possession of the Cup for a fourth year.

The rest of the period up to 1973 belonged mainly to the Welsh, and it was appropriate that their dominance should start in 1969 as that was the last season for the Welch Regiment and the South Wales Borderers before they were amalgamated to form the Royal Regiment of Wales.

Both regiments were determined to get to the Army Final in that year and if possible win it, so another all-Welsh final looked very likely. They had, after all, met each other twice in earlier finals.

On their records anything could happen, as the 1st Battalion SWB had won the Cup five times and so had both the 1st and 2nd Battalions of the Welch Regiment. The 1st Battalion Welch, you may recall, beat 2nd Battalion SWB in 1909 and again in 1935. Many distinguished players had worn their red or green jerseys. Whose name would be on the Cup, if either, to welcome in the RRW players with their green jerseys to be emblazoned with the red dragon?

A little piquancy was added to the sitation by the fact that 1st Battalion Welch had in their team two very good South Wals Borderers, Lieut Mike Howes and Lieut Chris Ensor, while Maj David Cox, a distinguished Welch Regimental player, was currently with 1st Battalion SWB! It turned out that Maj Cox was in the right side. The 1st Battalion Welch could get no further than the UK quarter-final. Reduced to fourteen men for most of the game, they were beaten 19-11 by a very strong 7th Regiment RHA team.

In the next round, however, the Gunners, after taking an early lead, lost 11–6 to the SWB and in the UK Final the Welsh Guards could not prevent the Borderers from winning a very close game 9–8.

The BAOR Cup had gone to 7 Signal Regiment, a very useful side, and in the Army Final they took an early lead over 1st SWB with a penalty goal by Thomson. But a fine try by O'Brien and a penalty from Williams gave the SWB a 6–3 edge at half-time and in the second half they attacked strongly. A try by Llewellyn, converted by Williams, produced the ultimate score of 11–3 to give the SWB their first win of the trophy since 1928 and make a fitting end to a great rugby regiment.

The new Royal Regiment of Wales made a very good beginning in 1970 when they reached the Army Final, but there they were beaten 18–6 by the 1st Battalion Welsh Guards. RRW had won 17–3 over 2nd Royal Tank Regiment in the BAOR semi-final and they beat 7 Signal Regiment 14–9 in the final there, but before they Army Cup Final five of their team, including their captain, Hodges, went down with a virus complaint, and the Guards, who had defeated the School of Electronic Engineering, REME, 19–3 in the UK Final fairly easily, were clearly the better balanced team.

Although it was disappointing that only two tries were scored in the 24 points – both on the Guards' side – the match was nonetheless 'one of the best'. Neck, who had a good game at fly-half, scored one of the tries, a good individual effort, and also dropped a goal. Jones scored the other try from a line-out. Evans kicked two penalties for the Guards and Davies two for the RRW, then the Guards finished the scoring with a third penalty.

Although the 1st Battalion RRW had moved to the UK before 1970 and the 1st Battalion Welsh Guards went to BAOR, they still managed to meet again in the Army Final. Going in via the UK Final that year enabled 1st Battalion RRW to win the trophy they themselves had donated on their formation. They beat the SEE, REME, 16–6.

But they were still not to win the Army Final, as the Welsh Guards triumphed again, but by a smaller margin, 6–3. Once again RRW had illness problems, being without their captain and having their fly-half on the sick list, which meant a major reshuffle, with Davies moving from full-back to fly-half and Evans going into the centre.

The match took place in dreadful conditions and the ground was a quagmire, but these favoured the Guards in an extremely hard mauling game. At full time the scores were level, from each side kicking a penalty goal, Williams for the Guards and Davies for RRW. It was not until the last period of extra time that the Guards' Williams kicked the winning penalty.

This second win was a great triumph for Hearne, the Guards' captain, whose experience, skill and leadership had played an outstanding part in their success – he was the proud holder of five winners' medals. The Cup was presented that year by Sir William Ramsay, President of the Rugby Football Union.

For 1972 the RRW reached their third final, only to find their considerably younger and far less experienced team up against the returning 1st Battalion Duke of Wellington's Regiment, who beat them 15-8.

Both RRW and the Welsh Guards were in BAOR that season and they met for the third year running, but in the BAOR Final, the RRW at last managed to win over those opponents. The Guards were leading 6-3 after eighty minutes, but in the fifth minute of injury time Llewellyn, the RRW scrum-half, scored a brilliant try in the corner. The DWR won the UK Cup 12-6 against the SEE, REME.

Seven of the Dukes' pack had played in one or other of their earlier four successive Cup wins, and both sides had a number of talented players. None of the RRW men had Cup winners' medals, but Davies, Chinnock and Llewellyn had all played for the Army.

At first things all went the Dukes' way as Cuss kicked a penalty goal, then Parrott, their left wing, scored in the corner and Cuss converted, which was followed by another try that Cuss also converted. But despite being behind 15-0 RRW suddenly came to life and played the most exciting rugby of the day. Llewellyn was making some very telling breaks from the base of the scrum and the forwards began to gain superiority over the Dukes' pack. With twenty minutes to go Rees initiated a wonderful passing movement and O'Brien scored a brilliant try, then ten minutes later another dazzling try by Beard put RRW within striking distance. Some fine passing movements were stopped by some desperate tackling and good covering, however. The Dukes were left with a deserved win but RRW certainly went down with their Colours flying.

In 1973 the Dukes were beaten 19-3 by 1st Battalion Welsh Guards in the UK Final and 1st Battalion RRW lost out to 7 Royal Signal Regiment in the BAOR semi-final, after which the Signallers went on to meet the Welsh Guards.

The Army Final was spoilt by a stream of infringements but the Guards eventually won 22-9. The Signallers got ample possession in the first half, only their finishing was poor and their few points at half-time were from two penalty goals kicked by Abbott their full-back. Jones replied with a penalty for the Guards and then he sold a perfect dummy, took a return pass from Seldon, and sent Davies the right wing crashing over for a try.

GUNNERS AND SAPPERS TRIUMPHANT
1974-1985

Despite constant changing of units, and problems in Northern Ireland, entries for the Army Cup competition have generally increased and continue to do so. This is very encouraging for the Army Rugby Union, because for all the hopeful units starting out the pattern at the top remains virtually the same. In these twelve years the finalists were more often than not the 1st Battalion Royal Regiment of Wales or the 1st Battalion Duke of Wellington's Regiment, sometimes both!

In 1973/74 the 1st Battalion DWR and the holders, the 1st Battalion Welsh Guards, were stationed in Northern Ireland, but the Dukes decided not to enter the contest that season. The Guards began to defend their title but had the misfortune to have their full-back, L/Sgt Jones, gravely ill after a land mine explosion, and they lost 20-0 in an early round to the 1st Battalion RRW.

The UK Final of 1974 was between the 1st Battalion RRW and the SEE, REME, with RRW winning narrowly after a very close game. The SEE, having now reached several finals without success, were apparently destined to be eternal runners-up.

From BAOR 7 Signal Regiment qualified for a second year but they too were again out of luck facing Welsh opposition. No details of the play could be discovered but RRW won the Army Final 15-12.

By 1975 the RRW had lost a lot of experienced players, so they did well to reach the UK Final once more, doing so from Northern Ireland. There was a good incentive for them when the match was honoured by the presence of their Colonel-in-Chief, the Prince of Wales, but they were up against the 1st Battalion DWR, who had their own distinguished supporter in the present Duke of Wellington. The teams could only lay on a disappointing, scrappy game, which DWR won 12-6.

The Dukes had enjoyed a much more exciting game in the second round, where they only just managed to beat the SEME 6-4. The lone try of the match was scored by the SEME, but to their dismay they missed the conversion from in front of the posts.

Meanwhile in BAOR 3rd Base Ammunition and Petrol Depot, RAOC, were sweeping all opposition aside to earn the right to face the Dukes in the Army Final. Although lacking experience, 3rd BAPD were full of enthusiasm and an attacking spirit and in the earlier rounds they had a ration of 213 points to 15.

There was, therefore, certainly no disgrace for 3rd BAPD when they lost 12–6 to the 1st Battalion Duke of Wellington's Regiment in the final. When Mike Cuss opened the scoring with a penalty for the Dukes BAPD came back fiercely and DWR gave away some penalties to find themselves 6–3 down. McCarthy kicked two BAPD penalties and hit the post going for a third. If BAPD had possessed a better kicker they could well have doubled their score.

But despite giving notice that they were a team to be reckoned with, a fine performance from a Depot of little more than 300 soldiers, BAPD could not match the all-round ability of the Dukes and at last, after a quick heel and some smart passing, Robinson got a try and Cuss converted for the Dukes to go ahead again, and they finished off with another penalty by Cuss. This final meant that Sgt Dickens of the Dukes received his sixth Cup winners' medal.

The Royal Regiment of Wales moving from Northern Ireland to BAOR, while the 1st Battalion DWR remained in the UK, enabled the two to meet again in the 1976 Army Final, where this time the 1st Battalion RRW won 10–4.

In BAOR they had beaten the 1975 runners-up 3rd BAPD 13–4 before the BAOR Final, which they then won 16–4 over 7 Signal Regiment. The RRW had a tremendous boost from a tour of Wales, during which they were delighted to be invited to Cardiff as opposition in a training session with the National side before Wales played Scotland.

The 1st Battalion DWR met the Guards Depot in the UK Final and won 30–6 after the Guards had led 6–0 at half-time. The Guards were captained by I S Smith of the RADC, the former Army and Scotland player.

Fierce and uncompromising defence by both sides resulted in attacks breaking down before they became dangerous in the Army Final that became, at times, over-heated and brought a stream of penalties. Despite that, after Rees opened the scoring for RRW with a beautiful penalty fifteen minutes from the start there was to be no more success until about twenty minutes from the end.

Then, after extreme pressure on the RRW line, the Dukes' back row went over for a try to put their side 4–3 ahead, but Rees kicked another and RRW began to get on top. It was Rees again who destroyed any chance the Dukes had. He kicked the ball high in the air towards the Dukes' corner flag and raced after it, the defence faltered, and Rees swept in to score, giving RRW a well-earned victory. Rees had an outstanding game and Sergeant, the other half, also played especially well. The RRW team spirit and determination made up for any short-comings in skill.

The RRW had little difficulty in retaining the Cup in 1977, sweeping through the competition from BAOR, where they had beaten the still luckless 7 Signal Regt 31–10 in their semi-final and 3rd BAPD 45–12 in the final. There was some chance for Signallers to gain revenge in the Army Final, the opposition being 8 Signal Regiment as UK champions. They had defeated the Guards Depot 16–0 in an interesting UK Final where no score appeared at all by full time, but in extra time the Signallers suddenly found three tries and converted two.

In a somewhat scrappy Army Final, however, the 1st Battalion RRW won 22–9 without much trouble. It became a kicking duel and good hard tackling by both teams prevented either from scoring a try until ten minutes before the end, when one came for Rees of the RRW. Prior to that, though, the penalties came thick and fast. The Signallers scored three and were in the lead twice, but fly-half Rees was having another excellent game, his try only rounding off his six penalties – he probably created a record by scoring all his side's points.

Once again the RRW had shown what excellent teamwork and a determined team spirit could achieve on the rugby field, and they were now poised for a hat-trick less than ten years after their formation, but it did not come off.

The 1st Battalion RRW returned to the UK in 1978 by way of a tour in Belize and the Duke of Wellington's Regiment had gone to BAOR, which somehow made it inevitable that they would be meeting in another final. The Dukes won through to the BAOR Final quite comfortably and there beat 7th Regiment RHA 16–8. The Gunners kept going to the bitter end and gave everything they had, but it was just not good enough.

The UK Final found the 1st Battalion RRW facing 8 Signal Regiment again and that year they laid on a most exciting game, played in front of RRW's Colonel-in-Chief, the Prince of Wales. Things went better for RRW than when they were before him in 1975, as they won this time, 13–6, but it was a very close call.

The Welsh forwards controlled the mauls, line-outs and set scrums, but their backs could not penetrate the devastating covering defence of the Signals' team. They did lead 4–3 at half-time from a try by Goddard to a penalty for the Signallers by Abbott, but in the second half the Signallers, who had missed a number of penalties, were able to go ahead when Abbott secured one more, and they were still holding that lead with two minutes to go. However, Rees calmly kicked an RRW penalty from a comparatively difficult position and there was a lively period of injury time to show that the game was by no means over, but to the Signallers' dismay another penalty right in front of the posts was missed and almost immediately A'Hearne raced in to give RRW a try, which Rees converted. RRW gave away a lot of penalties and there was little doubt that if the Signals' kicker had been on form they could have come out easy winners.

When RRW went to BAOR to meet the 1st Battalion DWR for the Army Final it was their turn to be thwarted again. They were leading at half-time but were eventually pipped by one point, losing 13–12.

Closing stages of the competition in 1979 were in the nature of 'action replays' all round: the 1st Battalion RRW versus 8 Signal Regiment in the UK Final; 1st Battalion DWR against 1st Battalion RRW in the Army Final. Nothing, however, was to change hands.

In BAOR the Dukes reached the final to come up against their old rivals the 1st Battalion Welsh Guards and won 12–9, while in the UK Final the 1st Battalion RRW beat 8 Signal Regiment 6–3. The latter was a typical Cup game played in good spirit but ona very cold, wet and miserable day. The Signallers, having won the toss and elected to face the wind, looked like turning that to advantage later on, yet the expected did not happen. RRW took every opportunity afforded by the breeze in the first half for Rees to drop goal and later increase their score with a penalty. At first the Signallers missed an easy penalty in front of the post, but before half-time another chance came along and that time Abbott made no mistake. The second half was exciting but the Signals' team could not run riot with the wind behind them. There was no further scoring at all.

One of the the best Army Finals for years resulted from the 1979 meeting of the 1st Battalion RRW and the Dukes, with the holders from BAOR keeping the trophy 12–7.

Both sides missed penalties from a long way out, but after a lot of pressure the Dukes opened the scoring when a splendid three quarter movement was finished off by Dixon with a try. The Welsh backs began to get more possession and made some dangerous breaks, which finally brought them a try, A'Hearne scoring in the right-hand corner after a superb movement. The game was kept flowing by referee Peter Lillington playing the 'advantage' rule very well.

A mix-up between the back and the scrum-half enabled Walker to nip in for another Dukes' try, but Jones missed a fairly easy conversion and Rees gave RRW a penalty to bring them nearly level once more. Landell went over for the Dukes' third try, however, and despite constant pressure from RRW they held out on that.

It looked like becoming a habit when the 1st Battalion RRW and

8 Signal Regiment met yet again in the 1980 UK Final. Could the Signallers at last gain their revenge? They must have had hopes when they put out the holders, 1st Battalion DWR, 18-6 in their semi-final, the Dukes being at that time in Northern Ireland. RRW won 19-10 over 42nd Survey Engineer Regiment, RE, in the other semi-final.

But the UK Final went to the RRW 12-9. With eight Army players in their side to the Signallers' three they were clear favourites, but in a game of two distinct halves both teams had their chances. Wintry cold and wet weather, with plenty of mud, were against good play and so was a strong wind blowing straight from the clubhouse – where many spectators wished they had remained!

RRW failed to make use of the wind in the first half and could have regretted that when 8 Signal Regiment tried to swing the game in the second, but in a final wholly of penalties the kicking of 'Nipper' Rees again stood them in good stead. He scored all four for them before forty minutes were up, which was just about the time the Signallers first got into the RRW 22 metre area. Signals' full-back Charlie Abbott pulled one back just before half-time and added two more in the second half, but he also missed two and a drop goal that could have given his team the match. The Signallers pinned RRW down in the second half, but perhaps not quite to the same extent as was done to them, and their tactics puzzled spectators as they spurned some kicks in order to run the ball when one at least, right in front of the posts, Abbott could hardly have fluffed. Only one try looked possible for either side throughout and both teams lacked a 'tactical general', but RRW deserved their win narrowly on the kicking of Rees and hard work by lock Harry Rundle.

The Army Final that year was in BAOR, at Bad Lippspringe, and the location was appropriate when the Cup went to 3rd Base Ammunition and Petrol Depot, RAOC, after their earlier near-misses. Having previously been BAOR runners-up to 1st Battalion RRW this was their year of satisfaction as they won 10-9.

On an open ground, very windy weather disrupted play, but it was an exciting game and no one would have thought that 3rd BAPD would win when RRW were leading until the last minute from three penalties by 'Nipper' Rees and seemed to have the trophy 'in the bag'. The Ordnance team, however, who had scored a try in the opening three minutes and later added a penalty, played energetically with very good pace and spoiling tactics and they scraped home with a penalty in injury time. RRW had one apparent try by A'Hearne disallowed, and another chance was thrown away when Rees made a break to the line but the final pass was dropped.

The 1980/81 competition was the first under new sponsorship from the distillers Whyte and Mackay and this was marked by a return to an RRW and DWR UK Final which experienced spectators considered was one of the better matches they could recall. The Dukes had arrived from a 52–0 third round win over the 2nd Battalion the Royal Irish Fusiliers, a 16–6 defeat of the SEME in the fourth round, and a 7–3 semi-final win against the Queen's Dragoon Guards, while RRW had beaten the 1st Battalion Cheshires 31–3, annihilated 42nd Survey Engineer Regiment, RE, 75–6, and defeated the 1st Battalion Welsh Guards 13–3.

A splendid UK Final had them level-pegging at 16–16 on full-time, but in extra time the Dukes won 26–19. It was not a typical cup match, but was hard, clean and skilled. The Dukes led 16–7 with only fifteen minutes left, but RRW made a late rally to earn extra time.

With luck RRW could have kept hold of the UK trophy, but they lost two players and that put them at a disadvantage when they needed to tilt the balance. On the other hand DWR would have been unlucky to lose as their pack was generally on top, especially in the tight. Tries for the Dukes came from skipper Bill Atkinson, Drake and Rance. Shuttleworth kicked three penalties and Atkinson one, while scorers for RRW were A'Hearne and Hughes with a try each, and 'Nipper' Rees with a conversion and three penalties. Rees kicked well throughout as usual and kept his line moving in a good way, with Rundle also prominent for RRW in line-outs, mauls and rucks. For the Dukes Tim Sinclair won scrums at a ratio of about five to one and Williams was outstanding as a flanker in all aspects of the game.

The Dukes went on to beat 7th Regiment RHA 20–0 in the Army Final that year. After the UK Final spectators observed that the Army one would have difficulty producing anything like as good, and although no details of the later match are available the score suggests they might have been right.

Until 1981/82 the various rounds of the contest had spread over the winter, culminating in the finals in the spring, but for this season it was decided to have the UK section completed by Christmas so that there could be concentration on Army matches, which mostly build up from the New Year. However in 1985 they reverted to the previous method.

The title went undefended as the Dukes did not enter, thus leaving the way free for another all Welsh UK Final.

Neither the 1st Battalion RRW nor the 1st Battalion Welsh Guards came into the contest before the fourth round because of earlier byes, but they paced each other into the UK Final from then on. In the semi-finals the RRW beat the 1st Battalion Queen's Dragoon Guards and the Welsh Guards won 34-6 over the 1st Battalion Gloucesters, having previously defeated 8 Signal Regiment 33-9.

When they met, the two Welsh teams both put up stolid defences that checked most attempts at a breakthrough and the game was decided entirely on penalties. Although RRW had been affected by injuries, which forced them to draft in some of their older players, the first half was even enough and ended 3-3. Hughes had opened with a penalty for RRW but Evans replied for the Guards. In the second half, however, the Guards started to press harder and come on as the stronger team, going ahead with another penalty by Evans and getting a third later to win 9-3.

The 1982 Army Final did have one link with that of 1907 in that a team of Sappers were involved, from 21st Engineer Regiment, RE. They emerged as BAOR champions on total points of 137 to 30 but had some close calls, notably in the BAOR Final where they just beat 7th Regiment RHA 9-8, and despite playing the Army Final over there they were no luckier than Sappers of former days. 21st Engineer Regiment, RE, were to be worthy runners-up, but the Guards were even worthier winners at 12-6, in front of a large crowd that included about 250 Guards' supporters from their UK base and a good muster of patriotic backing from the 1st Battalion Royal Welch Fusiliers, stationed in Germany, who themselves lost 39-8 to the Sappers in a BAOR semi-final.

Very good springlike weather greeted the game at Bad Lippspringe and the Sappers raised their supporters' hopes when they applied early pressure and Isham scored a penalty after only about ten minutes. A penalty was missed on both sides later, but the Guards made up for theirs with a very good try by Walker, who got the ball for touch down when things went badly for the Sappers from the back of a line-out.

Exchanges became fast and furious, with play surging from end to end in good open rugby. At first, as the Welsh Guards explored every avenue, Blomquist cleared the RE line time after time but the Guards gradually proved to be the stronger side. The Sappers were handicapped by injuries to their flankers Lamb and Wright, part of a strong back row, and although they kept pressing right to the end they fell further behind and could not catch up. Another try was scored for the Guards when Davis 28 chipped the ball ahead inside their '22' and gathered the bounce to hand off the full-back and go over in the corner, and Keeping added a third from a loose ruck on the Sapper line some ten minutes from the end. As the Sappers fought back, a neat drop goal by Wilson enabled them to narrow the gap, but a possible chance for extra time with a late try was denied them when one pass was deemed forward. Evans was the Guards' 'man of the match'.

Gen Sir George Cooper, the Adjutant General and President of the Army Rugby Union, presented the trophies.

The Guards' first win since 1973 was to be tragically marred only a few weeks later.

On 2 April 1982, Argentina invaded the Falkland Islands and Britain sent a Task Force to the South Atlantic to recapture the territory. The 1st Battalion Welsh Guards set sail later in the QE2 as part of the 5th Infantry Brigade reinforcements.

While troops were being landed from smaller ships at a place called Bluff Cove on 8 June they were bombed, resulting in terrible causualties, especially for the Guards.

Among those killed were two members of the rugby team, Gdsmn Andrew 'Yorkie' Walker, aged twenty, who had scored one of the tries in the final, and Sgt Cliff Elley, aged twenty-nine who was also an Army player.

One of the other players, Cpl Cordy, was badly injured and the unit rugby officer, Capt Glyn White, himself a player in Cup Final sides up to 1970, suffered burns.

The 1st Battalion Welsh Guards overcame their tragedy by stoutly defending their Cup title as far as the UK Final of 1982/83, but there fell foul of the returning 1st Battalion DWR, who just beat them 9–8 to recover the trophy.

Everything appeared set for another Guards' win, so that they could be in the Army Final again. They were the favourites, were dominant throughout in ball and ground advantage, and could have swung the game on any or all of five kicks, but hapless full-back Evans 34, despite a calm day, veered too far left each time. The Dukes, with most of the play in their half, some of it within five yards of their line for one particularly exciting spell of seven minutes that saw two line-outs, could only otherwise hold on by brilliant tackling and resolute defence.

The Dukes scored first from a penalty, and although Guards' pressure brought a try for Davis to give them the lead it changed hands again for half-time. Flanker Preston of the DWR snatched an opportunist try in the thirty-eighth minute, breaking to intercept a pass well in his own half and making a long run to cross the line. Jones converted.

In the second half the Dukes were hard-pressed to preserve the 9–4 lead as the Guards hammered away at them. About twenty minutes from the end Walford got through for a try, but it was not converted and no amount of further pressure could add to the Guards' points.

Hearts were in mouths on both sides right at the end of a fine game when the Dukes, over-eager to clear a danger, gave away a penalty, but that kick went the way of all the others. Williams and Gilbert were outstanding for the 1st Battalion DWR and Peacock for the Guards.

Over in BAOR the contest was shaping up to another final between 7th Regiment RHA and 21st Engineer Regiment. The former won 19-15 against the 1st Battalion Royal Regiment of Wales in one semi-final and the Sappers defeated 7 Signal Regiment 15-11.

There was a long wait before the BAOR Final, but for a second year the teams provided a final worth waiting for. In 1982 they had fought out extra time and then a replay, and it looked as if the same pattern was emerging again. In extra time in 1983, however, 7th Regiment RHA denied themselves a replay by missing a late kick and 21st Engineer Regiment were Army finalists again, 10-7.

Journeying to Aldershot for the big match was to be very worthwile for the Sappers. Throughout this history it has been seen that, for all their attempts and long rugby tradition, no Royal Engineers' unit could win the Army Cup. 1983 was the year that one at last did so! The Sappers beat the more experienced Dukes 8-4 in extra time.

At first, on a miserable wet day, the Sappers failed to take advantage of territorial supremacy and missed two early penalty chances, so it was the Dukes who went ahead when Kay scored a try after snapping up a loose ball from the Sapper full-back's only mistake. In their efforts to equalise, the Sappers exerted great pleasure and were twice nearly over, only to be thwarted, but right on half-time Cherryman did make it 4-4.

If anything, it was the Sappers who looked to have the edge in the match, but a dour second-half tussle brought no change in the score. That was left for a good period of extra time, when Spawforth, a minute into the first part, found the try that was to be the winner.

An interesting thing about this final was that not only did it make Corps' history for the Royal Engineers – a point referred to by ARU president Gen Sir George Cooper, himself a Sapper, when, for another year, he presented the trophies – but that it was also a distinct parallel with the first final of 1907 between the RE Training Battalion and the Dukes' predecessors of the 2nd Battalion West Riding Regiment.

But while the similarity to the opening of this section was very marked, so too were the differences. In 1983 it was the Dukes who had eight officers in their team and several Army players. The Sappers, all other ranks, included several known useful men, but no particular stars.

*   *   *

What neither 21st Engineer Regiment, nor anyone else, could know then was that this first Sapper win opened a door to others kept out by the giants of the Army Cup competition. The teams who had been the also-rans for so long were at last to have their day. First to take advantage were 7 Signal Regiment in the 1984 final.

The change to come was not immediately apparent when the 1st Battalion Welsh Guards again powered their way to the UK Final and won it 17-9 over the RAOC Training Centre. The Dukes did not enter that season as they went to Gibraltar. After a first round bye, the 1st Battalion Welsh Guards won through the second 28-12, then quarter-finals were delayed because some of the participant units were on duty at the US air base at Greenham Common, where anti-nuclear demonstrators were protesting about the siting of Cruise missiles. Eventually, however, the contest got going once more for a Guards' win at 45-7. In the semi-finals they beat the 1st Battalion Devonshire and Dorset Regiment 19-10 and the RAOC Training Centre, who had amassed 95 points to only 21 conceded in three earlier ties, defeated 22nd Special Air Service Regiment 40-10.

Two tries for the Guards in the first twelve minutes of the UK Final made the result rather a foregone conclusion, but it was still a good game on a nice day. Whitehouse and Walford did the early scoring and Jones later kicked three penalties, earning himself some distinction as he was the prop! RAOC points came from two penalties by Millward and one by Dover.

An odd situation arose when the 1st Battalion Welsh Guards were posted to BAOR before the Army Final, but as it was to be in Germany that year they could cut down on travel and, with the UK Title settled by Christmas, could watch the later stages of the BAOR contest to weigh up their most likely opponents.

The strongest teams, as so often, soon looked to be 7 Signal Regiment and 7th Regiment RHA, but there could have been a differ-outcome when an extra match had to be inserted after the quarter-final stage, to accommodate the 1st Battalion Royal Regiment of Wales who had been in Northern Ireland. By the luck of the draw it was 7 Regiment RHA who had to play them and they had a thrilling game that was touch and go, but 7th Regiment RHA just pipped the 1st Battalion RRW 15-13 in the last few minutes. Two good semi-finals followed, one a real fight again, between 7th Regiment and 17th/21st Lancers, before 7th Regiment RHA won 16-9, and the other matching 7 Signal Regiment and the 3rd Royal Tank Regiment. Although they battled hard, the 3rd RTR were outclassed and lost 34-4.

In the BAOR Final 7th Regiment RHA led 7-6 at half-time, but a close game could have gone either way and in the second half flurry both sides missed penalties, until 7 Signal Regiment turned the game their way with one near the end, to win 9–7. Their points came from three penalties, all kicked by Fife, the second a long penalty against the wind to pull his team up for half-time, which drew from one spectator the comment that it was 'as good a kick as I have seen for a long time!'

As they went into the Army Final, 7 Signal Regiment could not help but be aware that the Welsh Guards had a long tradition of winning, while they themselves had struggled long and hard only for final disappointment, and that no Signals' team had won the Cup for about twenty five years. In excellent conditions at Sennelager, however, their persistence paid off and they beat the 1st Battalion the Welsh Guards 9–3.

Like the Sappers the year before – whom, incidentally, 7 Signal Regiment had knocked out in an early BAOR round – the Signallers were not daunted by their opponents' reputation. In fact the teams were well matched and each had good backing in the crowd of many hundreds.

It appeared that referee Lieut-Col Mike Dickinson, Army Catering Corps, who came over from the UK, began the game two minutes early, but there were no complaints from 7 Signal Regiment, for a superbly-taken penalty by Andy Fife put them three points up in that time! The Guards hit back with one by Jones, though, in the twelfth minute, and battle was fairly joined, albeit, it was lamented, with more kicking than running. Wood gave the Signallers the lead for half-time with a dropped goal, but the Guards were unlucky with two penalty chances towards the end of the first half, one missing and the other hitting an upright and bouncing away.

Growing in confidence, 7 Signal Regiment fought off a lot of Welsh attacks and themselves dominated as much as they could, as both teams tried to run the ball. The winning points came when the Signallers opted for running a penalty and Showell kicked a well-taken dropped goal, the crowd uncertain at first whether it had succeeded, until the flag went up and so did supporters' cheers – a lot of berets were thrown in the air in delight! The Welsh Guards naturally reacted strongly, but they were just held and had to look to their defence again at the close.

Triumphant captain Andy Hickling earned his reward for managing his pack well and Atkins had a fine game at full-back for the Signallers. The Guards, a young side, were without their skipper John Davies to rally them on the field, as he was forced into a spectator role by a knee injury. But after the often dour yet sporting match he promised that the Welsh Guards would bounce back!

Gen Sir George Cooper flew over to present the trophies at this final too and also attending was Maj-Gen Archie Birtwistle, recently ARU Deputy President, who was once CO of 7 Signal Regiment and had also played for the 1st Training Regiment Royal Signals in 1950.

The holders were to be pitching in well in the later BAOR stages of the 1984/85 season, surrounded by former champions, but like the Sappers before them they were not to be allowed more than one year of glory. Now it was someone else's turn to come in from the cold.

Disappointment for 7th Regiment RHA in 1983/84 had been acute, because they were on the point of leaving BAOR to return to the UK and looked for rugby honours as part of their farewell. But preparations for their move probably affected their performance in the final push and the Gunners, who had never done better than being BAOR champions once and before that UK champions once, were left as runners-up yet again.

The return to Aldershot for the 7th Regiment RHA, to resume their former role with the new 5th Airborne Brigade, was, however, to completely change their luck.

In the UK contest the old formula was reverted to, the final no longer being settled by Christmas. This meant that some later ties in January and February, 1985, were delayed by snow, but there was not such a long wait between UK and Army finals.

Life was easy for 7th Regiment RHA when they had a preliminary round bye and did not have to play in the first round either due to a walkover! So they came in fresh at the second round to beat the 1st Battalion Royal Welch Fusiliers 21–9, then after an 8–3 quarter-final victory over the 1st Queen's Dragoon Guards they defeated the Northern Ireland winners, the 1st Battalion Devonshire and Dorset Regiment, 14–6 in the semi-finals.

A significant factor for 7th Regiment RHA in this competition may have been, though, a quarter-final between two other teams, the SEE and the 1st Battalion DWR. In the two other Army Finals they had reached 7th Regiment RHA had been up against the Dukes, as seen earlier, to lose both times. The SEE had been in four UK Finals years before without any success. This season they too had enjoyed a preliminary round bye and a first round walkover, before beating the Guards Depot 25–0 in the second. They took on the mighty Dukes in a frantically close and exciting game and just beat them 10–9.

UK runners-up of the season before, the RAOC Training Centre, had to be overcome in the other semi-final and they were not about to give up without a great fight either. In fact it was two fights, for the first encounter ended 3-3 even with extra time. But in the replay the SEE got their act together for a 20-7 victory.

Predictions were for 7th Regiment RHA to have an easy win in the UK Final, but the SEE had other ideas. Despite this game following only three days after their hard replay and having to alter their team because of injuries received there, the SEE, who also surmounted the loss of their number eight during the final, looked to be taking the game. They scored first and when 7th Regiment RHA took the lead with a try it was not converted, so a runaway try put the SEE ahead again. They made it 10-4 with another penalty. The Gunners found a penalty for 10-7. Reply to that from the SEE was another penalty to make it 13-7, and many thought the Gunners had left it too late. But they rallied in the last ten minutes with two more tries and a second penalty, to eventually win 18-13. The SEE, who had not been in a final for ten years, would have to wait for another day to put their name on the Cup.

Meanwhile in BAOR their final stages were shaping up as a battle of champions, with the holders, 7 Signal Regiment, taking on 1st Battalion Welsh Guards again and 21st Engineer Regiment facing 1st Battalion RRW. An all-Welsh final resulted when the Guards beat the Signallers 8-4 and 1st Battalion RRW put out the Sappers 12-6. In the final 1st Battalion RRW overcame 1st Battalion Welsh Guards 16-10, but in a thoroughly sporting match between two fine teams which could have gone either way. It was 6-6 at half-time of a game with great open play and resolute tackling, the Guards scoring from a dropped goal and a penalty and 1st Battalion RRW with a stylish try superbly converted. But the Guards were to regret other penalty misses, for although they went ahead again in the second half with try the 1st Battalion RRW narrowed the gap with a penalty and took the lead back with another. Both sides went on the attack then and the Welsh Guards thwarted two try chances, but the RRW succeeded with one more to take the match.

Almost continuous rain made the Army Final at Aldershot a damp prospect and the ball very slippery, but two well-matched teams – and also far from being strangers to each other – took the field. The 1st Battalion RRW had ended 7th Regiment RHA hopes on past occasions. Could the Gunners follow the Sappers and Signallers in making it three in a row for those so used to being eternal runners-up, and be themselves third-time lucky in going for the big one? So many times, as will be seen in the Reference Section, the 1st Battalion RRW had had their name inscribed on the Cup, but never once had a Royal

Artillery team done so. It was close, but in 1985 the Gunners achieved the longed-for 'first'. They defeated RRW 7–6.

Their opening points came after only three minutes, when King kicked a penalty from about 30 yards. The Welsh were slow to settle but in the eleventh minute Beattie ran from the halfway line and produced a splendid dummy to score between the posts, James converting the try. At half-time it was still 6–3 to 1st Battalion RRW, remaining honours being about even in excellent open play. On balance the RRW forwards were given the edge against the powerful RHA pack, and Withers and Ponting defended well in the centre, not letting anything through, but the running and handling of the Gunner halves was better.

Astute spectators, however, noticed that 7th Regiment RHA seemed to be gaining dominance and at the start of the second half they beat back all RRW pressure. Gunner skipper Martin Lewis then set off in a fine run, but was brought down three yards short of the line. The Welsh attacked again but could not score and the Gunners took control. Awarded a penalty some five yards out they opted to run the ball and to Lewis fell the winning try when he dived over midway between the posts and the corner. They could not make the lead more secure, but neither could RRW pull back, for all that they looked dangerous towards the end. RHA gained ground and were not about to yield, for a narrow but thoroughly deserved win.

RRW captain C/Sgt Mason, one of two brothers in their side, expected to be retiring with this final, after around seventeen years in the Regimental team, and several others would also be giving up, so RRW would need to rebuild. They would probably echo the Welsh Guards, though, in saying 'We'll be back'!

The new ARU president, Lieut-Gen Sir Charles Huxtable, presented the trophies and captain Lewis held the Army Cup aloft to the delight of the largely home crowd, among whose more distinguished ranks was the Director of the Royal Artillery, Maj-Gen 'Bill' Cornock, a former CO of 7th Regiment RHA.

So, for a third year, a team on the fringes of greatness heretofore proved that history can be made of one keeps plugging away. This should encourage enormously any others whose frequent good runs have ended every time when they were oh so close to the top. However, the giants may only be sleeping. Future years may see the Dukes, the Welsh Guards and RRW monopolising again. Who can tell?

It is every unit's ambition to win the Army Cup. This history has shown that some were more likely to do so than others. The last three years broke a mould.

UNRELATED SNIPPETS FROM ARMY RUGBY UNION MINUTES

1908 It was decided that the Colours for the Army team should be: Red jersey – white collar – white badge formed of the letters ARU with 'Royal Cypher' above, also in white, stockings: red with white tops (5 inches). White knickers.

The following were elected to serve on the Committee of the ARU:
Capt. B.A. Hill, AOC
W.B. Purdon, RAMC
G.H. Birkett, South Wales Borderers
W.C. Wilson, Leicestershire Regt.

1909 The action of the Secretary in forbidding the Welsh Regiment to come to Aldershot two days before the Army Cup match was upheld by the meeting.

1913 It was decided to ask Sir John French and Sir Douglas Haig to become Vice-Presidents of the ARU. Sir John French to act as President during the absence of HRH The Duke of Connaught in Canada.

1919 The Hon Secretary reported that owing to the Varsity match the Queen's Club ground was not available for matches on December 3 and 6. The Hon Secretary was instructed to write to the Queen's Club pointing out that their attitude was most unsatisfactory and that the ARU must insist upon a proper agreement in future. Having to change the venue of the ground being a financial loss to the ARU, a great inconvenience to the Army players and the clubs we were playing against and at the same time to the rugby public.

1920 A letter from the Yorkshire Rugby Union asking for the support of the ARU in proposing an International match be played in the North next season to assist Rugby Football in the North in their fight with the Northern Union.

It was resolved that the Representative of the ARU on the Rugby Football Union be empowered to vote as he considered best after hearing the case put forward.

1920   The Hon Secretary reported that a case has ben referred to him by the Army Football Association, of an NCO named Sergeant Farewell who had been suspended by them for foul play, being allowed to play rugby and the AFA desired to know whether the ARU will take steps to prevent this. It was decided that the NCO should *not* be allowed to play rugby football in the Army so long as he was under suspension by the Army Football Association. To refer the subject to the Army Sport Control Board with a view to arranging that in this and any future case of this nature all Army Associations should take similar action.

At a later meeting the Hon Secretary reported: That a reply had been received from the Army Sport Control Board to the effect that they could not see their way to recommend the suspension of Sgt Farewell from playing all games.

1923   At a General Committee meeting of the ARU held in December, 1923, the Hon Secretary read a letter from the Blackheath Rugby Club in which the Secretary states that the club have started some gymnasium training and that CSM H Giles, who is an Army player and also on the Committee of the Army Rugby Union, was the physical training instructor in the gymnasium where they trained. Blackheath Rugby Club wish to pay Giles for his services, but are first asking whether this is in order. In their opinion any salary he earns as physical training instructor does not in any way cut across his amateur status in rugby football.

The question was discussed and the Chairman (Lieut-Gen Sir Charles Harington) thought that any payment would not affect Giles' status as he was only assisting a club to get its players fit, but he thought that the question should be referred to the Rugby Football Union in order that they might know what was being done. The meeting was of the opinion that any salary paid to Giles for acting as an instructor of physical training would not affect his status as an amateur.

1929   The Inter-Services' Rugby Football Dance will be held at the Hyde Park Hotel on March 2, 1929, after the Royal Navy v Army match. The price of tickets will be £1.1.0 each. Seventeen complimentary tickets (will be provided) for use of each service.

1929   The president before closing the meeting remarked on the tendency to unnecessary roughness in Army Unit football due largely to a lack of knowledge of the laws which seem to exist, and hoped that

Officers in Charge of Rugby would do all in their power to see that their teams are well instructed in the Laws of the Game, ignorance of which has probably caused this tendency to roughness.

1932–33   So much football talent has now been developed that it is not an exaggeration to say there is material for another XV which would be little inferior to the one which represented the Army in the Services' Championship and the Committee commiserate with those unfortunates who by reason of remarkable material available have not yet obtained the Army Cap which they would probably have gained in a leaner year.

1933–34   The accounts for the season disclose a somewhat disquieting state of affairs the net profit having dropped from £377 in the year 1932–33 to £301 in 1933–34.

1934   A request from 1st Bn. Duke of Wellington's Regt. that personnel posted from the Battalion may be allowed to play for the Depot immediately on joining was refused.

1937   A proposal by the Southern Command "That an early trial and experiment should be made to reduce spoiling by Wing Forwards, and that the policy of no Wing Forwards until the ball is heeled, as tried in the Richmond and United Services' game last season, be further experimented". It was agreed that the ARU could not take action as the matter was in the hands of the Rugby Football Union (it is assumed they mean no Wing Forwards leaving the scrum).

1945   We receive great courtesy and assistance from the Press, both National and Provincial. Although space is restricted in these days the Press gives the Army a dignified publicity on all occasions, and we would especially record our cordial relations with Mr. Norman Preston (Press Association) who is most helpful in every respect.

1946   The RMA, Sandhurst, are desirous of playing in Red Jerseys, a similar colour to the Army jerseys, the College had asked the Army Rugby Union if they had any objections. The Committee decided that there should be no objection.

1947   The Army Rugby Union gave a small dinner at the Cafe Royal after the French Army match. The French Army team were taken to the Tower of London and Windsor Castle, and to a theatre and stayed at the Grosvenor Hotel.

1968   The outbreak of foot and mouth disease (in the scrum?) and an unusual high number of injuries to players in general made the selectors' task more difficult.

Misconduct   It has come as a surprise when reading the Minutes of Meetings to note the steady stream of players who were ordered off the field during the 1920s and 30s. Almost every season players were suspended or cautioned for various types of misconduct. This was a period when sending off a player was far less prevalent than today so perhaps ignorance of the laws accounted for some of the misdemeanours, or was the degree of foul play more than we are frequently led to believe?

BRITISH ARMY OF THE RHINE

As stated elsewhere the Army first played a BAOR Representative XV as early as 1945 and this match signalled the start of over a third of a century of Rugby activity in the Rhine Army. From modest beginnings a full, competitive and colourful fixture list has developed and European and North African National sides supplement a fixture list which already includes annual fixtures against West Germany and the Netherlands. The latter countries provide sides of a comparable standard to the BAOR side and the results through the years show a fairly even balance of results. An annual fixture is held against RAF(G) with generally a win to the Army though the results have become closer in recent years. The sternest test of the season, the match against the French Armed Forces, has provided a succession of wins for the French side though some contests have been a close run thing, regrettably with the decision invariably going in the opposite way to that enjoyed by Wellington.

Two stern fixtures are undertaken against Welsh opposition, one against the Welsh Districts XV and the other for the Lord Parry Trophy against the South Glamorgan Institute of Higher Education. Both of these fixtures, played on an alternate home and away basis provide attractive open rugby. Touring first-class clubs generally feature each year and notable opponents have been Bath, Blackheath, Llanelly, Abertillery and London Welsh. In recent years the grand finale of the season has been supplied by the visit of the Public Schools Wanderers when Brig Rolph James has produced a side of famous names invariably orchestrated into a fine display of running rugby.

The story of the BAOR side is laden with names of famous International players who played in their National Service days, and members of both codes brought their talents to enrich the game. The list is long but vivid memories remain of the immature but exciting skills of Malcolm Phillips, later of England and of Glyn Davidge and Norman Morgan who subsequently played with such distinction for Wales. The BAOR side has often contained names of those who have played for their Country, Combined Services and and the Army.

This short account of the progress of BAOR rugby could not be concluded without reference to the great debt owed to sponsorship through the kind offices of Great Universal Stores, without whose assistance the present fixture list could not be undertaken nor would the side be as well equipped, dressed or as comfortably transported.

Important features of the BAOR scene are the Army Rugby Union Challenge Cup and the BAOR Cup, closely linked in 1952 since when the BAOR winner has played the United Kingdom winner to decide the Army Championship. In the 31 finals since that date BAOR has provided the winner on 15 occasions but as 25 of the 31 finals have been won by either the Welsh Guards, the Duke of Wellingtons or the Royal Regiment of Wales it has so often depended on where those regiments were stationed. This should in no way detract from the performance of the other famous sides particularly 7 Signal Regiment who have promised so often and contrive to slip at the vital time but have made such a great contribution to Rugby Football, nor from the contribution of 7th RHA who have competed so successfully since their arrival in 1976. The Kings Own Scottish Borderers with two Scottish Internationals John MacDonald and Brian Shillinglaw had two fine notable victories in the sixties and rarely has one man had such an effect as 'Jones the Boot' in the Royal Welch Fusiliers' successes of the mid fifties. Unrivalled however remain the achievements of the Dukes who won both BAOR and the Army in the four years 1965–68. When again will we see a cup winning side which includes twelve officers?

With over sixty major units competing each season and with the loss of a couple of months due to frozen pitches it is no easy matter to produce the two finalists in time and with operational and training commitments conflicting with the demands of the competition it appears that the negotiating skills of Commanding Officers are as important as a well-trained pack.

BAOR MAJOR UNITS CUP

WINNER		RUNNER-UP
1946	4th Bn Welch Regiment	5th Royal Tank Regiment
1947	Royal Horse Guards	2nd Royal Tank Regiment
1948	2nd Royal Tank Regiment	HQ BAOR Camp
1949	1st Bn Parachute Regiment	42nd Field Regiment RA
1950	Royal Horse Guards	1st Bn Manchester Regiment
1951	1st Bn Welsh Guards	1st Bn York and Lancaster Regiment

1952	1st Bn Welsh Guards	1st Bn York and Lancaster Regiment
1953	1st Bn Welsh Guards	77th HAA Regiment RA
1954	1st Bn South Wales Borderers	6th Royal Tank Regiment
1955	1st Bn South Wales Borderers	1st Bn Royal Welch Fusiliers
1956	1st Bn Royal Welch Fusiliers	77th HAA Regiment RA
1957	1st Bn Welch Regiment	1(BR) Corps Tpt Col RASC
1958	1(BR) Corps Tpt Col RASC	3rd Royal Tank Regiment
1959	1st Bn Royal Scots	7th Royal Tank Regiment
1960	1st Bn Kings Own Scottish Borderers	1st Regiment RHA
1961	1st Bn Kings Own Scottish Borderers	1st Bn Welsh Guards
1962	1st Bn Welsh Guards	1st Bn Welch Regiment
1963	1st Bn Welsh Guards	1st Bn Lancashire Fusiliers
1964	1st Bn Somerset and Cornwall Light Infantry	19th Regiment RA
1965	1st Bn Duke of Wellington's Regiment	1st Somerset and Cornwall Light Infantry
1966	1st Bn Duke of Wellington's Regiment	2nd Royal Tank Regiment
1967	1st Bn Duke of Wellington's Regiment	7 Signal Regiment
1968	1st Bn Duke of Wellington's Regiment	7 Signal Regiment
1969	7 Signal Regiment	32nd Armd Engr Regiment
1970	1st Bn Royal Regiment of Wales	7 Signal Regiment
1971	1st Bn Welsh Guards	1st Div HQ & Sig Regiment
1972	1st Bn Royal Regiment of Wales	1st Bn Welsh Guards
1973	7 Signal Regiment	49th Field Regiment RA
1974	7 Signal Regiment	49th Field Regiment RA
1975	3rd BAPD	4th Div HQ & Sig Regiment
1976	1st Bn Royal Regiment of Wales	7 Signal Regiment
1977	1st Bn Royal Regiment of Wales	3rd BAPD
1978	1st Bn Duke of Wellington's Regiment	7th Regiment RHA
1979	1st Bn Duke of Wellington's Regiment	1st Bn Welsh Guards

1980	3rd BAPD	7th Signal Regiment
1981	7th Regiment RHA	7th Signal Regiment
1982	21st Engineer Regiment	7th Regiment RHA
1983	21st Engineer Regiment	7th Regiment RHA
1984	7th Signal Regiment	7th Regiment RHA
1985	1st Bn Royal Regiment of Wales	1st Bn Welsh Guards

The Ellis Cup provides an annually contested competition between RTC, RAMC, RAOC and REME with the latter generally being the team to beat. RAC, RA, RE and RCS also run Corps sides and have full fixture lists and compete with each other every year for an unofficial championship. There is now a move to start a competition between these sides on the same basis as the Ellis Cup, which should serve to ease the continual BAOR problem of fixture conjestion.

Another contribution is made by the Garrison sides, generally organised on the lines of a civilian club and regular success has been enjoyed by Rheindahlen Rhinos and Düsseldorf Dragons, with Bielefeld Javelins, Munster Rams, Hameln Rats, and Honne Hornets thriving at those times when enthusiasts are present.

A BAOR coaching organisation has prospered and developed for many years. Courses are held at least once a year and suitable candidates are sponsored on more advanced courses in the United Kingdom. Considerable assistance has been given during the years to aid the development of West German and US Forces rugby.

THE TERRITORIAL ARMY

The contribution of the Territorial Army deserves a history of its own and it is only possible here to mention some of the highlights.

It was in 1931 that the TA first placed a representative rugby XV in the field and on 25 February of that year they played their first match against the Army, at the Memorial Ground, Bristol, where the TA won an exciting game 10-9. TA units have constantly been brimful of Internationals, county and top-class club players, as can be seen by a look at their team on that occasion, with the fully representative side that the Army put out against them:

TA: 2nd Lieut E C P Whiteley* (Hon Artillery Company), Sgt R Clayton (North Somerset Yeomanry), Lieut H H Lindop (5th Bn South Staffordshire Regt), Pte G S Hoghton (HAC), Pte R G Turnbull (London Scottish), Lieut E M M Henderson (London Scottish), 2nd Lieut J P McArthur* (7th Bn King's Regt), Capt D J McMyn (RAMC), 2nd Lieut D A Kendrew* (Leicestershire Regt), Lieut E J Bruford (5th Bn Somerset Light Infantry), Pte K J Stark* (HAC), Lieut W B Allen (7th Bn Durham Light Infantry), Capt E Coley* (4th Bn Northamptonshire Regt), Lieut J R W Swayne (North Somerset Yeomanry), 2nd Lieut D Crichton-Miller* (Royal Scots Fusiliers).

Army: 2nd Lieut E W F de V Hunt* (Royal Artillery), 2nd Lieut A L Novis* (2nd Bn Leicestershire Regt), 2nd Lieut J R Cole (2nd Bn The Loyal Regt), 2nd Lieut J A M Rice-Evans (2nd Bn Royal Welch Fusiliers), Lieut A G Martin (South Wales Borderers), Lieut E L Marsh-Villett (Royal Engineers), 2nd Lieut F W Simpson (RE), Lieut Rew* (Royal Tank Corps), 2nd Lieut A Vaughan-Jones* (RA), Cpl C Townend (1st Bn Duke of Wellington's Regt), 2nd Lieut R G S Hobbs* (RA), Lieut E P Sewell (Northamptonshire Regt), 2nd Lieut G Taylor (1st Bn West Yorkshire Regt), 2nd Lieut B W Reynolds (1st Bn DWR), L/Cpl E H Sadler* (Royal Corps of Signals).

It is interesting to see that Kendrew played for the TA and not the Army. He, Whiteley, Stark, Coley and Crichton-Miller were already Internationals and McArthur was capped for Scotland a year later. On the Army side Hunt, Novis and Rew were existing Internationals and Vaughan-Jones, Hobbs and Sadler gained their honours later.

* = Internationals at time of match or later.

The Army dominated the first half of the game but could not penetrate a very sound defence and the only score then was a penalty goal kicked for them by Townsend.

Early in the second half the Army went further ahead after Novis made an opening to send Sadler for a try, and another try, scored by Rice-Evans, put them nine points up. However the TA pack began to look superior both in the scrum and the loose. They reduced the deficit after a brilliant swerving run by Hoghton, when Clayton scored a try which was converted. In the last minute, amid great excitement, Henderson and McArthur, a lively pair of half-backs, produced the move that resulted in Henderson crashing over the line to score, the successful conversion gave his side a well-deserved victory.

The following four years all brought wins for the Army, then in 1936 a game played in snow and sleet inded in a pointless draw. For 1937, at the Waterloo ground, Blundellsands, the TA nearly pulled off a surprising victory and it was only the brilliance of Leyland that ensured an Army win. Not only did he score a dazzling individual try but he made the opening for Cowey to go over in the corner, the conversion being kicked by Howard-Jones. Gerrard got a penalty goal for the TA and Huskisson scored a try after a blind-side break by Goldschmidt, leaving a narrow victory for the Army at 8-6.

At last, in 1938 at Bedford, the TA beat the Army again, and in a convincing manner by 17 points to nine. The TA pack was magnificent and their quick heeling and speed in the loose played havoc with the Army's attack and defence. To begin with the points for both teams kept pace fairly well. Huskisson kicked a penalty goal for the TA, but Allen and Arengo-Jones put the Army ahead with two tries. Wilton then scored a try for the TA and Huskisson converted. Again the Army replied, with a try by Bradley. But Forrester, the TA centre, clinched the match for them with a try, converted by Huskisson, followed by a drop goal.

The final game before the Second World War was played at Bath in very heavy conditions. It was hard and bruising. MacCrae and Candler combined to score a fine try for the TA and Garrett added another, with Parker converting both and kicking a penalty goal, for the TA to win 13-3, Bevis scoring the only Army try.

Play resumed after the war in 1949 and the Army won the first nine matches. Three in particular were memorable.

In 1951 the TA fought hard against a far faster attack and, though scoring first, were well beaten 22-5. For the Army Hardy and Shuttleworth were in scintillating form, as was Scott, the centre.

Boston, the Army and Rugby League centre, scored four tries for the Army when they defeated the TA 23–8 in 1954. Three of his tries came after he ran nearly the length of the ground. Bazley, the England wing, gave the Army a further try and Edwards helped their convincing win with four conversions. Bruce-Thomas got a try for the TA and Delight converted, also kicking a penalty.

In 1956 at Leicester the TA lost a hard game 13–8, but put up another good fight against a strong Army side that had Scotland and Shuttleworth at half-back. Gilbert-Smith scored a try for the Army after a break by Regan, and then Hopkins went over for a try that was converted by Southward. Fallon gave the TA a fine try and that was converted by Peter Mitchell, of the 5th Battalion Duke of Cornwall's Light Infantry, the Cornish scrum-half, who had previously played for the Army against the Navy when an officer cadet in 1954, just missed an attempted drop goal. A further try for the Army came from Thomas, with Southward converting, and the TA could only narrow the gap a little more with a late score by Power.

The Army continued to be more successful that not. In the 1960s they only lost twice, 11–8 in 1963 and 6–3 in 1966. Around 1967 the TA name was changed to Territorial Army and Volunteer Reserve, which was to apply until 1979.

For the 50th anniversary match in 1981 the two sides met at Twickenham for a new BP Challenge Trophy, of which the Army became the first winners by 20 points to 11.

TERRITORIAL ARMY RESULTS v ARMY

1931	Territorial Army 10	v	Army	9	Bristol
1932	Territorial Army	5	v	Army 19	Coventry
1933	Territorial Army 11	v	Army 23	Aldershot
1934	Territorial Army	6	v	Army 12	Woolwich
1935	Territorial Army	3	v	Army 18	Taunton
1936	Territorial Army	0	v	Army	0	Leicester
1937	Territorial Army	6	v	Army	8	Blundellsands
1938	Territorial Army 17	v	Army	9	Bedford
1939	Territorial Army 13	v	Army	3	Bath

Territorial Army: played 9, won 3, drew 1, lost 5, pts for 71, pts against 101

1949	Territorial Army	3	v	Army 20	Northampton
1951	Territorial Army	5	v	Army 22	Bath
1952	Territorial Army	5	v	Army 15	Coventry
1953	Territorial Army	6	v	Army 13	Newcastle
1954	Territorial Army	8	v	Army 23	Aldershot
1955	Territorial Army	0	v	Army	6	Birkenhead Park
1956	Territorial Army	8	v	Army 13	Leicester
1957	Territorial Army	3	v	Army	8	Cardiff

1958	Territorial Army 8	v	Army 11	Aldershot
1959	Territorial Army 8	v	Army 6	Harrogate
1960	Territorial Army 8	v	Army 22	Chatham
1961	Territorial Army 9	v	Army 24	Bath
1962	Territorial Army 6	v	Army 21	Chatham
1963	Territorial Army 11	v	Army 8	Coventry
1964	Territorial Army 12	v	Army 13	Woolwich
1965	Territorial Army 0	v	Army 15	Richmond
1966	Territorial Army 6	v	Army 3	Blackheath
1967	T & AVR, 3	v	Army 19	Oxford
1968	T & AVR, 9	v	Army 11	Sandhurst
1969	Cancelled			
1970	T & AVR 9	v	Army 37	Sandhurst
1971	T & AVR 3	v	Army 79	Old Paulines
1972	T & AVR 4	v	Army 11	Sandhurst
1973	T & AVR 11	v	Army 17	Armoury House
1974	T & AVR 6	v	Army 37	Aldershot
1975	T & AVR 6	v	Army 26	Sandhurst
1976	Cancelled			
1977	T & AVR 10	v	Army 18	Cardiff
1978	T & AVR 10	v	Army 36	Sandhurst
1979	Territorial Army 12	v	Army 0	Old Paulines
1980	Territorial Army 10	v	Army 7	Aldershot
1981	Territorial Army 11	v	Army 20	Twickenham
1982	Territorial Army 3	v	Army 13	Aldershot
1983	Territorial Army 0	v	Army 40	Oxford
1984	Territorial Army 0	v	Army 35	Aldershot
1985	Cancelled			

Territorial Army: played 33, won 5, drew 0, lost 28, pts for 216, pts against 649

REFEREES

After the First World War the Army Rugby Union (ARU) turned its attention to the question of referees for Army and Unit matches. The matter was recorded at Minute 6 of the General Committee Meeting on 29 November 1921 and read:

> It was agreed that this was a matter of vital importance and, for the furtherance of Rugby on sound lines, it was necessary that not only should a sufficient number of officials within the Army exist but that uniformity should be obtained in the definition of rules by the formation of a Central Army Rugby Referees Society. A sub-committee, as under, was appointed to take immediate steps for the setting up of such an organisation: Major B.C. Hartley, Army Sport Control Board, Capt. O.G. Philby, RMC Sandhurst, Capt A.H. MacIlwaine, RMA Woolwich and Major R.W. Ling, ASCB (Secretary).

The first list of Army referees published in 1931 showed that there were sixty registered throughout the world. In the main these were officers but only a season later, in 1932, although the total had dropped to fifty-one, the ranks varied from Lieutenant-Colonel to Sergeant. The former H C ('Tiny') Harrison, was an instructor at the Imperial Defence College and the latter, E Grainger, was serving in the Coldstream Guards. 'Tiny' Harrison's career in Rugby was outstanding by any standards. He played for England from 1909 to 1914 and then took up refereeing. He emulated his success as a player with his selection to referee France versus Scotland in 1922 and, in 1928, he refereed the final of the Army Rugby Union Challenge Cup Competition (ARUCCC).

Also recorded at about this time is the name of Capt W D C Greenacre. He was the first Army referee to represent the ARU in the London Society of Referees. This was the beginning of what was to prove a most rewarding and profitable relationship on both sides and one which remains strong to the present day. From the appointment of Honorary Secretary to the ARU, Greenacre was selected as the first Chairman of the Army Rugby Union Referees Society (ARURS) in 1939.

Many of the records for the years 1934 to 1942 were destroyed by fire during the war but one interesting document for the year 1938 remains. The book *Games and Sports in the Army* was becoming more sophisticated year by year, and by the winter of 1938 was able to produce a supplementary list of referees by districts and commands world-wide. Included in this list are such illustrious names as the Rev V J Pike (Ireland 1931–34), 2nd Lieut C O'N Wallis (Ireland 1936), Lieut 'Bun' Cowey (Wales 1934–35), Lieut D A Kendrew (England 1930–36) and Capt C K T Faithful (England 1924–26).

In 1948 the ARURS was reconstituted and continued to function for the next seven years on a similar basis to that of pre-war years, under the Chairmanship of Brig T H Clarke (1948–49) and Lieut-Col R B S Eraut (1950–54). These were difficult years for referees. Not only was the standard of refereeing unsatisfactory, but records of referees and their qualifications were incomplete or non-existent. Nor was all well in the playing enclosure. More than once in those years was it necessary for the ARU and the ARURS to express displeasure over the standard of behaviour on the field.

Nevertheless, it was in those seven years that the ARURS put into effect an outline structure of the Society which remains virtually unchanged today. In 1950 three classes of referee were introduced. Until the early fifties it was accepted practice for Command Rugby representatives to act as members of the ARURS Committee; the Chairman of the ARURS was but an ex-officio member of the ARU and then only on those occasions when refereeing was being discussed.

In September 1955 a meeting of Command representatives was called by Rev Ken Oliver as Chairman of the Society. For the first time the minutes of an Army referees meeting were produced and these record two interesting facts. Firstly, there still remained a number of referees who were neither qualified nor registered and it was quite clear that, if the ARURS was to function as such, referees must either be members or opt out of refereeing. Secondly, up to this date units were rarely notified of the names of qualified referees within their Commands. Action was taken on both points as the season progressed.

In 1956 came the announcement by the ARU that the Chairman of the ARURS should henceforth be considered a full member of their General Committee. The referee was no longer a second-class citizen within Army Rugby. The new status was to prove vital in the years to come as a great number and cross-section of all ranks participated in the game.

In the same year, with the Committee under its new Chairman, Col S Moore-Coulson, the ARURS expanded on the sound formula evolved in the previous season. This expansion was to have far reaching consequences it is, therefore, important to dwell for a moment on the decisions taken.

Certain County associations had made it clear to the Committee that the standard of senior Army referees did not match that of their County-grade referees. The remarks were neither ill-timed nor ill-considered. An unequivocal statement was made by the Chairman to the effect that only the Chairman of Command Rugby, one senior Army and one civilian referee of equivalent status could upgrade a referee to Class I; thus was taken the first major step towards obtaining the right standard of referee in top class Army Rugby. But it was one thing to restrict selection to Class I, another to ensure that the right standard of referee was developed and encouraged at lower levels.

By early 1958 not only was the ARURS in a position to control its own members but it was able to ask the ARU to instruct units that only registered Army referees should be appointed to ARUCCC games. A position of some strength? Well, it was an improved one with 171 registered and graded referees and forty-one probationary members and it had become normal practice for at least one vacancy to be allotted to the ARURS for the annual national Rugby Football Referees' course at Bisham Abbey.

As the 1950s reached their close the records reveal the name of Maj John Ledsham who was to achieve wide recognition in later years. On this particular occasion, in 1959, he was appointed to referee the final of the ARUCCC. At the same time to the Committee was added a representative from Northern Ireland, another former international player, Capt D W Shuttleworth (England 1951).

The ARURS moved into the 1960s with, for the first time ever, a grand total of 301 referees registered and graded, a far cry from the original sixty in 1931.

The decision of the Conference of County Referees to include Army personnel officiating in their areas on the County panel was followed swiftly by the selection of Maj Ledsham to the Cheshire County panel. As he made his first appearance in the records as the referee for the ARUCCC Final so did a comparative unknown of the time, WO2 Peter Lillington, appear as the nominated referee for the UK final.

Of importance in 1961 was the announcement in January of the first Society Dinner to be held in the following March at the famous 'Printers Devil', Fetter Lane. However, sadness tinged this great event since it was followed by the retirement of the Chairman, Moore-Coulson, now Maj-Gen, from the Committee and from the Army. In this short account, only too little space can be given to his achievements. He had overseen the transformation of the ARURS from a humdrum, if enthusiastic, body of referees of varying talent into a highly organised Society, finally and justly accepted in the higher grades by the County Panels. He handed over to Maj-Gen E B Stockdale.

As the next few years passed it appears that the ARURS received plaudit upon plaudit. The Army was asked to provide a representative on the County Championship Referees panel and John Ledsham was selected for the Eastern Counties versus Middlesex match. At the same time he accepted an invitation to take over as Secretary of the ARURS. Until then the task had been fulfilled by the Secretary of the Army Rugby Union who not unreasonably, as the record states, was finding difficulty in carrying out his normal military duties.

Maj Ledsham assumed his duties in the following spring under the new Chairman, 'Bun' Cowey, now Brigadier. At his first meeting guide lines for referees' courses were laid down with a view to the first Annual Convention to be held in 1964, when there were to be considerable changes in the laws. This new type of course was a success, but the plan for one central convention was found impossible to implement so the principle of area conventions at Chester, Chatham and Larkhill was evolved.

An astonishing decision of the Army Rugby Union in 1961, which ruled against the selection of Army referees as touch judges for Inter-Service games in which the Army were playing, was reversed in 1965 and at the same time a comparatively young officer, Capt Christ Tyler (later Brig Tyler, ARURS Chairman), made his first appearance in the minutes on being upgraded to Class I. Anomalously, he had already been on the County Championship Panel from 1957 to 1959 but that was whilst with the Cambridge Society.

The next two years were a logical development of the previous three. Civilian societies boasted some sixty-four Army members and this figure did not include those who had failed to register with the Army for a variety of reasons. As the annual conventions developed with international panel referees and players as speakers, so did the number of exchange fixtures between Army and civilian societies, particularly in Kent, Dorset and Wilts, London, Sussex, Berkshire and Cheshire.

The standards of refereeing improved all the time but were never taken for granted. Going from strength to strength, the ARURS had the honour of providing the touch judge and reserve referee for the Combined Services versus Australia match, namely Chris Tyler. Of no small consequence at this time, 1967, was the decision of the ARURS to issue an annual Newsletter which was received with enthusiasm by all concerned and grew in popularity in the years to come. This year was also particularly notable for the advances made by the ARURS to recruit and build up the junior ranks of referees. Some seventy per cent of Class II referees were appointed to senior fixtures and fifteen per cent of them were upgraded to Class I. At the same time referees were being strongly urged to join civilian societies, cementing the bond that had grown between them and ARURS.

At this stage record must be made of the formation by the Rugby Football Union of its Referee Advisory Panel, which as its title suggests is responsible for advising the RFU Referee Sub-Committee on the appointments of referees. One representative was drawn from each of the five divisional areas of the County Championships and one from the Combined Services. John Ledsham was primarily responsible for persuading the RFU to form the Panel and it was most fitting that he was chosen to be its first Hon Secretary. He was so successful in that capacity that the RFU have since made the Services representative the ex-officio Hon Secretary.

The work John Ledsham put in to further the recognition of rugby referees in general, and the ARURS in particular, was enormous. To mark this superlative contribution to Army rugby he was honoured by the award of the MBE on his retirement from the Army. The Secretaryship was taken over by Peter Lillington, now a Captain, who, having left the Dorset and Wilts area, was back in the fold and regularly represented the ARURS on and off the field of play at the highest levels.

The first major change to the original tenets which had survived from the Society's formative years was in the field of referees' gradings. Over the years referee societies had been increasingly aware of the difficulties in placing referees correctly when they moved into the area of operation of another society, either on a permanent basis or on an exchange appointment. Both factors had particular significance with respect to the ARURS and its constantly moving population. In 1975 the RFU Referee Sub-Committee and its Advisory Panel devised a national scale of gradings. This was welcomed by the ARURS as it enabled them to move within the UK or return from overseas without always starting at the foot of any civilian society 'ladder'.

Through the 1970s the ARURS scaled even greater heights by the achievements of its senior referees. Chris Tyler, in addition to refereeing many touring teams, accompanied the England XV on the 1971 Far East Tour; and Peter Lillington, now Major, and WO2 David Williams refereed at every senior standard up to 'B' Internationals. Peter Lillington remained on the A1 List for seven seasons and must have been very close indeed to the International Panel. For his out-standing services to Army rugby, he was elected an Honorary Vice-President of the ARU. Many other referees regularly achieve A2, 3 or 4 status.

In the mid-eighties the ARURS face the future with confidence. The Annual Conventions deserve their national acclaim with vacancies on them being sought eagerly by civilian societies and by the RFU's inter-national guests. ARURS members are well established on the RFU 'A' Lists and in the upper echelons of civilian societies. The foresight of that ARU Sub-Committee in 1921 has been well rewarded.

RUGBY TODAY ...

The Army has a full and interesting list of fixtures throughout each rugby season, but it has only been possible to touch on a few of those here, while considering in detail the closing Inter-Service matches to which they all lead.

There are, too, other competitions besides the Army Major Units' Cup. That is the main trophy, but there is a Minor Units' Cup as well (for units with a strength of 299 or under), which has a similar structure and, while not as well known, is a valuable part of Army rugby today. That contest has been going for twelve years.

Junior Units have three separate competitions and the Youth Cup has been in existence for twenty-five years. The Junior Major Units' Cup was first played for in 1954/55 and the Junior Minor Units' Cup began in the 1970s.

At the very end of the season there is a popular seven-a-side contest for more trophies.

Apart from the main Army team there is an Under 21 side and a Colts XV (under 19) to bring on newcomers. Some forty or more potential players attend the Army Under 21 trials at the start of every season, bidding for places in regular fixtures against such opposition as the RMA, Sandhurst; Hampshire; London Irish; Surrey; the Royal Military College of Science, Shrivenham; and Blackheath. The Colts also have their own fixture list and enjoy regular tours to various parts of Britain. The Army Junior Committee, most recently under the chairmanship of Lt-Col P A Salisbury, can be well satisfied and proud of their achievements with the Colts, particularly as they can be deprived of continuity and playing ability in shortage of experienced players due to unit commitments. In 1981 it was encouraging to note the number of Under 19 players who went up into the Army team.

The organisation of Army rugby caters for both beginners and the experienced player. A surprising number of players who had never seen a rugby ball before joining the Army have developed into first-class players and reached Army and County standard. At the other end of the scale, some players reached International level before joining the Army, a recent example being Peter Warfield (RAEC), who was capped for England six times between 1973 and 1975.

During the past few years a great deal has been done to improve the standard of coaching. Maj Noel Slater (RAEC, Army, Oxford University, Cheshire) was coach of the Junior Army XV from 1974–77, and he then went on to coach the Army XV from 1977–80. The culmination of his hard work and enthusiasm was the Army winning the 1980 Inter-Service Tournament. He is now Chairman of the Coaching Committee.

Coaching courses are held in the UK and BAOR, and in addition the introduction of conventions has given a considerable boost to the coaching programme. In 1977 S/Sgt (SSI) J Millward (APTC), was the first Army coach to pass the Rugby Football Union coaching course at Bisham Abbey. Six Army coaches attended in 1978 the RFU course run especially for the Combined Services, though only S/Sgt Frobisher (REME) was successful there. The Army Rugby Union holds an annual award course and the RFU preliminary award course is well attended. Over 100 soldiers have received the Award, though only about half are now actively coaching.

Army rugby affairs are managed by an Executive Committee which meets quarterly. It is the direct descendant of the committee mentioned in the first pages of this History.

It consists of a Chairman, currently Brig P V Crooks, the Secretary, the Director ASCB, Treasurer, Chairman of Selectors at each level, Chairman Army Referees, Chairman Coaching and District representatives.

Executive Committee

Chairman: Brig P V Crooks
DASCB: Brig P D F Thursby OBE
ARVRS: Brig C Tyler
Chairman under 21: Lieut Col M J Dickinson
Hon. Treasurer: Lieut Col H L C Radice MBE
Chairman Colts: Lieut Col P A Salisbury
BAOR RcP: Lieut Col S Thomas
Chairman Selectors: Lieut Col D Mc F Hathorn MBE
UKLF Rep: Lieut Col A Payne
PR: Maj J Quin
Secretary: Maj H C Greatwood

... AND TOMORROW

Discerning readers will have realised, as this history has unfolded, that it is to a degree a mirror of life in general in Britain over the past hundred years or so. Full-scale wars and lesser conflicts would be expected to feature, but so do civilian strikes. Then there is the evolvement from what are generally known as 'the good old days' through the Victorian and Edwardian eras with all the triumphs and tragedies and the move away from clear-cut class divisions.

It was inevitable, therefore, that in these modern times Army rugby should be affected by the economic climate and re-organisation of the Army. There is no longer a huge pool of soldiers around the world in which to fish for stars and there has been a decline in several areas. Aldershot Services, who used to run four sides and won the Hampshire Cup in 1972/73 before there was even a trophy in its name, have found so much difficulty getting enough players for one XV on Saturday afternoons to meet regular fixtures that they have carried on only with a Colts' side until 1983/84, when even that folded. Coming up to their seventy-fifth anniversary season in 1979/80 United Services, Chatham, wondered if they would still be in existence to celebrate it.

Saturday games had problems because players often went off to appear for first-class clubs in London and elsewhere, believing, it was thought, that they had a better chance of selection for the Army or Combined Services if they were seen in such company against quality opposition rather than in a lesser fixture. Their time was their own over the weekend in what had largely become a 'five-day-week Army'. When that phrase appeared in a newspaper a hard-pressed officer commented that he wished they would lead him to it as he would like to join!

Army rugby has naturally had to adapt to these problems and the fact that money was not so readily available for any projects. A way of solving the latter difficulty was to seek sponsors.

Soldiers have been known to take a drop or two of beer from time to time, rugby players perhaps more than most, and it was appropriate that the first of the Army's sponsors should be the brewers Courage (Central) Ltd. They stepped in with financial assistance in 1972 for the Army Seven-a-side Contest, which was known as the Courage Army

Sevens and was one of the highlights of the season, growing increasingly popular. Army players did not need much encouragement to down a few tankards of the firm's wares in return. Exactly how many may or may not be recorded, but the Army might match or better the tally of a civilian club in 1974. It is not known who the brewers were, but the club's annual meeting reported a bar consumption for the year of 71,000 pints of bitter, 3,500 of those in one day alone! Courage continued sponsorship until 1984, when Bulmers the well-known cider firm took over, but as a final gesture made a contribution towards this History.

Sponsorship of the Inter-Services' match between the Army and the Navy was accepted in 1977 by the firm of Stewart Wrightson Assurance Consultants Ltd, who manage pension schemes for both Services. The firm gives an annual grant to both sides for the game, and holds a pre-match lunch at Twickenham, having begun by donating a splendid trophy for the senior game and one for the colts. The firm has also been more than generous in contributing towards the publication of this History.

The Army Cup competitions for both Major and Minor Units are now under the sponsorship of the distillers Whyte and Mackay Ltd and this sponsorship also includes prizes. Furthermore Whyte and Mackay also have generously contributed to the publication of this book.

Great Universal Stores give financial assistance to the BAOR representative side. The ARU is indebted to all of these sponsors, whose help has provided great stimulus for our game throughout the Army at all levels.

Events of course need organisers and whatever else has changed over the years, this is as true today as when the Army Rugby Union was formed in 1906. In many sports it is the devoted few who keep the game going. High spots arrive when someone comes along who is a great inspiration to everyone else. For the rest of the time the sport may be just ticking over.

Rugby is a flourishing sport in today's Army and the enthusiasm for the game can clearly be seen at every level.

It is encouraging that in 1985 The Army has for the first time since 1969 a player who has gained International honours. Capt Brian McCall (REME) came on as a replacement for Ireland in their match against France.

FACTS AND FIGURES

ARMY CAPTAINS 1907–1939

A R Aslett	Kings Own R Regt	threequarter	12
A L Novis	Leicestershire Regt	threequarter	10
G J Dean	TRC	scrum half	5
R Mack Scobie	RE	forward	3
G D Young	Welsh Guards	forward	3
C M Usher	Gordons	forward	3
W S D Craven	RFA	forward	2
B A Hill	AOC	forward	2
R F A Hobbs	RE	forward	2
C C McCreight	RA	fly-half	2
A H MacIlwaine	RFA	forward	2
H J M Sayers	RA	forward	2
H L V Day	RFA	threequarter	1
B M Dunn	Welch Regt	forward	1
H Gardner	RFA	fly-half	1
D A Kendrew	Leicestershire Regt	forward	1
L Robertson	Cameron H	fly-half	1
C M Usher	Gordon H	forward	1
		Total	54

A R Aslett had the remarkable record of winning eleven of the twelve matches when captain.

ARMY CAPS 1907–1939 (eight matches or more)

*A R Aslett	Kings Own R Regt	20
J R Cole	Loyal Regt	17
*W F Browne	DWR	16
*H Rew	RTR	15
J A Ross	HLI	15
G J Bryan	RE	14
*A L Novis	Leicestershire Regt	14
*H J Sayers	RA	13
*H H C Withers	RE	13
*G V Palmer	Queen's Regt	12
*G J Dean	RTR	11
*E W F de V Hunt	RA	11
T G Rennie	Black Watch	11
G D Young	Welsh Gds	11
*C K T Faithfull	DWR	10
*R G S Hobbs	RA	10
G D Townend	DWR	10
*E J Unwin	Middlesex Regt	10
*C M Usher	Gordons	10
*J B Worton	Middlesex Regt	10
*A T Young	RTR	10

* Internationals

*P E R Baker-Jones	RFA	9
A T Boast	Welsh Gds	9
E E Cass	KOYLI	9
S T A Ratcliffe	RE	9
D S Jones	SWB	8
*R Leyland	Army Ed Corps	8
C C McCreight	RA	8
*C L Melville	Black Watch	8
*R K Miller	RE	8

* Internationals

ARMY CAPS 1907–1939

Infantry and Foot Guards	108
Royal Artillery	45
Royal Engineers	31
RAMC	13
Royal Tank Corps	10
Indian Army and IMS	7
Army Service Corps	4
Royal Marines and RMLI	4
Royal Corps Signals	3
Army Ordnance Corps	2
R Army Chaplains' Dept	2
Army Dental Corps	1
Army Educational Corps	1
Royal Military College	1
Life Guards	1
10th Hussars	1
	234

INFANTRY AND FOOT GUARDS

Welch Regt	16	KRRC	1
Duke of Wellington's Regt	13	East Yorkshire Regt	1
Welsh Guards	8	KOYLI	1
Leicestershire Regt	7	Hampshire Regt	1
King's Own R Regt	5	Loyal Regt	1
SWB	4	R Berkshire Regt	1
Gloucestershire Regt	4	Dorset Regt	1
Middlesex Regt	4	Sherwood Foresters	1
Queen's Regt	3	Border Regt	1
Cameron Highlanders	3	R Scots	1
Coldstream Guards	2	Beds & Herts	1
Northumberland Fus	2	Inniskilling Fus	1
Seaforth Highlanders	2	Royal Welch Fus	1
KSLI	2	Worcestershire Regt	2
Northamptonshire Regt	2	HLI	2
Dublin Fusiliers	2	Manchester Regt	1
Black Watch	2	Suffolk Regt	1

KOSB	1	Warwickshire Regt	1
DLI	1	E Surrey Regt	1
West Yorkshire Regt	1	R West Kents	1
Gordon Highlanders	1	Guards Depot	1
		Total	108

ARMY CAPS 1907–1939

List of players who have represented the Army against the Royal Navy, Royal Air Force and the French Army.

Aitken W H H	RE	RN 1924 RAF 1924 FA 1924
Allan A E	AD Corps	RN 1938–39 RAF 1938
Anderson R P G	RE	RN 1925–26 RAF 1925 FA 1925
Annesley G W	DWR	RAF 1931
Arengo-Jones A J A	Gloucestershire Regt	RN 1939 RAF 1939
Arnott S	RAMC	RN 1922 RAF 1922
Aslett A R	Kings Own Regt	RN 1921–22–24–25–26–28–29 RAF 1921–22–24–25–27–28–29 FA 1922–24–26–27–28–29
Baker C A	SWB	RN 1913–24 RAF 1924 FA 1924–25
Baker-Jones P E R	RFA	RN 1920–21–22–23 RAF 1920–21–23 FA 1920–23
Bastin G E R	RA	RN 1928 RAF 1928–29 FA 1928
Beaty-Pownall C C	Leicestershire Regt	FA 1930–31 RAF 1931
Begbie R P G	RGA	RN 1908–09–11–12
Bentley E	DWR	RAF 1931
Bevis D	CRA	RN 1939 RAF 1939
Bloxham G C	RFA	RN 1921
Boast A T	Welsh Guards	RN 1933–34–35–36–37 RAF 1933–34–35–37
Bolton C A	Manchester Regt	RN 1909–10
Bond I R B	Suffolk Regt	RN 1907
Bonham-Carter A L	KRRC	RN 1912
Bowerman E R M	E Yorkshire Regt	RN 1934–37 RAF 1937
Bowie J D	RAMC	RN 1911
Bowman J H	Coldstream Guards	RAF 1937
Boyd E F	Northumberland Fus	RN 1914
Brock A W S	Leicester Regt	RN 1909
Brookes V H	Indian Army	RN 1938
Brown R L	RE	RN 1921 RAF 1921
Browne W F	DWR	RN 1924–25–26–27–28–29 RAF 1924–26–27–28 FA 1924–25–26–27–28–29

Bryan G J	RE	RN 1924–25–26–27–28
		RAF 1924–25–26–27–28
		FA 1925–26–27–28
Bulkeley H I	RE	RN 1909
Caddell E D	RAMC	RN 1907–08
Campbell G C	RE	RN 1909
Carbutt N J O	RFA	RN 1921
Carleton C A S	Welch Regt	RN 1911
Cary F J L	RA	RN 1938 RAF 1938–39
Cass E E E	KOYLI	RN 1925–26–27 RAF 1925–
		26–27 FA 1925–26–
		27
Chamberlain d'E G	Hampshire Regt	RAF 1927 FA 1927
Chambers J L	RASC	RAF 1939
Champion A M	Welch Regt	RN 1939
Churcher G M	RGA	RAF 1921
Clarke T H	Gloucestershire Regt	RN 1932 RAF 1932
Clinch J D	Middlesex Regt	RN 1926 RAF 1926
		FA 1926
Cole J R	Loyal Regt	RN 1928–29–30–31–32–33–
		35–36
		RAF 1928–29–30–32–33–35
		FA 1928–29–30
Courtenay D H D	RTC	RN 1934 RAF 1934
Cowey B T V	Welch Regt	RN 1935 RAF 1934
Craven W S D	RFA	RN 1910–11–12–13
Crawford J A	RE	RN 1932–33–34
		RAF 1932–33–34–35
Crawford K N	RE	RAF 1921
Cross D	10th Hussars	RN 1920 RAF 1920
		FA 1920
Croston A J	RE	RN 1933 RAF 1933
Davies R I	R Berkshire Regt	RN 1922 RAF 1923
Day H L V	RFA	RN 1920–22–23 RAF 1922
		FA 1922
Dean G J	RTC	RN 1934–35–36–37–38
		RAF 1933–34–35–36–37–
		38
Dearden F	RFA	RN 1923 RAF 1922–23
		FA 1922–23
Delaney J	Welch Regt	RN 1939
De Smidt A G C	ASC	RN 1907–08
Devitt Sir T G Bart	Seaforth H	RN 1928–30 RAF 1928
		FA 1928
Down E E	Dorset Regt	RN 1926 RAF 1926
		FA 1926
Dunn B M	Welch Regt	RN 1925–26 RAF 1925–26
		FA 1922–24–25
Dobbs G E B	RE	RN 1907
Dowas F	DWR	RAF 1927 FA 1927
Duncan C S	Camerons	RN 1921 FA 1923
Evans J	Kings Own Regt	RN 1938 RAF 1938

Faithfull C K T	DWR	RN 1924-27-28
		RAF 1924-26-27-28
		FA 1924-26-28
Farmer E W	Gloucestershire Regt	RN 1939 RAF 1939
Fenton G C J	RA	RAF 1931
Fitzmaurice J G	RTC	RAF 1920 FA 1920
Ford F J V	Welch Regt	RN 1938 RAF 1938-39
France R L	RE	RAF 1939
Furber L D	KSLI	RN 1908-09
Gardner H	RFA	RN 1910-11-12-14
Gibbons P E	Welsh Guards	RN 1928 RAF 1928
Giles H G	Grenadier Guards	RN 1923 FA 1926
Glass H P L	Foresters	RAF 1936-37
Gordon R E	RFA	RN 1913
Gowlland G C	RE	RN 1907-09-10-13-14
Graham I S	Seaforth H	RAF 1936
Gransmore F W	Welch Regt	RN 1909
Green M A	Northamptonshire Regt	RN 1925 RAF 1925
		FA 1925
Grieve C F	DWR	RN 1938 RAF 1938
Griffith A L P	RFA	RN 1911-12
Grischotti W	KSLI	RN 1907-08-09
Hardy J C	R Signals	FA 1929
Harris L J	RE	RN 1931
Harrison E G W W	RFA	RN 1920
Harrison H C	Royal Marine Artillery	RN 1910-11-14
Harrison J	DWR	RN 1938 RAF 1938-39
Heale A S	RAMC	RN 1912
Heath L M	Indian Army	RN 1912
Hedderwick G	RTC	RN 1920 RAF 1920-21
		FA 1920
Hemphill R	RAMC	RN 1913
Herbert K L	Border Regt	RN 1921-23-25
		RAF 1923-25 FA 1925
Hill B A	AOC	RN 1907-08-09
Hinde H M	RASC	RN 1921-22-23
		RAF 1921-22 FA 1922-23
Hobbs P G	RA	RN 1933-34-35-36
		RAF 1933-34-35
Hobbs R F A	RE	RN 1907
Hobbs R G S	RA	RN 1929-30-31-32
		RAF 1929-30-31-32
		FA 1929-30
Holmes R N B	RE	RN 1939 RAF 1939
Honeyman P E C	R Scots	RN 1923-25 RAF 1923-25-26
		FA 1925-27
Howard-Jones S I	Royal Military College	RN 1936-37 RAF 1936-37
Huggan J L	RAMC	RN 1913-14
Hunt E W F de V	RA	RN 1929-30-31-32
		RAF 1929-30-31-32
		FA 1929-30-31

Huntingford W L	Royal Marine Artillery	RN 1908
Hutchison C R M	RHA	RN 1913–14
Hyland C	Life Guards	RN 1920–21 RAF 1920–21
Ibbitson H	Welch Regt	RN 1939 RAF 1939
Ievers F R	RA	FA 1931
Inglis W M	RE	RN 1937–38
		RAF 1936–37–38
Jackson A M	RE	RN 1914
Jackson F C	IMS	RAF 1932
Jones C W	Welch Regt	RN 1920–22 RAF 1922–23
		FA 1922–23
Jones D	SWB	RN 1926–27–28
		RAF 1926–27–28 FA 1926–28
Jones R L	Welch Regt	RAF 1923
Kavanagh G C MacM	RE	FA 1923
Kellie R H A	RGA	RN 1912
Kendrew D A	Leicester Regt	RN 1932–33–34–35–36
		RAF 1933–34
Kilgour I J	Northumberland Fus	RN 1922 RAF 1921–22
		FA 1922–23
King Q E M A	RFA	RN 1921–23 RAF 1921
Kitton L H	Bedfordshire &	FA 1922
	Hertfordshire Regt	
Lacey F H	Welch Regt	RN 1913
Lawless P H	Middlesex Regt	RN 1920 RAF 1920
		FA 1920
Leyland R	AEC	RN 1936–37–38–39
		RAF 1936–37–38–39
Liddell C G	Leicester Regt	RN 1912
Ling R W	RFA	RN 1913–14
Loch I G	RE	RAF 1925 FA 1925
MacIlwaine A H	RFA	RN 1913–14–21 RAF 1921
Maclear B	Dublin Fus	RN 1907
Macnamara G B	Inniskilling Fus	RN 1922–27 RAF 1922
		FA 1922
Mann W E	RFA	RN 1911
Marriott J H	Leicester Regt	RN 1937 RAF 1936–37
Marshall H G	RAChD	RN 1910
Martin A G	SWB	RN 1931 RAF 1931
		FA 1931
Maxwell R B	RAOC	RN 1927 RAF 1927
		FA 1927
McCall B E W	Welch Regt	RN 1936
McCreight C C	RA	RN 1930–34
		RAF 1929–30–31–34
		FA 1930–31
McIntyre K J	RTC	RN 1930–35 RAF 1930–35
		FA 1930
McVicker H	RAMC	RN 1927–28 RAF 1927
		FA 1927
Melville C L	Black Watch	RN 1936–37–38–39
		RAF 1936–37–38–39

Melville J L	Cameron H	RAF 1939
Middleton J A	RASC	RN 1922–23
		RAF 1921–22–23 FA 1922
Miles H G P	DWR	FA 1931
Millar R K	RE	RN 1923–24–25
		RAF 1923–24–25
		FA 1923–24
Montgomery R H	Welch Regt	RN 1909
Morgan R L	RAMC	RN 1934 RAF 1934
Morton W A	King's Own Regt	RN 1928–29
		RAF 1928–29–30
		FA 1928–29
Neave A C W	Indian Army	RN 1914
Newton A W	Dublin Fus	RN 1907–08
Nott D H	Worcestershire Regt	RN 1929–30 RAF 1929–30
		FA 1929–30
Novis A L	Leicestershire Regt	RN 1929–30–31–32–33–35
		RAF 1929–30–31–32–33–35
		FA 1929–30
Oliphant G W	DWR	RN 1914
Owen C R	Welch Regt	RN 1936–37–39
		RAF 1936–37–39
Palmer G V	The Queen's Regt	RN 1922–27–28
		RAF 1922–23–27–28
		FA 1922–23–24–27–28
Partridge J E C	Welch Regt	RN 1907–08–09–10
Pates F A	Welsh Guards	RN 1921–24 RAF 1923–24
		FA 1923
Peddie G	RA	RN 1930 RAF 1930
		FA 1930
Penney W R C	R Signals	RAF 1920 FA 1920
Penney E C	RFA	RN 1920 RAF 1920
		FA 1920
Phillips R M	Welch Regt	RN 1925–26 RAF 1925–26
		FA 1925–26
Phillips	Welsh Guards	RAF 1936
Pike V J	RAChD	RN 1933–34 RAF 1933–35
Powell W C	Welsh Guards	RN 1925 RAF 1925
		FA 1925
Proudlock J L	RA	RN 1927
Purdon W B	RAMC	RN 1908
Pym J A	RGA	RN 1910–11–12
Quill B C	The Queen's Regt	RN 1911–12
Radcliffe S T A	RE	RN 1932–33–34–35
		RAF 1932–33–34–35
		FA 1931
Ramsay N W	RE	RN 1939
Rawlence J R	RE	RN 1936 RAF 1936
Rees T E	Welsh Guards	RN 1926–28 RAF 1926–28
		FA 1926–28
Reeves G C	RTC	RAF 1934

Rennie T G	Black Watch	RN 1921–23–24–25
		RAF 1921–23–24–25
		FA 1923–24–25
Rew H	RTC	RN 1929–30–31–32–33–34
		RAF 1929–30–31–32–33–34
		FA 1929–30–31
Reynolds B W	DWR	RN 1931 RAF 1931
		FA 1931
Reynolds F J	DWR	RN 1937 RAF 1937–38
Rice-Evans J A M	RWF	RN 1929–30–31
		RAF 1929–30–31
Rideout E S	RE	RN 1913
Robertson L	Cameron H	RN 1908–09–10–12–13–14
Robinson T T H	RAMC	RN 1907
Roderick W B N	Coldstream Guards	RN 1920 RAF 1920
		FA 1920
Rodham C H B	Indian Army	RN 1930 RAF 1930
		FA 1930
Rogers W L Y	RA	RN 1908
Rohde J H	RE	RN 1910
Ross J A	HLI	RN 1922–23–24–25–26–27
		RAF 1922–24–25–27
		FA 1922–24–25–26–27
Sadler E H	R Signals	RN 1931–32–33
		RAF 1931–32–33 FA 1931
Sanders G A P	RA	RN 1924 RAF 1924
		FA 1924
Saunders H R	RA	RN 1926 RAF 1926
		FA 1926
Sayers H J	RA	RN 1933–34–35–36–37–38–39
		RAF 1932–34–35–37–38–39
Scobie R MacK	RE	RN 1914–20–23 RAF 1920
		FA 1920
Sewell E P	Northamptonshire Regt	RN 1927–31 RAF 1927
		FA 1927
Shewen W G M	KOSB	RN 1920 RAF 1920
		FA 1920
Simpson F W	RE	RN 1931–32–33–35
		RAF 1932–35
Simpson R B Y	Durham LI	RN 1920 RAF 1920
		FA 1920
Simson J R	HLI	RN 1907
Simson J T	RAMC	RN 1910–11
Simson R F	RFA	RN 1911–12–13
Stevens L M	Worcestershire Regt	RN 1908
Stevenson W H	Indian Army	RN 1925 RAF 1925
Stone J S W	RE	RN 1920 FA 1920
Sydenham P S B	RE	FA 1923
Tagg E J B	Royal Marines	RN 1910
Tarrant V F D	Gloucestershire Regt	RN 1938–39 RAF 1938

Taylor G	W Yorkshire Regt	RN 1931 RAF 1931–33–37 FA 1931
Teacue J C J	RMLI	RN 1909
Tennant T B L	RGA	RN 1921 RAF 1921–22 FA 1922–24
Thomas L G	RE	RN 1924 RAF 1924 FA 1924
Thomas W	SWB	RN 1927 RAF 1927
Thomson J N	RA	RN 1911–13
Townend G	DWR	RN 1928–29–30 RAF 1928–29–30 FA 1928–29–30–31
Troop C L	DWR	RN 1931–32–33 RAF 1931–32–33 FA 1931
Tucker B H G	Indian Army	RN 1924–27 RAF 1924–27 FA 1927
Turner F T	RAMC	RN 1907–08
Turquand Young D	RTC	RN 1926 RAF 1925–26 FA 1925–26
Tyler A W	RA	RN 1932–33 RAF 1932–33
Unwin E J	Middlesex Regt	RN 1934–35–36–37–38–39 RAF 1934–35–36–38
Usher C M	Gordon H	RN 1912–13–14–22 RAF 1920–22–23 FA 1920–22–23
Vaughan-Jones A	RA	RN 1932
Wade-Geary R H	RGA	RN 1910–12
Wainwright J W	RA	RN 1929 RAF 1929–30 FA 1929–30–31
Walker H J I	Warwickshire Regt	RN 1914
Wallis C O'N	E Surrey Regt	RN 1937–38 RAF 1936–38
Watson A J A	The Queen's Regt	RN 1934–35–36–37 RAF 1934–35
Whelpton J W	King's Own Regt	FA 1928
Whitcombe F W	RE	RN 1935 RAF 1935
Whitty J H H	R W Kent Regt	RN 1937 RAF 1936–37
Wilcox I	Welsh Guards	RN 1935–36 RAF 1935–36
Wilkins W C	RTC	RAF 1920 FA 1920
Wilkinson J	RE	RAF 1923
Williamson M J	RAMC	RN 1910
Wilson W C	Leicester Regt	RN 1907–08–09–10–11
Withers H H C	RE	RN 1929–30–31–32 RAF 1928–29–30–31–32 FA 1928–29–30–31
Worton J B	Middlesex Regt	RN 1921–22–23–24 RAF 1922–23–24 FA 1922–24–29
Wright K M	RA	RN 1929–30 RAF 1929–30 FA 1927–29–30
Wright R F	RA	FA 1923

Young A T	RTC	RN 1926–27–28–29
		RAF 1926–27–28
		FA 1926–27–28
Young G D	Welsh Guards	RN 1920–22–23–24
		RAF 1920–22–23–24
		FA 1920–23–24

ARMY CAPTAINS 1946–85

Inter-Service Matches–French Army

A J Hoon	RE	forward	8
N S Bruce	RAOC	forward	6
R D H Bryce	RE	forward	6
M J Campbell-Lamerton	DWR	forward	6
F H Coutts	KOSB	forward	6
J M H Roberts	Welsh Guards	full-back	6
K H S Wilson	R Sussex	scrum-half	5
H G Greatwood	E Surreys	forward	5
J M Bowles	RCT	forward	4
G Davies	APTC	scrum-half	4
F R Beringer	RE	forward	3
A B Edwards	RAEC	full-back	3
J P Fisher	RADC	forward	3
C J W Gilbert	DWR	forward	3
H M Inglis	RA	forward	3
B A Neale	RA	forward	3
D W Shuttleworth	DWR	scrum-half	3
T Sinclair	DWR	forward	3
C R Bruce	RA	outside half	2
N C G Raffle	RE	forward	2
R E Rae	RAMC	forward	2
R Roe	RAChD	forward	2
N T Slater	RAEC	forward	2
P J Warfield	RAEC	threequarter	2
S G Jackson	RAMC	threequarter	1

Inter-Service matches	80
French Army	13
	93

ARMY CAPS 1946–1985 (ten or more caps)

*N S Bruce	RAOC	27
A J Hoon	RE	22
*D W Shuttleworth	DWR	22
*A B Edwards	RAEC	17

*B A Neale	RA	17
G Davies	QDG/APTC	16
P A Eastwood	RAPC	15
H G Greatwood	E Surrey Regt	15
G O W Williams	DWR	14
J M Bowles	RCT	13
D S Boyle	Parachute Regt	13
R D H Bryce	RE	13
*M J Campbell-Lamerton	DWR	13
R J Moyle	REME	13
J M H Roberts	Welsh Gds	13
*F H Coutts	KOSB	12
*D S Gilbert-Smith	DWR	12
N J Gray	RE	12
G D Lilley	RCT	12
D Spawforth	REME	12
R Braybrooke	RE	11
M R Handfield-Jones	RE	11
*E M P Hardy	DWR	11
S G Jackson	RAMC	11
J H Morgan	REME	10
N C G Raffle	RE	10
I P Reid	DWR	10
K A'Hearne	RRW	10
B Neck	Welsh Guards	10

ARMY CAPS 1946–1985

Infantry And Foot Guards	102
Royal Engineers	40
Royal Signals	40
Royal Artillery	37
Royal Electrical and Mechanical Engineers	36
Royal Army Medical Corps	25
Royal Army Ordnance Corps	20
Royal Army Educational Corps	19
Royal Army Service Corps/Royal Corps of Transport	18
Royal Armoured Corps	15
Parachute Regt	5
Army Physical Training Corps	5
Corps of Royal Military Police	4
Royal Army Dental Corps	3
Royal Army Pay Corps	2
Indian Army	2
Royal Military Academy Sandhurst	2
Mons (OCTU)	1
Total	376

Royal Armoured Corps
Royal Tank Regt   7
13th/18th Royal Hussars   3
14th/20 King's Hussars   3
16th/5th Queen's Royal Lancers   1
1st Queen's Dragoon Guards   1
                                                                  ——
                                          Total   15

When players have received Army caps having changed their Corps or Regiments both units have been credited with the cap.

THE INFANTRY AND FOOT GUARDS

Duke of Wellington's Regt   29
Royal Regt of Wales   13
Welsh Guards   11
King's Own Scottish Borderers   6
Light Infantry   4
Gloucestershire Regt   3
Royal Hampshire Regt   3
Welch Regt   3
Coldstream Guards   2
Cameronians (Scottish Rifles)   2
Northamptonshire Regt   2
Royal Welch Fus   2
Royal Sussex Regt   2
South Wales Borderers   2
Cheshire Regt   1
Devonshire and Dorset Regt   1
East Surrey Regt   1
East Lancashire Regt   1
Grenadier Guards   1
King's Own Royal Border Regt   1
Lancashire Fus   1
Queen's Lancashire Regt   1
Queen's Own Royal West Kent Regt   1
The Buffs (Royal East Kent Regt)   1
Queen's Regt   1
Royal Northumberland Fus   1
Royal Highland Fus   1
Royal Leicestershire Regt   1
Royal Scots   1
Royal Anglian Regt   1
Rifle Brigade   1
Scots Guards   1
                                                                  ——
                                          Total   102

ARMY CAPS 1946-1985

List of players who have represented the Army against the Royal Navy, Royal Air Force and the French Army.

Abbott B J	REME	RAF 1978-82 RN 1982
Anderson J H	Welsh Guards	FA 1958
Arnold S R	DWR	RN 1959 RAF 1959
Armstrong S	REME	RN 1979-80 RAF 1979-80
Ashcroft J S	RE	RAF 1970-71 RN 1971
Asquith A E	RA	RN 1951
Atkins E	R Signals	RN 1985 RAF 1985
Atkinson W A N	DWR	RAF 1977-78 RN 1977-78
Audrain R	RAOC	RN 1982 RAF 1982
Bale C G	RAMC	RN 1967-69-71 RAF 1967
Barker E	RA	RN 1965 RAF 1965
Barstow H B W	Queen's Regt	RAF 1968-69 RN 1969
Bartlett J T	RE	RN 1947
Bassom K	RE	RN 1979-82-84
		RAF 1979-82-84
Batten H P	14/20H	RN 1951 RAF 1951
		FA 1951
Baume J L	R Northumberland Fus	RN 1950-51-53
		RAF 1950-53 FA 1950
Baxter J	RA	RN 1978-79 RAF 1978
Bazley R C	RE	RN 1954-55 RAF 1954-55
		FA 1955
Bearne K R F	RE	RN 1956 RAF 1956
		FA 1956
Beazley N	RA	RN 1985
Bedford R	RE	RAF 1983
Bell R G	RMA/13/18H	RN 1974 RAF 1976
Bellows M L	RASC	RAF 1956 FA 1956
Bennett G K	RAEC	FA 1959
Beringer F R	RE	RN 1951-53-54
		RAF 1951-53-54
		FA 1951-53-54
Bevan D	Gloucestershire Regt	RN 1948 RAF 1948
		FA 1948
Bird P G	DWR	RN 1972
Blomquist M	RE	RN 1984
Boston W J	R Signals	RN 1954 FA 1954
Bott W E	RE	RN 1976 RAF 1976
Bowen D T	Welsh Guards	RN 1968-73 RAF 1968
Bowles J M	RCT	EN 1973-76-77-78-79-80-81-82
		RAF 1973-77-78-79-80-81-82-84
Boyle D S	Parachute Regt	RAF 1967-68-69-70-71-72-73
		RN 1968-69-70-71-72-73

Blackmore M W	RAPC	FA 1956–57
Black W P	RAMC	RN 1952–53 RAF 1952–53
		FA 1952–53
Blackett G	R Signals	RN 1959 RAF 1959
		FA 1959
Bland D F	REME	RN 1952–53 RAF 1952–53
		FA 1952
Blinkhorn H	RAOC	RN 1963 RAF 1963–64
Brewer T J	R Signals	RN 1953 RAF 1953
		FA 1953–54
Brook J	R Signals	FA 1952
Broome J	RAOC	RN 1952–53 RAF 1952–53
		FA 1952–53
Brown J K	RAOC	RN 1984 RAF 1984
Brown R T	RA	RN 1964 RAF 1964
Bruce C R	RA	RN 1946 RAF 1946
Bruce N S	RAOC	RN 1955–56–57–59–60–61–62–63–64–67–68
		RAF 1955–56–57–59–60–61–62–63–64–67–68
		FA 1955–56–57–58–59
Bryce R D H	RE	RN 1964–65–66–67–68–69–70–71
		RAF 1964–67–69–70–71
Braybrooke R	RE	RN 1961–62–63–64–65–67
		RAF 1961–62–63–64–67
Burcher A C	CRMP	RAF 1947 FA 1947
Byrne J	REME	RN 1982 (R)–83–84–85
		RAF 1982–84–85
Cairns I	R Signals	RN 1970–71–72–73
		RAF 1972
Cameron A	RA	RN 1948–49 RAF 1948–49
		FA 1948–49
Campbell G B L	RE	RAF 1965–67–69
		RN 1967–69–70
Campbell R G C	RCT	RN 1975–76 RAF 1975–76
Campbell-Lamerton M J	DWR	RN 1960–61–62–63–64–65–66
		RAF 1960–62–63–64–65–66
Campbell-Lamerton J	Scots Guards	RN 1981 RAF 1981
Carroll J	RAMC	RAF 1971–75 RN 1972–75
Castleton N	RMAS	RN 1985
Chapman I L	Parachute Regt	RN 1964
Chapman J M D	RA	RN 1954 FA 1954
Chisnall R	RA	RN 1957–58 RAF 1957–58
Christopher C	RAOC	RN 1981–82–83–84
		RAF 1981–82–83–84–85
Chapple A	REME	RAF 1981
Cleaver P D	REME	RN 1955
Clesham B P	Light Infantry	RAF 1977
Clancy J D	RAEC	RN 1949 RAF 1949
		FA 1949

Colgate T K	RAEC	RN 1965 RAF 1965
Collins K	REME	RAF 1970
Cockcroft J C	Welsh Guards	RAF 1962
Collier R S	REME	RN 1975 RAF 1975
Coutts F H	KOSB	RN 1947–48–49–50
		RAF 1947–48–49–50
		FA 1947–48–49–50
Crooks P V	REME	RN 1960–61–62–63
		RAF 1960–61–62
Cross R	R Signals	RN 1949–50 RAF 1949–50
		FA 1949–50
Cuss M	DWR	RN 1973–75 RAF 1973–75
Danby T	RAOC	RN 1947 FA 1947
Davies E W	RASC	RN 1961
Davies G G	RCT	RAF 1974–75 RN 1974–75
Davies G	QDG/APTC	RN 1977–78–79–81–82–83
		84–85
		RAF 1977–78–79–81–82–83
		84–85
Davies G R	R Signals	RN 1948 RAF 1948
		FA 1948
Davies J	RRW	RN 1971–72 RAF 1971–72
Davies J	Welsh Guards	RAF 1976
Davies P J	DWR	RN 1959–60 RAF 1959
		FA 1959
Davies P M	13/18H	RN 1972–73–74–75
		RAF 1972–73–75
Davies R	RA	RN 1959 RAF 1959
		FA 1959
Denham D	RAOC	RN 1976–77
Dorey R F	R Hampshire Regt	RN 1950–52 RAF 1950–52
		FA 1950
Drew R J	RA	RN 1970–72
Drummond C W	KOSB	RN 1946
Drummond J D	RHF	RN 1966 RAF 1966
Drummond N W	RAChDept	RN 1977 RAF 1977
Eastwood P A	RAPC	RAF 1963–64–65–66–67–68–69–74
		RN 1964–65–66–67–68–69–74
Edgecombe G J B	Buffs	RN 1958–60
		RAF 1958–60–61
		FA 1958–59
Edwards A B	RAEC	RN 1952–53–54–55–56
		RAF 1951–52–53–54–55–56
		FA 1951–52–53–54–55–56
Edwards C G J	DWR	RN 1964–65–66–67–68
		RAF 1964–65–66–67
Elsbury D	Welch Regt	RAF 1966
Elwill P	DWR	RN 1976
Elkan H	R Signals	RAF 1973 RN 1981
		RAF 1981

Evans E	RA	RAF 1946 RN 1946
Evans P J	REME	RN 1962
Evans R	R Signals	RAF 1954 RAF 1955
		FA 1954
Fisher J P	RADC	RN 1965–66–67
		RAF 1965–66–67–68
Fleming R M	RA	RN 1946 RAF 1946
Friend M	Devon & Dorset	RN 1964–65 RAF 1964–65
Gabbitas B	R Signals	RN 1954–55 RAF 1954–55
		FA 1954
Gilbert C J W	DWR	RAF 1966–76–77
		RN 1968–72–76–77
Gilbert-Smith D S	DWR	RN 1952–56–58
		RAF 1951–52–56–58
		FA 1951–52–55–56–58
Glean H	R Signals	RN 1980–81 RAF 1980–81
Gloag I S	R Signals	RN 1948 RAF 1948
		FA 1948
Goddard D	RRW	RN 1982
Godson A	R Signals	RN 1957–58 RAF 1957–58
		FA 1957
Godwin H O	R Leicestershire Regt	RN 1960 RAF 1959–60
Gordon I A	Cameronians	RAF 1965
Gray N J	RE	RAF 1974–75–76–77–78–79
		RN 1974–75–76–77–78–79
Greatwood H G	E Surrey Regt	RN 1955–57–58–59–62
		RAF 1953–55–57–58–59–62
		FA 1953–55–57–58
Greenhalgh M	RA	RAF 1983 RAF 1985
Greenwood D G	RE	FA 1955
Gregory J A	RAMC	RN 1946 RAF 1946
Grieve C F	DWR	RAF 1977
Griffiths P A D	RTR	RN 1966
Griffiths P	Welsh Guards	RN 1975 RAF 1981
Guthrie C R L	Welsh Guards	RN 1964 RAF 1964
Hall J W	R Signals	RN 1949 RAF 1949
		FA 1949
Hall N M	R Signals	RN 1949 RAF 1949
		FA 1949
Hancock J H	REME	RN 1954–55 RAF 1954–55
		FA 1954–55
Handfield-Jones M R	RE	RN 1959–60–61–62–63–64
		RAF 1960–61–62–63–64
Hardy E M P	DWR	RN 1950–51–52–55
		RAF 1950–51–52
		FA 1950–51–52–55
Hartley M J	RE	RN 1956 RAF 1956
		FA 1956
Hart A I	RA	FA 1957
Harvey C	DWR	RN 1983–84–85
		RAF 1983–84–85

Hathorn D Mc F	Cameronians	RN 1966 RAF 1966
		FA 1967
Hazel B J B	RAEC	RN 1951–52 RAF 1951–52
		FA 1951–52
Hearn D	Welsh Guards	RAF 1962 RAF 1969
Hearne K'A	RRW	RN 1978–79–80–81–82
		RAF 1978–79–80–81–82
Heath M H S	RE	RN 1961–62 RAF 1961–62
Higgins R	R Signals	RN 1954 RAF 1954
Hill F C H	CRMP	RN 1946 RAF 1946
Hitchcock I	RE	RN 1983
Hoon A J	RE	RN 1966–67–68–69–70–71–
		72–73–74–78–79
		RAF 1966–67–68–69–70–71–
		72–73–74–78–79
Horsell F G	RA	RN 1946 RAF 1946
Horton L	RE	RN 1982
Houghton H J	RAMC	RAF 1947 FA 1947
Howard-Jones S I	RTR	RN 1947 FA 1947
Hughes J	REME	RN 1957 RAF 1957
Hutt M J	REME	RN 1958
Hyde J P	Northamptonshire Regt	RN 1950–51 RAF 1950–51
		FA 1950–51
Ince R P P	RCT	RAF 1974 RN 1974
Inglis H M	RA	RN 1956–57 RAF 1956–57
		FA 1956–57
Innes J R S	RAMC	RN 1946 RAF 1946
Isles D E	DWR	RAF 1950 FA 1950
Jackson P	R Signals	RAF 1954 RN 1955
		RAF 1955
Jackson T G H	R Signals	RN 1948–49–51
		RAF 1946–48
Jackson S G	RAMC	RN 1975–76–77–78–79–81
		RAF 1976–77–78–79–81
Jeffray J S A	RA	RN 1967–72
		RAF 1967–68–72
Jenkins M	RRW	RN 1978–80 RAF 1978–80
Johnson D	RWF	RN 1983–84–85
		RAF 1983–84
Johnson P M	RAEC	RAF 1972–73 RN 1976
Johnstone G	RAMC	FA 1955
Jones A G C	RE	RN 1950–51 RAF 1950–51
		FA 1950–51–52
Jones J M	RA	RN 1963 RAF 1963
Jones R	REME	FA 1956
Jones R	Welsh Guards	RAF 1970
Jones W O	REME	RN 1947 RAF 1947
Joy A E P	REME	RN 1947 RAF 1947
		FA 1947
Kaged M	RRW	RN 1980 RAF 1980
Kay A	DWR	RN 1983 RAF 1983

Keeling J H	RADC	RN 1950 RAF 1950 FA 1950
Kelly R V	RA	RN 1968
Kennedy G E	RAMC	FA 1958
Kerr D J	RAOC	RAF 1974–76 RN 1976
Kessell	R Signals	RN 1985 RAF 1985
Kirk J	RAMC	RN 1946 RAF 1946
Kirke N	RA	RAF 1965
Knight M	16/5 Lancers	RAF 1983
Knowles J E	RCT	RAF 1974
Lapidus D	RCT	RN 1966 RAF 1966
Lees C A	Lancashire Regt	RN 1963 RAF 1963
Leleu J	Parachute Regt	RN 1955 RAF 1955
Lennox R	RAOC	RN 1970
Leonard R J N	RE	RN 1960 RAF 1960
Lerwill A T D	Light Infantry	RAF 1970
Lerwill J A W	Indian Army	FA 1947
Lewis M	RA	RN 1985 RAF 1985
Lightfoot R	RASC	RN 1958–59 RAF 1958 FA 1958–59
Lilley G D	RCT	RN 1968–69–70–71–73–77 RAF 1968–69–70–71–72–73
Lloyd M	RAOC	RN 1983R
Lockitt P	REME	RN 1983–85 RAF 1984–85 RN 1984R
Lougher G	RAEC	RN 1965
Lowdon S A	RA	RN 1954 RAF 1955
Lowis I J A	KOSB	RN 1967
Lovegrove G	QDG	RN 1981
Luckey C	RA	RN 1972–73 RAF 1972
Lysaght P	RA	RN 1955 RAF 1955 FA\1955
Lytollis P	R Signals	RAF 1980–81–82 RN 1980–81
McCall B	REME	RN 1983–84 RAF 1983–84–85
MacDonald J D	KOSB/RCT	RAF 1961–64–66–67 RN 1965–66–67–70
MacDonald R	RAMC	RN 1953 RAF 1953
Machie C G	RAMC	RN 1947–48 RAF 1948 FA 1948
Mackay A	RCT	RAF 1984–85 RN 1985
Mackie N O	R Signals	FA 1954
Major W C	Welch Regt	RN 1951 RAF 1951 FA 1951
Marriot V R	RAEC	RN 1961–62 RAF 1962
Marques R W D	RE	RN 1954 RAF 1954 FA 1954
Marshall T R	R Signals	RN 1949 RAF 1949 FA 1949
Martin L	RE	RN 1967 RAF 1967–68
Martin P J S	SWB	RN 1947 RAF 1947 FA 1947
Mason A	RRW	RN 1982

Matthews J	RAMC	RN 1947–48 RAF 1947–48 FA 1948
Matthews R J	RE	RN 1978–79 RAF 1978–79
McCrae A R	R Signals	RAF 1954 FA 1954
McCracken D	CRMP/APTC	RN 1977–78–83 RAF 1983
McFarlane B	RCT	RAF 1982 RN 1984 RAF 1984
McLean K	RAMC	RN 1958 RAF 1958 FA 1958
McLeod H F	R Scots Greys	RN 1954–55 RAF 1954–55 FA 1954–55
McPartlin J J	RA	RN 1959 RAF 1959
Michell P J B	Mons OCTU	RN 1954
Michie E J S	RE	RN 1956–57 RAF 1956 FA 1956–57
Mills J B	REME	RAF 1976 RAF 1977
Mills P M S	Parachute Regt	RN 1977 RAF 1977
Miller G	RAEC	RN 1970–74 RAF 1970–71–74
Mitchell P R B	RASC	RN 1949 RAF 1949 FA 1949
Molloy M G	RAMC	RN 1968–70–74 RAF 1969–70–72–73–74
Morgan H J	REME	RN 1957–58 RAF 1957–58 FA 1957
Morgan J H	REME	RAF 1973–74–75–76–80 RN 1973–74–75–76–80
Moroney T A	RAMC	RN 1964–66–69–71 RAF 1966–68–69–71
Moyle R J	REME	RN 1957–58–59–61–62–63 RAF 1957–58–61–62–63 FA 1957–58
Munroe W H	R Signals	RN 1946 RAF 1946
Murphy J G M W	RAChDept	RN 1957 RAF 1957 FA 1957
Murray W	R Signals	FA 1957
Neale B A	RA	RN 1949–50–51–52–53 RAF 1948–49–50–51–52–53 FA 1948–49–50–51–52–53
Neck B	Welsh Guards	RN 1969–70–71–72–73 RAF 1969–70–70–72–73
Neild G	RE	RN 1983–84 RAF 1983–84
Newell N J	DWR	RN 1974
Newmarsh G W C	Light Infantry	RN 1976
Noel-Smith M	Gloucesters	RN 1982–83 RAF 1982–83
O'Flaherty M A	RTR	RAF 1960 FA 1959
Oulton P H	Cheshire Regt	RAF 1961 RN 1962
Outram C S	RA	RAF 1956
Owen J R	RAMC	RN 1955 RAF 1955 FA 1955
Owen S G	REME	RN 1952–53 RAF 1952
Parker G D	RAEC	RN 1960–61 RAF 1960–61

Paterson H McI	R Signals	RN 1959
Payne G W	RE	RN 1960–61 RAF 1961
Peacock S	R Signals/APTC	RN 1975–84–85
		RAF 1975–76–83–84–85
Peart T G A H	RA	RN 1956 RAF 1956–57
		FA 1956
Phillips D V	RAC	RN 1946 RAF 1946
Phillips J R	RE	RN 1948 RAF 1948
		FA 1948
Phillips W K	REME	RN 1952 RAF 1952
		FA 1952
Philp M H	Light Infantry	RAF 1969
Phipps G C	R Hampshire Regt	RN 1950–52 RAF 1950–52
		FA 1950–52
Pontin K	RE	FA 1957
Preston R T	RAEC	RN 1969 RAF 1969
Priest W R	APTC	RN 1946 RAF 1946
Prosser M	RRW	RAF 1980 RN 1980
Prowse D	REME	RAF 1978
Purdy S J	RAEC	RN 1959–60 RAF 1959–60
Raffle N C G	RE	RN 1957–58–59–60
		RAF 1957–58–59–60
		FA 1957–59
Rapley A	REME	RN 1980 RAF 1980
Rea RE	RAMC	RAF 1973–74–75
		RN 1973–74–75
Rees D F	R Signals	RN 1953–55 RAF 1953
		FA 1953–55
Rees P	RRW	RN 1980 RAF 1980
Rees R K	REME	FA 1959
Reeves P B	R Signals	RN 1949–50 RAF 1949–50
		FA 1949–50
Redwood-Davies A R	DWR	RN 1971
Regan J	RAMC	RAF 1955–56 RN 1955–56
Reid I P	DWR	RAF 1962–63–64–65
		RN 1962–63–64–65–66–67
Relph G C	RA	RAF 1971
Renilson C	DWR	RN 1961 RAF 1961
Reynolds D B	REME	RAF 1975–77–78–79–80R
		RN 1977–78–79–80
Richards E A	RAOC	RN 1962 RAF 1962–63
Richardson C	R Scots	RN 1981 RAF 1981
Richardson T E	R Signals	RAF 1947 FA 1947
Ricketts A F	REME	RN 1958 RAF 1958
		FA 1958
Robins R J	R Signals	RN 1953 FA 1953
Robinson P	DWR	RAF 1975–76 RN 1975
Roberts J M H	Welsh Guards	RN 1949–50–51–52
		RAF 1948–49–50–51–52
		FA 1948–49–51–52
Roche A	RAEC	RAF 1949 FA 1949
Roche G G	RE	RN 1950

Roddan H	RE	RN 1957 RAF 1957
		FA 1957
Roe R	RAChD	RN 1956–57–63
		RAF 1956–57–63
		FA 1956
Rose M J	RTR	RN 1965 RAF 1967
Rosser D W A	RAEC	RN 1960–61–62
		RAF 1960–61
Rowlands D S	RAMC	RN 1948
Rundle H	RRW	RN 1980 RAF 1980
Sausmarez de P W D	Coldstream Guards	RAF 1966
Saunders D W	RE	RN 1966 RAF 1966
Saville B	DWR	RAF 1958
Scarr D P R	14/20 H	FA 1950
Scotland K J F	R Signals	RN 1956–57 RAF 1956–57
		FA 1956–57
Scott D M	RAEC	RN 1950 RAF 1950–51
		FA 1950–51
Scourfield J R	RAMC	RN 1958
Scroby J	DWR	RN 1959 RAF 1959
Sexton C	RE	RN 1977
Sharp G	R Signals	RN 1960–61 RAF 1960–61
Shaw I	RAOC	RN 1984
Shillinglaw R B	KOSB	RAF 1960
Shuttleworth D W	DWR	RN 1949–50–51–52–53–55–
		56
		RAF 1949–50–51–52–53–56–
		58
		FA 1949–50–51–52–53–55–
		56–58
Shuttleworth G	DWR	RAF 1981
Silcox P	Grenadier Guards	RN 1983
Simpson C P	R Anglian Regt	RN 1965–68
		RAF 1963–65–68
Sinclair T C	DWR	RN 1975–80 RAF 1975–80
Slater N T	RAEC	RN 1972–74 RAF 1972–74
Smith D W C	RAMC	RN 1949 RAF 1949
		FA 1949
Smith J V	Gloucestershire Regt	RAF 1948 FA 1948
Smith M J C L	Parachute Regt	RN 1967
Smith P D	RAOC	RN 1977–79
		RAF 1977–78–79
Smith I S G	RADC	RAF 1969–70 RN 1970–71
Southward I	RA	RN 1956–57 RAF 1956–57
Spawforth D	REME	RAF 1968–69–71–72–73–74
		RN 1969–70–71–72–73–76
Spring R	Coldstream Guards	RAF 1977–79 RN 1979
Spurrell R A	REME	RAF 1975–76 RN 1976
Spowart C	RE	RN 1982 RAF 1982
Stancombe R M	RE	RN 1963–64–65
		RAF 1964–65
Steele I	RA	RN 1985 RAF 1985

Stephenson J R	R Sussex	FA 1959
Stevens D E	RE	RN 1978-79 RAF 1979
Stevens W H F	R Hampshire Regt	RAF 1963
Stobart G	Indian Army	RN 1947 RAF 1947 FA 1947
Stone G A	REME	RAF 1963 RN 1963
Swan J S	REME	FA 1953-54 RN 1954 RAF 1954
Taggart H G R	RE	RN 1969
Tarr T	RAOC	RAF 1981 RN 1981
Taylor P J	DWR	RN 1951 RAF 1951 FA 1951
Taylor R M	RASC	RAF 1962
Taylor T	RAMC	RAF 1953 FA 1953
Thomas A R	RASC	FA 1959 RN 1959 RAF 1959
Thomas E	RASC	RAF 1959 FA 1959
Thomas D W	Welch Regt	RN 1966 RAF 1966
Thomas H	APTC	RN 1947 RAF 1947 FA 1947
Thomas N B	RAEC	RN 1968-69-70 RAF 1968-70
Thomas T	RA	FA 1956 RN 1956
Thomson I H M	R Signals	RN 1953 RAF 1953 FA 1953
Thorn J	DWR	RN 1973 RAF 1973
Thurgood W P G	RA	FA 1958
Tippett A M	Rifle Bde	RN 1953-54 RAF 1953 FA 1953
Titterington S	REME	RAF 1981-82 RN 1981-82-83
Townsend W E	RAEC	FA 1953 RN 1956
Travers R	RAOC	RN 1982-84-85 RAF 1982-85
Treadwell D J	RTR	RN 1968 RAF 1968
Turner B	RAOC	RN 1971 RAF 1971
Turner D M	QOR West Kent Regt	RN 1954 RAF 1954 FA 1954
Turner J A	R Signals	FA 1954
Turk A S	RTR	RAF 1973-74 RN 1973-74
Tyler B	REME	RN 1979 RAF 1979
Valentine D D	KOSB	RN 1947 RAF 1947 FA 1947
Vaux J E	RE	RN 1961-62-63 RAF 1961-62
Walter S T J	RA	RAF 1947 RN 1948
Waqabaca T	DWR	RN 1963-64-68 RAF 1964
Ward E	Lancashire Fus	RN 1946 RAF 1946
Warfield P	RAEC	RN 1981-84 RAF 1983-84
Watchorne D	RAMC	RN 1954 RAF 1954 RAF 1955
Watling S		RAF 1985

Watt A G M	RAMC	RN 1948 RAF 1948 FA 1948
Watts T R	RAOC	FA 1958
White D F	Northamptonshire Regt	RN 1946–47–48 RAF 1946–47–48 FA 1947–48
Whitehorn A	RE	FA 1955–59 RAF 1959
Willcox J G	E Lancashire Regt	RN 1958 RAF 1958 FA 1958
Williams D A	R Signals	RAF 1959–60 FA 1959 RN 1960
Williams D R	RWF	RN 1975 RAF 1975
Williams F A	RA	RAF 1965–71–72 RN 1972
Wiliams G O W	DWR	RN 1976–78–80–81–82–83–85 RAF 1976–78–79–80–82–83–85
Williams J K	R Signals	RN 1947–48 RAF 1947–48 FA 1947–48
Williams P	RRW	RN 1980 RAF 1980
Williams P R G	Welsh Guards	RN 1958
Williams T L	SWB	RN 1969
Wilkinson R	RAOC	RAF 1971–72
Wilson D	RE	RN 1970–71 RAF 1970–71
Wilson K H S	R Sussex	RN 1946–47–48 RAF 1946–47–48 FA 1947–48
Wood A G I	R Signals	RN 1952 RAF 1952
Wright C L G	R Signals	RAF 1974–77 RN 1974
Wright P J	King's Own R Border Regt	RAF 1976 RN 1977–78
Young P M	RASC	RN 1949 RAF 1949 FA 1949
Young R E	REME	RAF 1958 FA 1958
Zaidman I	RAOC	RN 1951 RAF 1951 FA 1951–52

INTERNATIONAL HONOURS

The Honours List includes all players who gained International caps during their Army Service. Players who were capped before their Army Service and did not play for their Country whilst serving are not included; likewise players who were capped after leaving the Service are omitted. This means that such distinguished players as W C Powell (Welsh Guards and Wales) and C F Grieve (Duke of Wellington's Regiment and Scotland) are not included.

The records up to 1914 make it difficult to be certain whether some players were serving in the Army when they gained International honours. In such cases the players have been given the benefit of the doubt.

The abbreviation (capt) signifies players who captained their Country. The regiment or corps are those in which players were serving when they played International rugby.

INTERNATIONAL HONOURS

Year	Name	Country	No caps	Regt/Corps
1871	C W Sherrard	England	2	RE
1871	C A Crompton	England	1	RE
1872	F B G d'Aguilar	England	1	RE
1872	R P Maitland	Scotland	1	RA
1872	F T Maxwell	Scotland	1	RE
1872	H W Renny Tailyour	Scotland	1	RE
1873	C H Rickards	England	1	RA
1874	C W Crosse	England	2	KDGs
1874	F L Cunliffe	England	1	RA
1874	W F H Stafford	England	1	RE
1874	A K Stewart	Scotland	2	AMS
1874	A H Young	Scotland	1	Inniskilling Fus
1875	A P Cronyn	Ireland	3	Royal West Kent Regt
1875	J W Dunlop	Scotland	1	RA
1876	W C W Rawlinson	England	1	Lincolnshire Regt
1877	H H Johnston	Scotland	2	AMS
1877	H W Murray	Ireland	3	IMS
1877	E I Pocock	Scotland	2	Indian Army
1878	E W D Croker	Ireland	1	A & SH
1879	W W Pike	Ireland	5	AMS
1881	R D Garnons-Williams	Wales	1	R Fusiliers
1882	W N Bolton	England	11	Wiltshire Regt

1882	J B Buchanan	Ireland	3	AMS
1882	R G Thompson	Ireland	1	AMS
1882	F S Heuston	Ireland	3	AMS
1883	R S F Henderson	England	5	AMS
1884	W Edgeworth-Johnstone	Ireland	1	R Irish Regt
1885	T W Irvine	Scotland	10	IMS
1887	C M Moore	Ireland	3	AMS
1888	A Walpole	Ireland	2	RE
1893	P Maud	England	2	RE
1894	T J Crean	Ireland	9	AMS
1894	W G Neilson	Scotland	1	A & SH
1895	T H Stevenson	Ireland	7	AMS
1896	G O Turnbull	Scotland	5	Indian Army
1897	R H Mangles	England	2	Queen's Royal West Surrey Regt
1897	P E O'Brien Butler	Ireland	6	ASC
1898	R O'H Livesay	England	2	Queen's Royal West Surrey Regt
1898	F F S Smithwick	Ireland	2	AChD
1898	C E Wilson	England	1	Queen's Regt
1899	E F Campbell	Ireland	4	AChD
1899	R F A Hobbs	England	2	RE
1902	J C Pringle	Ireland	2	RE
1902	E D Simson	Scotland	17	IMS
1903	G A D Harvey	Ireland	5	RAMC
1903	B A Hill	England	9	Ord Services
1903	J E C Partridge	South Africa	1	Welch Regt
1903	R S Smyth	Ireland	3	RAMC
1904	E D Caddell	Ireland	13	RAMC
1904	C G Robb	Ireland	5	RAMC
1904	T T H Robinson	Ireland	10	RAMC
1904	E J Ross	Scotland	1	Indian Army
1905	W M Grylls	England	1	Indian Army
1905	B Maclear	Ireland	11	R Dublin Fus
1905	H G Monteith	Scotland	8	RAMC
1905	W L Y Rogers	England	2	RA
1906	F Casement	Ireland	3	RAMC
1906	G E B Dobbs	England	2	RE
1906	W B Purdon	Ireland	3	RAMC
1906	J T Simson	Scotland	7	RAMC
1906	M White	Ireland	6	RAMC
1907	A W Newton	England	1	R Dublin Fus
1907	W C Wilson	England	2	Leicestershire Regt
1908	G C Gowlland	Scotland	7	RE
1908	L Robertson	Scotland	9	QO Cam H
1909	C A Bolton	England	1	Manchester Regt
1909	E C Deane	Ireland	1	RAMC
1909	H C Harrison	England	4	RM
1910	H Berry	England	4	Gloucestershire Regt
1910	C T O'Callaghan	Ireland	7	10th R Hussars
1910	A S Taylor	Ireland	4	RAMC
1911	W E Mann	England	3	RA

1911	A R Ross	Scotland	4	RMA
1911	R F Simson	Scotland	1	RA
1912	W V Edwards	Ireland	2	R Irish Fus
1912	R Hemphill	Ireland	4	RAMC
1912	A H MacIlwaine	England	5	RA
1912	J A Pym	England	4	RA
1912	C M Usher	Scotland (Capt)	16	Gordon H
1913	T C Bowie	Scotland	4	RAMC
1913	J J Clune	Ireland	6	AVC
1913	R E Gordon	Scotland	3	RA
1913	J B Minch	Ireland	5	RAMC
1913	A W P Todd	Ireland	3	RAMC
1914	J C A Dowse	Ireland	3	RAMC
1914	J L Huggan	Scotland	1	RAMC
1914	R Mac K Scobie	Scotland	3	RE
1920	H L V Day	England	4	RA
1920	C W Jones	Wales	3	Welch Regt
1920	J T Smyth	Ireland	1	RAMC
1921	P E R Baker Jones	Wales	1	RA
1921	I J Kilgour	Scotland	1	Northumberland Fus
1921	Q E M A King	England	1	RA
1922	J A Middleton	England	1	RASC
1923	J D Clinch	Ireland	30	Middlesex Regt
1924	C K T Faithful	England	3	DWR
1924	R K Millar	Scotland	1	RE
1924	W J Stewart	Ireland	10	IMS
1924	A T Young	England	18	RTR
1925	W F Browne	Ireland	12	DWR
1925	W H Stevenson	Scotland	1	Indian Army
1926	A R Aslett	England	6	KORR
1926	Sir Thomas Devitt	England	4	Seaforth H
1926	T E Rees	Wales	4	Welsh Guards
1926	J R B Worton	England	2	Middlesex Regt
1927	H McVicker	Ireland	5	RAMC
1928	G V Palmer	England	3	Queen's R Regt
1928	D Turquand Young	England	5	RTR
1929	A L Novis	England (Capt)	7	Leicestershire Regt
1929	H Rew	England	10	RTR
1929	K M Wright	Scotland	4	RA
1930	E W F de Vere Hunt	Ireland	5	RA
1930	D A Kendrew	England (Capt)	10	Leicestershire Regt
1931	G J Dean	England	1	RTR
1931	V J Pike	Ireland	13	RAChD
1931	H H C Withers	Ireland	5	RE
1932	R G S Hobbs	England	4	RA
1932	A Vaughan-Jones	England	3	RA
1933	E H Sadler	England	2	R Signals
1933	C L Troop	England	2	DWR
1934	B T V Cowey	Wales	4	Welch Regt
1934	J A Crawford	Scotland	1	RE
1935	R Leyland	England	3	AEC

1935	H J Sayers	Ireland	10	RA
1936	C O'N Wallis	Ireland	1	East Surrey's
1936	B E W McCall	Wales	3	Welch Regt
1937	W M Inglis	Scotland	6	RE
1937	C L Melville	Scotland	3	Black Watch
1937	F J Reynolds	England	3	DWR
1937	E J Unwin	England	4	Middlesex Regt
1939	F J V Ford	Wales	1	Welch Regt

1947	F H Coutts	Scotland	3	KOSB
1947	G R Davies	Wales	11	R Signals
1947	T G H Jackson	Scotland	12	R Signals
1947	J Matthews	Wales (Capt)	17	RAMC
1947	D D Valentine	Scotland	2	KOSB
1947	A G M Watt	Scotland	6	RAMC
1947	D F White	England	14	Northamptonshire Regt
1947	N M Hall	England (Capt)	17	R Signals
1948	A Cameron	Scotland (Capt)	17	RA
1949	D W C Smith	Scotland	8	RAMC
1949	W C Major	Wales	2	Welch Regt
1950	J L Baume	England	1	R Northumberland Fus
1950	J P Hyde	England	2	Northamptonshire Regt
1950	G C Phipps	Ireland	5	R Hampshire Regt
1950	D M Scott	Scotland	10	KRRC
1951	E M P Hardy	England	3	DWR
1951	B A Neale	England	3	RA
1951	D W Shuttleworth	England	2	DWR
1951	I H M Thomson	Scotland	7	R Signals
1952	D S Gilbert-Smith	Scotland	1	DWR
1952	R C Bazley	England	10	RE
1952	J G M W Murphy	Ireland	6	RAChD
1952	R Roe	Ireland	21	RAChD
1953	R J Robins	Wales	13	R Signals
1953	J S Swan	Scotland	17	REME
1954	R Higgins	England	13	R Signals
1954	H F McLeod	Scotland	40	R Scots Greys
1954	E J S Michie	Scotland	15	RE
1955	A B Edwards	Wales	2	RAEC
1955	J H Hancock	England	2	REME
1956	N M Campbell	Scotland	2	RAMC
1957	K J F Scotland	Scotland (Capt)	27	R Signals
1958	N S Bruce	Scotland	31	RAOC
1958	H J Morgan	Wales	27	REME
1959	H O Godwin	England	11	R Leicestershire Regt
1960	G W Payne	Wales	3	RE
1960	G Sharp	Scotland	4	R Signals
1960	R B Shillinglaw	Scotland	5	KOSB
1961	M J Campbell-Lamerton	Scotland (Capt)	23	DWR
1963	J P Fisher	Scotland (Capt)	25	RADC
1964	T A Moroney	Ireland	3	RAMC
1965	C P Simpson	England	1	R Anglian Regt
1966	J D MacDonald	Scotland	8	RCT

1966	M G Molloy	Ireland	27	RAMC
1969	I S G Smith	Scotland	8	RADC
1985	B W McCall	Ireland	1	REME

Corps and Regiments

Infantry	55 capped players
Royal Army Medical Corps	35 capped players
Royal Artillery	20 capped players
Royal Engineers	20 capped players
Indian Army	10 capped players
Royal Corps of Signals	9 capped players
Royal Army Chaplain's Dept	5 capped players
Royal Tank Regiment	4 capped players
Royal Electrical and Mechanical Engineers	4 capped players
Royal Corps of Transport	3 capped players
Royal Armoured Corps (Cavalry)	3 capped players
Royal Army Ordnance Corps	2 capped players
Royal Army Educational Corps	2 capped players
Royal Army Dental Corps	2 capped players
Royal Marines	1 capped player
Royal Army Veterinary Corps	1 capped player
Royal Military Academy	1 capped player
Total	177 capped players

The title given is the present title of the Corps or Regiment

INTERNATIONAL HONOURS – INFANTRY

Regiment	Caps		Player
Inniskilling Fus	1	1874	A H Young
Royal West Kent Regt	1	1875	A P Cronyn
Lincolnshire Regt	1	1876	W C W Rawlinson
Royal Fus	1	1881	R D Garnons-Williams
Wiltshire Regt	1	1882	W N Bolton
Royal Irish Regt	1	1884	W Edgeworth-Johnstone
Argyll & Sutherland Highlanders	2	1878	E W D Croker
		1894	W G Neilson
Queen's Regt/Queen's R Regt	2	1898	C E Wilson
		1928	G V Palmer
Queen's Royal West Surrey Regt	2	1897	R H Mangles
		1898	R O'H Livesay
Welch Regt	6	1903	J E C Partridge
		1920	C W Jones
		1934	B T V Cowey
		1936	B E W McCall
		1939	F J V Ford
		1949	W C Major

Royal Dublin Fus	2	1905	B MacLear
		1907	A W Newton
Leicestershire & R Leicestershire Regt	4	1907	W C Wilson
		1929	A L Novis
		1930	D A Kendrew
		1959	H O Godwin
Queen's Own Cameron Highlanders	1	1908	L Robertson
Manchester Regt	1	1909	C A Bolton
Gloucestershire Regt	1	1910	H Berry
Royal Irish Fus	1	1912	W V Edwards
Gordon Highlanders	1	1912	C M Usher
Northumberland/R Northumberland Fus	2	1921	I J Kilgour
		1950	J L Baume
Middlesex Regt	3	1923	J D Clinch
		1926	J R B Worton
		1937	E J Unwin
Duke of Wellington's Regt	8	1924	C K T Faithfull
		1925	W F Browne
		1933	C L Troop
		1937	F J Reynolds
		1951	E M P Hardy
		1951	D W Shuttleworth
		1952	D S Gilbert-Smith
		1961	M J Campbell-Lamerton
King's Own Royal Regt	1	1926	A R Aslett
Seaforth Highlanders	1	1926	Sir Thomas Devitt
Welsh Guards	1	1926	T E Rees
East Surrey Regt	1	1936	C O'N Wallis
Black Watch	1	1937	C L Melville
King's Own Scottish Borderers	3	1947	F H Coutts
		1947	D D Valentine
		1960	R B Shillinglaw
Northamptonshire Regt	2	1947	D F White
		1950	J P Hyde
Royal Hampshire Regt	1	1950	G C Phipps
King's Royal Rifle Corps	1	1950	D M Scott
Royal Anglian Regt	1	1965	C P Simpson

55

INTERNATIONAL HONOURS

Royal Army Medical Corps and AMS   35 caps

1874	A K Stewart	1882	F S Heuston
1877	H H Johnston	1883	R S F Henderson
1879	W W Pike	1894	T J Crean
1882	J B Buchanan	1895	T H Stevenson
1882	R G Thompson	1903	G A D Harvey

1903	R S Smyth		1913	J B Minch
1904	E D Caddell		1913	A W P Todd
1904	C G Robb		1914	J C A Dowse
1904	T T H Robinson		1914	J L Huggan
1905	H G Monteith		1920	J T Smyth
1906	F Casement		1927	H McVicker
1906	W B Purdon		1947	J Matthews
1906	M White		1947	A G M Watt
1906	J T Simson		1949	D W C Smith
1909	E C Deane		1956	N M Campbell
1910	A S Taylor		1964	T A Moroney
1912	R Hemphill		1966	M G Molloy
1913	T C Bowie			

Royal Artillery   20 caps

1872	R P Maitland		1920	H L V Day
1873	C H Rickards		1921	P E R Baker-Jones
1874	F L Cunliffe		1921	Q E M A King
1875	J W Dunlop		1929	K M Wright
1905	W L Y Rogers		1930	E W F de Vere Hunt
1911	W E Mann		1932	R G S Hobbs
1911	R F Simson		1932	A Vaughan-Jones
1912	A H MacIlwaine		1935	H J Sayers
1912	J A Pym		1948	A Cameron
1913	R E Gordon		1951	B A Neale

Royal Engineers   20 caps

1871	C W Sherrard		1906	G E B Dobbs
1871	C A Crompton		1908	G C Gowlland
1872	F B G D'Aguilar		1914	R MacK Scobie
1972	F T Maxwell		1924	R K Millar
1872	H W Renny Tailyour		1931	H H C Withers
1874	W F H Stafford		1934	J A Crawford
1893	A Walpole		1937	W M Inglis
1893	P Maud		1953	R C Bazley
1899	R F A Hobbs		1954	E J S Michie
1902	J C Pringle		1960	G W Payne

Indian Army and Indian Medical Services   10 caps

1877	H W Murray		1902	E D Simson
1877	E I Pocock		1904	E J Ross
1885	T W Irvine		1905	W M Grylls
1887	C M Moore		1924	W J Stewart
1896	G O Turnbull		1925	W H Stevenson

Royal Corps of Signals   9 caps

1933	E H Sadler		1953	R J Robins
1947	G R Davies		1954	R Higgins
1947	T G H Jackson		1957	K J F Scotland
1947	N M Hall		1960	G Sharp
1951	I H M Thomson			

Royal Army Chaplain's Dept   5 caps

1898   F F S Smithwick
1899   E F Campbell
1931   V J Pike
1952   J G M W Murphy
1952   R Roe

Royal Tank Regt   4 caps

1924   A T Young
1928   D Turquand-Young
1929   H Rew
1931   G J Dean

Royal Corps Transport   3 caps
RASC and ASC

1897   P O'Brien-Butler
1922   J A Middleton
1966   J D MacDonald

Royal Armoured Corps (Cavalry)   3 caps

1874	C W Crosse	KDG
1910	C T O'Callaghan	10H
1954	H F McLeod	Scots Greys

Royal Electrical and Mechanical Engineers   4 caps

1953   J S Swan
1955   J H Hancock
1958   H J Morgan
1985   B W McCall

Royal Army Ordnance Corps   2 caps
Ordnance Services

1903   B A Hill
1958   N S Bruce

Royal Army Educational Corps   2 caps
AEC

1935   R Leyland
1955   A B Edwards

Royal Army Dental Corps   2 caps

1963   J P Fisher
1969   I S G Smith

Army Veterinary Corps   1 cap

1913   J J Clune

Royal Military Academy   1 cap

1911   A R Ross

Royal Marines   1 cap

1909   H C Harrison

International Caps

England	60 caps
Scotland	52 caps
Ireland	50 caps
Wales	14 caps
South Africa	1 cap
Total	177 caps

Captains

A L Novis	England
D A Kendrew	England
N M Hall	England
C M Usher	Scotland
A Cameron	Scotland
M J Campbell-Lamerton	Scotland
K J F Scotland	Scotland
J P Fisher	Scotland
J Matthews	Wales

BRITISH ISLES – BRITISH LIONS

					tests
1896	South Africa	T J Cream	RAMC	Ireland	–
1930	New Zealand and Australia	D A Kendrew	Leicestershire Regt	England	–
1930	New Zealand and Australia	A L Novis	Leicestershire Regt	England	3
1930	New Zealand and Australia	H Rew	RTC	England	4
1938	South Africa	C F Grieve	DWR	Scotland	1
1938	South Africa	R Leyland	AEC	England	–
1938	South Africa	F J Reynolds	DWR	England	2
1938	South Africa	E J Unwin	Middlesex Regt	England	2
1955	South Africa	H F McLeod	R Scots Greys	Scotland	–
1955	South Africa	E J S Michie	RE	Scotland	–
1955	South Africa	R Roe	RAChD	Ireland	–
1959	New Zealand and Australia	H F McLeod	R Scots Greys	Scotland	6
1962	South Africa	M J Campbell-Lamerton	DWR	Scotland	2
1966	New Zealand and Australia	M J Campbell-Lamerton	DWR	Scotland	4

SUMMARY OF RESULTS OF INTER-SERVICE MATCHES

RN v Army (Results 1878–1985)

Year	Team	Score	Year	Team	Score	Year	Team	Score
1878	RN	1G 1T 1G	1934	Army	16–8	1963	Army	11–3
1907 (Feb)	RN	15–14	1935	Army	11–8	1964	Army	8–0
1907 (Dec)	RN	15–0	1936	Army	12–3	1965	Army	5–3
1909	RN	25–0	1937	Army	14–3	1966	RN	10–9
1910	RN	19–10	1938	RN	10–9	1967	Army	6–3
1911	Army	22–13	1939	Drawn	6–6	1968	Army	9–6
1912	RN	16–8	1946	Army	11–6	1969	Drawn	3–3
1913	RN	18–8	1947	Army	19–11	1970	RN	15–9
1914	Army	26–14	1948	RN	9–8	1971	RN	11–9
1920	RN	23–11	1949	Army	23–3	1972	Army	13–3
1921	RN	11–10	1950	Army	16–6	1973	RN	10–7
1922	RN	7–3	1951	RN	11–0	1974	RN	25–3
1923	RN	16–11	1952	Army	11–3	1975	RN	19–0
1924	Army	19–5	1953	Army	3–0	1976	Army	15–6
1925	Army	11–8	1954	RN	8–6	1977	RN	16–0
1926	Army	24–10	1955	RN	8–3	1978	RN	17–16
1927	RN	6–3	1956	Army	6–3	1979	Army	10–3
1928	Army	11–5	1957	Army	6–3	1980	Drawn	0–0
1929	Army	17–11	1958	RN	14–0	1981	RN	7–3
1930	Army	16–10	1959	RN	6–0	1982	Army	11–7
1931	RN	6–0	1960	Army	12–3	1983	Army	10–9
1932	Army	11–0	1961	RN	6–3	1984	Army	13–6
1933	Army	19–0	1962	Army	9–6	1985	Army	11–6

Results not including 1878 match:
Army 36   RN 29   drawn 3

ARMY V RAF (Results 1920–1985)

Year	Team	Score	Year	Team	Score	Year	Team	Score
1920	Army	21–9	1937	Army	29–9	1960	Army	6–3
1921	RAF	26–3	1938	Army	15–7	1961	RAF	19–11
1922	Army	23–8	1939	RAF	18–3	1962	RAF	19–14
1923	RAF	13–5	1946	Army	11–6	1963	Army	8–6
1924	RAF	8–3	1947	RAF	8–0	1964	Army	19–6
1925	drawn	6–6	1948	Army	15–8	1965	drawn	11–11
1926	Army	11–0	1949	drawn	3–3	1966	RAF	12–3
1927	Army	22–0	1950	Army	11–3	1967	Army	17–6
1928	Army	18–6	1951	Army	14–0	1968	drawn	3–3
1929	Army	27–0	1952	Army	9–6	1969	Army	26–21
1930	Army	14–8	1953	Army	11–3	1970	RAF	15–12
1931	RAF	16–5	1954	Army	16–3	1971	drawn	6–6
1932	Army	21–4	1955	drawn	6–6	1972	Army	14–6
1933	Army	12–3	1956	RAF	26–9	1973	Army	19–9
1934	Army	14–3	1957	Army	14–9	1974	RAF	9–4
1935	RAF	6–3	1958	drawn	3–3	1975	Army	41–13
1936	Army	16–3	1959	RAF	11–3	1976	Army	6–3

1977 Army	19–13	1980 Army	26–7	1983 Army	16–7
1978 Army	16–6	1981 Army	6–4	1984 RAF	15–9
1979 RAF	10–3	1982 RAF	10–6	1985 RAF	15–12

Army 35   RAF 18   drawn 7

ROYAL NAVY v RAF (Results 1920–1985)

1920 RN	12–3	1946 RAF	9–6	1966 RN	11–3
1921 RN	33–3	1947 drawn	5–5	1967 RN	5–3
1922 RN	9–6	1948 RAF	16–11	1968 RN	17–15
1923 RAF	3–0	1949 RAF	11–0	1969 RAF	9–5
1924 RN	16–9	1950 drawn	6–6	1970 RN	13–6
1925 RAF	3–0	1951 RN	6–5	1971 RAF	17–6
1926 RN	8–3	1952 RN	6–0	1972 RN	18–4
1927 RN	8–3	1953 drawn	3–3	1973 RN	15–0
1928 RN	5–0	1954 RAF	12–6	1974 RN	23–13
1929 RN	8–3	1955 RAF	6–3	1975 RAF	20–7
1930 RN	8–3	1956 RN	11–9	1976 RN	21–13
1931 RN	16–0	1957 RN	8–6	1977 RN	15–9
1932 RN	22–5	1958 RAF	14–3	1978 RAF	15–8
1933 RN	14–3	1959 RAF	12–9	1979 RAF	23–6
1934 RN	36–0	1960 RN	8–0	1980 RAF	16–7
1935 RN	13–8	1961 RN	9–3	1981 RN	15–12
1936 RAF	3–0	1962 RAF	12–6	1982 RAF	16–14
1937 drawn	3–3	1963 RAF	3–0	1983 RAF	8–4
1938 RN	10–6	1964 RN	5–3	1984 RN	10–9
1939 RN	8–3	1965 RN	15–6	1985 RAF	29–23

RN 35   RAF 21   drawn 4

INTER-SERVICES TOURNAMENT CHAMPIONS 1920–1985

1920	RN	1936	Army	1958	RAF
1921	RN	1937	Army	1959	RAF
1922	RN	1938	RN	1960	Army
1923	RAF	1939	RN	1961	RN
1924	Triple Tie	1946	Army	1962	RAF
1925	{ Army / RAF	1947	RAF	1963	Army
		1948	Triple Tie	1964	Army
1926	Army	1949	{ Army / RAF	1965	Army
1927	RN			1966	RN
1928	Army	1950	Army	1967	Army
1929	Army	1951	RN	1968	Army
1930	Army	1952	Army	1969	Army
1931	RN	1953	Army	1970	RN
1932	Army	1954	Triple Tie	1971	RAF
1933	Army	1955	RAF	1972	Army
1934	Army	1956	Triple Tie	1973	RN
1935	Triple Tie	1957	Army	1974	RN

1975	Triple Tie	1979	RAF	1983	Army
1976	Army	1980	Army	1984	Triple Tie
1977	RN	1981	RN	1985	RAF
1978	Triple Tie	1982	RAF		

The Army outright winners 25 times
The Royal Navy outright winners 15 times
The Royal Air Force outright winners 10 times

BRITISH ARMY v FRENCH ARMY 1920–1931

1920	Army	6	v	French Army 15	Paris
1922	Army	13	v	French Army 6	Paris
1923	Army	6	v	French Army 15	Twickenham
1924	Army	21	v	French Army 17	Paris
1925	Army	9	v	French Army 9	Twickenham
1926	Army	19	v	French Army 13	Paris
1927	Army	12	v	French Army 6	Blackheath
1928	Army	10	v	French Army 29	Paris
1929	Army	21	v	French Army 8	Twickenham
1930	Army	5	v	French Army 0	Paris
1931	Army	21	v	French Army 12	Twickenham

pd	won	drawn	lost	pts for	pts ag
11	7	1	3	143	130

1947–1959

1947	Army	3	v	French Army 16	Paris
1948	Army	6	v	French Army 0	Twickenham
1949	Army	10	v	French Army 13	Paris
1950	Army	8	v	French Army 12	Twickenham
1951	Army	17	v	French Army	Paris
1952	Army	22	v	French Army 11	Twickenham
1953	Army	6	v	French Army 19	Paris
1954	Army	27	v	French Army 0	Twickenham
1955	Army	0	v	French Army 6	Paris
1956	Army	0	v	French Army 18	Twickenham
1957	Army	6	v	French Army 8	Paris
1958	Army	6	v	French Army 6	Twickenham
1959	Army	3	v	French Army 20	Paris

pd	won	drawn	lost	pts for	pts ag
13	4	0	9	111	138

THE ARMY CUP 1907–1939

1907	2nd Bn West Riding Regt (DWR)	5	v	Training Bn Royal Engineers	0
1908	1st Bn The Leicestershire Regt	5	v	1st Bn Welch Regt	4
1909	1st Bn Welch Regt	6	v	2nd Bn South Wales Borderers	0
1910	2nd Bn Gloucestershire Regt	3	v	1st Bn Leicestershire Regt	0
1911	1st Bn Leicestershire Regt	14	v	2nd Life Guards	0

1912	1st Bn Leicestershire Regt	6	v	2nd Bn Welch Regt	3
1913	2nd Bn Welch Regt	9	v	1st Bn Gloucestershire Regt	3
1914	2nd Bn West Riding Regt (DWR)	6	v	1st Bn Gloucestershire Regt	3
1915–19					
1920	2nd Bn Welch Regt	9	v	2nd Life Guards	0
1921	2nd Bn Welch Regt	31	v	Training Bn Royal Engineers	3
1922	2nd Bn Welch Regt	27	v	1st Bn Gloucestershire Regt	8
1923	1st Bn Welsh Guards	6	v	2nd Bn Welch Regt	0
1924	2nd Bn Welch Regt	7	v	1st Bn Welsh Guards	3
1925	1st Bn South Wales Borderers	16	v	Royal Horse Guards	3
1926	1st Bn South Wales Borderers	10	v	1st Bn Welsh Guards	3
1927	1st Bn South Wales Borderers	9	v	Royal Engineers ((Aldershot)	8
1928	1st Bn South Wales Borderers	15	v	1st Bn King's Own Royal Regt	14
1929	1st Bn King's Own Royal Regt	21	v	1st Bn Welsh Guards	9
1930	1st Bn King's Own Royal Regt	3	v	Training Bn Royal Engineers	0
1931	1st Bn Duke of Wellington's Regt	21	v	Taining Bn Royal Engineers	0
1932	1st Bn Welsh Guards	11	v	2nd Bn Leicestershire Regt	3
1933	1st Bn Duke of Wellington's Regt	19	v	2nd Bn Leicestershire Regt	8
1934	1st Bn Welsh Guards	4	v	5th Bn Royal Tank Corps	0
1935	1st Bn Welch Regt	11	v	2nd Bn South Wales Borderers	0
1936	5th Bn Royal Tank Corps	11	v	2nd Bn King's Own Royal Regt	0
1937	1st Bn Welch Regt	13	v	1st Bn Prince Wales Volunteers	7
1938	2nd Bn Gloucestershire Regt	3	v	1st Bn Welsh Guards	0
1939	1st Bn Welch Regt	6	v	2nd Bn Gloucestershire Regt	3

THE ARMY CUP 1947–1985

1947	RAMC Depot & Trg Est	10	v	2nd Bn Welsh Guards	3
1948	Royal Signals (Catterick)	6	v	Royal Engineers (Hameln)	0
1949	1st Trg Regt Royal Signals	31	v	9th Indep Airborne Sqd RE	3
1950	1st Trg Regt Royal Signals	36	v	RAMC Depot & Trg Est	0
1951	1st Trg Regt Royal Signals	9	v	1st Guards Indep Para Coy (Parachute Regt)	6
1952	1st Bn Welsh Guards	14	v	RAMC Depot & Trg Est	0
1953	1st Trg Regt Royal Signals	35	v	1st Bn Welsh Guards	0
1954	1st Trg Regt Royal Signals	11	v	1st Bn South Wales Borderers	6
1955	RAMC Depot & Trg Est	16	v	1st Bn South Wales Borderers	0
1956	1st Bn Welch Regt	9	v	1st Bn Royal Welch Fusiliers	8
1957	1st Trg Regt Royal Signals	15	v	1st Bn Welch Regt	3
1958	1st Bn Duke of Wellington's Regt	23	v	1st (BR) Corps Troops Col RASC	5
1959	1st Trg Regt Royal Signals	12	v	1st Bn The Royal Scots	9
1960	1st Bn King's Own Scottish Borderers	9	v	1st Bn Duke of Wellington's Regt	0
1961	1st Bn King's Own Scottish Borderers	6	v	1st Bn Duke of Wellington's Regt	3
1962	1st Bn Welsh Guards	9	v	1st Bn Duke of Wellington's Regt	6
1963	1st Bn Welsh Guards	9	v	28th Coy RAOC	6
1964	1st Bn Welsh Guards	25	v	1st Bn Somerset & Cornwall Light Infantry	3
1965	1st Bn Duke of Wellington's Regt	11	v	1st Bn Welsh Guards	6
1966	1st Bn Duke of Wellington's Regt	9	v	63rd Para Squadron RCT	3

1967	1st Bn Duke of Wellington's Regt	14	v	7th Regt Royal Horse Artillery	3
1968	1st Bn Duke of Wellington's Regt	20	v	1st Bn Welsh Guards	3
1969	1st Bn South Wales Borderers	11	v	7 Signal Regt Royal Signals	3
1970	1st Bn Welsh Guards	18	v	1st Bn Royal Regt Wales	6
1971	1st Bn Welsh Guards	6	v	1st Bn Royal Regt Wales	3
1972	1st Bn Duke of Wellington's Regt	15	v	1st Bn Royal Regt Wales	8
1973	1st Bn Welsh Guards	22	v	7 Signal Regt Royal Signals	9
1974	1st Bn Royal Regt Wales	15	v	7 Signal Regt Royal Signals	12
1975	1st Bn Duke of Wellington's Regt	12	v	3rd BAPD RAOC	6
1976	1st Bn Royal Regt Wales	10	v	1st Bn Duke of Wellington's Regt	4
1977	1st Bn Royal Regt Wales	22	v	1st Bn Duke of Wellington's Regt	9
1978	1st Bn Duke of Wellington's Regt	13	v	8 Signal Regt Royal Signals	12
1979	1st Bn Duke of Wellington's Regt	12	v	1st Bn Royal Regt Wales	7
1980	3rd BAPD RAOC	10	v	1st Bn Royal Regt Wales	9
1981	1st Bn Duke of Wellington's Regt	20	v	7th Regt Royal Horse Artillery	0
1982	1st Bn Welsh Guards	12	v	21st Engineers Regt RE	6
1983	21st Engineers Regt RE	8	v	1st Bn Duke of Wellington's Regt	4
1984	7 Signal Regt Royal Signals	9	v	1st Bn Welsh Guards	3
1985	7th Regt Royal Horse Artillery	7	v	1st Royal Regt Wales	6

THE INTER UNIT ARMY CHALLENGE CUP WINNERS

1st Bn Duke of Wellington's Regt	12 ⎫	
2nd Bn West Riding Regt	2 ⎭	14
1st Bn Welch Regt	5 ⎫	
2nd Bn Welch Regt	5 ⎭	10
1st Bn Welsh Guards		11
1st Trg Regiment Royal Signals	7 ⎫	
1 Signal Regt Royal Signals (Catterick)	1 ⎬	9
7 Signal Regt Royal Signals	1 ⎭	
1st Bn South Wales Borderers		5
1st Bn Leicestershire Regt		3
Royal Regt of Wales		3
1st Bn Gloucestershire Regt		2
1st Bn King's Own Royal Regt		2
1st Bn King's Own Scottish Borderers		2
Royal Army Medical Corps Depot & Trg Est		2
5th Bn Royal Tank Corps		1
Royal Army Ordnance Corps 3 BAD		1
21st Engineers Regt Royal Engineers		1
7th Regt Royal Horse Artillery		1
	Total	67

PRESIDENTS ARMY RUGBY UNION

1908	Maj A J TURNER
1909–14	Maj-Gen C E HEATH CVO
1914–19	Maj-Gen C E HEATH CVO CB
1919–23	Maj-Gen Sir V A COUPER KCB
1923–27	Maj-Gen Sir Charles H HARINGTON GBE KCB DSO
1927–31	Gen Sir D WHIGHAM KCB KCMG DSO
1931–34	Field Marshal Sir G F MILNE GCB GCMG DSO DCL LLD
1934–38	Gen Sir Cyril J DEVERILL KCB KBE ADC
1938–39	Maj-Gen B A HILL CB DSO
1939–40	Gen Sir Walter M St KIRK GCB CMG DSO
1940–43	Lieut-Gen Sir Clive LIDDELL KCB CMG CBE DSO
1943–47	Lieut-Gen Sir H COLVILLE B WEYMISS KBE CB DSO MC
1947–48	Lieut-Gen Sir Frederick A M BROWNING KBE CB DSO
1949–53	Lieut-Gen Sir Kenneth N CRAWFORD KCB MC
1953–56	Lieut-Gen Sir A Dudley WARD GCB KBE DSO
1957–63	Gen Sir Hugh C STOCKWELL GCB KBE DSO ADC
1964–68	Maj-Gen R G S HOBBS CB DSO OBE
1968–71	Gen Sir George BAKER GCB CMG CBE MC
1972	Field Marshall Sir George BAKER GCB CMG CBE MC
1973	Gen Sir Mervyn BUTLER KCB CBE DSO MC
1974	Maj-Gen W N R SCOTTER OBE MC
1975–76	Gen Sir Peter HUNT GCB DSO OBE ADC
1977–80	Lieut-Gen Sir William SCOTTER KCB OBE MC
1981	Maj-Gen J A WARD-BOOTH OBE
1982–84	Gen Sir George COOPER KCB MC
1985	Lieut-Gen Sir Charles Huxtable KCB CBE

SECRETARIES ARMY RUGBY UNION

1908–14	Capt J R HANNAY
1919–20	Maj J R RAINSFORD-HANNAY DSO
1920	Lieut S H WRAY
1920–26	Maj R W LING CBE DSO MC
1926–27	Capt F W SIMPSON
1927	Capt G D D'ATH MC
1927–31	Lieut Col B A HILL DSO
1931–34	Lieut Col W B PURDON DSO OBE MC
1934–38	Maj R F WALKER MC
1938–39	Lieut Col E H C FRITH MBE
1942–45	Maj F A SLOAN MC
1946–47	Col R G S HOBBS DSO OBE
1948–51	Brig R G S HOBBS DSO OBE
1952–53	Brig G PEDDIE DSO MBE
1953–54	Lieut Col F W SIMPSON DSO
1954–56	Maj C O'N WALLIS MC
1957–58	Col F W SIMPSON DSO OBE
1959–63	Lieut-Col J KELSEY
1964–65	Lieut Col H J H GATFORD

1966–71   Lieut Col J H DALRYMPLE OBE
1972–85   Lieut Col P E Y DAWSON
1985–   Maj H G GREATWOOD

Mr E L (Ted) Savage was assistant Secretary for the period 1959–63 and contributed a great deal to ARU administration. Previously he was Secretary to the manager Surgeon-Capt L B Osborne on the 1950 British Lions tour to Australia and New Zealand.

PRESIDENTS OF NATIONAL RUGBY FOOTBALL UNIONS

RUGBY FOOTBALL UNION
Maj-Gen B A Hill CB DSO	1937–39
Col B C Hartley CB OBE	1947–48
Maj-Gen R G S Hobbs CB DSO OBE	1961–62
Brig D W Shuttleworth OBE ADC	1985–

SCOTLAND
Brig F H Coutts CBE DL	1977–78

CONCLUSION

This history of Army rugby to date would not be complete without both an assessment of the current state of our game and a look into the future. So what state are we in today after these many past years of great teams and great players? It is most heartening to record that despite the now small size of the Army, disappearance of old regiments and increasing pressure to do more with fewer men, rugby is still flourishing at all levels. In many areas the playing standards have not kept up with those in top civilian clubs but they compare favourably with the majority. At Colts and Under 21 levels the Army competes on equal terms with the best civilian standards and at senior level, bearing in mind all the problems and the fact that the Army XV does not begin playing until after Christmas in each season, the teams usually can at least hold their own and are rarely completely outclassed.

Career demands make it very difficult now for Army players to meet the commitments required by first-class clubs. However in recent years a significant number of our top players somehow have made those commitments and have shown themselves well able to compete. Unfortunately at the very top level only one Army player in the past fourteen years has gained an International cap and this situation is unlikely to change significantly.

Overall, both at home and abroad, Army competitions are well supported and keenly contested, unit teams and Corps teams play full fixture lists, and representative honours are much prized. The Army continues to play everywhere from Hong Kong to the Falkland Islands and from Belize to Berlin, maintaining the best traditions of rugby and the comradeship resulting from it.

As for the foreseeable future, reductions in number and increasing pressures seem likely to continue but, unless there are radical changes, Army rugby should be able to maintain its present levels of activity, enthusiasm and commitment. It is worrying that most of the administrators and most of the representative players now come from Corps rather than Regiments but perhaps this is inevitable. So long as Regiments take part whenever and wherever they can and everyone involved does their utmost to keep the spirit of our game alive, rugby will remain one of the Army's premier sports.